The Role of Foreign Direct Investment in East Asian Economic Development

NBER–East Asia Seminar on Economics
Volume 9

National Bureau of Economic Research
Tokyo Center for Economic Research
Korea Development Institute
Chung-Hua Institution for Economic Research
Hong Kong University of Science and Technology
National University of Singapore

The Role of Foreign Direct Investment in East Asian Economic Development

Edited by **Takatoshi Ito and Anne O. Krueger**

The University of Chicago Press

Chicago and London

TAKATOSHI ITO is professor in the Institute of Economic Research at Hitotsubashi University, Tokyo, and a research associate of the National Bureau of Economic Research. ANNE O. KRUEGER is the Herald L. and Caroline L. Ritch Professor of Economics, senior fellow of the Hoover Institution, and director of the Center for Research on Economic Development and Policy Reform at Stanford University, and a research associate of the National Bureau of Economic Research.

The University of Chicago Press, Chicago 60637
The University of Chicago Press, Ltd., London
© 2000 by the National Bureau of Economic Research
All rights reserved. Published 2000
Printed in the United States of America
09 08 07 06 05 04 03 02 01 00   1 2 3 4 5
ISBN: 0-226-38675-9 (cloth)

Library of Congress Cataloging-in-Publication Data

The role of foreign direct investment in East Asian economic development / edited by Takatoshi Ito and Anne O. Krueger.
     p. cm. — (NBER–East Asia seminar on economics ; v. 9)
    ISBN 0-226-38675-9 (cloth : alk. paper)
    1. Investments, Foreign—East Asia—Congresses. I. Ito, Takatoshi, 1950– II. Krueger, Anne O. III. NBER–East Asia seminar on economics (Series) ; v. 9.

HG5770.5.A3 R65 2000
332.67′3′095—dc21

                                                    99-086531

Contents

Acknowledgments

This volume contains edited versions of papers presented at the NBER–East Asia Seminar on Economics ninth annual conference, held in Osaka, Japan, on 25–27 June 1998.

We are indebted to members of the program committee who organized the conference, and to Chung-Hua Institution, Taipei; the Hong Kong University of Science and Technology; Korea Development Institute, Seoul; the National University of Singapore; and the Tokyo Center for Economic Research.

Professor Shinji Takagi, Professor Yuzo Honda, and their colleagues in the Economics Department at the University of Osaka were the local hosts. They did a superb job in making all the local conference arrangements, and all participants are indebted to them for a most enjoyable venue for the conference and an excellent opportunity to become acquainted with Osaka and Kyoto.

The Center for Global Partnership of the Japan Foundation provided major financial support for the conference, which is gratefully acknowledged. The National Bureau of Economic Research provided logistical support. Travel support by All Nippon Airways for some participants is very much appreciated. We are greatly indebted to the NBER, the Center for Global Partnership, and the Asian institutions that supported the research and the conference.

Introduction

Takatoshi Ito and Anne O. Krueger

One of the hallmarks of the 1990s has been the enormous increase in the international flow of long-term private capital. The architects of the postwar economic system (the Bretton Woods system) based their plans on the assumptions that private capital markets had been almost entirely destroyed by the upheavals of the Great Depression and that, in the future, most capital flows would consist either of short-term trade credits or of official flows. Over the intervening forty years, private capital flows gradually reemerged, first among the industrialized countries and then among most of the countries of the world. By the 1980s, some developing countries were relying more on private capital flows than on official flows, and by the 1990s, private capital flows had dwarfed official flows for most countries.

Different components of private capital flows grew at different rates. Among them, many observers focused on foreign direct investment (FDI) as an important contributor to growth. According to the International Monetary Fund (1998), FDI to developing countries rose steadily from US$18 billion in 1990 to $138 billion in 1997. Even in the wake of the currency crises of 1994–95 in Mexico and 1997–98 in Asia, FDI has been credited for its stability relative to other forms of capital flows.

Interestingly, in the 1950s and 1960s, few developing countries attempted to attract private foreign capital. What efforts there were usually

Takatoshi Ito is professor in the Institute of Economic Research at Hitotsubashi University, Tokyo, and a research associate of the National Bureau of Economic Research. Anne O. Krueger is the Herald L. and Caroline L. Ritch Professor of Economics, senior fellow of the Hoover Institution, and director of the Center for Research on Economic Development and Policy Reform at Stanford University, and a research associate of the National Bureau of Economic Research.

were intended to attract investment into "import substitution" industries. Indeed, in many countries private foreign capital was subject to strong political attacks for being an instrument of "exploitative" Western capitalism. When that attitude changed in the late 1980s and early 1990s, policymakers in many of the same countries sought private foreign capital. In a complete reversal, by the mid-1990s, many policymakers came to regard private foreign capital, and especially FDI, as a major and essential source, if not the key source, for accelerating economic growth.

Asian countries have had varying experiences with private foreign capital. Taiwan and Singapore sought private foreign capital early in their development efforts at a time when few other countries did so. Japan and Korea received little equity capital (FDI or portfolio) during their years of rapid development, although Korea accessed commercial banks to a considerable extent. Countries of Southeast Asia began encouraging FDI by the 1970s, as they began their rapid outward-oriented development effort. Later on, Japan, Korea, and Taiwan became exporters of private capital to other countries, although there were substantial inflows as well as outflows. The Southeast Asian countries have continued to be predominantly recipients of inflows, especially from the East Asian countries.

International economists have long taught that a negative current account balance is the counterpart to capital flows and enables a country to invest more than it saves. This truism led most economists to believe that net capital flows were in the interests of both capital exporters and capital importers. Until recent years when private capital flows increased, however, little attention was paid to their causes and effects, and to differences between types of capital flows.

However, at the same time as private capital flows had greatly increased in importance, financial crises in countries such as Mexico, and later in Asia, raised concern about the stability of these flows. In very short periods of time, private capital outflows threatened to overwhelm central banks, forcing rapid action and changes in policies on the part of a number of governments.

These recent developments thus raise a number of questions. What is the role of private capital (inflows or outflows) in resource allocation and in affecting economic growth? What determines the direction and composition of capital flows? What are the contributions of different types of capital flows? Researchers have been turning their attention to these issues as the importance of private long-term capital flows has increased, and as policymakers have attached increasing importance to them. But in fact, little is known about these capital flows and their causes and effects. Questions arise at many levels—micro- and macroeconomic determinants and effects of capital flows in general and of different types of capital flows.

For that reason, and also because capital flows are so important to countries in East Asia, the ninth annual NBER–East Asia Seminar on

Economics (EASE) focused on FDI in and from East Asian countries and its microeconomic determinants and effects. FDI plays a number of roles in different countries. For Japan, FDI has mostly been directed outward; about one-quarter of it has been directed to other Asian countries. Korea, Taiwan, and to a lesser extent Singapore and Hong Kong have both inward and outward FDI flows. In the early years of their phenomenal growth, inward FDI predominated; more recently, outward investment has taken place as industries earlier established in those places have pursued cost advantages in countries with lower wage rates for unskilled workers. In 1996, for example, outward FDI from Korea and Taiwan was US$4.7 billion and $3.8 billion, respectively, while inward FDI was $2.3 billion and $1.9 billion. Thus "net" FDI amounted to $2.4 billion, or 0.5 percent of GDP, in Taiwan and $1.4 billion, or 0.7 percent of GDP, in Korea. For still other countries, most notably in South and Southeast Asia, FDI has been mostly inward.

Economists have long agreed that capital flows, from countries where capital per worker is abundant and has a relatively low real rate of return to countries where capital per worker is scarcer and has a higher real rate of return, could benefit both capital-sending and capital-receiving countries. Moreover, in the context of the standard Heckscher-Ohlin-Samuelson model of international trade, where comparative advantage derives in large part from differences in relative factor endowments, capital flows (in the form of current account deficits) to a country can serve as a substitute for trade in goods. Thus a relatively capital-poor country could benefit either from exporting labor-intensive goods and exchanging them for capital-intensive goods or from having a current account deficit to enable it to increase its relative stock of capital.

In either case, the country would obtain a bundle of goods and services with larger capital inputs than would be achievable in the absence of trade in goods and capital flows. But if "trade in capital" is all that is involved in capital flows, the form of the capital flow should be immaterial— whether long-term bonds issued in the receiving country, long-term commercial bank lending, foreign purchase of equities in the local share market, or FDI. In fact, many observers have claimed that these forms of capital flow are distinctly different, both in terms of their microeconomic impact on the sending and receiving countries and in terms of the degree to which they render the receiving economy vulnerable. This latter concern has been highlighted by events in Mexico at the end of 1994 and again by the Asian crisis of 1997–98. Many of the issues are macroeconomic as, for example, when it is claimed that FDI is less likely to result in financial instability than is portfolio investment, which can be withdrawn much more easily and quickly.

Many papers investigating the determinants (or early warning indicators) of currency crisis in the aftermath of the Mexican and Asian crises point out that a higher ratio of FDI to total flow reduces the probability of currency crisis. The reason is thought to be that FDI is a steady flow of long-term capital that, once invested, is not likely to be quickly withdrawn, while portfolio flows are volatile and foreign investors can quickly sell them. It has been debated whether capital controls erected against short-term portfolio flows by developing countries serve the purpose of lowering the vulnerability of these countries, but there is a consensus that accepting (expanding) FDI normally reduces vulnerability to large shifts in flows.

While issues relating to the macroeconomic effects of different types of capital flows are being addressed by many economists and financial analysts throughout the world, a prior question relates to the differing effects of each of these types of capital flows. Questions arise as to when investments will be undertaken and financed by purchases of equity (as in instances of acquisitions or simply purchases of shares in the open market), by various forms of long-term lending and borrowing, or by FDI. If all that capital flows do is enable additional investment in the receiving country, the form of the capital flow might not matter. Even then, issues relating to the volatility of different types of capital flows might arise. This subject is addressed below.

But observers have suggested that FDI provides people in the recipient country with much more than simply a larger amount of capital with which to work. One of the early efforts to ascertain what these broader effects are was made by Kiyoshi Kojima (1978, esp. chaps. 4 and 7), who suggested that Japanese FDI and American FDI in Southeast Asia were quite different, with the Japanese investing more in industries that produced goods to be used by Japanese industry and Americans investing more in industries that produced goods for the home market.

In recent years, it has often been said that FDI enables managers and workers in the recipient country to acquire know-how and technology faster than would otherwise be possible. It may also enable new entrants to learn about export markets, stimulate competition with local firms, and provide training for workers. While these ideas have been put forth, many questions remain. What is "technology"? What attributes are "transferred" through FDI that could not otherwise be attained by, for example, sending students abroad or through licensing and royalty agreements? Even at the theoretical level, a number of questions arise. But there is a dearth of empirical evidence, which could help to shed light on these issues.

It was to consider how FDI in fact affects host and recipient countries at the microeconomic level that the ninth annual EASE was held. Questions addressed included: How different are foreign-owned (or joint venture) firms from local firms, and in what ways? What are the effects of the entrance of foreign firms into a domestic market? Do foreign firms enable all firms to achieve mastery of advanced technologies, or are those technologies adapted only in foreign-owned local firms?

The first set of papers examines characteristics of Japanese FDI in Asia. Belderbos, Capannelli, and Fukao examine Japanese FDI to Asia in the electronics sector, analyzing practices with regard to local procurement and technology transfer. Urata and Kawai's paper covers Japanese FDI to the rest of the world in textiles, chemicals, general machinery, electronic machinery, and transport equipment to test for effects on intrafirm productivity enhancement and local procurement. Kimura examines Japanese FDI to Asia and North America in both manufacturing and nonmanufacturing sectors. His goal is to test whether the industrial sector of a subsidiary is the same as that of its parent. Branstetter examines Japanese FDI in the United States in chemicals, machinery, electronics, transportation equipment, and precision instruments with a view to seeing whether FDI helps innovation in local production.

Belderbos et al. analyze in chapter 1 the determinants of local content for 157 Japanese electronics manufacturing subsidiaries in Asia. Local content is the sum of in-house value added and local outsourcing and is considered to be the component of output that yields benefits to the host country via technology transfers. Belderbos and his coauthors find that local content is generally lower in greenfield subsidiaries, subsidiaries of R&D-intensive parents, and export-oriented subsidiaries in the ASEAN-4 countries and China. In contrast, local content is higher in export-oriented subsidiaries in the newly industrialized economies, those subsidiaries that have higher domestic sales ratios, and subsidiaries of vertical *keiretsu* firms with strong intra-*keiretsu* supplier relationships.

In chapter 2 Urata and Kawai measure technology transfer by comparing the level of total factor productivity of overseas affiliates with that of parent firms. The smaller the gap between the two, they believe, the greater the extent of intrafirm technology transfer. Urata and Kawai find that the capability to absorb technologies, as reflected in educational attainment in host countries, is a key explanatory variable for intrafirm technology transfer. In some cases, experience in industrial activities is also shown to contribute to intrafirm transfers of technology.

We tend to think that FDI is a locational decision for reproducing production facilities. Kimura points out in chapter 3 that FDI is not necessarily undertaken in the same industry. Sector switching between parent and FDI affiliate is the focus of his study. The research is motivated by the observation that many Japanese trading firms invest in downstream and upstream industries abroad. Kimura finds that large Japanese manufacturing parent firms tend to have both manufacturing affiliates (all over the world) and nonmanufacturing affiliates (mainly in North America and Europe). Small manufacturing parent firms concentrate on production activities (do less sector switching) at their affiliates, particularly in East Asia. Large nonmanufacturing parent firms, such as general trading companies (*sogo shosha*), have extensive networks of production and wholesale trading all over the world. For manufacturing firms, factors that promote FDI, such as size, foreign sales, and R&D expenditures, also promote sector switching.

Branstetter examines FDI as a channel for R&D spillovers in chapter 4. He constructs and uses panel data for individual Japanese firms to measure the quantitative impact of FDI on firms' innovation activities. He asks: How does Japanese FDI enable Japanese firms to acquire knowledge in the United States? To answer this question, he regresses "innovation" (as measured by the number of U.S. patents owned by a firm) on the firm's own R&D expenditures, foreign spillovers (measured by R&D expenditures by technologically related U.S. firms), and foreign spillovers times FDI (greenfield investments in the United States). The coefficient on the interaction of FDI with foreign spillovers is significantly positive, and Branstetter concludes that Japanese firms with FDI in the United States experience higher productivity from those spillovers than firms without FDI.

The first four chapters center on Japanese FDI; another interesting issue is contrasts between Japanese and American FDI in the Southeast Asian region. Lipsey addresses that subject in chapter 5. He notes that the composition of exports has changed markedly in East Asian countries, moving away from the "typical developing country" composition of labor-intensive commodities toward one more like that in advanced countries. U.S. FDI is found to have played an important part in this shift because it was directed largely toward the newer group of export industries. As experience with exports in the new industries was gained, U.S. firms reduced their concentration on exportable production and tended to produce more for home markets. Lipsey finds that Japanese firms invested in industries that had already demonstrated comparative advantage and exported. However, he also finds that over time U.S. and Japanese affiliates have become more alike.

In chapter 6 Abe and Zhao build a theoretical model to consider the benefits and costs of customs union between developed and developing countries. They derive conditions for a profit-increasing (for the firm) customs union and show the policy implications of developing countries' use of subsidies to promote joint ventures. These subsidies work in the same way as a reduction in tariffs on intermediate goods and can, under their assumptions, improve welfare.

In chapter 7 Cheng and Kwan consider the determinants of FDI in China, using data from twenty-nine Chinese regions for the period 1986–95. They attempt to distinguish between the agglomeration effect (under which new investment follows old investment to the same destinations) and other factors (such as wage levels) that influence choice of location for foreign investors. They find that both sets of factors are important. Investors are more likely to flock to a location where others have already gone. However, other factors can offset this tendency. They find that good infrastructure, for example, attracts FDI and that higher wage costs deter

FDI. Measures to encourage FDI (such as those taken in China's Special Economic Zones) have had large positive effects, while other measures to attract FDI have had smaller, but still positive effects.

Another interesting question pertains to the determinants of the overall level of FDI directed to China, as contrasted with other emerging markets. In chapter 8 Wei addresses this question. He first notes the very large absolute value of investment in China but then points out that a sizable part originates in Hong Kong. He argues that this is "false" foreign investment because it is investment by mainland Chinese who send their capital to Hong Kong to receive the benefits accorded to foreign investors. Once investment from Hong Kong is netted out, Wei uses a cross-country model to examine the extent to which FDI in China is the same as for other emerging markets. He finds that China is a "significant underachiever," given its size and other attributes, relative to other countries. He also finds that corruption within China is a major deterrent and can explain a significant portion of the shortfall in foreign investment. In addition, he believes that the regulatory burden in China may weigh heavily on the FDI decision.

Korea has also had an interesting experience with foreign investment. In chapter 9 June-Dong Kim and Sang-in Hwang investigate the effect of inward FDI on the productivity of Korean industries and also the effect on the likelihood of currency crisis. They find that FDI in Korean manufacturing sectors had a positive, but statistically insignificant, effect on the productivity of these sectors. In a sample of ninety developing countries in the 1990s, they found that FDI inflows lower the incidence of both currency crashes and IMF rescue loans. The explanation, they believe, is that FDI is less mobile than short-term portfolio flows so countries with higher FDI ratios are better able to withstand adverse macroeconomic shocks than countries with relatively less FDI.

In chapter 10 Seungjin Kim also considers Korean FDI but analyzes the impact of outward FDI from Korea. Some observers have feared that investing overseas may drain home firms of investment resources that could otherwise be used to increase productivity in Korea. However, Kim finds no evidence of any such effects and notes that the relatively small size of Korean FDI, combined with the access of Korean firms to the international capital market, probably implied that FDI occurred in addition to home investment and was not a substitute for it.

For Taiwan, Chen and Ku analyze in chapter 11 the effects of FDI by examining the microeconomic aspects of FDI in one industry: Taiwanese textiles. They study the pattern of change at the level of individual firms over the years 1992–95. During that period, extensive restructuring of the industry was going on, much of it entailing large investments. Most firms reduced the number of product lines in which they engaged, even changing the principal commodities they produced, so that by 1995 almost half of sales revenue came from products introduced after 1992. Firms that had undertaken FDI were found to have restructured more dramatically in Taiwan than those that had avoided FDI.

In chapter 12 Chan analyzes the role of FDI in the growth of Taiwan's manufacturing industries. Controlling for the growth of human capital, gross capital formation, and exports in two-digit manufacturing industries, Chan investigates the links between FDI and growth in each manufacturing sector. Pooling time-series and cross-sectional data, Chan finds a link between FDI in individual manufacturing sectors and growth but no link between FDI and fixed investment or exports. The suggested interpretation is that FDI's impact on manufacturing growth probably came directly through technological improvements resulting from FDI rather than through any indirect channel.

References

International Monetary Fund. 1998. *International capital markets: Developments, prospects and key policy issues.* Washington, D.C.: International Monetary Fund, October.
Kojima, Kiyoshi. 1978. *Direct foreign investment.* Guildford, England: Billings.

1

The Local Content of Japanese Electronics Manufacturing Operations in Asia

René Belderbos, Giovanni Capannelli, and Kyoji Fukao

1.1 Introduction

Foreign direct investment (FDI) may increase host country productivity through improved resource allocation, increased competition, and expansion of local capabilities through a transfer of (technological) know-how (e.g., Caves 1995; Wang and Blomström 1992). Expansion of local capabilities occurs if FDI introduces superior organizational practices and technologies and if this know-how spills over to and is assimilated by local suppliers and customers, the local workforce, and local rival firms. The scope for such spillovers depends on the underlying innovative capabilities of the investing firm, the degree to which these are transferred to the foreign venture, and the extent of integration of the foreign firm into the host economy. In addition, a condition for substantial spillovers is sufficient "absorptive capacity" of the local economy, for example, the sophistication of local suppliers and the skill level of the workforce (Cohen and Levinthal 1990; Capannelli 1997a, 1997b). Integration in this context is the degree of interaction with the local workforce, local suppliers, customers, government institutions, industry associations, educational institutions,

René Belderbos is a Royal Netherlands Academy of Arts and Sciences Research Fellow at Maastricht University, Netherlands. Giovanni Capannelli is fellow in residence at the University of Malaya European Studies Programme, Kuala Lumpur, Malaysia. Kyoji Fukao is professor of economics at Hitotsubashi University, Tokyo.

This research was conducted as part of the project "Economic Analysis Based on MITI Survey Data" in liaison with the Institute of International Trade and Industry (ITI) and sponsored by the Japanese Ministry of International Trade and Industry (MITI). The authors are grateful to the ITI for the data compilations. They are also grateful to Ashoka Mody, David Wheeler, and Krishna Srinivasan for providing the Business International data and to the volume editors and conference participants for their helpful comments. This paper is partly based on Belderbos, Capannelli, and Fukao (1996).

and research centers (Turok 1993; De Arcos et al. 1995; Lall 1995). Since integration is achieved through country-specific investments in building relationships with the local economy, highly integrated foreign firms are less likely to divest in the future and the long-term viability of FDI increases.

The empirical literature on spillovers and productivity growth has produced mixed evidence on the impact of FDI. Industry-level studies have generally shown positive effects of FDI on labor productivity (Globerman 1978) and product and process innovations (Bertschek 1995). Firm- and establishment-level studies have given less support. Haddad and Harrison (1993) did not find evidence of productivity-increasing technology spillovers from foreign-owned subsidiaries to local firms in Morocco.[1] Aitken, Hanson, and Harrison (1997) found evidence of a more limited form of spillover from multinational investment in Mexico. The presence of exporting multinational firms was found to increase the probability that domestically owned firms start export activities, suggesting the presence of spillovers in the form of informational externalities and access to overseas distribution channels. Okamoto (1997) and Chung, Mitchell, and Yeung (1996) failed to find a direct impact on the productivity of North American car component suppliers from their forward linkages with Japanese assemblers.[2] These two studies did show substantial improvements in the productivity of U.S.-owned component suppliers (partly as a result of inventory reductions), suggesting that Japanese FDI had an indirect positive effect on productivity by increasing competition.[3] However, another recent study of the impact of Japanese FDI on the productivity of locally owned Chinese firms found almost opposite effects (Kinoshita 1996). Here the results did not support indirect spillover effects of FDI on local firms' productivity but provided evidence that direct buyer or supplier linkages with foreign firms led to higher productivity levels.

The debate about spillovers and other benefits from FDI appears to be particularly intense where it concerns Japanese FDI in Asia, which is the

---

1. Although this conceivably may have been due to a relative lack of absorptive capacity of local firms.

2. Okamoto (1997) failed to find productivity-increasing effects of supplier relationships with Japanese assemblers located in the United States throughout the 1980s but did obtain weakly significant coefficients in the early 1990s.

3. The findings may also be taken to indicate that U.S.-owned firms have been able to increase productivity by actively introducing organizational practices such as "just in time" delivery systems pioneered by Japanese automobile producers. It is conceivable that introduction of these practices was facilitated by the "demonstration" effect of plants set up by Japanese assemblers and suppliers, which is a particular form of spillover. Similarly, Oliver and Wilkinson (1992) found that a majority of U.K. firms in their sample had successfully introduced such "Japanese" manufacturing management practices as just-in-time delivery, quality circles, and flexible manufacturing techniques by the early 1990s. The U.K. firms were able to emulate these practices after Japanese plants set up in the United Kingdom in the mid-1980s had demonstrated that they could be successful in the U.K. environment.

subject of this paper. One reason is the perception that Japanese FDI is somehow less likely to generate spillovers to local economies because of the idiosyncratic behavior of Japanese multinational firms. Another reason is the economic importance of the activities of Japanese multinational firms in Southeast Asian countries. As shown in table 1.1, Japanese manufacturing affiliates play a principal role in East Asian economies. In three ASEAN countries (Indonesia, Philippines, and Malaysia), Japanese firms are responsible for almost a third of employment in the electronics and transport machinery industries.

In the discussion of the role of Japanese FDI, two contrasting views can be discerned. The positive view of Japanese FDI holds that it promotes economic development in Asia because the production processes and know-how transferred correspond closely to the absorptive capacity of the Asian economies. Products and components manufactured with the most standardized and mature technologies are produced in the ASEAN countries and, more recently, China, where cheap and low-skilled labor is relatively abundant. Goods of intermediate technology are produced in the newly industrialized economies (NIEs), where labor is more expensive but also more skilled. The most technologically advanced and capital-intensive production takes place in Japan. In this "flying wild geese" representation of Japanese FDI, Japan's technological leadership pulls along the industrialization of other Asian economies (e.g., Yamazawa et al. 1993; Urata 1991). The specialized nature of Japanese FDI in different Asian countries in accordance with differences in comparative advantage promotes intraregional and intraindustry trade. In this view, an important role is played by the "regional core networks" established by the larger Japanese multinational firms: networks of interrelated manufacturing plants for final goods and components, with different capital, labor, and skill intensities (Belderbos and Sleuwaegen 1996; Gold, Eonomou, and Tolentino 1991).

A contrasting and less benign view of Japanese FDI points out that the centralized nature of management in Japanese multinational firms and the reliance of Japanese firms on long-term dedicated supplier relationships discourages substantial integration in local economies. Japanese firms exercise strict control over overseas ventures (Mason and Encarnation 1994), are slow in appointing local staff to managerial positions (Westney 1996; Belderbos 1997), and are among the least internationalized in terms of overseas R&D activities (Patel 1995). A number of studies have presented evidence of relatively closed supply chains. Japanese affiliates in the United States rely more on imported components from their parent companies than do other foreign investors (Graham and Krugman 1990; Froot 1991; Murray, Wildt, and Kotabe 1995), and Japanese affiliates in Australia rarely use open tenders for machinery procurement but routinely buy from long-standing suppliers in Japan (in contrast with European and

Table 1.1   Share of Japanese Manufacturing Subsidiaries in Host Country Employment, 1995

Country	Electrical Machinery			Transport Machinery			All Manufacturing[a]
	Total Employment	Employment of Japanese Subsidiaries	Japanese Share (%)	Total Employment	Employment of Japanese Subsidiaries	Japanese Share (%)	Japanese Share (%)
South Korea	436,385	12,740	2.9	314,000	7,908	2.5	1.2
Taiwan	377,877	34,780	9.2	127,764	22,825	17.9	3.6
Singapore	100,111	38,809	38.7	34,672	1,243	3.6	13.5
Indonesia	132,484	49,373	37.3	123,842	42,510	34.3	1.8
Philippines	118,560	45,106	38.0	n.a.	26,515	n.a.	3.6
Malaysia	452,422	127,475	28.2	45,487	14,051	30.9	8.8

Source: Authors' calculations based on MITI (1998a) and Asian Development Bank (1998).

[a]Shares in all manufacturing are for 1997.

U.S. affiliates; Kreinin 1992). Evidence on Japanese subsidiaries in the Malaysian electronics industry shows that Japanese firms buy an overwhelming share of local components from Japanese-owned component suppliers, including those within the same corporate group or vertical *keiretsu* (Capannelli (1993, 1997b).[4] In a recent paper, Hackett and Srinivasan (1998) argued that Japanese firms face higher supplier-switching costs because of their intensive use of cooperative subcontractor relationships with established Japanese suppliers, in particular, suppliers within vertical *keiretsu*. This implies that Japanese firms are less eager to switch to local suppliers for their overseas manufacturing operations. Hackett and Srinivasan's empirical evidence suggesting that Japanese firms are less inclined than U.S. firms to invest in countries that impose strict local content requirements on foreign investors is consistent with the hypothesis of higher switching costs. However, it appears to be an open question whether differences in investment and procurement behavior are due to the idiosyncratic organization of Japanese multinational firms or are a temporary phenomenon due to a "vintage effect": the relatively late internationalization of Japanese firms (Mody and Srinivasan 1997; Westney 1996; Belderbos 1997, chap. 10).

In this paper, we contribute to the discussion by examining the determinants of Japanese firms' decisions to establish vertical linkages in Asian economies. Vertical linkages, that is, the local content of manufacturing operations, have been a focal point of host country concern. Several Asian countries have instituted formal local content requirements for foreign investors; others have made preferential investment status conditional on local content or have put informal pressure on foreign investors to extend their vertical linkages (Japan Machinery Center for Trade and Investment 1997; Commission of the European Communities 1998). Local content rules exist because increased local content is believed to provide a number of benefits to the host economy. If increased local content is achieved by sourcing materials and components from local suppliers, it may involve transfer of know-how to, and promote growth of, the local supplying industry. If local content is increased, on the other hand, through greater vertical integration of manufacturing operations (by producing more components in-house), it may be associated with an upgrading of employee skills, in particular, if the production of components is more technology and know-how intensive. In either case, increased vertical linkages are likely to enhance the local employment and trade balance effects of the investment project. In addition, the increased cost of divestment associated with greater investment and linkages to the local economy may positively affect the longevity of FDI.

In this paper we analyze procurement behavior at the micro level, that

---

4. Capannelli (1997b, 172–73) estimated that a mere 6.4 percent of local procurement was from Malaysian-owned firms in 1995.

is, at the level of individual firms, using subsidiary-level data from the Ministry of International Trade and Industry's (MITI's) 1992 survey of Japanese multinationals. We develop an empirical model that aims to explain the local content of Asian manufacturing operations by Japanese subsidiaries in the electrical and electronics industry. The model specifies determinants at the parent, subsidiary, and host country levels. Three main determinants, among others, are included: the presence of local content rules, the role of dedicated supplier linkages in vertical *keiretsu,* and the vintage effect. The effect of local content rules is measured at the subsidiary level, by utilizing a question in the MITI survey that inquires whether such regulations were applied. The effect of supplier relationships within vertical *keiretsu* is measured directly by estimating for each parent firm the intensity of transactions within the vertical *keiretsu* in Japan. The vintage effect is taken into account by including a variable for the operating experience of the subsidiary in the country of investment. The data set used contains information on 157 Asian subsidiaries in the electronics industry. The electronics industry is the largest Japanese investor in Asia and makes extensive use of subcontracting relationships outside and within vertical *keiretsu.* However, empirical research on Japanese subcontracting relationships to date has focused almost solely on the automobile industry.

Our main interest in this paper is the potential benefits of Japanese FDI for host economies that are derived from extended vertical linkages. The empirical analysis therefore focuses on the local (host country) content of electronics manufacturing subsidiaries in Asia. Local content includes both the value added of manufacturing subsidiaries (in-house production of components) and the value of components and materials sourced from local (Japanese and third country owned, as well as locally owned) suppliers. We chose not to focus on procurement alone because ignoring intra-subsidiary value added could lead to biased results: there is conceptually little difference between in-subsidiary production of components (value added) and procurements from nearby component plants of affiliated firms belonging to the same vertical *keiretsu.* The difference could merely be one of legal subsidiary boundaries. On the other hand, a distinction between procurements from locally owned suppliers and those from related suppliers would be useful because the former are likely to be associated with greater technology transfer and the stimulation of local entrepreneurship (e.g., Lim and Fong 1983). Unfortunately, our data do not allow us to estimate the importance of local procurement from locally owned firms.[5]

---

5. The MITI data do contain information on procurement from subsidiaries owned by the same parent firm ("intragroup procurement" in the MITI terminology), which is a narrower definition than intra-*keiretsu* procurement. However, no distinction is made among procurements from third country, Japanese, and locally owned suppliers, and the question on intragroup procurement has a low response rate.

The remainder of the paper is organized as follows. Section 1.2 briefly reviews the literature on subcontracting and supplier relationships of Japanese firms and previous work on vertical linkages of foreign-owned affiliates. Section 1.3 develops hypotheses concerning the determinants of the local content ratio of Japanese manufacturing operations in East Asia and describes the empirical model and data. Section 1.4 presents the empirical results. Section 1.5 summarizes our findings and offers concluding remarks.

1.2 Previous Literature: Vertical Linkages, Japanese Supplier Networks, and Local Content Rules

We are not aware of any recent systematic empirical analysis of the vertical linkages of foreign-owned firms in host economies. There is a research tradition on vertical linkages of foreign firms in the economic geography literature. O'Farrell and O'Loughlin (1981), for instance, statistically analyzed local procurement levels of foreign-owned affiliates in Ireland. In a more recent study, Turok (1993) investigated local sourcing by firms under foreign (including Japanese) ownership in the Scottish electronics industry ("Silicon Glen") in 1992 and concluded that the level of vertical linkage was low.[6] The only recent attempt to provide a more comprehensive explanation of local sourcing decisions in this tradition was Reid (1995), but this study was primarily concerned with the effect of just-in-time delivery systems on the spatial clustering of suppliers. Reid found that the use of just-in-time systems by 239 Japanese-owned manufacturing plants in the United States is positively associated with the proportion of material inputs procured at the county level (but not at the state or national levels).

Apart from the descriptive evidence presented in Kreinin (1992), Graham and Krugman (1990), and Froot (1991), which emphasized the reliance of Japanese overseas affiliates on component and material imports from Japan, a number of (case) studies have examined local procurement by Japanese firms. Hiramoto (1992) presented a case study of the subcontracting and sourcing relationships of Japanese television and VCR assemblers in Asia and Europe. He found that Japanese assemblers have often failed in their attempts to establish long-lasting subcontracting relationships with local parts suppliers similar to those they have with Japanese suppliers. Major obstacles were the lack of an orientation toward continuous improvement, the lack of emphasis on quality and reliability, the dominant position of the assembler-buyer, and the buyer's preference for the use of relatively ambiguous contracts. Belderbos (1997, chap. 8) examined aggregate data on procurement and value added of Japanese electronics subsidiaries in the European Union and the United States. While the local

6. Only 12 percent of components were supplied from Scotland and another 30 percent from the rest of the United Kingdom (Turok 1993, 406).

(European and North American) content of manufacturing operations was substantial (in the range of 40 to 60 percent), the role of locally owned firms in the supply chain was limited. Comparable findings were obtained by Capannelli (1993, 1997b) for Malaysia. These results are consistent with earlier work by Lim and Fong (1982) for Japanese investors in Singapore.

On the other hand, there is some evidence that reliance on in-house components and procurement from Japanese affiliates is declining. Baba and Hatashima (1995) and Chia (1995) argued that there has been a recent move from the use of firm-specific components developed internally or within the vertical *keiretsu* toward the open purchase of standard components. Greater competitive pressures have forced Japanese firms to redesign products in order to facilitate the procurement of cheaper mass-produced components in Asia. Baba and Hatashima (1995) described a number of cases in which Japanese electronics firms have extended local design activities in Southeast Asia.[7] Chia (1995) showed that an increasing number of Japanese firms have set up regional procurement offices in Singapore to facilitate cost-effective sourcing of components made in Asia.

Recent empirical work on Japanese FDI has explored the role of supplier and subcontractor linkages in the decision to invest abroad and the location of investments. Belderbos and Sleuwaegen (1996) found that vertical linkages between firms are an important factor in the decision to invest in Asia: subcontractor firms within vertical *keiretsu* are more likely to invest in Asia if the parent firm operates a large number of plants (a "regional core network") in the region. Using location data on Japanese manufacturing affiliates in the United States, Head, Ries, and Swenson (1995) found that Japanese plants were more likely to be set up in a state, the greater the number of existing Japanese plants in that state in the same industry. The existence of plants set up by parent firms or suppliers in the same vertical automobile *keiretsu* exerted an additional positive effect on location decisions by firms in the *keiretsu*. Horiuchi (1989) and Cusumano and Takeishi (1991) reported that Japanese automobile manufacturers actively help their *keiretsu* component suppliers to set up plants near their assembly operations abroad.

Empirical work on Japanese subcontracting and buyer-supplier relationships has been concerned primarily with establishing the role of risk sharing as well as the correlation between relationship-specific investments and the performance of suppliers and assemblers. These studies have focused on the automobile industry. Asanuma and Kikutani (1992) and Okamuro

---

7. Matsushita Electric and Seiko Epson are reported to have recently transferred part of their die-making activities to Southeast Asia in order to reduce costs and reduce the period from design to delivery of new models. Matsushita Electric makes dies for television parts and cabinets in Singapore and Malaysia, and Seiko Epson is producing dies for computer printers in Hong Kong. See "Manufacturing Technology Leaving Its Stamp on Asia," *Nikkei Weekly*, 23 June 1997.

(1995) provided evidence that the intensity of long-term supply relationships is positively correlated with the stability of performance. Dyer (1996) found evidence that automobile assemblers are more profitable, the greater the proximity (spatial clustering) of their suppliers. Proximity is associated with suppliers' dedicated investment in production facilities, greater sharing of know-how, and more intense communication. These are found to be correlated with faster design changes, improved quality, and increased return on investment. For the consumer electronics industry, Capannelli (1997a) found that technology transfer by Japanese assembly firms to their input suppliers is positively related to specific investments to enhance the former's technological capability and the latter's absorptive capacity and negatively related to the bargaining power of suppliers. The effectiveness of technology transfer was found to be greater in the case of lower end production inputs.

Studies of component procurement and supply chain management in the strategic management literature have also focused on the relation between sourcing strategies and firm performance. Kotabe and Omura (1989) examined sourcing strategies of a group of foreign (including Japanese) multinational firms in the United States and found that the extent of internal sourcing of major components is positively related to U.S. market performance of the product. Murray et al. (1995) surveyed 104 foreign-affiliated manufacturing subsidiaries in the United States in 1993 and found weak evidence that reliance on nonstandardized components and internal sourcing was related to better market performance as measured by sales growth. They also reported significant differences in procurement behavior between European- and Japanese-owned subsidiaries in the United States in 1991. Japanese subsidiaries sourced a significantly smaller share of the value of components in the United States and combined greater reliance on nonstandardized components with significantly higher levels of intrafirm sourcing.

A last research tradition has been concerned with formal analysis of the welfare and strategic effects of local content requirements (e.g., Belderbos and Sleuwaegen 1997; Jie-A-Joen, Belderbos, and Sleuwaegen 1998; Richardson 1993). The effect of local content requirements has been found to depend on, among other things, the market power of local parts suppliers, the cost competitiveness and level of vertical integration of local competitors in the assembly industry, and whether the requirements induce FDI in component production. Despite the wealth of theoretical studies, the only empirical study of the effect of content regulations is Hackett and Srinivasan (1998). Their finding that local content regulations exert a significantly negative effect on Japanese FDI would imply that, on balance, the negative effect on FDI in assembly industries is much stronger than any positive effect on FDI by assemblers and related suppliers in local component production to satisfy the requirements. However, they also found a positive and significant effect of the stock of Japanese FDI on new investments. This is consistent with the finding of strong agglomeration economies by Head et al. (1995) and may in fact measure a partly off-setting positive effect on FDI by subcontractors in response to previous investments by assemblers facing local content regulations.

1.3   Data and Empirical Model

This section develops an empirical model explaining the extent of vertical linkages of Japanese manufacturing subsidiaries in Asia. The dependent variable is the local content ratio (LOCON), defined as sales of the subsidiary, minus components and materials imported from abroad, divided by subsidiary sales.[8] Since the dependent variable is restricted to the interval [0,1], two-limit Tobit analysis is used to relate the local content ratio to a set of explanatory variables.

We first introduce the data set and discuss the use of the dependent variable. This is followed by a discussion of the explanatory variables at the parent firm and subsidiary levels. We will start by estimating a set of empirical models including these variables while controlling for country characteristics through a set of country dummies. This helps us to focus on the estimates of variables at the level of the firm. Since our data set only includes nine Asian countries, the variation is not large enough to allow inclusion of a comprehensive set of country variables. Nevertheless, in a second set of extended models we do employ a set of country variables expected to have an impact on local content. Country variables are discussed in the last part of subsection 1.3.3.

1.3.1   Data

Subsidiary data are drawn from MITI's 1992 basic survey of Japanese multinational enterprises and account for operations in the fiscal year through March 1993. A representative number of 157 subsidiaries in the electronics industry had sufficient information on local content and a basic set of explanatory variables. Eighty-three of these were established in the four NIEs and 67 in the ASEAN-4 countries (Indonesia, Thailand, Philippines, and Malaysia), and 7 subsidiaries operated in China. Further details on the data selection as well as the definitions of the dependent and explanatory variables are provided in the appendix.

Table 1.2 shows the origins of procurements by Asian electronics subsidiaries of Japanese firms. Japan is the most important origin of procurements (46 percent), followed by the host country (39 percent) and other Asian countries (12 percent). Asian countries other than Japan are important sources of parts and components for subsidiaries in the ASEAN-4

---

8. When a subsidiary also imported finished goods, we deducted the value of such imports from both the total sales value and the total import value.

Table 1.2   **Distribution of Procurement by Asian Manufacturing Subsidiaries of Japanese Electronics Firms over Regions of Origin, 1992**

Country	Local (%)	Japan (%)	Asia (%)	Other (%)	Subsidiaries (number)
Hong Kong	48	34	18	0	8
South Korea	46	50	4	0	25
Singapore	40	43	15	2	27
Taiwan	50	43	6	1	38
NIEs	46	44	9	1	98
Indonesia	63	17	20	0	5
Malaysia	34	44	16	6	40
Philippines	16	42	42	0	4
Thailand	28	55	15	2	34
ASEAN-4	32	47	17	4	83
China	23	72	0	5	7
Asia-9	39	46	12	3	188

Source: Authors' calculations based on MITI (1994).

Note: From 188 subsidiaries with complete imformation (see appendix). Percentages are shares of total procurement.

Table 1.3   **Local Content Ratio of Asian Manufacturing Subsidiaries of Japanese Electronics Firms, 1992 (percent)**

Country	Local Procurement / Sales (A)	Value Added / Sales (B)	Local Content Ratio (A + B)
Hong Kong	33	36	69
South Korea	23	44	67
Singapore	30	39	69
Taiwan	29	44	73
NIEs	28	43	71
Indonesia	44	28	72
Malaysia	23	34	57
Philippines	10	44	54
Thailand	18	34	52
ASEAN-4	22	34	56
China	18	36	54
Asia-9	24	38	63

Source: Authors' calculations based on MITI (1994).

Note: From 188 subsidiaries with complete information (see appendix).

countries, Singapore, and Hong Kong, but less so for Taiwan, South Korea, and China.

Table 1.3 shows the average local content ratio by country. The local content ratio averaged 71 percent for the NIEs and 56 percent for the ASEAN-4 countries. Higher local content ratios in the NIEs are achieved through both greater local sourcing (28 percent) and higher value added (43 percent).

1.3.2   Dependent Variable

Foreign-owned subsidiaries can achieve higher local content in a number of ways: (1) increasing the value added of the assembly activity, (2) increasing intrasubsidiary production of components, (3) increasing procurement of components and materials from Japanese suppliers in the same *keiretsu* that are producing in local plants, (4) increasing procurement from locally established independent Japanese firms, (5) increasing procurement from local subsidiaries of third country firms, and (6) increasing procurement from locally owned suppliers. The local content ratio of a subsidiary measures how much value its activity creates in the local economy, that is, to what extent the value chain is established locally. However, a potential measurement problem is associated with the local procurement share of the local content ratio. In particular, when local suppliers are foreign owned, these suppliers in turn will source part of their subcomponents and materials from abroad. The value added that is generated locally must be less than the price paid for the components. Hence, our local content measure (and the figures in table 1.3) overestimates the contribution to the local economy. There is evidence that this overstatement of actual local content is not negligible. Belderbos (1997, 326) reported that the local content ratio of Japanese electronics subsidiaries drops from 66 to 55 percent if the non-European content of components manufactured by Japanese suppliers in the European Union is deducted. Although this is an important qualification to our analysis, it is less likely to introduce a systematic bias into the empirical results concerning the determinants of local content. At the country level, the same factors that positively affect value added of final goods manufacturing will also have a positive impact on the value added of locally manufactured components. We did not find evidence that the local content of the electronic component subsidiaries in our sample is determined differently from the local content of final goods subsidiaries.[9] Hence, our measured local content ratio and actual local content will be strongly correlated.

A Japanese firm's decisions concerning the sourcing of components and materials for its manufacturing operations in Asia can be subdivided into two decision problems: (1) whether to procure the components in-house (or intra-*keiretsu*) and (2) whether to procure the components in Japan or overseas (in Asia). The "internalization" decision of problem 1 reflects the trade-off between the quality and reliability benefits of in-house produc-

---

9. In addition, our results appeared robust with respect to the choice of the dependent variable (including or excluding value added): we obtained very similar results with local procurement as the dependent variable. If the local procurement share of measured local content were systematically biased, we would expect differences in these results.

tion of components of proprietary design versus the cost reduction benefits of sourcing standard components. If a firm chooses external sourcing of components to maintain a competitive cost structure, it will be more likely to choose components produced in low-cost Asian locations (produced by locally owned firms or independent Japanese transplants). If a firm chooses proprietary component manufacturing, it is still possible that overseas manufacturing activities reach high local content levels. A condition is that the overseas manufacturing location allow cost-effective production of the components within the assembly plant or in a dedicated component manufacturing subsidiary established by the assembler or its related component suppliers. The local content level reached will therefore reflect both the importance of transactions costs associated with arm's-length trade and the attractiveness of Asian countries in component manufacturing.

1.3.3   Explanatory Variables

Parent Firm Level

We posit that the *R&D intensity* of the parent firm, R&DINT, has a negative effect on local content. R&D-intensive firms make greater use of proprietary designs and in-house know-how, and they possess more intangible assets related to capabilities in the manufacture of high-technology components. They are less likely to transfer the production of these components to external suppliers. Since production of in-house developed components is generally capital and technology intensive, it is less likely that Asian manufacturing locations provide substantial cost advantages for R&D-intensive firms. There is some evidence for this assertion: Fukao et al. (1994) found that R&D intensity has a significantly negative impact on the stock of FDI in Asia by Japanese electronics firms. We hypothesize that R&DINT is negatively correlated with the local content ratio. We also test whether the effect is stronger for the ASEAN-4 countries and China compared to the NIEs since the greater technological capabilities of the latter make them more attractive for R&D-intensive manufacturing operations.

Japanese firms differ in the intensity of long-term cooperative subcontracting and supplier-assembler relationships (e.g., Sako 1992; Dyer 1996). In particular, firms that are member of large vertical *keiretsu* with a substantial number of related component manufacturers will make intensive use of these relationships. Intra-*keiretsu* procurement is based on long-term relationships characterized by intensive interaction between supplier and assembler involving dedicated investments in equipment and human resources and requires the implementation of just-in-time delivery and total quality control systems. There is evidence that these relationships enhance performance and reduce risk (Dyer 1996; Asanuma and Kikutani

1992; Okamuro 1995). Since the assembler-supplier system is one of the bases for the competitiveness of Japanese firms, they have followed a strategy of emulating it abroad. In practice, however, it has proved difficult to involve locally owned suppliers in such relationships (Hiramoto 1992). Moreover, supplier-switching costs are higher for *keiretsu* firms given the sunk investments in existing relationships with Japanese suppliers (Hackett and Srinivasan 1998). Supplier networks have therefore often been replicated abroad through the establishment of overseas manufacturing plants by existing Japanese manufacturers of parts and components, in which the latter were often assisted by the "core" firm of the *keiretsu* (Belderbos and Sleuwaegen 1996).

The consequences of *keiretsu* membership for the local content of overseas operations are not unambiguous. On the one hand, the higher switching costs of *keiretsu* member firms may lead to a greater continuing reliance on inputs from long-standing suppliers located in Japan. On the other hand, if the supplier has followed the assembler abroad, *keiretsu* firms may be able to reach higher local content than independent firms. The possibility of replicating supplier networks abroad may be a particular advantage in locations where local or third country component manufacturers are lacking. We therefore examine whether the effect of *keiretsu* intensity is stronger in countries that have less developed indigenous electronic parts industries, such as the ASEAN-4 countries and China.

Since a substantial share of investment in Asia is done by the core firms of *keiretsu* or by member firms of *keiretsu,* membership in a vertical *keiretsu* itself is not a distinctive characteristic. Instead, we devised a measure of the intensity of supplier-assembler relationships. We used Toyo Keizai's publication *Nihon no Kigyou Guruupu* (Japanese Corporate Groups), to establish for each Japanese investor whether it belonged to a vertical *keiretsu.* Then we proxied the intensity of supplier-assembler relationships for *keiretsu* members by taking the ratio of the size (measured by paid-in capital) of all Japanese subsidiaries and related firms in manufacturing (*kogaisha* and *kankeigaisha*) to the size of the core firm of the *keiretsu* in Japan. We call this *variable keiretsu intensity, KEIRINT.* The values for KEIRINT corresponded well to our intuition concerning the strength of supplier networks, with, for example, the highest ratios for Matsushita and Fujitsu and the lowest for Sharp. Unfortunately, we were not able to identify *keiretsu* intensity for all Japanese investors, and the inclusion of KEIRINT reduces the number of valid observations by seventeen.

Subsidiary Level

At the subsidiary level, *experience* in manufacturing in a country is likely to be an important determinant of the extent of vertical linkages. Finding suitable local suppliers and establishing links with these firms is time consuming, in particular, if the suppliers have to adapt to the demands of Japanese assemblers in terms of quality and delivery schedules. In other cases, redesign of the product is necessary to allow the use of locally made standardized components. O'Farrell and O'Loughlin (1981) found a positive effect of operating experience on the level of local procurement by foreign-owned subsidiaries in Ireland, but Reid (1995) could not establish a similar effect for Japanese firms in the United States. One reason for the latter result may be that no distinction was made between greenfield establishments and acquisitions. In cases where a local subsidiary was acquired by a Japanese investor, it is natural to assume that the subsidiary was relatively deeply embedded in the local economy at the time of the acquisition; the number of years of operation under Japanese ownership is not likely to have an important additional impact on local content. In fact, it is conceivable that under Japanese ownership, a restructuring of manufacturing activities takes place, which may involve a switch to the use of Japanese-made components. In our analysis of Japanese subsidiaries in Asia, the distinction between acquisitions and greenfield plants is of very limited importance because the role of acquisitions in Asia is marginal: only four subsidiaries in the sample were acquired. This small number does not allow us to test for a different effect of experience for acquired firms. We therefore use only one variable, EXPER, the number of months since operations started in the manufacturing subsidiary under Japanese control.[10]

As mentioned above, the *entry mode* is likely to have an impact on integration in the local economy. Acquired subsidiaries are likely to have higher local content given their local ownership and preacquisition operating experience. We also expect that joint ventures facilitate higher levels of local content than wholly owned subsidiaries, ceteris paribus. This is because the local joint venture partner or its related firms may have accumulated expertise either in electronic component manufacturing or in procuring components from local suppliers. Taking the wholly owned greenfield subsidiary as the base case, we include two dummy variables in the model, ACQUIS when the subsidiary was acquired and JV when the subsidiary is a joint venture with a local partner.

A feature of the operations of Japanese electronics firms in Asia is a certain dichotomy between subsidiaries producing for export markets and subsidiaries primarily selling on the local market. The *export versus local sales strategy* may have an impact on vertical linkages of the subsidiary. If the subsidiary focuses on the local market it is likely that (1) it produces relatively mature and low-priced products for this local market and not the most sophisticated products or models and (2) it has an incentive to

---

10. We tested a model that included both EXPER for greenfield and EXPER for acquired firms. As expected, the latter had a small and insignificant coefficient, while the coefficient of the former was only marginally different from the EXPER coefficient for all subsidiaries.

adapt the products to local tastes and circumstances. The more mature the products, the more likely it is that locally produced low-cost standard components can be used. Adapting products to the local market is likely to involve redesign, which allows the use of locally made components. Furthermore, subsidiaries selling price-sensitive products on the local market are more vulnerable to currency swings if they rely on procurement from Japan. In sum, we expect that subsidiaries with higher local sales ratios have higher local content. LOCSALES measures the percentage of subsidiary turnover destined for the local market. We expect this positive effect to be greatest for the ASEAN-4 countries and China, where demand is less sophisticated than in the NIEs.

Industry characteristics will have an effect on the extent of vertical linkages. High local content ratios may be more difficult to achieve in high-technology industries such as telecommunications than in the more mature consumer goods sectors. Subsidiaries manufacturing products that use components with a low value-to-weight ratio will be more inclined to use local components because transportation costs associated with imports are relatively high. We control for such possible systematic differences by including industry dummies. We regrouped the industry classification used in the MITI survey into four subclasses in the electronics industry: consumer goods, semiconductors and electronic parts, telecommunications and computer equipment, and other electronic and electrical equipment. We use consumer goods as the reference case and include three dummies: TELCOMP, PARTS, and OTHERIND.

Country Level

The first country characteristic affecting local integration is the availability of locally established component suppliers. We used data from Elsevier's *Yearbook of World Electronics Data* to calculate the *value of electronic parts and component production* in each country in 1992 (Elsevier 1995). As explanatory variable we took the natural logarithm of the production value, SUPPLIERS. The variable SUPPLIERS measures the availability of locally owned suppliers as well as Japanese-owned suppliers. It will also generally reflect the attractiveness of a country as a place to establish component manufacturing operations.

The extent to which *Japanese suppliers* play a role in the local component industry will also affect vertical linkages. By using long-standing suppliers from Japan established near the overseas manufacturing base, firms can avoid switching costs and emulate best practice in Japan. There may be important economies of agglomeration once a substantial number of Japanese suppliers have set up local manufacturing subsidiaries. Reduced input costs can result from increased specialization and training of local personnel. We used MITI survey data to establish the total turnover of Japanese electronic parts manufacturing subsidiaries in each country in

1992. We employ as an indicator of the presence of Japanese suppliers, JRATIO, the log of total turnover by Japanese subsidiaries divided by SUPPLIERS. We also hypothesize that firms with extensive supplier linkages within their *keiretsu* in Japan are likely to benefit most from the availability of Japanese suppliers. Hence we test for the cross-effect of JRATIO and KEIRINT.

The cost advantage of using a local network of suppliers also depends on the *quality of infrastructure.* Good infrastructure facilitates physical transport of components within the country and communication between assembler and suppliers. The perceived quality of infrastructure, as measured by a survey of U.S. multinational firms conducted by Business International Corporation, has been found to have a significantly positive impact on inward investment (Wheeler and Mody 1992; Hackett and Srinivasan 1998). We use the rating provided by Business International (1989) as an indicator of the quality of infrastructure in 1989: INFRA measures this quality on a scale of 0 to 10. We include INFRA as a moderating factor on the effect of SUPPLIERS. Hence we include SUPPLIERS * INFRA.

An important issue is to what extent *local content rules* directed at increasing the local content of (foreign-owned) manufacturing operations are successful in enhancing vertical linkages. We examined in some detail the available information at the country level on local content regulations and import restrictions on components and materials (Japan Machinery Center for Trade and Investment 1997; Commission of the European Communities 1998). We found that very few formal rules specifying local content requirements applied to the electronics industry. Most existing requirements apply to automobile and machinery manufacturing. The only country that regularly imposes local content and export performance requirements on foreign-owned firms is China; often these are part of trade-balancing requirements that link import restrictions to export performance. In some ASEAN-4 countries, preferential treatment given to foreign investment projects is contingent on local content (among other requirements). Malaysia, for instance, grants "pioneer status" (a right to tax exemptions) if the investment meets a number of conditions, among which are local content requirements. In Indonesia import tariff reductions can be made dependent on local content. Overall, we concluded that import requirements and local content rules in Asia, if applied, are mostly part of incentive schemes. Such schemes and the conditions vary with each investment project, and this introduces a degree of discretion into the application of local content rules. The schemes may link import restrictions or local content requirements to export requirements.

Based on these findings, we decided to use two alternative indicators of local content requirements: besides an indicator of local content requirements at the *country* level, we also use a measure at the level of the individual *subsidiary.* At the country level, the presence and strictness of local content regulations and import restrictions is measured by the ratings given by U.S. multinational firms provided by Business International (1989). We averaged the ratings for the extent of component and material import restrictions and the use of local content requirements to construct the variable REGULATION. When local content requirements and import restrictions are made contingent on export requirements, subsidiaries with a local sales orientation will face stricter requirements than export-oriented firms. To control for this characteristic, we also include the cross-effect of LOCSALES and REGULATION. Both the cross-effect and REGULATION are expected to have a positive effect on the local content ratio.

The subsidiary-specific indicator of local content requirements is taken from the MITI survey. Subsidiaries are asked to indicate whether local content rules affect their manufacturing operations. If they indicate yes, the dummy variable for subsidiary-specific local content requirements, REGUSUB, takes the value one. Because REGUSUB varies by subsidiary, we also include the variable in the country dummy model. The dummy variable REGUSUB has the disadvantage that it does not indicate the strictness of the requirements. Given that local content rules tend to be stricter in the ASEAN-4 countries and China than in the NIEs, we attempted to remedy this to some extent by including REGUSUB separately for both groups of countries. We expect a stronger positive effect of REGUSUB for the ASEAN-4 countries and China. In addition, we include the cross-effect of REGUSUB and LOCSALES to test whether subsidiaries with a local sales orientation face stricter requirements.

1.4   Empirical Results

After presenting the results of the country dummy model, we analyze the results of the model with country variables. Finally, the results of a number of tests are discussed.

1.4.1   Country Dummy Model

Table 1.4 shows the results of five Tobit models explaining the local content ratios of Asian manufacturing subsidiaries of Japanese electronics firms. The first two equations do not include KEIRINT and are estimates based on 157 observations. Equation (1) is used as the basic model while equation (2) tests whether procurement behavior differs between subsidiaries located in the NIEs and those located in the ASEAN-4 countries and China. Equations (3), (4), and (5) include KEIRINT; its inclusion reduces the number of observations to 133.

In accordance with our expectations, the parent firm's R&D intensity negatively affects local content. R&D-intensive firms make greater use of

Table 1.4 **Determinants of Local Content Ratios of Asian Subsidiaries: Tobit Estimates with Country Dummies**

Variable	(1)	(2)	(3)	(4)	(5)
R&DINT	−1.28 (−2.41)**		−1.23 (−2.21)**	−1.32 (−2.40)**	−1.25 (−2.24)**
R&DINT*NIES		−1.23 (−1.58)			
R&DINT*(1 − NIES)		−1.10 (−1.54)			
KEIRINT			0.17 (3.21)***	0.19 (3.47)***	
KEIRINT*NIES					0.20 (2.21)**
KEIRINT*(1 − NIES)					0.16 (2.49)**
EXPER	0.0006 (2.68)***	0.0005 (2.58)**	0.0006 (3.03)***	0.0007 (3.32)***	0.0006 (3.04)***
ACQUIS	0.29 (1.81)*	0.24 (1.50)	0.24 (1.55)	0.20 (1.36)	0.24 (1.56)
JV	0.05 (1.28)	0.04 (1.14)	0.05 (1.14)	0.05 (1.20)	0.04 (1.09)
LOCSALES	0.12 (2.25)**				
LOCSALES*NIES		0.01 (0.18)	−0.01 (−0.16)	−0.04 (−0.48)	−0.01 (−0.13)
LOCSALES*(1 − NIES)		0.23 (3.06)***	0.17 (2.20)**	0.10 (1.23)	0.18 (2.22)**
REGUSUB	0.06 (1.37)				
REGUSUB*NIEs		0.00 (0.01)	−0.05 (−0.63)	−0.14 (−1.59)	−0.05 (−0.60)
REGUSUB*(1 − NIES)		0.10 (1.74)*	0.15 (2.69)***	0.08 (1.31)	0.15 (2.61)***
REGUSUB*LOCSALES				0.34 (2.16)**	
TELCOMP	−0.06 (−0.71)	−0.05 (−0.67)	−0.09 (−1.12)	−0.07 (−0.88)	−0.09 (−1.16)
PARTS	−0.05 (−1.33)	−0.03 (−0.72)	−0.02 (−0.38)	−0.02 (−0.44)	−0.02 (−0.43)
OTHERIND	−0.06 (−1.00)	−0.06 (−1.00)	−0.04 (−0.57)	−0.05 (−0.62)	−0.04 (−0.59)
Indonesia	0.24 (1.78)*	0.14 (0.97)	0.13 (0.89)	0.15 (1.01)	0.14 (0.93)
South Korea	0.12 (1.13)	0.11 (1.04)	0.14 (1.23)	0.13 (1.16)	0.14 (1.22)
Malaysia	0.11 (1.02)	0.00 (0.01)	0.00 (−0.01)	0.01 (0.09)	0.01 (0.05)
Philippines	0.08 (0.55)	−0.05 (−0.31)	−0.03 (−0.21)	−0.01 (−0.07)	−0.03 (−0.16)

(continued)

Table 1.4   (continued)

Variable	(1)	(2)	(3)	(4)	(5)
Singapore	0.15	0.14	0.16	0.17	0.16
	(1.43)	(1.36)	(1.48)	(1.59)	(1.43)
Thailand	0.06	−0.06	−0.08	−0.06	−0.07
	(0.55)	(−0.45)	(−0.58)	(−0.47)	(−0.50)
Taiwan	0.19	0.17	0.20	0.20	0.20
	(1.88)*	(1.71)*	(1.83)*	(1.85)*	(1.82)*
China	0.13	0.01	0.04	0.03	0.05
	(0.97)	(0.07)	(0.25)	(0.21)	(0.30)
Constant	0.44	0.50	0.43	0.43	0.43
	(4.17)***	(4.65)***	(3.65)***	(3.73)***	(3.65)***
N [censored]	157 [6]	157 [6]	140 [4]	140 [4]	140 [4]
Log likelihood	19.04	21.49	25.84	28.15	25.91
χ^2	49.52	54.41	58.19	62.80	58.32

Note: Numbers in parentheses are t-values.
*Significant at the 1 percent level.
**Significant at the 5 percent level.
***Significant at the 10 percent level.

nonstandardized and technology-intensive components, often developed and produced by the firm in Japan. There is no evidence, on the other hand, that this effect is significantly stronger in the ASEAN-4 countries and China. The estimated coefficients for R&DINT do not differ markedly in equation (2), while the standard error of the separate estimates is substantially higher.

The results show a robust positive and significant effect of operating experience on the local content ratio. Operating experience in the host country increases the vertical linkages of subsidiaries in the local economy, because the switch to local suppliers and the process of adaptation to the new environment require time. However, the estimated coefficient of EXPER suggests that this effect in itself is limited: one additional year (twelve months) of local operating experience increases the local content ratio by 0.6 percentage points. The results can only be taken as partial confirmation of the role of Japanese firms' relatively late internationalization in procurement behavior.

Our expectation that the entry mode of the subsidiary has an impact on the input-sourcing strategy is partly confirmed. Both ACQUIS and JV consistently have positive signs, but their significance is low. ACQUIS is significant (at the 10 percent level) in equation (1).

The hypothesis that local content increases if sales are destined for the local market is confirmed by the positive and significant coefficient of LOCSALES in equation (1). The results of equations (2), (3), and (5) show that this effect is largely driven by the procurement behavior of subsidiaries in the ASEAN-4 countries and China: LOCSALES is significant for subsidiaries in these countries but insignificant for subsidiaries located in the NIEs. This suggests that for countries with relatively unsophisticated markets, focusing on local markets helps subsidiaries to achieve lower dependence on imports of technology-intensive parts and components.

REGUSUB, the variable indicating local content requirements at the subsidiary level, has a positive sign but is insignificant in equation (1). However, if the effect is split between the NIEs and the ASEAN-4 countries and China, it appears that these requirements have an insignificant effect on the local content ratio of subsidiaries located in the former countries but a positive and significant impact on that of subsidiaries in the latter. This indicates that relatively strict local content requirements have changed procurement behavior in the ASEAN-4 countries and China but such restrictions play no role in influencing sourcing decisions of subsidiaries in the NIEs. In equation (4), it is also tested whether local content regulations have a greater impact on subsidiaries selling on local markets. The cross-effect of LOCSALES and REGUSUB is positive and significant, suggesting that local-market-oriented subsidiaries indeed face stricter requirements. Inclusion of the cross-effect increases the standard errors of the coefficients of LOCSALES and REGUSUB, which become insignificant.

The effects of the inclusion of the *keiretsu* intensity variable, KEIRINT, in equation (3) confirm that *keiretsu* linkages have a major impact on vertical integration and local procurement. KEIRINT has a positive sign and is highly significant. Moreover, inclusion of KEIRINT clearly improves the fit of the model: the χ^2 increases by a substantial margin. Separating the effect of KEIRINT for subsidiaries in the NIEs and subsidiaries in the ASEAN-4 countries and China in equation (5) shows a slightly higher coefficient for the NIEs. Hence, we do not find evidence that *keiretsu* firms are able to reach higher local content ratios in countries with less developed local supply infrastructures. Perhaps investments in local manufacturing plants by *keiretsu* suppliers are also less viable in these countries than in the NIEs.

After controlling for subsidiary and parent firm characteristics, there is not much additional variation in local content ratios across countries. Only the dummy for Taiwan is consistently significant (at the 10 percent level), indicating that Taiwanese subsidiaries reach higher ratios than subsidiaries in Hong Kong, ceteris paribus. The coefficient of the Indonesia dummy is positive and significant at the 10 percent level in equation (1), but this appears to be related to the local sales orientation of Indonesian subsidiaries and stricter local content requirements. The Indonesia dummy becomes insignificant if the models include separate (and higher) estimates for local sales orientation and local content rules in the ASEAN-4 countries and China.

Nor does the industry of the subsidiary exert a strong independent influence on the local content ratio. The coefficients for TELCOMP, PARTS, and OTHERIND are negatively signed, indicating that subsidiaries producing consumer goods tend to have higher local content, but the coefficients are not significant.

We conclude that the results generally confirm our hypotheses concerning the effects of parent firm and subsidiary characteristics on local content. Almost all coefficients have the predicted signs and reach conventional significance levels in most equations; for subsidiary-specific local content regulations and local sales orientation this only applies to the ASEAN-4 countries and China. The only unexpected result is the lack of geographic differentiation in the effects of R&D intensity and *keiretsu* intensity.

1.4.2   Country Variable Model

Table 1.5 shows the estimated coefficients of equations (6) through (10), which include host country variables. A general observation is that the estimated effects for most parent and subsidiary variables do not differ markedly from the estimates of the country dummy model. R&DINT and EXPER remain significant, ACQUIS is significant at the 10 percent level in all equations, and REGUSUB (eqs. [7], [9], and [10]) and LOCSALES (eqs. [9] and [10]) remain positive and significant for the ASEAN-4 countries and China.

The results for the host country variables are generally less unambiguous. In equation (6), the size of the host country's electronic parts industry, SUPPLIERS, has the expected positive sign but is far from significant. SUPPLIERS does affect local procurement conditional on good quality of host country infrastructure: SUPPLIERS * INFRA becomes significant in equation (7).

In equation (8), the country-specific indicator of local content regulations and import restrictions, REGULATION, is substituted for REGUSUB. In addition, the cross-effect of REGULATION and LOCSALES is included. REGULATION has the expected positive sign but is insignificant, while its cross-effect with LOCSALES is insignificant with the wrong (negative) sign.[11] Taken together with the results for REGUSUB, this suggests that local content regulations vary considerably between foreign subsidiaries in a country and have a greater impact on the procurement behavior of specific subsidiaries (presumably those that apply for some form of favorable investment status) rather than affecting local content of all investors.

In equation (9), the indicator for the presence of Japanese suppliers,

---

11. Nor does REGULATION reach significance if the cross-effect with LOCSALES is excluded.

Variable	(6)	(7)	(8)	(9)	(10)
Table 1.5		**Determinants of Local Content Ratios of Asian Subsidiaries: Tobit Estimates with Country Variables**			
R&DINT	−1.57	−1.66	−1.77	−1.40	−1.49
	(−2.89)***	(−2.84)***	(−3.06)***	(−2.40)**	(−2.56)**
KEIRINT	0.19	0.22	0.20	0.14	
	(3.33)***	(3.84)***	(3.54)***	(2.29)**	
EXPER	0.0009	0.0008	0.0008	0.008	0.0008
	(4.44)***	(4.04)***	(3.79)***	(4.07)***	(4.23)***
ACQUIS	0.29	0.26	0.31	0.24	0.24
	(1.93)*	(1.73)*	(1.91)*	(1.65)	(1.66)*
JV	0.03	0.03	0.03	0.01	0.01
	(0.86)	(0.89)	(0.65)	(0.32)	(0.23)
LOCSALES*NIES	0.07	0.01	0.08	0.01	0.01
	(0.98)	(0.15)	(0.63)	(0.14)	(0.19)
LOCSALES*(1 − NIES)	0.10	0.09	0.20	0.18	0.20
	(1.28)	(1.10)	(1.01)	(1.97)*	(2.14)**
REGUSUB*NIEs	0.00	−0.02		−0.04	−0.03
	(−0.06)	(−0.32)		(−0.54)	(−0.39)
REGUSUB*(1 − NIES)	0.09	0.12		0.13	0.12
	(1.64)	(2.02)**		(2.30)**	(2.10)**
REGULATION			0.02		
			(0.91)		
REGULATION*LOCSALES			−0.03		
			(−0.68)		
SUPPLIERS	0.04				
	(1.33)				
SUPPLIERS*INFRA		0.0033	0.0030	0.0049	0.0037
		(2.29)**	(1.92)*	(3.01)***	(2.08)**
KEIRINT*SUPPLIERS*INFRA					0.004
					(1.58)
JRATIO				0.12	0.15
				(0.51)	(0.65)
KEIRINT*JRATIO					−0.14
					(−0.68)
TELCOMP	−0.08	−0.10	−0.08	−0.08	−0.09
	(−1.07)	(−1.33)	(−1.04)	(−1.01)	(−1.14)
PARTS	−0.03	−0.04	−0.03	−0.02	−0.02
	(−0.74)	(−0.91)	(−0.78)	(−0.54)	(−0.61)
OTHERIND	0.03	0.03	0.02	0.03	0.04
	(0.36)	(0.37)	(0.26)	(0.28)	(0.41)
Constant	0.19	0.29	0.27	0.09	0.14
	(0.83)	(2.73)***	(1.65)	(0.37)	(0.60)
N [censored]	140 [4]	133 [4]	133 [4]	128 [2]	128 [2]
Log likelihood	18.90	19.79	18.14	26.31	27.24
χ^2	44.30	46.59	43.28	47.44	49.31

Note: Numbers in parentheses are *t*-values.
*Significant at the 1 percent level.
**Significant at the 5 percent level.
***Significant at the 10 percent level.

JRATIO, is introduced. It has the expected positive sign but is not significant. Nor does the inclusion of cross-effects of KEIRINT with SUPPLIERS and JRATIO in equation (10) give significant effects.[12] In light of the strong positive effect of the KEIRINT variable, these results are puzzling. Given the higher switching costs for firms with intensive intra-*keiretsu* supplier relationships, we expected the positive effect of KEIRINT to work through the replication of *keiretsu* supplier networks abroad. We can think of a number of reasons why the results do not bring this out. First, the variable JRATIO may not be an accurate proxy for the strength of the local Japanese supply base. JRATIO is derived from MITI survey data with a limited response rate, and response rates may differ by country. Furthermore, JRATIO measures sales of responding component subsidiaries and hence includes exports, while export-oriented subsidiaries may not have been set up to supply local manufacturers. We are not able at this point to remedy these potential problems. Second, we may not be able to estimate country variable effects precisely enough because the number of countries (seven) in our country variable model is small. Third, in theory we should include an indicator for the local presence of suppliers *within the same keiretsu* instead of a proxy for the presence of Japanese suppliers overall. These issues need further attention in future research.

1.4.3 Further Tests

We performed a number of other tests, the results of which are not shown. These do merit some discussion. We also hypothesized that the characteristics of the local market may have an impact on the local content of manufacturing operations. The more sophisticated the demand for electronic goods, the more firms will be inclined to adapt and redesign products for the local market, which may also involve a switch to higher value-added components produced locally. We used as a measure of demand sophistication, MARKET, the value of electronics sales in the country in 1992 (taken from Elsevier 1995) per capita. Market sophistication may moderate the effect of LOCSALES: the more sophisticated market demand, the more the market resembles the major export markets (the European Union, the United States, and Japan) and the smaller the effect of differences in local versus export sales strategy. The cross-effect of LOCSALES and MARKET had the expected negative sign but was not significant.

Another test involved adding a dummy variable that takes the value one if the investing firm is a core firm in the vertical *keiretsu*. The results did not support the hypothesis that core firms behave differently from member firms. Another consideration was that in the country dummy model, the strict regulations in China linking export and import requirements could

---

12. Including KEIRINT itself in eq. (10) does not change these results.

bias the effect of LOCSALES: the regulations are likely to increase the effect of LOCSALES on the local content ratio, compared with other Asian countries. We included a cross-effect of the China dummy with LOC-SALES. The coefficient was positive, as expected, but not significant.

We tested whether we could find evidence that transfer-pricing issues are affecting reported local content ratios. Affiliates located in host countries with higher tax rates may have an incentive to engage in transfer pricing and report a higher value of imports from the parent firm (and hence a lower local content ratio). We calculated host countries' effective tax rates by taking the pretax current profit minus after-tax current profit divided by pretax current profit for all Japanese subsidiaries reporting in the 1992 MITI survey.[13] We included this effective tax rate as an explanatory variable in an attempt to control for the effects of transfer pricing. The variable had a counterintuitive positive sign but was not significant, while the other coefficients remained unchanged.

A last test involved substituting the local procurement ratio (local procurement divided by total procurement) for the local content ratio as the dependent variable in the model. The estimated effects were very similar to those in the local content ratio models. The one important difference was that the country-specific measure of local content rules, REGULA-TION, did reach conventional significance levels in the model of equation (8). We took this result as further confirmation that local content rules in Asia have an impact on vertical linkages.

1.5 Conclusions

We examined the determinants of the vertical linkages, that is, the local content (intrasubsidiary value added and procurement of inputs from locally established suppliers), of 157 Asian subsidiaries of Japanese multinational firms in the electronics industry in 1992. Consistent with our theoretical considerations, we found that a number of characteristics, both at the parent firm level and at the subsidiary level, affect subsidiaries' local content ratios. Operating experience has a positive effect on the local content ratio. As subsidiaries gain operating experience in the local economy, they are able to deepen their vertical linkages. This result is consistent with the notion that the alleged lack of vertical linkages of Japanese multinational firms is the result of a "vintage effect": the relatively late internationalization of Japanese firms. However, the magnitude of the estimated experience effect is too small to take these results as more than a partial confirmation of the vintage effect explanation. The results indicate that

---

13. This gave us the following rates: Hong Kong, 0.138; Korea, 0.348; Singapore, 0.192; Taiwan, 0.207; Indonesia, 0.286; Malaysia, 0.112; Thailand, 0.369; Philippines, 0.217; and China, 0.065.

acquired subsidiaries are more integrated into the local economy and have higher local content ratios than greenfield subsidiaries. Subsidiaries of R&D-intensive parents rely more strongly on imports of (nonstandardized) components designed by the parent and have lower local content ratios. Subsidiaries located in the ASEAN-4 countries and China that sell a high percentage of manufactured output on the host market reach higher local content levels than export-oriented subsidiaries. A local market orientation is likely to be associated with the use of mature and standardized low-cost components procured from locally established suppliers, whereas an orientation toward sophisticated export markets is associated with technology-intensive components that are not typically available locally.

Membership of the parent firm in a vertical *keiretsu* with intensive supplier-assembler relationships has a robust positive impact on local content. We ascribed this to the ability of *keiretsu* members to stimulate the creation of a network of *keiretsu* component and parts manufacturers in host economies, which helps them to achieve higher local content levels. Apparently, this effect offsets a possible negative effect of *keiretsu* relationships on local content that may be due to the higher costs involved when switching to overseas suppliers outside the *keiretsu*. However, we could not establish with the data available that *keiretsu* firms reach higher local content in countries with a greater presence of Japanese suppliers.

Host country local content regulations have a positive and significant effect if measured at the subsidiary level but not if a more general measure is used at the country level. This finding is consistent with the observation that although there are few formal local content rules in Asian countries, preferential investment status programs give governments the discretionary power to demand changes in procurement behavior on a case by case basis. It should be noted, though, that the finding that local content requirements have been capable of changing procurement behavior does not tell us whether the benefits of these policies have outweighed their costs. Achievement of local content targets comes at the price of tax relief or investment subsidies, and perhaps more important, there is evidence that local content requirements reduce the total volume of foreign investment (Hackett and Srinivasan 1998).

In general, our attempt to establish the effects of host country characteristics on local content was less successful, which may be due to the limited number of countries represented in our sample. We did find that the size of the host country electronic parts and component manufacturing sector combined with the availability of good local infrastructure raises the local content of Japanese subsidiaries.

This study is a first attempt to shed some light on the determinants of vertical linkages by Japanese firms. In order to allow a better assessment of vertical linkages and potential spillovers to the local economy as well as the role of *keiretsu* supplier linkages, it may be necessary in future research to distinguish between local procurement from Japanese subsidiaries and local procurement from locally owned suppliers.[14] In addition, the effect of overseas supplier networks of vertical *keiretsu* should be analyzed directly by measuring the size of these networks for each *keiretsu* in each country. We are planning to examine these networks by combining the available information on *keiretsu* membership with databases on overseas subsidiaries. We expect that this approach will provide us with more robust evidence concerning the interaction of *keiretsu* linkages, local supply infrastructure, and local content. We are also planning to remedy the limited variation in host country characteristics by extending the study to more countries and, possibly, by adding data on local content and host country variables in 1995. An extension to 1995 is of interest because evidence exists that local procurement in Asia increased between 1992 and 1995 (MITI 1998a).

Another avenue for further research is to change the focus from the host country level to the regional level. In order to gain insight into the role of "regional core networks" in East Asia and their importance in Asian trade and industrial development, a perspective is needed that takes into account procurements from other Asian countries (excluding Japan). As can be seen from table 1.2, procurements from other Asian countries are not unimportant.

Japanese subsidiaries appear to have been quick to adjust to changing economic conditions after the Asian economic crisis in the summer of 1997. According to a recent MITI survey, Japan's manufacturing subsidiaries in the ASEAN-4 countries reduced their investment in tangible fixed assets by 21 percent and increased their exports to Japan by 11 percent from the last quarter of 1996 to the last quarter of 1997 (yen-based figures; MITI 1998b). Such changes are bound to have a substantial impact on procurement behavior. There are some indications that the increased cost of imported components due to the depreciation of Asian currencies has spurred firms to increase local procurement.[15] More insight concerning the procurement strategies of Japanese firms may be obtained by investigating changes in vertical linkages throughout the 1990s. We hope to be able to contribute to research in this area in the future.

---

14. It may be possible to study such local linkages in the future because MITI is planning to introduce such a distinction in the 1999 survey.

15. E.g., Hitachi Consumer Products in Thailand reportedly plans to raise the local content of its washing machine manufacturing operations from 43 percent (in early 1998) to 85 percent within a year. See "Local Procurement Up in Southeast Asia," *Nikkei Weekly*, 27 July 1998.

Appendix

Data Sources, Selection, and Description of Variables

Data Selection

Our data on local procurement and intrasubsidiary value added of overseas manufacturing subsidiaries of Japanese electronics firms are taken from MITI's fifth *Basic Survey on Foreign Direct Investment* (MITI 1994) and concern fiscal year 1992 (the year ending 31 March 1993). This MITI survey includes a total of 314 subsidiaries in East Asia. For a relatively large number of subsidiaries, the information on local procurement and procurement by region of origin was incomplete, and a first screening reduced the number of observations to 203. We further eliminated subsidiaries with fewer than ten employees and a few cases in which the data were unreliable (e.g., the value of total procurement exceeded that of total sales). This diminished the number of observations by 15, and we ended up with reliable information for a sample of 188 firms.

We matched these data with information on parent firms using fiscal year 1992 financial data from published financial reports (MOF 1993) for firms listed on the Tokyo Stock Exchange and Toyo Keizai's *Nihon no Kigyou Guruupu* (for *keiretsu* membership). We could not establish the parent firms of all Asian subsidiaries, and R&D and *keiretsu* information on parents was not available for all subsidiaries. This reduced the number of observations to 157 in the basic country dummy model and further, to 140, in models that included the *keiretsu* variable. The data on host country characteristics from Business International do not include information on China, which further reduced the sample to 133 in the country variable model, and the presence of Japanese suppliers could not be established for 5 more observations, reducing the number of observations to 128.

Variable Definitions

Table 1A.1 provides the definitions of the variables and the data sources.

Table 1A.1   **Variable Definitions and Data Sources**

Variable	Definition	Source
LOCON	Local content ratio: (total sales − total imports) / (total sales − imports of finished goods)	1
R&DINT	Parent firm R&D ratio: parent firm R&D expenditure / total sales	1, 5
KEIRINT	Intensity of supplier-assembler relationships within the vertical *keiretsu* in Japan; paid-in capital of the core *keiretsu* firm's manufacturing-related companies in Japan / paid-in capital of the core *keiretsu* firm. Core firms have at least 250 billion yen in sales.	2
Entry mode		1
Omitted dummy	Greenfield and 100% Japanese equity share (reference case)	
ACQUIS	Acquisition (100% Japanese equity share) of existing firm	
JV	Joint venture	
Industry dummies		1
Omitted dummy	Consumer goods	
TELCOMP	Telecommunications and computers	
PARTS	Electronic parts	
OTHERIND	Other electronic devices	
EXPER	Operating experience: number of months of production since start of operations until March 1993	1
REGUSUB	Subsidiary-specific local content requirements: dummy variable that takes value 1 if subsidiary reports that it faced such requirements	1
LOCSALES	Local sales ratio: sales in host country / total sales	1
SUPPLIERS	Size of local supply industry of electronic parts and components: natural log of host country's production of electronic parts	3
JRATIO	Presence of Japanese-owned suppliers in the local supply industry: natural log of total sales by Japanese subsidiaries manufacturing electronic parts / natural log of total production of host country electronic parts industry	1, 3
INFRA	Quality of infrastructure: indicated on a 0–10 range	4
REGULATION	Strictness of local content requirements and restrictions on component and material imports: indicated on a 0–10 range, where 0 means no regulation, 10 strict regulation	4

Sources: (1) MITI (1994). (2) Toyo Keizai Shinpousha, *Nihon no Kigyou Guruupu* (Japanese corporate groups; Tokyo, 1990). (3) Elsevier (1995). (4) Business International (1989). (5) MOF (1993).

References

Aitken, Brian, Gordon H. Hanson, and Ann E. Harrison. 1997. Spillovers, foreign investment, and export behaviour. *American Economic Review* 43:103–32.

Asanuma, Banri, and T. Kikutani. 1992. Risk absorption in Japanese subcontracting: A microeconometric study of the automobile industry. *Journal of the Japanese and International Economies* 6:1–29.

Asian Development Bank. 1998. *Key indicators of developing Asian and Pacific countries.* Manila: Asian Development Bank.

Baba, Yasunori, and Hiroyuki Hatashima. 1995. Capability transfer in the Pacific Rim nations: The case of Japanese electrical and electronics firms. *International Journal of Technology Management* 10:732–46.

Belderbos, René. 1997. *Japanese electronics multinationals and strategic trade policies.* Oxford: Oxford University Press.

Belderbos, René, Giovanni Capannelli, and Kyoji Fukao. 1996. Nikkei Kigyou Genchi Choutatsu Ritsu no Kettei Youin (Determinants of local procurement ratios by Japanese electronics firms). In *Dai 25-Kai Wagakuni Kigyou no Kaigai Jigyou Katudou (The twenty-fifth survey on Japan's direct investment abroad),* ed. Ministry of International Trade and Industry. Tokyo: Oukurashou Insatsu-kyoku.

Belderbos, René, and Leo Sleuwaegen. 1996. Japanese firms and the decision to invest abroad: Industrial groups and regional core networks. *Review of Economics and Statistics* 78:214–20.

———. 1997. Local content rules and vertical market structure. *European Journal of Political Economy* 13:101–19.

Bertschek, Irene. 1995. Product and process innovation as a response to increasing imports and foreign direct investment. *Journal of Industrial Economics* 43 (4): 341–57.

Business International. 1989. *Country assessment service.* New York: Business International Corporation.

Capannelli, Giovanni. 1993. Transfer of Japanese electronics industry to Malaysia. *Keizai Bunseki (Economic Analysis)* 129:67–118.

———. 1997a. Buyer-supplier relations and technology transfer: Japanese consumer electronics. *International Review of Economics and Business* 44, no. 3 (September): 633–62.

———. 1997b. Industry-wide relocation and technology transfer: A study on buyer-supplier relations in Malaysia. Unpublished Ph.D. diss., Hitotsubashi University, Tokyo.

Caves, Richard E. 1995. *Multinational enterprise and economic analysis,* 2d ed. Cambridge: Cambridge University Press.

Chia, Siow Yue. 1995. The international procurement and sales behaviour of multinational enterprises. In *Corporate links and foreign direct investment in Asia and the Pacific,* ed. Edward K. Y. Chen and Peter Drysdale. Pymble, Australia: Harper Educational.

Chung, W., W. Mitchell, and B. Yeung. 1996. Foreign direct investment and host country productivity: The case of the American automotive components industry. Ann Arbor: University of Michigan School of Business Administration. Mimeograph.

Cohen, W., and D. Levinthal. 1990. Absorptive capacity: A new perspective on learning and innovation. *Administrative Science Quarterly* 35:128–52.

Commission of the European Communities. 1998. Sectoral and trade barriers database. Available at http://mkaccdb.eu.int/mkdb/mkdb.pl.

Cusumano, Michael A., and Akira Takeishi. 1991. Supplier relations and management: A survey of Japanese, Japanese-transplant, and U.S. auto plants. *Strategic Management Journal* 12:563–88.

De Arcos, Luisa, et al. 1995. *Innovative capability, embeddedness, and the contribution of foreign firms to innovation in their host regions.* Report to the SPRINT Programme of the European Commission. Maastricht: MERIT.

Dyer, Jeffrey H. 1996. Specialized supplier networks as a source of competitive advantage: Evidence from the auto industry. *Strategic Management Journal* 17:271–91.

Elsevier Science Publishers. 1995. *Yearbook of world electronics data.* Oxford: Elsevier.

Froot, Kenneth A. 1991. *Japanese foreign direct investment.* NBER Working Paper no. 3737. Cambridge, Mass.: National Bureau of Economic Research.

Fukao, Kyoji, Toshiyasu Izawa, Morio Kuninori, and Toru Nakakita. 1994. R&D investment and overseas production: An empirical analysis of Japan's electric machinery industry based on corporate data. *BOJ Monetary and Economic Studies* 12:1–60.

Globerman, Steven. 1978. Foreign direct investment and "spillover" efficiency benefits in Canadian manufacturing industries. *Canadian Journal of Economics* 12 (1): 42–56.

Gold, David, Persa Eonomou, and Telly Tolentino. 1991. Trade blocs and investment blocs: The triad in foreign direct investment and international trade. Paper presented at the annual meeting of the Academy of International Business, Miami, 19 October.

Graham, Edward M., and Paul Krugman. 1990. *Foreign direct investment in the United States.* Washington, D.C.: Institute for International Economics.

Hackett, Steve C., and Krishna Srinivasan. 1998. Do supplier switching costs differ across Japanese and U.S. multinational firms? *Japan and the World Economy* 10:13–32.

Haddad, Mona, and Ann Harrison. 1993. Are there spillovers from direct foreign investment? Evidence from panel data for Morocco. *Journal of Development Economics* 42:51–74.

Head, Keith, John Ries, and Deborah Swenson. 1995. Agglomeration benefits and location choice: Evidence from Japanese manufacturing investments in the United States. *Journal of International Economics* 38:223–47.

Hiramoto, Atsushi. 1992. Subcontracting strategies of Japanese companies in Europe and Asia: A case study of the electronics industry. In *New impacts on industrial relations: Internationalization and changing production strategies,* ed. Shigeyoshi Tokunaga, Norbert Altmann, and Helmut Demes. Munich: Deutsches Institut für Japan Studien.

Horiuchi, T. 1989. The flexibility of Japan's small and medium-sized firms and their foreign direct investment. In *Japanese investment in the United States: Should we be concerned?* ed. Kozo Yamamura. Seattle: University of Washington, Society for Japanese Studies.

Japan Machinery Center for Trade and Investment. 1997. Ajia no Keizai Hatten to Boueki Toushi jou no Mondaiten (Economic growth and government interventions on trade and investment in Asia). Tokyo: Nihon Kikai Yushutsu Kumiai. Mimeograph.

Jie-A-Joen, Clive, René Belderbos, and Leo Sleuwaegen. 1998. Local content requirements, vertical cooperation, and foreign direct investment. Netherlands Institute of Business Organization and Strategy Research Memorandum no. 9801. Maastricht: Maastricht University.

Kinoshita, Yuko. 1996. Technology spillovers through foreign direct investment. New York: New York University, Department of Economics. Mimeograph.

Kotabe, Masaaki, and Glenn S. Omura. 1989. Sourcing strategies of European and Japanese multinationals: A comparison. *Journal of International Business Studies* 20:113–30.

Kreinin, Mordechai E. 1992. How closed is Japan's market? Additional evidence. *Journal of World Trade* 26:529–42.

Lall, Sanjaya. 1995. Industrial strategy and policies on foreign direct investment in East Asia. *Transnational Corporations* 4:1–26.

Lim, Y. C., and Pang Eng Fong. 1982. Vertical linkages and multinational enterprises in developing countries. *World Development* 7:585–95.

Mason, Mark, and Dennis Encarnation, eds. 1994. *Does ownership matter? Japanese multinationals in Europe.* Oxford and New York: Oxford University Press.

MITI (Japan Ministry of International Trade and Industry). 1994. *Dai 5-kai Kaigai Toushi Tokei Souran* (Basic survey on foreign direct investment no. 5). Tokyo: Okurashou Insatsukyoku.

———. 1998a. *Dai 6-Kai Kaigai Toushi Tokei Souran* (Basic survey on foreign direct investment no. 6). Tokyo: Okurashou Insatsukyoku.

———. 1998b. *Kigyou Doukou Chousa* (Survey of trends of enterprises). Tokyo: Ministry of International Trade and Industry.

Mody, Ashoka, and Krishna Srinivasan. 1997. Japanese and United States firms as foreign investors: Do they march to the same tune? Washington, D.C.: World Bank. Mimeograph.

MOF (Japan Ministry of Finance). 1993. *Yuuka Shouken Houkokusho* (Financial reports of listed firms). Tokyo: Okurashou Insatsukyoku.

Murray, J. Y., A. R. Wildt, and M. Kotabe. 1995. Global sourcing strategies of U.S. subsidiaries of foreign multinationals. *Management International Review* 35 (4): 307–24.

O'Farrell, P. N., and B. O'Loughlin. 1981. New industry input linkages in Ireland: An econometric analysis. *Environment and Planning* 13:285–308.

Okamoto, Yumiko. 1997. Multinationals, production efficiency, and spillover effects: The case of the U.S. auto parts industry. Kobe: Kobe University. Mimeograph.

Okamuro, Hiroyuki. 1995. Changing subcontracting relations and risk sharing in Japan: An econometric analysis of the automobile industry. *Hitotsubashi Journal of Economics* 36 (2): 208–18.

Oliver, Nick, and Barry Wilkinson. 1992. *The Japanization of British industry: New developments in the 1990s.* Oxford and Cambridge, Mass.: Blackwell.

Patel, Pari. 1995. Localized production of technology for global market. *Cambridge Journal of Economics* 19:141–53.

Reid, Neil. 1995. Just-in-time inventory control and the economic integration of Japanese-owned manufacturing plants. *Regional Studies* 29:345–55.

Richardson, Martin. 1993. Content protection with foreign capital. *Oxford Economic Papers* 45:103–17.

Sako, Mari. 1992. *Prices, quality, and trust: Inter-firm relations in Britain and Japan.* Cambridge: Cambridge University Press.

Turok, Ivan. 1993. Inward investment and local linkages: How deeply embedded is "Silicon Glen"? *Regional Studies* 27:401–17.

Urata, Shujiro. 1991. The rapid increase of direct investment abroad and structural change in Japan. In *Direct foreign investment in Asia's developing economies and structural change in the Asia-Pacific region,* ed. Eric D. Ramstetter. Boulder, Colo.: Westview.

Wang, Jian-Ye, and Magnus Blomström. 1992. Foreign investment and technology transfer: A simple model. *European Economic Review* 36:137–55.

Westney, Eleanor. 1996. Japanese multinationals in North America. In *Multinationals in North America,* ed. Lorraine Eden. Calgary: University of Calgary Press.

Wheeler, D., and A. Mody. 1992. International investment location decisions: The case of U.S. firms. *Journal of International Economics* 33:57–76.
Yamazawa, Ippei, et al. 1993. Dynamic interdependence among the Asia-Pacific economies, *Keizai Bunseki* (Economic Analysis), no. 129 (March). Tokyo: Economic Planning Agency, Economic Research Institute.

Comment   Toshihiko Hayashi

FDI is expected to be an important vehicle by which technology and know-how are transmitted from a home country to a host country. The transmission mechanism is commonly called spillover, perhaps borrowing from the similar concept well established in the local public finance literature. Belderbos, Capannelli, and Fukao (BCF) are interested in how the extent to which such spillover takes place varies among individual subsidiaries and what factors determine the scope of spillovers. BCF are also concerned with how Japanese FDI fares in Asia in this regard because it is often observed that Japanese subsidiaries in Asia are less likely to generate spillovers to local economies than are subsidiaries from other home countries.

Two contrasting hypotheses have been advanced to account for the alleged lack of enthusiasm for linkages in Japanese subsidiaries: the idiosyncrasy hypothesis and the vintage hypothesis. The idiosyncrasy hypothesis says that idiosyncratic behavior on the part of Japanese multinational corporations—reflecting *keiretsu*-oriented or inward-looking attitudes—leads to less interaction with local industrial communities in the host country, and thus less spillover. The vintage hypothesis says, to the contrary, that the idiosyncrasies are only temporary. The basic reason for less involvement by Japanese subsidiaries is simply that they are relatively new to the host country and hence less experienced. As vintage develops Japanese subsidiaries will gain experience in dealing with the local business community and workforce, deepening vertical linkages and increasing spillovers.

In my view, BCF's study reported here is no doubt an important contribution to this debate, although other facets of their findings merit no less recognition. Making use of the data set *Basic Survey on Foreign Direct Investment,* published by MITI in 1994, BCF try to decipher the relation between the local content ratio of Japanese electronics manufacturing subsidiaries and the characteristics of the parent company as well as the subsidiaries themselves. Through their methodologically sound and laborious work, several interesting findings emerge.

BCF Findings

BCF define local content to include "both the value added of manufacturing (in-house production of components) and the value of components

Toshihiko Hayashi is professor of international public policy at Osaka University.

and materials sourced from local (Japanese and third party owned, as well as locally owned) suppliers." They take this measure of local content and divide it by total sales of the subsidiary to get the local content ratio. By means of a Tobit model with the local content ratio as dependent variable and R&D intensity, intensity of supplier-assembler relationships (*keiretsu*), vintage, and other factors as explanatory variables, BCF obtain some very interesting results. Three of the most interesting findings are as follows:

1. Their prior conjecture that the parent firm's R&D intensity negatively affects the local content ratio is empirically verified. Their results give support to the view that "R&D-intensive firms make greater use of nonstandardized and technology-intensive components, often developed and produced by the firm in Japan."

2. *Keiretsu* intensity has a positive sign and is highly significant in their estimates, suggesting that "*keiretsu* linkages have a major impact on vertical integration and local procurement." BCF ascribe this finding to the "ability of *keiretsu* members to stimulate the creation of a network of *keiretsu* component and parts manufacturers in host economies, which helps them to achieve higher local content levels."

3. Operating experience has a positive effect on the local content ratio. From this BCF confirm, albeit cautiously, that the vintage effect is the cause of the alleged lack of vertical linkage of Japanese multinational firms.

Suggested Research Agenda

Though BCF's findings are extremely interesting by themselves, I would learn more if they followed up their analyses along the lines suggested below.

In the course of their analyses BCF carefully distinguish the factors that affect the parent firm side and those that affect the subsidiary side. However, their final estimation is based on a kind of reduced-form model. It would help me understand the nature of the problem better if they presented a structural form model and obtained estimates for structural coefficients.

If BCF had shifted from econometrics to case studies to substantiate their analyses, they would have encountered a richer reality. For example, they make use of the ratings given by U.S. multinational firms provided by Business International to proxy an explanatory variable, REGULATION. Though it may tell us something about the country-wise degree of freedom to invest, the index seems to provide only tangential information if any to the parent firm contemplating FDI. It seems to be often the case that for Japanese firms searching for investment opportunities, the choice is between Dalian and Shanghai rather than between China and India. And if the chosen location is Dalian, should it be downtown Dalian or the Economic and Technological Development Zone in the suburbs?

Policy Implication

This leads me to the question BCF pose at the outset. They seem to be concerned with the spillover effects that FDI is expected to bring to the host country. However, their study concentrates on the degree of local content of foreign subsidiaries, based on the hypothesis that higher local content will be correlated with greater spillover effects.

It goes without saying that the degree of vertical linkage is an important piece of information. However, from a policy perspective, it would be just as important to know whether spillovers are taking place in the market. The question is whether spillovers are a case of pecuniary externalities or a case of technical externalities.

If vertical linkages create increased demand for local products and labor, which induces or encourages productivity-enhancing measures in indigenous industry, the host country government would have to be concerned with the amount of higher linkage FDI and little else.

However, if spillovers are more technical in nature, such as foreign subsidiaries acting as role models, demonstration effects, or increased opportunities for local spinoffs, the presence and the magnitude of FDI itself would be important. In that case it may be necessary for the host country government to encourage or give additional incentives to foreign firms with greater or lesser degrees of linkage to invest in the host country. Also, the role of Japanese electronics manufacturing subsidiaries in Asia would have to be evaluated in this context as well.

Comment   Lee Branstetter

I found this to be an extremely interesting, original, and ambitious paper. Belderbos, Capannelli, and Fukao, individually and together, have been among the most important and prolific contributors to the burgeoning literature on the economic analysis of Japanese FDI at the micro level. This paper is an important addition to that record of research, and I believe that the research agenda that grows out of this paper will yield many interesting results. I should also note that I am quite envious of the wealth of data to which these authors have been allowed access.

The authors begin by noting that economists have little systematic evidence on the determinants of local sourcing activity by multinational firms. The authors utilize unusually rich data collected by the Japanese General Management and Coordination Agency that is rarely provided to outside researchers. This data set includes information at the subsidiary

Lee Branstetter is assistant professor of economics and director of the East Asian Studies Program at the University of California, Davis, and a faculty research fellow of the National Bureau of Economic Research.

level on local sourcing and other variables, information on parent firms, and information on *keiretsu* linkages among parent firms and their affiliates. The authors then analyze the determinants of local sourcing at the micro level, using Tobit regression techniques. They find some results consistent with their initial predictions. I found the empirical work in the paper to have been well executed, and I do not question the results. Therefore, I will actually concentrate most of my initial remarks not on the body of the paper but on the motivation outlined in the first few pages.

One important element of that motivation can be summarized as follows. A primary benefit of FDI is technology spillover or technology transfer from the multinational firm to host country enterprises. However, the amount of technology spillover that actually accrues to the host country may depend in part on the "embeddedness" of Japanese subsidiaries in Asia. Therefore, in order to get a sense of the long-term benefits of Japanese FDI for the host countries, one needs to look at this embeddedness, as measured by the local sourcing activity of Japanese affiliates at the subsidiary level. These views are not unique to these authors. In fact, similar views color much of the current debate among policymakers concerning the costs and benefits of FDI in developing countries. The authors also contend that even if the link between embeddedness and technology transfer is not so strong or direct, the economics of local procurement are an interesting and important topic.

I think that technology spillovers and technology transfer are fascinating and important phenomena. My own contribution to this volume, chapter 4, examines the role Japanese FDI may have played in fostering R&D spillovers between Japan and the United States. However, "traditional" international economic analysis emphasizes other benefits of FDI, which have little to do, at least directly, with technology or embeddedness. Viewed through that analytical lens, the chief benefit of FDI is the same as the chief benefit of trade: namely, the ability to obtain goods (or factor services) at lower opportunity cost than that available under autarky.[1] The additional benefit from FDI over trade is that a capital-scarce country can obtain the factor services of capital directly (and more cheaply) even when the indirect trade of factor services through trade in goods may be limited or may fail to achieve factor price equalization.[2] With a free trade and investment regime, the resource cost of a given basket of consumption goods is likely to decline substantially, and the saved resources can be reallocated to other sectors in which their marginal product is higher.

---

1. Helpman and Krugman (1985) presented this sort of model in a useful form.
2. To be more precise, one can construct an equilibrium in which trade in goods alone fails to bring about factor price equalization. However, allowing for FDI pushes the global economy toward factor price equalization, allowing the capital-scarce country access to the factor services of capital at the new world price, which would be lower than the price available under autarky *or* free trade without FDI. If there is some natural or artificial barrier to trade in goods, then the role of FDI in the model could become even more pivotal.

These are, if you will, the direct benefits of FDI. These benefits are likely to be substantial. Furthermore, these benefits do not depend on embeddedness, as the authors have acknowledged. In fact, embeddedness could impede this kind of benefit. Let us consider the following example. Imagine that a Japanese auto producer decides to establish a manufacturing subsidiary within a certain country. Let us further imagine that this producer is "forced" to source parts and services from local firms, due to restrictive local content requirements. Now, these restrictions are designed to raise the embeddedness of the Japanese firm. However, these restrictions, by forcing the Japanese firm to rely on high-cost, inefficient domestic producers, could actually raise the price and lower the quantity (and quality) of the final good sold by the Japanese firm in the domestic market. Attempts to increase embeddedness could actually reduce the welfare of the host country. This speaks to the "less benign view" of Japanese FDI mentioned by the authors. I am concerned that Japanese firms in Asia may be unfairly criticized for an insufficient level of embeddedness, and the response to this criticism could very well be something that winds up making the host country worse off rather than better off.[3]

Even if we were to focus solely on the benefits brought by FDI through improved levels of productivity in the host country industry, these can arise through multiple channels, as the authors have acknowledged. One potential channel is, of course, technology transfer to local firms in the host country through the sorts of supply chain relationships stressed in this paper. However, it is also true that simply through their presence in the host country market, Japanese affiliates can bring about improved productivity in the host country at the industry and firm level by raising the level of competitive pressure on domestic incumbents. The least efficient local firms are forced out of the market, and the more efficient local firms are forced to become yet more efficient in order to withstand the competitive pressure of the foreign affiliates. This competition improves resource allocation within the host country industry and raises the level of productivity, even if supply relationships with domestic firms are completely absent.[4]

Having pointed out that important benefits from FDI will accrue to the host country even in the absence of local sourcing, we can also question the extent to which foreign affiliates can be expected to function as channels of technology spillover or technology transfer. This is something the authors acknowledge, but it is also a point worth reemphasizing. Using microlevel data and careful econometric analysis, Haddad and Harrison

---

3. I do not mean to imply here that the linkages between multinationals and domestic firms are unimportant. For a theoretical treatment that formalizes the concept of "linkages" and highlights their potential importance, see Rodríguez-Clare (1996).

4. This point has been raised by a number of other researchers, including Richard Caves (1974).

(1993) and Aitken and Harrison (1999) found *no* evidence that the presence of foreign affiliates accelerated the productivity growth of domestic firms in Morocco and Venezuela. In fact, the latter paper found a negative effect of the presence of foreign affiliates on domestic firm productivity in Venezuela. This seems to at least call into question the view that technology transfer or spillover is an important or inevitable consequence of multinational activity in the host country industry.

In a similar fashion, we might also question whether technology spillovers are proportional to the density of commercial transactions, as the authors suggest. To illustrate this point, let me use a trivial example. I purchase much more from my physician, my landlord, and my mechanic than I do from other economists. Yet I receive relatively little in the way of "knowledge spillovers" or technology transfer from these transactions. On the other hand, I purchase very little from my fellow economists, yet I learn a great deal from reading their papers and interacting with them at conferences. Now let me note a more substantive example, which the authors also mention. Chung, Mitchell, and Yeung (1996) investigated the impact of Japanese FDI in the U.S. auto component industry using plant-level data. They found that the increased Japanese FDI in this industry after 1985 was associated with increased productivity growth. However, the productivity of U.S. component plants supplying Japanese assembly plants grew *more slowly* than that of firms with no ties to the Japanese plants. Here embeddedness actually apparently retarded the technological development of plants with closer supply relationships. Chung et al. concluded that the positive impact on productivity identified in the data was due to competitive pressure from Japanese entrants rather than technology transfer mediated through supply relationships.

Now let us turn briefly to the definition of the dependent variable. The numerator of the authors' measure of local sourcing, LOCON, is simply the value of subsidiary sales minus the value of imported parts and components. This measure does not distinguish between the subsidiaries' own production and the sourcing of parts to local (i.e., host country owned) firms, as the authors freely acknowledge. My own concern is that this measure could differ between countries for reasons that have little or nothing to do with "sourcing strategy." For instance, let us say that Japanese affiliates in one host country experience a surge in overall domestic demand that drives up demand for the output of the affiliates in that country. This increase in demand could be met partly by an increase in price (and profits). This leads to a larger measured level of local sourcing in this country even though the local sourcing strategy has not changed. In contrast, let us suppose that the currency of a second host country depreciates with respect to the Japanese yen. This means that the value of imported components relative to the local currency value of sales will be higher, and the measured level of local sourcing correspondingly lower, than was the case before the currency fluctuation. However, the sourcing strategy has not changed.[5] In more general terms, the authors' inference is limited by sample size and by the use of a single cross section.

However, it is clear that this data source and the authors' basic approach could yield substantial insights with data from more than one year. This would allow for the use of panel data techniques. The authors could focus on differences in behavior of a given affiliate over time, allowing for a more precise identification of the kind of relations the authors are seeking to examine. The authors also suggest that their data could provide some insight into the development of the East Asian financial and economic crisis, and I heartily agree. It is probably obvious to every participant in this conference that the speed with which that crisis is resolved and its ultimate human and financial cost will depend in a vital way on the response of the Japanese firms operating in these countries. The authors' data and approach are tailor-made for examining the evolution of this response across industries and countries. Such an examination could provide crucial information for policymakers and academics alike, and I hope that the authors are able to proceed in this direction as soon as possible.

Again, I feel that this is an interesting and important paper. I look forward to future work by the authors along these lines.

References

Aitken, Brian, and Ann Harrison. 1999. Do domestic firms benefit from foreign direct investment? Evidence from Venezuela. *American Economic Review* 89 (3): 605–18.

Caves, Richard. 1974. Multinational firms, competition, and productivity in host-country markets. *Economica* 41:176–93.

Chung, Wilbur, Will Mitchell, and Bernard Yeung. 1996. Foreign direct investment and host country productivity: The case of the American automotive components industry. Ann Arbor: University of Michigan School of Business Administration. Working paper.

Haddad, Mona, and Ann Harrison. 1993. Are there positive spillovers from direct foreign investment? Evidence from panel data for Morocco. *Journal of Development Economics* 42:51–74.

Helpman, Elhanan, and Paul Krugman. 1985. *Market structure and foreign trade.* Cambridge, Mass.: MIT Press.

Rodríguez-Clare, Andrés. 1996. Multinationals, linkages, and economic development. *American Economic Review* 86 (4): 852–73.

5. I should note that these criticisms are not so important in the present paper. The problems I raise in this paragraph are presumably taken care of in those regressions in which the authors use country-specific fixed effects, since they only have a single cross section. In the context of a panel data set, these concerns could be dealt with by including data on host country wages, demand shocks, and exchange rate fluctuations.

2

Intrafirm Technology Transfer by Japanese Manufacturing Firms in Asia

Shujiro Urata and Hiroki Kawai

2.1 Introduction

Foreign direct investment (FDI) by multinational enterprises (MNEs) contributes to the economic development of countries receiving the FDI, or host countries, through several channels. FDI not only brings financial resources for capital formation to host countries but also expands their production, employment, and foreign trade. Furthermore, FDI transfers to host countries technology and managerial know-how (hereafter, the term "technology" is used broadly to include managerial know-how), which play a crucial role in promoting economic development. Besides FDI, technology may be transferred internationally through such channels as international trade in technology in the forms of patents and licenses, international trade in capital goods embodying technologies, and international movement of skilled labor. Among these means, FDI has increased its importance significantly in recent years, as MNEs have expanded their FDI activities rapidly. Recognizing the important contributions that FDI makes in host countries, many countries are interested in attracting FDI. In particular, host countries eagerly expect MNEs to transfer technology. Technology transfer is also a main concern for MNEs, as its success or failure is an important element in determining the outcome of their overseas operations.

Shujiro Urata is professor of economics at Waseda University and a research fellow at the Japan Center for Economic Research, both in Tokyo. Hiroki Kawai is associate professor of economics at Keio University and a visiting researcher at the Economic Planning Agency of the Government of Japan.

The authors thank E. Ogawa, H. T. Chun, T. Ito, and other conference participants for helpful comments and discussions.

In the analysis of international technology transfer by MNEs, two types of technology transfer have been examined in previous studies. One is technology transfer from parent firms of MNEs to their overseas affiliates, and the other is technology transfer from overseas affiliates of MNEs to local firms. The former type of technology transfer is described as intra-firm technology transfer, the latter as technology spillover. Intrafirm technology transfer is carried out by various means, including provision of training programs to local employees and purchase of technologies from parent firms. Technology spillover may be realized in different forms. Technology may be transmitted from foreign firms to local firms, when local workers who have acquired knowledge from working at foreign firms move to local firms or start new businesses. Local firms may acquire technology from foreign firms by imitating production methods practiced by foreign firms.

The objective of this paper is to analyze the extent of intrafirm technology transfer achieved by Japanese manufacturing firms and to identify the explanatory factors. Measuring the extent of technology transfer is difficult because technology is not easily quantifiable. Previous empirical studies on intrafirm technology transfer did not directly measure the extent of technology transfer undertaken. Instead, indirect measures have been used to examine technology transfer. For example, the value of patent and licensing transactions is often used to measure the international flow of technology. Some researchers have estimated the costs involved in technology transfer, while others have examined R&D activities at overseas affiliates. These indicators measure the efforts or activities related to technology transfer, but they do not measure the extent of technology transfer achieved. To remedy the problem of the indirect nature of the indicators used in previous analyses, we measure the extent of technology transfer achieved by comparing the level of total factor productivity (TFP) of an overseas affiliate with that of its parent firm. The smaller the gap between them according to our interpretation, the greater the extent of intrafirm technology transfer achieved.

An analysis of the determinants of intrafirm technology transfer is useful not only for researchers but also for MNEs and policymakers because successful intrafirm technology transfer benefits both MNEs and host countries. The paper is organized as follows. Section 2.2 presents a brief discussion of recent developments in Japanese FDI, to set the stage for the following analysis. Section 2.3 begins with a brief review of previous studies and then carries out statistical analyses estimating the extent of intrafirm technology transfer achieved by Japanese firms and its determinants. Section 2.4 concludes the paper.

2.2   Japanese Foreign Direct Investment in Recent Years

Japanese FDI grew in scale and underwent major changes in its regional and sectoral composition in the latter half of the 1980s (figs. 2.1 and 2.2). The number of FDI cases increased sharply from around 2,500 in the early 1980s to more than 6,000 in the second half of the decade. As dramatic as the size of the boom was the pace at which the number of FDI cases declined after peaking in 1989. The decline in annual FDI cases continued through 1994, when the number of FDI cases amounted to less than 40 percent of those recorded in 1989. The number of FDI cases remained around 2,500 through 1996.

One identifies both "push" and "pull" factors in the rapid expansion of Japanese FDI. Push factors are those in the investing country—Japan in this case—while pull factors are those in the recipient countries. We discuss these factors in turn below.[1]

Several push factors were responsible for the rapid growth of Japanese FDI in the latter half of the 1980s. The rapid and steep appreciation of the yen against other currencies was the most important macroeconomic factor. The yen appreciated by 37 percent between 1985 and 1988 on a real effective basis. This drastic appreciation stimulated Japanese FDI in two ways. One was the dramatic "relative price" effect; the other was the "liquidity" or "wealth" effect. The relative price effect substantially reduced the international price competitiveness of Japanese products, depressing Japan's export volume. To cope with the new international price structure, a number of Japanese manufacturing firms moved their production bases to foreign countries, especially to East Asia, where production costs were lower.

Yen appreciation had a positive impact on Japanese FDI through the liquidity or wealth effect as well. To the extent that yen appreciation made Japanese firms more "wealthy" in the sense of increased collateral and liquidity, it enabled them to finance FDI more cheaply than their foreign competitors. A number of FDI projects in real estate were undertaken by Japanese firms taking advantage of the liquidity effect.

Another important push factor was the emergence of the "bubble" economy in Japan. Indeed, the liquidity effect discussed above was strengthened by the bubble economy, in which the prices of assets such as shares and land increased enormously. Average share prices more than doubled in the four years from 1985 to 1989, as the index of share prices increased from 45.7 in 1985 to 117.8 in 1989. The Bank of Japan injected liquidity into the economy to deal with the recessionary impact of the drastic yen appreciation. Active fiscal spending also for the purpose of reflating the economy was another factor leading to the bubble economy.

1. This section draws on Kawai and Urata (1998).

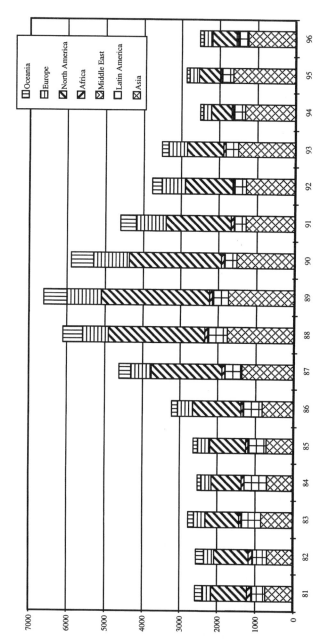

Fig. 2.1   Japanese FDI by region (number of cases)
Source: Ministry of Finance, reported statistics on FDI.

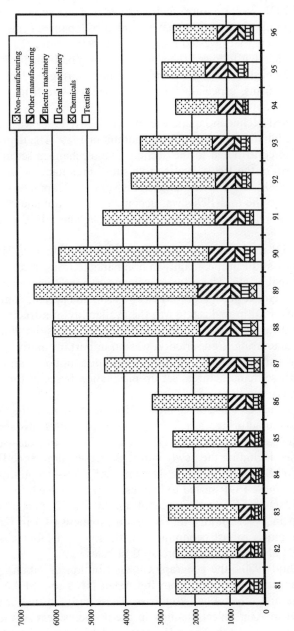

Fig. 2.2 Japanese FDI by industry (number of cases)
Source: Ministry of Finance, reported statistics on FDI.

A general rise in Japanese firms' technological and managerial capabilities in international business, accumulated through past experience in exporting and FDI, was a natural factor underlying the surge in Japanese FDI. It is also important to note that a number of Japanese firms followed business customers that invested overseas. A case in point is FDI by subcontracting firms that followed their parents, which had undertaken FDI, to maintain the business. Furthermore, the labor shortage in Japan forced some Japanese firms, especially small and medium-size firms, to move their operations abroad.

The continued decline in Japanese FDI in the early 1990s was the result mainly of the bursting of the bubble economy in 1989. The depreciation of the yen also contributed to the decline. The mechanism set in motion in the latter half of the 1980s, leading to a substantial increase in FDI, reversed in the 1990s. The drastic change in the volume of Japanese FDI from the mid-1980s to the mid-1990s was accompanied by notable changes in the regional as well as sectoral distribution of Japanese FDI during the period.

Japanese FDI in the second half of the 1980s was directed largely to North America and Europe, mainly in nonmanufacturing sectors such as services and real estate. These two developed regions together absorbed more than 50 percent of Japan's FDI cases during the period. A main pull factor in active FDI in real estate was the availability of attractive assets, which satisfied the speculative demand of Japanese investors. For investment in manufacturing, trade friction was an important motive. To cope with such restrictive measures as antidumping duties imposed on Japanese exports, Japanese manufacturers set up production bases in Europe and North America.

Although a smaller share of Japan's FDI went to Asia, in the 1980s investment in manufacturing was relatively active. The 1990s have seen some changes in the pattern of Japan's FDI. First, the share of Asia—particularly East Asia, including the newly industrialized economies (NIEs), the Association of South East Asian Nations (ASEAN-4) countries, and China—in Japanese FDI started to increase sharply. Indeed, the share of Asia in total Japan's FDI cases increased rapidly from 25 percent in 1990 to 57 percent in 1995. Major pull factors in Japanese FDI in East Asia include the region's robust economic growth, low unit labor costs, and trade and FDI liberalization and pro-FDI policies.

Since the mid-1980s, the geographical distribution of Japan's FDI in Asia has changed significantly, from the Asian NIEs to ASEAN-4, and then to China and other Asian countries. These shifts in the location of Japanese FDI in Asia reflect changes in the attractiveness of the Asian countries as hosts to FDI. The NIEs attracted FDI until the late 1980s through FDI promotion policies. However, they started to lose some of their cost advantages after rapid wage increases and currency appreciation in the late 1980s. Firms in Japan and other advanced economies therefore started to look to other East Asian countries, such as the ASEAN-4 countries, as hosts for investment. One important factor in attracting FDI in manufacturing to ASEAN-4 has been the ASEAN-4 countries' shift from inward-oriented to outward-oriented strategies, which were carried out through their unilateral liberalization of trade and FDI policies. Such regime changes have been prompted by the earlier success of outward-oriented policies in the NIEs.

FDI inflows into China have also grown quickly since 1990 due to China's gradual but persistent economic reforms, liberalization in trade and FDI policies, and political and social stability despite the Tiananmen Square incident in 1989. As of 1996, China was the largest recipient of Japanese FDI in Asia. China has recently become more attractive as a host to FDI because some ASEAN countries have lost their attractiveness after rapid increases in production costs including wages, material, and service costs, which were in turn the result of currency appreciation, shortage of manpower, emergence of serious bottlenecks in infrastructure, and other factors.

The sectoral distribution of Japanese FDI went through significant changes. In terms of the number of FDI cases, manufacturing increased its share in the total from 30 percent in the 1980s to 50 percent in the mid-1990s. Among manufacturing subsectors, electric machinery and textiles registered very rapid expansion, developments particularly noticeable for FDI in Asia. The rapid expansion of FDI in electric machinery and textiles in Asia reflected the strategy chosen by Japanese firms to deal with high production costs in Japan, which were in turn due to yen appreciation and high labor costs. Faced with high production costs in Japan, Japanese textile and electric machinery firms, whose production requires labor-intensive technologies and processes, set up manufacturing plants in Asia.

2.3   Intrafirm Technology Transfer

Technology transfer within MNEs from parent companies to overseas affiliates, or intrafirm technology transfer, is important not only for MNEs but also for their host countries.[2] The performance of overseas affiliates depends crucially on the success or failure of intrafirm technology transfer because efficient production and management cannot be carried out unless technologies are transferred. Host countries are also concerned about the outcome of intrafirm technology transfer because successful technology transfer improves the technological capability of local workers, thereby contributing to economic growth. Indeed, host governments as well as

---

2. Reddy and Zhao (1990) and Caves (1996) are good surveys of studies of international technology transfer.

employees working at the affiliates of foreign firms have often expressed dissatisfaction with the slow pace of technology transfer by MNEs.

This section examines the extent of international intrafirm technology transfer achieved by Japanese firms and attempts to discern its determinants. Before carrying out the analysis, we briefly review previous studies of the subject.

2.3.1   A Brief Review of the Determinants
of Intrafirm Technology Transfer

Several studies have examined the patterns of intrafirm technology transfer from parent firms to their overseas affiliates.[3] Most of these studies examined the resources or costs expended for intrafirm technology transfer by utilizing information obtained from case studies. Davies (1977) studied 119 cases of technology transfer by British companies in India. He found that British companies expend more resources for technology transfer, in the form of providing such tangibles as designs and components as well as sending personnel, to their joint ventures with Indian firms than to local Indian firms.

Based on information about the resource costs associated with twenty-six technology transfer projects undertaken by U.S. firms in chemicals and petroleum refining and machinery, Teece (1977) found that the costs of technology transfer were higher when technology recipients were joint ventures than when they were wholly owned foreign subsidiaries. He also found that the costs were higher when technology suppliers were less experienced in technology transfer and when recipients were less experienced in manufacturing. In addition to these observations derived from both chemicals and petroleum refining and machinery, some differences were observed between these industries. For example, past experience in technology transfer reduces the costs of technology transfer for chemicals and petroleum refining but not for machinery. Teece attributed this difference to the characteristics of the technologies used in these industries. Process technologies used in chemicals and petroleum refining cannot be modified without massive reconstruction of the plant; therefore, previous experience in technology transfer is effective in transferring technology. By contrast, production technologies used in machinery can be modified flexibly, making previous experience obsolete in a relatively short period for technology transfer.

Ramachandran (1993) found a similar relation between equity ownership and the resources used for technology transfer in his study of the characteristics of technology transfer agreements signed by Indian firms and MNEs from the United States, United Kingdom, and western Eu-

---

3. For empirical investigations of technology spillover, see, e.g., Globerman (1979), Aitken and Harrison (1994), Haddad and Harrison (1993), and Harrison (1996).

rope. Analyzing the data aggregated into fourteen industries, he found that MNEs spent more resources, in the form of sending engineers and training local employees in the MNEs' home countries, for technology transfer involving wholly owned subsidiaries than in the case of joint ventures, while they spent the least resources in the case of technology transfer to independent firms. In addition, R&D by licensees was found to reduce the amount of resources spent for technology transfer, indicating that high technological capability of the technology recipient facilitates technology transfer.

Wakasugi (1996) adopted a similar approach to study the costs of technology transfer by Japanese firms. Using information on resources expended for intrafirm technology transfer for 104 Japanese firms, Wakasugi performed statistical analyses to discern the determinants of the costs and lengths of time required for transferring technology. Similar to the findings of other studies, he found that the greater the equity participation by the parent firm, the more resources spent for technology transfer. Past experience in technology transfer was found to lower the costs of technology transfer. The level of technology to be transferred was found to affect the costs of technology transfer, in that transferring high technology tends to cost more.

Although a very important issue regarding intrafirm technology transfer is to identify the circumstances and environments in which technology can effectively be transferred, the earlier studies did not address this issue directly. They instead examined the costs or resources involved in technology transfer. However, costs or resources spent for technology transfer do not indicate the extent of technology transfer achieved. An increase in resources expended for technology transfer does not realize technology transfer if the resources are spent wastefully. To deal with this problem, Urata (forthcoming) adopted a different approach. He evaluated the extent of technology transfer achieved by assessing who, either staff from the parent firm or local staff, has responsibility for managing technologies. Technology transfer is deemed to have been achieved if local staff is in charge of managing technologies. Using a sample of 133 cases of intrafirm technology transfer by Japanese MNEs to their Asian affiliates, he found a positive correlation between the extent of technology transfer and the degree of equity holding by the parent company only in the case where the technologies involved are simple, such as those related to the maintenance of machines. The opposite relation was found when the technologies involved were sophisticated, such as design technologies, development of new machines, and development of new technologies. His interpretation was that Japanese MNEs are reluctant to transfer sophisticated technologies to their foreign affiliates, and they transfer these technologies under pressure from local joint venture partners. Urata also found that technology transfer is successfully carried out when Japanese MNEs adopt measures specifically intended to promote technology transfer, such as providing manuals in the local language and holding seminars in local areas.

2.3.2   Intrafirm Technology Transfer by Japanese Firms

Characteristics of Sample Firms

Our analysis of intrafirm technology transfer uses firm-level data compiled from a survey conducted by the Ministry of International Trade and Industry (MITI) in 1993.[4] A brief discussion of the sample firms is in order before we examine the extent of intrafirm technology transfer they have achieved. The sample consists of 266 parent firms and 744 overseas affiliates in textiles, chemicals, general machinery, and electric machinery (table 2.1). Electric machinery has the largest representation, followed in descending order by chemicals, general machinery, and textiles. Out of 266 parent firms, 178 firms, or 67 percent of the total, are large firms with paid-in capital exceeding 1 billion yen. Of the remaining 181 parent firms, 52 firms (20 percent) are medium-size firms with paid-in capital ranging from 100 million to 1 billion yen, and 36 are small firms with paid-in capital of less than 100 million yen.

The sectoral distribution of the 744 overseas affiliates is similar to that of the parent firms; electric machinery has the largest number of affiliates, followed by chemicals, general machinery, and textiles. As for the geographical distribution of overseas affiliates, 59 percent are located in Asia, while the shares of the affiliates in North America and the European Community are 19 and 15 percent, respectively. In Asia, the NIEs and ASEAN-4 host 29 and 24 percent of all affiliates, respectively; China hosts only 5 percent. Among the 744 affiliates, 486 affiliates, or 65 percent of the total, started operations before 1985, while 258 affiliates, or 35 percent of the total, started operations after 1986. These shares vary notably across regions. Within Asia, the share of affiliates that started before 1985 is highest for affiliates in the NIEs, followed by the ASEAN-4 countries, and then by China. These sectoral and geographical patterns of overseas affiliates of Japanese firms in our sample are similar to those observed for overall Japanese FDI in an earlier section. For approximately 70 percent of affiliates, the Japanese parent firm holds majority ownership, while for the remaining 30 percent, the Japanese firm has a minority position. The share of minority ownership is significantly greater for affiliates in Asia than for those in developed countries. Within Asia, China has the largest share of minority-owned affiliates, at 53 percent. China is followed by the ASEAN-4 countries and the NIEs. These differences in the patterns of

---

4. MITI conducts a comprehensive survey of the overseas activities of Japanese firms every three years. In the 1993 survey, a questionnaire was sent to 3,378 Japanese MNEs, 1,594 of which responded. The respondents covered the activities of 7,108 overseas affiliates.

Table 2.1   Characteristics of Sample Firms, 1993

	Parent Firms: Firm Size[a]				Overseas Affiliates: Initial Year of Operation				Equity Held by Parent Firm (%)		
	Total	Small	Medium	Large	Total	Up to 1985	1986–90	1991 or After	0–50	51–75	76–100
Total	266	36	52	178	744	486	200	58	242	80	422
Industry											
Textiles	42	5	8	29	94	58	24	12	40	16	38
Chemicals	78	4	20	54	222	153	50	19	110	23	89
General machinery	52	8	7	37	116	74	38	4	20	10	86
Electric machinery	94	19	17	58	312	201	88	23	72	31	209
Host regions/countries											
North America					142	79	51	12	30	5	107
European Community					110	76	23	11	20	7	83
Asia					436	281	123	32	181	57	198
NIEs					214	153	58	3	78	28	108
Hong Kong					26	12	14	0	4	3	19
Korea					53	37	15	1	34	5	14
Singapore					45	36	9	0	4	3	38
Taiwan					90	68	20	2	36	17	37
ASEAN-4					180	111	49	20	79	23	78
Indonesia					25	21	2	2	9	9	7
Malaysia					73	43	21	9	25	9	39
Philippines					14	11	3	0	6	0	8
Thailand					68	36	23	9	39	5	24
China					34	12	14	8	18	5	11

Source: MITI, *Kaigai Jigyo Katsudo Kihon Chosa* (Comprehensive survey of overseas activities of Japanese firms), no. 5 (Tokyo, 1993).

[a]Firm size is classified by amount of paid-in capital: small firms have less than 100 million yen, medium between 100 million and 1 billion yen, and large more than 1 billion yen.

equity ownership largely reflect the FDI policies pursued by these countries. Developing countries tend to have more restrictive FDI policies than developed countries, hence their large share of minority-owned affiliates.

Intrafirm Technology Transfer Achieved

To measure the extent of intrafirm technology transfer undertaken by Japanese firms, we adopt a different indicator from previous studies. We compare the technological level of a foreign affiliate of a Japanese firm to that of its parent firm in Japan by using the following equation:[5]

$$\ln TFP_a - \ln TFP_p = \ln VA_a - \ln VA_p$$
$$- \alpha(\ln L_a - \ln L_p) - \beta(\ln K_a - \ln K_p),$$

where TFP is total factor productivity, VA is value added, L is labor inputs (number of employees), K is capital inputs (value of fixed assets), α is the simple average of labor shares in value added for the parent firm and the foreign affiliate, β is the simple average of capital shares in value added for the parent firm and the foreign affiliate, p is the parent firm, and a is the foreign affiliate.

Value added is computed by subtracting the value of procurement from the value of sales. Admittedly calculated value added does not accurately represent value added in production, but this is the best approximation possible given the information available. Labor inputs are measured by the number of employees, and capital inputs by the value of fixed assets. Factor shares are taken from the international input-output table for 1990 constructed by the Institute of Developing Economies in Tokyo. The international input-output table has information on factor shares for the four industries examined in our analysis for eight East Asian countries (Korea, China, Taiwan, the Philippines, Malaysia, Singapore, Thailand, and Indonesia), Japan, and the United States. For sample countries other than those included in the international input-output table, factor shares for countries included in the table with similar per capita income are used.

To make a comparison of technological levels meaningful, we only considered overseas affiliates engaged in the same production activity as their parent firms. In many cases, tasks assigned to a parent firm and to its affiliates differ. For example, there are cases where a parent firm specializes in product development while its overseas affiliates carry out manufacturing activities. In some cases, a parent firm manufactures products and its overseas affiliates distribute them. We did not consider such cases.

The results of our computation of the extent of intrafirm technology

5. Jorgenson and Nishimizu (1978) used this methodology to compare the TFP levels of Japan and the United States. One should note that TFP computed in this way as a residual may not reflect the level of technology alone. It may include other elements influencing the level of output, such as the level of capacity utilization, scale economies, and managerial know-how.

transfer achieved are shown in table 2.2. The difference in level of technology between affiliate and parent firm is expressed as the ratio of their technological levels.[6] Judging from the average for all affiliates, intrafirm technology transfer has advanced most in electric machinery, followed by general machinery, and then by textiles.[7] Intrafirm technology transfer has been lagging in chemicals. For all industries except textiles, a greater extent of intrafirm technology transfer has been achieved at affiliates in developed countries than at those in developing countries. For textiles, affiliates in Asia achieved a greater extent of intrafirm technology transfer than those in the European Community. Although a number of irregular observations occur at the individual country level, we observe a consistently regular pattern among the Asian countries in that the extent of intrafirm technology transfer has been most advanced in the NIEs in all industries. The positions of the ASEAN-4 countries and China in terms of the extent of intrafirm technology transfer achieved differ for different industries. In textiles and electric machinery, the ASEAN-4 countries register higher levels of intrafirm technology transfer than China, but the opposite pattern is observed in chemicals and general machinery. These observations indicate that high-income countries provide a better environment for intrafirm technology transfer than low-income countries. Furthermore, one may infer from the results for the ASEAN-4 countries and China, in heavy industries such as chemicals and general machinery, experience in heavy industrialization, such as that accumulated in China, enhances intrafirm technology transfer.

Having discussed the extent of intrafirm technology transfer achieved using average values for industries and countries, we should note that large standard deviations of the values among sample firms make a meaningful comparison of the averages difficult. To deal with this problem, in the next subsection we analyze through statistical analyses the determinants of the extent of intrafirm technology transfer achieved by Japanese firms.

The Determinants of Intrafirm Technology Transfer: The Hypotheses

We have seen variations in the extent of intrafirm technology transfer achieved by Japanese firms to their overseas affiliates. In this subsection we attempt to discern the factors that explain these variations and to identify the determinants of intrafirm technology transfer. One may divide the possible explanatory factors into two groups.[8] One group of factors concerns the characteristics and strategies of the Japanese parent firms

6. The ratio is constructed in such a way that the value is unity when the technological level of the affiliate is the same as that of its parent firm.

7. Some ratios in the table exceed unity, indicating that the level of technology at the affiliate is higher than at its parent. Such "overachieving" is not unrealistic, because in many cases MNEs use the most efficient technologies at their affiliates, thereby achieving very high productivity.

8. Appendix tables 2A.1 and 2A.2 show the characteristics of the explanatory variables used in the statistical analyses.

Table 2.2   Level of Intrafirm Technology Transfer Achieved from Japanese Parent Firms to Overseas Affiliates, 1993

Host Region or Country	Textiles			Chemicals			General Machinery			Electric Machinery			Total		
	Average	S.D.	No. of Affiliations	Average	S.D.	No. of Affiliations	Average	S.D.	No. of Affiliations	Average	S.D.	No. of Affiliations	Average	S.D.	No. of Affiliations
North America	1.376	0.492	6	0.781	0.588	44	0.852	0.386	35	1.114	0.801	57	0.932	0.666	142
European Community	0.798	0.170	5	0.600	0.489	26	1.203	0.752	30	1.190	0.400	49	1.081	0.505	110
Asia	0.873	0.672	67	0.511	0.370	138	0.622	0.543	42	0.685	0.728	189	0.687	0.675	436
NIEs	1.060	0.865	19	0.684	0.371	63	0.761	0.597	31	0.748	0.804	101	0.776	0.769	214
Hong Kong	1.157	1.001	9	0.915	0.296	3	0.870	0.000	1	1.906	1.796	13	1.663	1.596	26
Korea	0.803	0.773	5	0.586	0.301	18	0.945	0.726	7	0.341	0.147	23	0.461	0.393	53
Singapore				0.925	0.197	11	0.682	1.285	6	1.038	0.667	28	1.019	0.637	45
Taiwan	1.618	0.931	5	0.611	0.467	31	0.615	0.475	17	0.572	0.259	37	0.705	0.535	90
ASEAN-4	0.755	0.451	33	0.394	0.285	63	0.234	0.085	9	0.551	0.459	75	0.576	0.442	180
Indonesia	1.004	0.461	11	0.280	0.292	11	0.277	0.000	1	1.251	0.354	2	0.838	0.524	25
Malaysia	0.164	0.086	8	0.426	0.335	17	0.267	0.000	1	0.540	0.507	47	0.503	0.484	73
Philippines	0.123	0.159	2	0.359	0.194	6	0.152	0.058	3	0.294	0.159	3	0.312	0.160	14
Thailand	0.565	0.239	12	0.445	0.267	29	0.115	0.137	4	0.532	0.332	23	0.516	0.289	68
China	0.137	0.069	15	0.523	0.332	8	0.327	0.038	2	0.171	0.094	9	0.248	0.178	34
World	0.868	0.643	94	0.679	0.533	222	0.922	0.545	116	0.977	0.677	312	0.887	0.640	744

Source: Authors' computation.

Note: Table reports total factor productivity (TFP) levels of overseas affiliates relative to the TFP levels of their parent firms (TFP level of parent firm = 1). S.D. = standard deviation.

and their overseas affiliates, and the other group concerns the characteristics of the host countries. We discuss these factors in turn below.

To begin with the characteristics of the parent firms, one would expect firm size to affect the pattern of technology transfer. Large firms are more able to transfer technology than small firms because large firms possess greater financial and human resources, which may be used for technology transfer. Following this argument, we would expect the size of the parent to have a positive effect on intrafirm technology transfer. In this study we use two dummy variables associated with firm size to test the effect of parent firm size on intrafirm technology transfer: SML for small firms with paid-in capital of less than 100 million yen and MDM for medium-size firms with paid-in capital ranging between 100 million and 1 billion yen. Since SML and MDM capture the effect of firm size on technology transfer in comparison to large firms, these variables are expected to have negative signs. Previous experience in transferring technology by parent firms should facilitate technology transfer. Indeed, several studies reviewed earlier have confirmed this effect (e.g., Teece 1977; Wakasugi 1996). Because appropriate information is lacking in the MITI survey, we use the number of overseas affiliates owned by a parent firm as a measure of previous experience (EXP) in intrafirm technology transfer. Since parent firms accumulate experience in intrafirm technology transfer by getting involved in the operations of overseas affiliates, EXP is expected to have a positive effect on intrafirm technology transfer.

Turning to the characteristics of overseas affiliates, which depend largely on the strategies of their parent firms, especially in the case of Japanese firms, one can think of several variables that could affect the extent of intrafirm technology transfer. The length of operation (YRS) is likely to be an important factor. The longer an affiliate has been operating, the greater the extent of technology transfer expected. Local staff at overseas affiliates accumulate experience over time, which makes it easier for them to absorb technology. Experience has an important effect on intrafirm technology transfer particularly for Japanese firms, since on-the-job training plays a particularly important role in transferring technology inside Japanese firms.[9] Based on this argument, we expect YRS to have a positive sign. The share of equity held (EQY) by parent firms has been shown by previous researchers to affect the pattern of intrafirm technology transfer, as discussed earlier. Several studies have shown that the cost of intrafirm technology transfer declines as the share of equity holding by the parent firm increases (see Teece 1977; Ramachandran 1993). The reason behind this relation is that the threat of misuse of technologies declines with the

9. Koike and Inoki (1987) presented a detailed discussion of the importance of on-the-job training for skill formation in Japanese firms. Yamashita (1991) also found that on-the-job training is important as a means of technology transfer for Japanese firms.

increase in the share holding by parent firms, since the monitoring capability of parent firms on the use of technologies by affiliates increases with the level of equity holding by parent firms. Following these arguments, we expect EQY to have a positive effect.

The technical capability of foreign affiliates affects the extent of intrafirm technology transfer achieved. Technology transfer is likely to take place at overseas affiliates whose technical capability is high. We measure the technical capability of overseas affiliates with two indicators, the ratio of R&D expenditures to sales (R&D) and the ratio of royalty payments to sales (ROY). Both of these variables are expected to have a positive influence on technology transfer. We also include two variables that reflect the strategy for technology upgrading adopted at the affiliates. As noted above, it is widely recognized that Japanese firms rely heavily on on-the-job training as a method of technology transfer, while Western firms rely more on manuals containing detailed technical descriptions. These contrasting patterns are reflected in differences between Japanese and Western firms in the position of personnel from the parent firms in their overseas affiliates; the ratio of personnel from the parent firm to total employment at overseas affiliates is higher for Japanese firms than for Western firms.[10] We include the share of Japanese staff from the parent firm in total employment at an overseas affiliate (JPL) as an explanatory variable to test whether on-the-job training by Japanese firms is effective in transferring technology. A number of firms conduct training programs to upgrade the capability of local employees, including lectures and study trips to the parent firm. We use a dummy variable for training programs (TRN) to examine the impact of such programs on technology transfer. TRN takes a value of unity if a training program is reported to be given and zero otherwise. We expect a positive sign on TRN. The quality of machines and equipment (capital goods) influences productivity. High-quality capital goods increase productivity. Capital goods that employees are accustomed to using in their activities also improve productivity. Based on this assertion we include the share of capital goods procured from the parent firm in total procurement of capital goods by an overseas affiliate as an explanatory variable (CAP). We expect CAP to have a positive effect on intrafirm technology transfer.

The other group of explanatory variables captures factors related to the host countries, such as educational level, experience in industrial activities, and policies toward FDI in general and toward technology transfer in particular. We expect the educational level of the host country to have a positive effect on intrafirm technology transfer, since the absorptive capability of local employees rises with educational level, here measured by

---

10. Beechler (1995) found that Japanese MNCs send more technical personnel to their affiliates in Southeast Asia than do U.S. MNCs.

the secondary school enrollment ratio (EDU). Accumulated experience in industrial activities in the host country would facilitate technology transfer. We include value added in industrial activity in the host country (IND) to capture this effect. We expect IND to have a positive effect on intrafirm technology transfer. The presence of local affiliates of Japanese firms in the host country would facilitate intrafirm technology transfer for several reasons. First, Japanese manufacturing firms regard the availability of a well-developed parts procurement system as important for achieving productive efficiency. In developing countries, where an efficient local procurement system has not been developed, the presence of local affiliates of Japanese firms is important. The second reason somewhat contradicts the first. Japanese firms in many cases compete against each other. Therefore, a large number of local affiliates of Japanese firms results in greater competition. In a competitive environment, firms would be interested in promoting intrafirm technology transfer, to beat their competitors. To test the validity of the preceding arguments, we include the accumulated number of Japanese FDI cases (FDI) in the host country and expect FDI to have a positive effect on intrafirm technology transfer. One of the policy measures that would affect the extent of technology transfer is a requirement on technology transfer (RTT) imposed by the host country government as a condition for obtaining approval for undertaking FDI. Such a measure would undoubtedly be intended to increase technology transfer, and accordingly we expect RTT to have a positive effect on technology transfer.

The Determinants of Intrafirm Technology Transfer: The Results

We conducted regression analyses to test the validity of the arguments presented above concerning the determinants of intrafirm technology transfer, which is expressed by the ratio of the TFP level of an overseas affiliate and that of its parent firm. The estimation was conducted for textiles, chemicals, general machinery, and electric machinery separately, and besides it was conducted for those industries combined with industry dummies. We applied White's heteroskedasticity-consistent covariance matrix estimator to deal with possible problems due to heteroskedasticity (Davidson and MacKinnon 1993). The results are shown in table 2.3. The explanatory variables chosen for the analysis explain 13 to 45 percent of the variation in intrafirm technology transfer for the cases where all affiliates are considered, while they explain 20 to 57 percent of the variation for the cases where only affiliates in Asia are considered.

The size of the parent firm is found to influence intrafirm technology transfer. The estimated coefficients of SML have negative signs in many cases, and in several cases they are statistically significant. These results indicate that small firms lag behind large firms in intrafirm technology transfer, as expected—probably because small firms are short of human,

Table 2.3 Determinants of Intrafirm Technology Transfer

Explanatory Variable	Total		Textiles		Chemicals		General Machinery		Electric Machinery	
					Affiliates in the World					
Characteristics of parent firms										
SML	-0.1336*	(-1.653)	0.0306	(0.148)	-0.0874	(-0.582)	-0.4165	(-1.595)	-1.1404**	(-2.236)
MDM	0.0108	(0.114)	-0.2580	(-1.562)	-0.0548	(-0.598)	0.0234	(0.080)	0.0594	(0.282)
EXP	0.0001	(1.138)	0.0009**	(2.171)	0.0001	(1.112)	0.0018	(1.381)	0.0018	(1.558)
Characteristics of affiliates										
YRS	0.0019***	(2.671)	0.0024**	(1.907)	0.0056**	(2.118)	0.0024*	(1.878)	0.0008**	(2.534)
EQY	0.0125**	(2.152)	0.3068	(1.258)	0.0241	(1.184)	0.0398	(1.142)	0.0982*	(1.876)
R&D	-0.1935	(-1.215)	6.1165***	(2.522)	0.2948	(0.413)	-0.6523	(-0.612)	-0.2291	(-1.146)
ROY	-0.0581	(-0.949)	-0.0359	(-1.666)	-0.0714	(-0.161)	-0.2852	(-0.175)	-0.7348	(-0.721)
JPL	1.4542**	(2.303)	3.0323**	(2.087)	0.3041*	(1.715)	1.7126***	(2.722)	3.8300***	(7.240)
TRN	0.0849	(1.499)	0.0574	(0.595)	0.1894*	(1.972)	0.0360	(0.197)	0.0887	(0.971)
CAP	0.1870**	2.312	0.1227**	(1.936)	0.0440	(1.351)	0.2542	(1.098)	0.2398*	(1.941)
D_textile	-0.1884***	(-2.562)								
D_chemical	-0.1084*	(-1.704)								
D_general machinery	0.0354	(0.404)								
Characteristics of host countries										
EDU	0.0057***	(4.582)	0.0078**	(2.057)	0.0023**	(2.236)	0.0109**	(2.710)	0.0046**	(2.247)
IND	0.0004	(1.523)	0.0009**	(2.304)	0.0003	(1.259)	0.0006	(0.914)	0.0003	(0.760)
FDI	0.0038*	(1.672)	0.0078**	(2.245)	0.0023	(1.011)	0.0080	(1.435)	0.0021	(0.645)
RTT	-0.1349**	(-2.293)	0.0087	(0.117)	-0.0632	(-0.718)	0.0441	(0.160)	-0.2652***	(-3.591)
Constant	0.0353	(0.316)	-0.0033	(0.015)	0.1984	(1.215)	-0.1742	(-0.417)	-0.0776	(-0.485)
R^2	0.1797		0.4537		0.1347		0.2039		0.3242	
F	7.03		11.98		1.47		2.53		9.08	
N	744		94		222		116		312	

Affiliates in Asia

	(1)		(2)		(3)		(4)		(5)	
Characteristics of parent firms										
SML	−0.1783**	(−2.294)	−0.3174**	(−2.128)	−0.0600	(−1.386)	−0.5285	(1.580)	−0.1441	(−1.281)
MDM	0.0060	(0.055)	−0.3284***	(−2.154)	−0.0934	(−0.807)	0.7976**	(1.928)	0.0693	(0.302)
EXP	0.0011	(1.285)	0.0009***	(1.959)	0.0016**	(2.145)	0.0149	(0.893)	0.0013	(0.853)
Characteristics of affiliates										
YRS	0.0002**	(2.017)	0.0036**	(2.461)	0.0013	(1.628)	0.0020**	(2.587)	0.0017	(1.246)
EQY	0.2186	(1.010)	0.5859**	(2.448)	0.1620**	(2.035)	0.4597	(1.206)	0.0824	(1.556)
R&D	−0.1690	(−0.206)	47.5415*	(1.754)	0.4744	(0.338)	4.8286	(1.632)	−2.0478	(−1.269)
ROY	−0.0241	(−1.444)	−0.0554**	(−2.236)	3.4431**	(2.108)	−1.2829	(−0.862)	−0.7781	(−0.623)
JPL	2.8036**	(3.448)	3.3729	(1.125)	0.1763***	(2.388)	10.3893***	(4.658)	3.5420***	(9.451)
TRN	0.0887	(1.412)	0.1173	(0.945)	0.2124*	(1.786)	0.0119	(0.050)	0.0385	(0.419)
CAP	−0.242	(−0.275)	−0.0540	(−0.536)	0.0445	(0.391)	0.0759	(0.199)	−0.0412	(−0.295)
D_textile	−0.1886**	(−2.270)								
D_chemical	−0.1380**	(−2.009)								
D_general machinery	−0.0451	(−0.389)								
Characteristics of host countries										
EDU	0.0077***	(6.079)	0.0093***	(2.902)	0.0060***	(3.055)	0.0228**	(2.553)	0.0093***	(5.119)
IND	0.0008***	(2.787)	0.0016**	(2.551)	0.0005	(0.694)	0.0012	(0.818)	0.0010**	(2.053)
FDI	0.0230***	(3.379)	0.0091	(1.020)	0.0012	(0.125)	0.1190*	(1.920)	0.0601**	(3.589)
RTT	−0.0187	(−0.301)	−0.0601	(−0.711)	−0.0360	(−0.371)	−0.0601	(−0.182)	−0.0789	(−0.988)
Constant	0.0161	(0.127)	0.5098	(1.445)	0.0858	(0.560)	−2.4237**	(−2.173)	−0.3875**	(−1.985)
R^2	0.2871		0.5696		0.2078		0.6985		0.4443	
F	7.21		5.02		2.39		6.69		20.08	
N	436		67		138		42		189	

Source: Authors' estimation.

Note: Dependent variable is the ratio of the TFP level of the affiliate to that of its parent firm. For explanatory variables involving characteristics of parent firms, affiliates, and host countries, see note to appendix table 2A.1. Industry dummy variables are D_textile, textile dummy; D_chemical, chemicals dummy; and D_general machinery, general machinery dummy. Numbers in parentheses are t-statistics.

*Significant at the 10 percent level.

**Significant at the 5 percent level.

***Significant at the 1 percent level.

financial, and other resources necessary for technology transfer. The results for MDM are more mixed, with limited statistical significance, indicating that the extent of intrafirm technology transfer achieved does not differ much between medium-size and large firms. The estimated coefficients on EXP are positive in all cases, and they are statistically significant for textiles (both for affiliates in the world and for those in Asia) and chemicals (for affiliates in Asia). These results indicate that past experience in intrafirm technology transfer on the part of parent firms facilitates intrafirm technology transfer in textiles and chemical. Our finding for chemicals, which is consistent with the finding by Teece (1977), can be explained by the type of technologies used in chemicals. The technologies used in chemicals do not change over short intervals because such change incurs substantial costs. This follows from the fact that these technologies are designed for use in large plants, and reconstruction of large plants incurs substantial costs. In this technological environment, past experience proves useful for intrafirm technology transfer. In the case of textiles, the fact that standardized technologies are used in many firms makes past experience in intrafirm technology transfer useful for intrafirm technology transfer.

Concerning the characteristics of overseas affiliates of Japanese firms, the estimated coefficients for length of operation (YRS) have positive signs in all cases, and they are statistically significant in most cases. This result, which is consistent with our expectations, indicates that accumulated experience at the affiliate plays an important role in executing intrafirm technology transfer. Equity participation by the parent firm has an important positive impact on intrafirm technology transfer, as the estimated coefficients on EQY are positive in all cases and statistically significant in four cases out of ten. These results confirm findings by other researchers, including Teece (1977) and Ramachandran (1993), that the amount of resources a parent firm spends for intrafirm technology transfer increases with the size of equity participation in the affiliate by the parent. Technical capability measured in terms of R&D spending (R&D) and in terms of royalty payments (ROY) is found to have an unexpectedly negative effect on intrafirm technology transfer in many cases, although the results of the estimation are statistically insignificant in most cases.

On-the-job training provided by Japanese employees appears to promote intrafirm technology transfer, as the estimated coefficients on JPL are positive in all industries, and statistically significant in all cases except Asian affiliates in textiles. This finding may be interpreted in a quite different way. One may interpret the results as indicating the limited degree of technology transfer from Japanese employees to local employees. Such an interpretation may be possible if one observes that Japanese employees, although capable of increasing productivity, hold important positions that determine the technological level of the affiliates, and they do not give local employees much responsibility for technological improvement. To shed more light on the role of Japanese employees in upgrading the technological level of overseas affiliates, a detailed analysis of this subject is required. The estimated coefficients on training programs (TRN) have positive signs in all cases, as expected, but they are statistically significant only for chemicals. Use of capital goods procured from the parent firm tends to promote intrafirm technology transfer, as expected, since the estimated coefficients on CAP are positive in all cases and statistically significant in three cases out of five, total industries, textiles, and electric machinery. For affiliates in Asia, we obtain mixed results.

Among the characteristics of host countries, the level of education (EDU) is shown to be very important in promoting intrafirm technology transfer, as the estimates on EDU are positive and statistically significant in all cases. This result is consistent with the finding by Borensztein, De Gregorio, and Lee (1998) that FDI from developed countries to developing countries contributes to economic growth when enough educated human capital is available in the host country. Experience in industrial activities (IND) is shown to have a positive effect on intrafirm technology transfer in textiles and in electric machinery (only for Asian affiliates). The estimated coefficients on cumulative FDI by Japanese firms (FDI) have positive signs in all cases, and they are statistically significant in textiles (for all affiliates), general machinery, and electric machinery (for affiliates in Asia). These findings indicate that in these industries the presence of local affiliates of other Japanese firms speeds up intrafirm technology transfer. However, it is not clear whether this is due to the role of other affiliates as parts suppliers or competitors.[11] A requirement on technology transfer imposed by the host country does not yield the expected outcome, as the coefficients on RTT are unexpectedly negative in many cases. One possible reason for this unexpected negative relation may be that it is countries with low technology levels that impose technology transfer requirements, in an attempt to extract as much technical capability as possible, and therefore the causality goes the other way. Unavailability of time-series data precludes us from testing the causal relationship.

2.4   Conclusions

Japanese firms have actively undertaken FDI in recent years. Although their FDI activities have slowed recently because of the sluggish economy at home and abroad, they are projected to recover and expand in the medium to long term. In light of such prospects and considering the benefits

---

11. One should note that IND and FDI are closely correlated with each other, as the computed correlation coefficient between them is as high as .97 (appendix table 2A.2). Such close correlation raises the problem of multicollinearity in the estimation, making it difficult to separate their effects on technology transfer.

that FDI brings to host countries, developing countries should make themselves attractive to prospective FDI. In this regard, it is useful to note that Urata and Kawai (1997) found that the availability of skilled labor, well-developed infrastructure, macroeconomic stability, and good governance play key roles in attracting Japanese FDI.

This study found that the capability to absorb technology reflected in educational level, in host countries is very important in promoting intrafirm technology transfer. In addition, in some cases experience in industrial activities is shown to contribute to intrafirm technology transfer. These findings suggest that upgrading educational attainment and particularly promoting skills such as engineering would have a high rate of return. Another important finding drawn from this study is that technology transfer takes time and experience. The evidence shows as well that the creation and maintenance of a stable economic environment is also conducive to improved economic performance. Reliance on parent firms in the forms of equity holding, personnel, and capital goods is shown to promote intrafirm technology transfer. The liberalization of FDI regimes and removal of restrictions on the activities of foreign firms encourages intrafirm transfer of technology.

In many cases, host developing countries maintain restrictions on the activities of foreign firms to promote local industries. One justification often given for such infant industry policy is the "successful" cases in Japan. For acquiring foreign technology, Japanese firms relied on the importation of technologies in the forms of patents and licensing rather than FDI, mainly because of government restrictions on FDI inflow. Japanese policies appear to have been effective in some industries such as automobiles but not in others such as chemicals. To evaluate the effectiveness of restrictive FDI policies in Japan, detailed and careful studies have to be performed. However, even if there turn out to have been successful cases of restrictive FDI policy in Japan in the past, restrictive FDI policies are not likely to be effective in the current economic and technological environment. The speed of technological progress is much faster now, and MNEs with frontier technologies have been rapidly expanding their global economic activities through FDI. In this global economic environment, pursuing a restrictive FDI policy would deter technological upgrading.

Use of firm-level data on Japanese MNEs and their overseas affiliates enabled us to analyze the extent of intrafirm technology transfer achieved by Japanese MNEs and its determinants. A number of important and interesting issues remain concerning the activities of MNEs, even if we limit our scope to technological issues. Some of them include time-series analysis of changes in the technological level of overseas affiliates and their determinants. Furthermore, it would produce useful information if we could undertake international comparisons regarding international technology transfer, that is, compare technology transfer patterns of Japanese firms with those of firms from other countries. To carry out an international comparison, internationally comparable data have to be constructed.

Appendix

Table 2A.1   **Characteristics and Sources of Data**

Variable	Affiliates in the World		Affiliates in Asia		Data Source
	Mean	S.D.	Mean	S.D.	
Characteristics of parent firms					
SML (%)	5.5	22.8	8.0	27.2	MITI
MDM (%)	9.1	28.8	12.6	33.2	MITI
EXP (no. of affiliates)	16.8	17.9	15.7	17.5	MITI
Characteristics of overseas affiliates					
YRS (years)	10.1	8.8	10.7	8.9	MITI
EQY (%)	74.0	35.6	62.9	33.8	MITI
R&D (%)	2.6	7.2	0.3	2.6	MITI
ROY (%)	0.7	2.8	1.2	4.4	MITI
CAP (%)	39.8	37.8	35.6	35.1	MITI
JPL (%)	1.4	2.2	1.1	1.8	MITI
TRN (%)	30.4	46.0	30.3	46.0	MITI
Characteristics of host countries					
EDU (%)	76.1	22.4	67.4	20.1	World Bank
IND (billion yen)	32,500	53,200	5,980	5,990	World Bank
FDI (no. of cases)	34.9	59.6	5.9	3.7	MOF
RTT (%)	12.8	33.4	17.4	38.0	MITI

Sources: MITI, *Kaigai Jigyo Katsudo Kihon Chosa* (Comprehensive survey of overseas activities of Japanese firms) no. 5, (Tokyo, 1993); World Bank, *World Development Indicators* (Washington, D.C., 1997), CD-ROM; MOF (Ministry of Finance), reported statistics on FDI.

Note: Characteristics of parent firms are SML, small firms with paid-in capital of less than 100 million yen; MDM, medium-size firms with paid-in capital of between 100 million and 1 billion yen; and EXP, experience in intrafirm technology transfer expressed by number of foreign affiliates. Characteristics of affiliates are YRS, length of operation measured in years; EQY, equity participation ratio defined as share of affiliate's equity held by parent firm; R&D, ratio of R&D expenditures to sales; ROY, ratio of royalty payments to sales; JPL, share of Japanese employees in total employees; TRN, training program—value is one when affiliate has a training program; and CAP, share of capital goods procured from parent firm in total capital goods procurement. Characteristics of host countries are EDU, secondary school participation ratio; IND, GDP of industry; FDI, cumulative number of FDI cases by Japanese firms in host country; and RTT, technology transfer requirements—value is one when requirement is imposed.

Table 2A.2   Correlation Coefficient Matrix of Variables Used in Regression Analyses

Variable	TFP	SML	MDM	EXP	YRS	EQY	R&D	ROY	CAP	JPL	TRN	EDU	IND	FDI
SML	-.0534	1												
MDM	-.0195	-.0766*	1											
EXP	-.0610	-.1387*	-.1697*	1										
YRS	.0892*	-.1007*	-.1197*	.0026	1									
EQY	.1023*	.0358	-.0985*	-.0116	-.0032	1								
R&D	-.0397	-.0229	-.0144	.0164	.0114	.0103	1							
ROY	-.0423	-.0175	-.0125	-.0256	-.0319	-.0326	-.0071	1						
CAP	.2009*	-.0806*	-.0671	-.1242*	.0539	.2069*	-.0192	-.0242	1					
JPL	.2032	.0198	.0428	-.0682	-.0568	.1081*	-.0033	.0395	.1264*	1				
TRN	.0350	.0582	.1252*	-.0510	-.1071*	.0310	.0177	-.0353	-.0173	.0826*	1			
EDU	.2773*	-.0414	-.0914*	-.0814*	.0469	.1441*	.0911*	-.0683	.1025*	.1636*	.0080	1		
IND	.1198*	.0384	-.0828*	-.0112	.0014	.1475*	.1728*	-.0118	.0354	.1707*	.0334	.4731*	1	
FDI	.1044*	-.0401	-.0832*	-.0024	.0076	.1590*	.1790*	-.0065	.0279	.1714*	.0465	.4379*	.9717*	1
RTT	-.1303*	.0488	.0044	-.0228	-.1087*	-.0435	-.0202	-.0038	.0056	-.0522	.0100	-.1910*	-.1296*	-.1327*

Source: Authors' computation.

Note: For variables, see note to table 2A.1.

*Significant at the 5 percent level.

References

Aitken, Brian, and Ann Harrison. 1994. Do domestic firms benefit from foreign direct investment? Evidence from panel data. Policy Research Working Paper no. 1248. Washington, D.C.: World Bank, Policy Research Department.

Beechler, Schon. 1995. Corporate strategies of Japanese and American MNCs in Southeast Asia: Key success factors. Paper presented for the conference Managing for Success: Japanese and U.S. Corporate Strategies in Southeast Asia, Columbia University, 9 November.

Borensztein, E., J. De Gregorio, and J. W. Lee. 1998. How does foreign direct investment affect economic growth? *Journal of International Economics* 45:115–35.

Caves, Richard E. 1996. *Multinational enterprises and economic analysis.* 2d ed. Cambridge: Cambridge University Press.

Davidson, Russel, and James G. MacKinnon. 1993. *Estimation and inference in econometrics.* New York: Oxford University Press.

Davies, Howard. 1977. Technology transfer through commercial transactions. *Journal of Industrial Economics* 26 (December): 161–75.

Globerman, Steven. 1979. Foreign direct investment and "spillover" efficiency benefits in Canadian manufacturing industries. *Canadian Journal of Economics* 12 (1): 42–56.

Haddad, Mona, and Ann Harrison. 1993. Are there positive spillovers from direct investment? Evidence from panel data for Morocco. *Journal of Development Economics* 42:51–74.

Harrison, Ann. 1996. Determinants and effects of direct foreign investment in Côte d'Ivoire, Morocco, and Venezuela. In *Industrial evolution in developing countries,* ed. Mark J. Roberts and James R. Tybout, 163–86. New York: Oxford University Press.

Jorgenson, Dale W., and Mieko Nishimizu. 1978. U.S. and Japanese economic growth, 1952–1974: An international comparison. *Economic Journal* 88, no. 352 (December): 707–26.

Kawai, Masahiro, and Shujiro Urata. 1998. Are trade and direct investment substitutes or complements? An analysis of the Japanese manufacturing industry. In *Economic development and cooperation in the Pacific Basin: Trade, investment, and environmental issues,* ed. Hiro Lee and David W. Roland-Holst, 251–96. Cambridge: Cambridge University Press.

Koike, Kazuo, and Takenori Inoki, eds. 1987. *Skill formation in Japan and Southeast Asia.* Tokyo: University of Tokyo Press.

Ramachandran, Vijaya. 1993. Technology transfer, firm ownership, and investment in human capital. *Review of Economics and Statistics* 75 (November): 664–70.

Reddy, N. Mohan, and Liming Zhao. 1990. International technology transfer: A review. *Research Policy* 19:285–307.

Teece, David J. 1977. Technology transfer by multinational firms: The resource cost of transferring technological know-how. *Economic Journal* 87 (June): 242–61.

Urata, Shujiro. Forthcoming. Intra-firm technology transfer by Japanese multinationals. In *Japanese multinationals in Asia: Regional operations in comparative perspective,* ed. Dennis J. Encarnation. Oxford: Oxford University Press.

Urata, Shujiro, and Hiroki Kawai. 1997. Governance and the flow of Japanese foreign direct investment. Paper presented at a World Bank workshop on Governance and Private Investment in East Asia, Hakone, Japan.

Wakasugi, Ryuhei. 1996. Gijutsu Iten no Kettei Yoin (The determinants of technology transfer). In *Kaigai Chokusetsu Toshi to Nihon Keizai* (Foreign direct investment and the Japanese economy), ed. Sueo Sekiguchi and Hiroshi Tanaka, 98–119. Tokyo: Keizai Shimpo Sha.

Yamashita, Shoichi. 1991. Economic development of the ASEAN countries and the role of Japanese direct investment. In *Transfer of Japanese technology and management to the ASEAN countries,* ed. Sohichi Yamashita, 3–22. Tokyo: University of Tokyo Press.

Comment   Eiji Ogawa

Urata and Kawai empirically analyze the patterns of technology transfer undertaken by Japanese firms by classifying technology transfer into "intrafirm technology transfer" and "technology spillover" in this paper. The former is technology transfer from parent firms to their overseas affiliates while the latter is technology transfer from overseas affiliates to local firms. The authors do regressions to clarify which factors affected both intrafirm technology transfer and technology spillover for Japanese affiliates in the world and in Asia.

They measure the extent of intrafirm technology transfer by calculating the relative total factor productivity of foreign affiliates with respect to that of parent firms. They regress the extent of technology transfer on several explanatory variables, which they classify into characteristics of parent firms, affiliates, and host countries.

They measure the extent of technology spillover by calculating the share of local purchases in total purchases by overseas affiliates, that is, a local procurement ratio. They regress the extent of technology spillover on almost the same explanatory variables as were used in the regression of intrafirm technology transfer.

The authors reach some findings from the regressions. First, such indicators of absorptive capability as educational level and industrialization have positive effects on both intrafirm technology transfer and technology spillover. Second, both kinds of technology transfer are affected by the time and experience variables, including period of operation, industrialization, and cumulative FDI. Third, a factor related to the affiliates, such as equity participation by parent firms in their overseas affiliates, has different effects on the two kinds of technology transfer. High equity participation tends to promote intrafirm technology transfer but discourage technology spillover.

I have four comments. The first is about the measure of technology spillover. Urata and Kawai regard the local procurement ratio as a measure of technology spillover in this paper. An assumption behind the measure

Eiji Ogawa is professor of commerce at Hitotsubashi University.

is that technology spillover from overseas affiliates to local firms would give the affiliates more incentive to procure inputs from local firms. In other words, technology spillover implies an increase in the local procurement ratio. Therefore, it is necessary to use change in the local procurement ratio as a measure of the extent of technology spillover in the regression.

My second comment is related to the causality relation between FDI and local procurement ratios. In this paper, it is assumed that FDI would affect the local procurement ratio through technology transfer. However, we can make another assumption: that parent firms tend to carry out FDI in countries where their affiliates can procure inputs from local firms. Here causality runs from a high local procurement ratio to FDI. If this is true, for example, a high educational level would lead to a high local procurement ratio and, in turn, high FDI. Therefore, we have another interpretation of the causality relation.

My third comment is related to characteristics of technology transfer in Asian countries. It seems to me that the regression results show little difference between affiliates in the world and those in Asia. Rather, we find differences in the regression results among industries. Urata and Kawai should identify what is characteristic of technology transfer in Asia and what factors determine those characteristics, if Asian countries do indeed have their own characteristic technology transfer.

Finally, I am interested in how the Asian currency and financial crises since last July have affected Japanese FDI and technology transfer in Asian countries. Urata and Kawai expect to use recent and future data to address this issue in the future.

Comment   Hong-Tack Chun

Urata and Kawai analyze technology transfer from Japanese parent firms to their overseas affiliates and identify determinants of the extent of such transfer. I thoroughly enjoyed reading this paper.

Earlier studies of intrafirm technology transfer mostly used the size of resources spent or costs incurred as a measure of intrafirm technology transfer. Although it is reasonable to assume that intrafirm technology transfer is positively related to the size of resources spent, this amount is, however, an indirect measure of intrafirm technology transfer.

Urata and Kawai directly measure the technological levels of overseas affiliates with respect to those of their Japanese parent firms. They use

Hong-Tack Chun is a senior fellow at Korea Development Institute.

TFP as a measure of technological level and apply the interpretation that the smaller the gap between the TFP of an overseas affiliates and that of its Japanese parent firm, the greater the extent of technology transfer from the parent firm to the affiliate.

Urata and Kawai compute technological levels of overseas affiliates relative to their Japanese parent firms using firm-level data for selected manufacturing sectors: textiles, chemicals, general machinery, and electric machinery. They find that the extent of intrafirm technology transfer is greater for affiliates in developed countries than for those in developing countries. Within developing Asian countries, a similar pattern is observed. In general, the level of intrafirm technology transfer is higher for affiliates in NIEs, followed by those in the ASEAN countries, and then by those in China.

These observations indicate that high-income countries provide a better environment for intrafirm technology transfer than low-income countries. Next, to examine the determinants of technology transfer, Urata and Kawai regress the extent of technology transfer using several explanatory variables, which are classified into characteristics and strategies of Japanese parent firms and their affiliates and characteristics of host countries.

They find that educational levels in host countries are very important in promoting intrafirm technology transfer. In addition, liberal FDI regimes without restrictions on the activities of foreign firms are conducive to intrafirm technology transfer. I have little disagreement with the authors except for two minor comments.

The technical capability of Japanese affiliates abroad, measured in terms of R&D spending, is found to have unexpectedly negative effects on intrafirm technology transfer in many cases, although the effects are usually insignificant. This result contradicts the findings by previous studies such as Ramachandran (1993).

The unexpected sign of the R&D variable might be due to the strategies of Japanese parent firms and their affiliates. Suppose that a Japanese parent firm sets a certain target intrafirm technology transfer level and its strategy is to increase R&D expenditures in the early years of the affiliate's operation to promote technology transfer. Suppose further that once the target level of technology transfer is achieved, the Japanese-affiliated firm reduces R&D expenditures to a normal level.

If this is the case, relatively old Japanese-invested firms, which had achieved their target levels of technology transfer, tend to have lower ratios of R&D spending to sales than newly invested firms. Thus intrafirm technology transfer would appear to be negatively associated with R&D expenditure. To shed more light on the strategies of Japanese parent firms and their affiliates regarding R&D expenditure, time-series analysis as well as international comparisons are needed.

Next, in addition to upgrading educational levels and providing liberal

FDI regimes, there may be other useful policies for countries aiming to capture productivity benefits from FDI. Some studies—for instance, Blomström (1986)—have suggested that important influences of MNCs on local firms operate through competition.

If the markets in which the products of foreign-invested firms are sold become more competitive, then the parent firms and their affiliates would make greater efforts to promote intrafirm technology transfer. Therefore, it would be interesting to include in the estimation a variable that measures the competitiveness of the markets in which Japanese-affiliated firms are competing and to see the effect of this variable on technology transfer.

References

Blomström, Magnus. 1986. Multinationals and market structure in Mexico. *World Development* 14:523–30.

Ramachandran, Vijaya. 1993. Technology transfer, firm ownership, and investment in human capital. *Review of Economics and Statistics* 75 (November): 664–70.

Location and Internalization Decisions
Sector Switching in Japanese Outward Foreign Direct Investment

Fukunari Kimura

3.1 Location and Internalization Decisions of Multinational Enterprises

The motivation for foreign direct investment (FDI) is often analyzed in the OLI framework (Dunning 1993). Considering an advantage based on the ownership (O) of firm-specific assets such as technology and managerial ability, a firm decides how far it internalizes activities (I) and where it locates them (L). The firm maximizes its profits by making decisions on internalization and location at the same time. The previous theoretical and empirical literature on FDI, however, has concentrated on location choices and has largely neglected internalization choices.

In theory, Horstman and Markusen (1992), for example, formalized endogenous investment decisions in the trade-off between arm's-length exports and FDI. However, they did not include possible vertical division of labor between a parent firm and a foreign affiliate. To the author's knowledge, the literature on vertical integration in industrial organization theory has not yet been incorporated into the international trade theory of division of labor in an operational format. As for empirical study, there is an extensive literature on location choices of FDI; Smith and Florida (1994) and Head, Ries, and Swenson (1995) are examples for Japanese multinational enterprises (MNEs) in the United States along this line. However,

Fukunari Kimura is professor of economics at Keio University.

The author thanks two discussants and other conference participants for useful comments and suggestions. Comments by an anonymous referee were also helpful. Research assistance provided by Takamune Fujii is acknowledged.

The MITI database used in this paper was prepared and analyzed in cooperation with the Research and Statistics Department, Minister's Secretariat, Ministry of International Trade and Industry, Government of Japan. However, opinions expressed in this paper are those of the author.

these studies generally treat location choices independent of internalization decisions. They analyze why an affiliate in a certain industry is located in country A instead of country B. However, they do not make any direct inference about the function of the affiliate in the business strategy of the firm group or the nature of transactions among the parent firms and affiliates. As Yamawaki (1998) argued, empirical studies of internalization have been much thinner and have not been fully integrated with studies of location.

Decisions about internalization take various forms in the international setting. A firm usually conducts a number of activities or functions. These consist of (1) a headquarters function including overall planning, financial management, personnel management, and legal services, (2) production activities including R&D, technology management, production control, quality control, and purchases and inventory control of parts and components, and (3) marketing activities including marketing surveys and planning, inventory control of products, logistics arrangement, advertisement, and others. Considering firm-specific assets and the saving of transaction costs, a firm decides what activities and functions are to be internalized and what to be left for other firms and at the same time geographically locates the internalized activities and functions. Particularly in the context of international operations, an important decision is whether the headquarters function is placed only at the parent firm or is partially dispersed across foreign affiliates. Internalization decisions about the value chain of production and distribution are also made while considering locational advantages all over the world. A firm decides the boundary of its activities over the value chain, slices the internalized activities, and disperses them over a number of locations. The upstream and downstream boundaries of the firm can be fuzzy if, for example, the firm has long-term outsourcing contracts with other firms.

Empirical studies of internalization face serious difficulties in statistical quantification. It is usually difficult to match statistical data for parent firms with those for their foreign affiliates. Even if we can match the data, it is almost impossible to obtain detailed information on differences in activities or functions of parent firms and affiliates. Moreover, we cannot quantify physical transactions between parent firms and their affiliates in many cases. In addition, internalization decisions are deeply rooted in the nature of firm-specific assets, and thus statistical aggregation is often difficult.

There is, however, statistically tractable internalization data in the case of Japanese MNEs. The Basic Survey of Business Structure and Activity conducted by Japan's Ministry of International Trade and Industry (MITI) provides detailed data on firms in Japan and their foreign affiliates with census coverage. The questionnaire-level microdata are matched between parent firms in Japan and their foreign affiliates. We can thus obtain information on what sorts of Japanese firms have how many and what sorts of foreign affiliates. We place our focus on sectoral choices of parent firms and foreign affiliates over manufacturing and wholesale or retail trade. Some manufacturing parent firms have only manufacturing foreign affiliates while others have wholesale or retail trade foreign affiliates. Some wholesale or retail trade parent firms have manufacturing foreign affiliates, and others do not. These differences in affiliate-holding patterns come from differences in internalization decisions.

When a manufacturing parent firm has one or more nonmanufacturing foreign affiliates, or when a nonmanufacturing parent firm has one or more manufacturing foreign affiliates, we say that "sector switching" occurs. Sector switching of course does not necessarily imply that foreign affiliates conduct activities completely different from those of their parent firms. Parent firms usually have broader activities than their affiliates, and the secondary activity of a parent firm may be identical to the activity of its affiliate. However, from the concordance and discordance of major activities we can infer the width of internalization along the value chain of production and distribution. By incorporating the characteristics of parent firms, we can analyze internalization decisions in the context of the international operation of MNEs. This approach does not cover all features of internalization, but it provides a precious trial to capture an important cross section of internalization decisions.

There are a number of studies on the choice of activities of MNEs in the literature on management and international business, but they are mostly based on case studies or anecdotal evidence. It is thus worthwhile to try to capture the internalization behavior of MNEs with comprehensive statistical data. In this sense, MITI's data are an indispensable resource that deserves careful investigation. This paper proves that internalization decisions are an essential element in analyzing the behavior of MNEs and are particularly important to understanding the characteristics of Japanese firms.

Section 3.2 gives an overview of manufacturing and nonmanufacturing sector switching by Japanese parent firms and foreign affiliates and claims that internalization and location choices reveal some key features of Japanese MNEs. Statistical figures for U.S. MNEs are also presented for comparison. Section 3.3 analyzes statistical data on sector switching from the foreign affiliate side, while section 3.4 approaches from the parent side. Section 3.5 summarizes the findings and lists agenda for future research.

3.2   Sector Switching by Japanese Multinational Enterprises

In both the academic and journalistic literature, Japanese MNEs are claimed to be different from MNEs of other nationalities in some important ways. There is a set of anecdotal "stylized facts" on Japanese MNEs.

Although they are stylized in the sense that rigorous empirical confirmation remains to be done carefully, it is of interest that most of them are related to sector switching and internalization decisions.

First, it is well known that many Japanese manufacturers have wholesale trade foreign affiliates, particularly in developed countries. A large proportion of these parent firms belong to the general machinery, electric machinery, and transport equipment industries, in which products are differentiated, fringe and aftercare services are important, and capturing local market niches is the key to selling products. Having foreign affiliates in the wholesale trade sector is an example of downward internalization. Yamawaki (1991) claimed that wholesale trade affiliates of Japanese firms in the United States help to expand Japanese exports to the United States. However, if we interpret the issue as simply whether to make arm's-length exports or to sell exported products through wholesale trade affiliates, we may misunderstand the current stage of globalization of Japanese firms. Since the latter half of the 1980s, the international activities of Japanese firms have expanded dramatically. Large Japanese manufacturers, typically in the automobile, consumer electronics, and office machine industries, do not just have wholesale trade affiliates for exported goods but establish foreign affiliates for both production and distribution while taking strong home country effects into consideration. Since major MNEs have constructed extensive worldwide networks of production and distribution, a simple story of export versus FDI may not be entirely relevant. It is necessary to specify the activities of foreign affiliates and analyze the overall strategy of Japanese MNEs.

Second, Japanese MNEs are often claimed to export a vertical *keiretsu* structure formed by multiple Japanese companies. The competitive edge of the Japanese manufacturing sector is found in industries in which efficient subcontracting arrangements are established. With efficient subcontracting arrangements, small and medium-size enterprises (SMEs) do not have to internalize a wide range of activities but can concentrate on production activities while keeping themselves slim. In the globalization era, it is observed that SMEs, particularly competitive ones, move their production plants to foreign countries together with their major clients. They try to keep subcontracting relationships with customers, which can be interpreted as loose internalization arrangements. In this sense, the no-sector-switching cases of SMEs—that is, manufacturing to manufacturing—are also related to internalization, in contrast to the sector-switching cases of large MNEs. Although the agglomeration effect of Japanese FDI to the United States has been pointed out by Smith and Florida (1994) and Head et al. (1995), we must examine it in more detail to see whether the effect is generated in a horizontal manner or in the form of vertical subcontracting systems. In East Asia, it is more important for Japanese MNEs to transplant subcontracting systems because local indigenous supporting industries are immature. In Malaysia and Thailand, for example, Japanese SMEs have formed the first and second layers of subcontracting systems upstream of large Japanese MNEs, particularly in the electric and electronic machinery industries.[1]

Third, in a recent phenomenon a number of Japanese wholesale and retail trade companies have established manufacturing plants abroad and imported from them, particularly from East Asian countries. This is an example of upward internalization, which probably is not often observed for MNEs of different nationalities. It may be based partly on the tradition of product development by Japanese trading companies and partly on the desire to avoid the rent-capturing or inefficient existing distribution system in Japan. Although Kimura and Kohama (1997) tried to quantify this type of sector switching to some extent, there is certainly room for more formal investigation.

Fourth, general trading companies (GTCs) are one of the major components of the Japanese economic system (Yoshino and Lifson 1986). GTCs establish their affiliates and branches all over the world and set up networks of information and distribution. As discussed in Kimura and Kohama (1997), they seek economies of scope in terms of the number of commodities to handle and the functions to conduct. The functions include not only commodity trading but also matchmaking in setting up joint ventures, finance and insurance, construction and management of industrial estates, among others. As theoretically formalized in Kimura and Talmain (1994), GTCs work as a device through which other, client companies can avoid internalizing distribution functions. Statistical, comprehensive analysis of the activities of GTCs, however, is yet to come.

It is thus obvious that internalization is one of the key concepts in understanding the globalization pattern of Japanese firms. Sector switching or nonswitching between manufacturing and nonmanufacturing reveals some of the major characteristics of Japanese MNEs. Past analyses of this topic, however, have not been statistically comprehensive but rather anecdotal. What this paper relies on is data from MITI's Basic Survey of Business Structure and Activity. This survey was first conducted in fiscal year 1991, then in fiscal year 1994, and annually afterward. The main purpose of the survey is to capture an overall picture of Japanese corporate firms in terms of their activity diversification, internationalization, and strategy on R&D and information technology. The strength of the survey is the comprehensiveness of its samples and the reliability of its figures.

---

1. Since the subcontracting relationship is long term in nature, it sometimes works as an obstacle to the restructuring of industrial organization in Japan. An interesting anecdotal observation is that the globalization of interfirm relationships reshuffles rigid subcontracting relationships. Even if the match between upstream and downstream firms is the same, the prices of parts and components typically become more competitive abroad than in domestic transactions.

We must, however, be careful because the survey only covers large domestic firms and large foreign affiliates in specific industries. The domestic firms covered have more than fifty workers, have capital of more than 30 million yen, and own establishments in the mining, manufacturing, wholesale and retail trade, or restaurant industry. The foreign affiliates must have more than 50 percent Japanese ownership and capital of more than $1 million and must conduct mining, manufacturing, or commerce activities.[2] We will use the questionnaire-level fiscal year 1994 data. Because the survey does not yet provide long time-series data, it is difficult to analyze entry and exit decisions directly. However, it yields precious information on the connection between parent firms in Japan and foreign affiliates.

Before moving forward, we take an overview of the data on manufacturing and commercial affiliates of Japanese firms in comparison with such affiliates of U.S. firms (see table 3.1).[3] The Japanese data are from MITI's published report on the 1994 Basic Survey of Business Structure and Activity (hereinafter BS94) while the U.S. data are derived from a publication of the Bureau of Economic Analysis, U.S. Department of Commerce (hereinafter FAUSF94).

Note that figures for foreign affiliates of Japanese firms (FAJFs) are not perfectly comparable with those for foreign affiliates of U.S. firms (FAUSFs). FAUSF94 covers finance and a wide range of other service industries while BS94 does not. "Gross product"[4] is used for value added in the case of FAUSFs while value added is calculated by subtracting purchases from sales in the case of FAJFs. We also have to be careful because FDI between Japan and the United States is so asymmetrical that we cannot directly compare figures for FAJFs with those for FAUSFs.[5]

Despite a number of statistical reservations, table 3.1 suggests several important differences between FAJFs and FAUSFs. First of all, combinations of manufacturing parents and wholesale trade affiliates are indirectly observed for both Japanese and U.S. MNEs. A difference, however, is that wholesale trade FAJFs have small value-added ratios and large value-added productivity, compared with FAUSFs, which may imply that FAJFs handle large amounts of commodities at low cost. In addition, the value-

---

2. The data allow us to distinguish Japanese affiliates of foreign firms, but we do not exclude them from our data set.

3. A similar table for 1991 is presented in Kimura and Baldwin (1998).

4. Gross product is defined as the sum of employee compensation, profit-type return, net interest paid, indirect business taxes, and capital consumption allowances. It is thus slightly different from that for FAJFs.

5. In addition, the data from BS94 may be imprecise for several reasons. First, the number of FAJFs looks too small, which suggests that parent firms may not report all of their foreign affiliates. Second, by-destination sales shares may be biased toward exports because FAJFs may report exports even if they export through local affiliates of Japanese trading companies. The same bias may exist in the case of by-origin purchase shares. Moreover, official, contractual flows of commodities do not necessarily coincide with physical commodity flows, and we are not sure on which FAJFs base their answers.

Table 3.1　　Comparison of Manufacturing and Commercial Affiliates: Japan and the United States, 1994

Industry	Affiliates		Sales		Value Added[a]		Employment		Average Number of Employees	Value-Added Ratio[b] (%)	Value-Added Productivity[c] ($)	By-Destination Shares in Sales (%)			By-Origin Shares in Purchases (%)	
	Number	Percent	Millions of Dollars	Percent	Millions of Dollars	Percent	Number	Percent				Local	Japan/U.S.	Third Countries	Local	Imports
					Foreign Affiliates of Japanese Firms (FAJFs)											
By parent companies' classification																
All industries	2,480	100.00	526,518	100.00	56,925	100.00	779,851	100.00	314	10.81	72,995	70.68	12.25	17.06	34.55	65.45
Manufacturing	1,769	71.33	197,698	37.55	40,204	70.63	587,797	75.37	332	20.34	63,398	80.03	5.35	14.62	28.07	71.93
Wholesale and retail trade	697	28.10	328,477	62.39	16,721	29.37	190,450	24.42	273	5.09	87,797	65.03	16.42	18.55	37.80	62.20
Wholesale	650	26.21	327,163	62.14	16,321	28.67	182,107	23.35	280	4.99	89,623	64.99	16.39	18.63	37.70	62.30
Retail	47	1.90	1,314	0.25	400	0.70	8,343	1.07	178	30.45	47,946	75.84	23.71	0.45	70.63	29.37
By affiliates' classification																
All industries	2,480	100.00	526,518	100.00	56,925	100.00	779,851	100.00	314	10.81	72,995	70.68	12.25	17.06	34.55	65.45
Manufacturing	1,524	61.45	130,592	24.80	34,659	60.89	679,366	87.11	446	26.54	51,017	74.40	8.34	17.27	33.77	65.23
Wholesale and retail trade	946	38.15	395,462	75.11	22,130	38.88	99,911	12.81	106	5.60	221,499	69.47	13.51	17.01	34.77	65.23
Wholesale	866	34.92	392,732	74.59	21,343	37.49	91,072	11.68	105	5.43	234,457	69.41	13.59	17.00	34.76	65.24
Retail	80	3.23	2,730	0.52	787	1.38	8,839	1.13	110	28.82	89,020	78.49	2.57	18.94	36.35	63.65
					Foreign Affiliates of U.S. Firms (FAUSFs)											
By parent companies' classification																
All industries	18,713	100.00	1,432,412	100.00	394,557	100.00	5,572,600	100.00	298	27.54	70,803	66.91	10.48	22.61	n.a.	n.a.
Manufacturing	13,370	71.45	1,161,856	81.11	331,965	84.14	3,996,400	69.03	299	28.57	83,066	64.07	11.25	24.68	n.a.	n.a.
Manufacturing excl. petroleum and coal products	12,318	65.83	973,045	67.93	246,797	62.55	3,846,500	69.03	312	25.36	64,161	62.37	11.31	26.31	n.a.	n.a.

(*continued*)

Table 3.1 (continued)

Industry	Affiliates		Sales		Value Added[a]		Employment		Average Number of Employees	Value-Added Ratio[b] (%)	Value-Added Productivity[c] ($)	By-Destination Shares in Sales (%)			By-Origin Shares in Purchases (%)	
	Number	Percent	Millions of Dollars	Percent	Millions of Dollars	Percent	Number	Percent				Local	Japan/U.S.	Third Countries	Local	Imports
Foreign Affiliates of U.S. Firms (FAUSFs)																
Wholesale and retail trade	1,399	7.48	92,476	6.46	13,117	3.32	553,400	9.93	396	14.18	23,703	n.a.	n.a.	n.a.	n.a.	n.a.
Wholesale	1,159	6.19	63,468	4.43	6,294	1.60	192,700	3.46	166	9.92	32,662	n.a.	n.a.	n.a.	n.a.	n.a.
Wholesale excl. petroleum wholesale	933	4.99	48,598	3.39	7,070	1.79	185,700	3.33	199	14.55	38,072	69.76	8.97	21.27	n.a.	n.a.
Retail	240	1.28	29,008	2.03	6,823	1.73	360,700	6.47	1,503	23.52	18,916	n.a.	5.79	n.a.	n.a.	n.a.
By affiliates' classification																
All industries	18,713	100.00	1,432,412	100.00	394,557	100.00	5,572,600	100.00	298	27.54	70,803	66.91	10.48	22.61	n.a.	n.a.
Manufacturing	7,073	37.80	776,257	54.19	244,345	61.93	3,401,700	61.04	481	31.48	71,830	62.08	12.99	24.92	n.a.	n.a.
Manufacturing excl. petroleum and coal products	6,998	37.40	694,666	48.50	197,535	50.07	3,353,000	60.17	479	28.44	58,913	59.55	13.88	26.57	n.a.	n.a.
Wholesale and retail trade	5,476	29.26	422,423	29.49	73,846	18.72	1,006,900	18.07	184	17.48	73,340	71.52	n.a.	n.a.	n.a.	n.a.
Wholesale	5,123	27.38	387,718	27.07	65,416	16.58	560,600	10.06	109	16.87	116,689	69.17	6.08	24.75	n.a.	n.a.
Wholesale excl. petroleum wholesale	4,789	25.59	296,549	20.70	47,367	12.01	526,400	9.45	110	15.97	89,983	68.69	5.25	26.06	n.a.	n.a.
Retail	353	1.89	34,705	2.42	8,430	2.14	446,300	8.01	1,264	24.29	18,889	97.77	n.a.	n.a.	n.a.	n.a.

[a]Value added: for Japan, sales minus purchases; for United States, gross product.

[b]Value-added ratio: (value added)/sales.

[c]Value-added productivity: (value added)/employment.

added share of wholesale trade FAJFs is as high as 37 percent while that of wholesale trade FAUSFs is only 17 percent. This suggests that efficient wholesale activities may be a source of profitability for Japanese MNEs. Second, wholesale trade parents have a much heavier weight among Japanese firms than among U.S. firms. The value-added share of foreign affiliates of Japanese wholesale trade parents is 29 percent while that of U.S. wholesale trade parents is only 2 percent; the wholesale parents are much more important MNEs in Japan than in the United States. It should also be noted that foreign affiliates of Japanese wholesale or retail trade parents export large amounts to Japan, which suggests that the wholesale and manufacturing activities involved in sending products back to Japan are important components of their operations. Overall, the comparison between FAJFs and FAUSFs again suggests that sector switching of parent firms and foreign affiliates may reveal the characteristics of Japanese MNEs.

3.3   Sector-Switching Analysis from the Foreign Affiliate Side

In the following, we will go into the analysis of sector switching between parents and foreign affiliates by using the questionnaire-level data underlying BS94 (hereinafter the "MITI database"). In this section, we look at the data from the affiliate side and try to connect our discussion with traditional location choice analysis.

Table 3.2 presents the number of FAJFs in East Asia, North America, and Western Europe, which covers more than 90 percent of all FAJFs in the world in terms of the number of FAJFs. The row denotes the industry of the parent firm, and the column denotes the industry of the FAJF.[6] For industry codes, see the appendix. Because many FAJFs belong to the same industries as their parents, large numbers are naturally found in the diagonal cells of the table. In East Asia 673 FAJFs out of 975 (69 percent) are in the diagonal cells, in North America 409 out of 728 (56 percent), and in Western Europe 283 out of 552 (51 percent). The rest of the FAJFs belong to industries different from those of their parents. Most sector switching between parents and foreign affiliates occurs between the manufacturing sector (industries 120 to 340) and the wholesale trade sector (industry 481). In North America and Western Europe, many wholesale trade FAJFs have manufacturing parent firms. In East Asia, a considerable number of manufacturing FAJFs have wholesale trade parent firms.

Table 3.3 presents reorganized information on the activities of FAJFs by location of FAJF and by industries of parent firm and FAJF. To simplify the table, industries are aggregated up to manufacturing (M) and

---

6. The questionnaire of BS94 asks for a detailed sales composition of each parent firm, and its industry is assigned by following its largest sold commodity item. The industry of each FAJF is answered directly in the form of industry code.

Table 3.2   Industries of Japanese Parent Firms and FAJFs, 1994 (number of foreign affiliates)

East Asia: All Asian Countries East of Pakistan

Industry of Parent Firm	Industry of FAJF																											Subtotal
	120	130	140	150	160	170	180	190	200	210	220	230	240	250	260	270	280	290	300	310	320	330	340	050	481	540	Other	
120	12																											12
130	2	1																							1			4
140			7	1																					1			10
150			2	9									1															12
160					2																							2
170						5																						5
180							2																					2
190								7																				10
200	1		14						71		4					1	2	3					1		10			106
210										1															1			2
220											25														1			28
230												15														1		16
240																												0
250														6											1			8
260									1						5	2	3	2	3						1			15
270																33	3		6						2			44
280																3	26	1	2									35
290												1			1			49	5	1	3		1		16			76
300			1						2		4						1	5	211	4	1		1		25			249
310																		1		45	1					1		53
320																					22				3			24
330																												1
340																	1						12		1			13
050																												0
481	4		3	10	3	1		2	3	1	7	1	1	7	5	1	6	6	56	2	4		5		94	2		224
540	1			1		1					1			1						1	2		1		2	13		20
Other				1																						1		4
Subtotal	20	1	27	22	5	7	2	9	77	2	41	17	2	14	12	40	42	69	283	52	33	0	21	0	159	18	0	975

North America: United States and Canada

Industry of FAJF

Industry of Parent Firm	120	130	140	150	160	170	180	190	200	210	220	230	240	250	260	270	280	290	300	310	320	330	340	050	481	540	Other	Subtotal
120	15	2																							2			19
130	1	9																							5	1		16
140			4																									4
150				1																					1	1		3
160					1						2																	3
170						1																	1					2
180							5	1																	1	1		8
190								4	1																2			7
200		2	2						27		2						2		1						17	1		54
210																												0
220											11	1														1		13
230											1	8													4	1		14
240																												0
250					1									11											2			14
260															6	2				1				3	3			15
270														2		9	1	1	1	3					2			19
280									2			1				2	13	1	2	1					2			24
290									1			1					1	37	1	1					48	2		92
300											1	1		1	1	1	2	1	41	1			1	1	33			85
310																				69	5				22			96
320																					5				18			23
330																									2			2
340																			1	6			1		9			17
050																												0
481	8				2			4	2		1	1		3	1	1	1	2	10	5	1		6		123	6		177
540																							1		3	9		13
Other				2																			2		3	1		8
Subtotal	24	13	6	3	4	1	5	9	33	0	18	12	0	15	7	13	19	46	57	89	10	0	11	4	303	26	0	728

(*continued*)

Table 3.2   (continued)

Western Europe: All Europe Excluding the Commonwealth of Independent States and Eastern European Countries

Industry of Parent Firm	Industry of FAJF																											Subtotal
	120	130	140	150	160	170	180	190	200	210	220	230	240	250	260	270	280	290	300	310	320	330	340	050	481	540	Other	
120	3								1																1			5
130		6							1																1			8
140			3																						1			4
150																									2	3		5
160											1																	1
170																									1			1
180																									1			1
190								1																	1			2
200			2						16		1					1			2						15			37
210																					1							1
220											5																	5
230												7													3			10
240																												0
250																		1	1									2
260																					1							1
270												1				6									5			12
280																4	3											7
290																		38	1						61			100
300									2		1							1	44	1	1				40	6		95
310																		2	1	14					20			37
320									1										2		5				13	1		22
330																												0
340																			1				4		14	2		21
050																												0
481		1							2		3			4			1	3	18	2	1		4		119	6		164
540																										9		9
Other																							2					2
Subtotal	3	7	5	0	0	0	0	1	23	0	11	8	0	4	0	11	4	44	69	17	9	0	10	0	299	27	0	552

Data source: MITI database.

Note: For industry codes, see the appendix.

Table 3.3   Foreign Affiliates of Japanese Parent Firms by Industries of Parent and Affiliate, 1994

Location of Affiliate and Industries of Parent and Affiliate[a]	Affiliates		Sales		Value Added		Employment		Average Number of Employees	Value-Added Ratio (%)	Value-Added Productivity ($)	By-Destination Shares in Sales (%)			By-Origin Shares in Purchases (%)	
	Number	Percent	Millions of Dollars	Percent	Millions of Dollars	Percent	Number	Percent				Local	Japan	Third Countries	Local	Imports
East Asia																
Total	975	100.00	116,313	100.00	13,099	100.00	415,035	100.00	426	11.26	31,561	58.42	13.99	27.58	38.57	61.43
M/M	660	67.69	33,949	29.19	9,106	69.51	288,310	69.47	437	26.82	31,582	50.48	18.71	30.80	32.38	67.62
M/N	67	6.87	8,711	7.49	540	4.12	4,651	1.12	69	6.20	116,087	46.86	17.30	35.84	7.51	92.49
N/M	138	14.15	12,330	10.60	4,014	30.64	110,244	26.56	799	32.55	36,406	59.85	23.17	16.98	15.03	84.97
N/N	110	11.28	61,324	52.72	(560)	-4.28	11,830	2.85	108	-0.91	(47,351)	64.17	9.07	26.76	48.32	51.68
North America																
Total	728	100.00	226,795	100.00	27,543	100.00	217,220	100.00	298	12.14	126,800	78.64	12.12	9.23	39.39	60.61
M/M	343	47.12	42,825	18.88	11,053	40.13	148,413	68.32	433	25.81	74,472	94.76	1.94	3.30	40.63	59.37
M/N	187	25.69	58,556	25.82	8,189	29.73	35,773	16.47	191	13.99	228,927	96.90	1.08	2.02	22.22	77.78
N/M	51	7.01	12,545	5.53	1,848	6.71	20,396	9.39	400	14.73	90,630	96.63	2.94	0.43	15.21	84.79
N/N	147	20.19	112,868	49.77	6,453	23.43	12,638	5.82	86	5.72	510,601	61.05	22.74	16.21	49.58	50.42
Western Europe																
Total	552	100.00	149,625	100.00	12,771	100.00	97,201	100.00	176	8.54	131,389	73.28	7.35	19.37	24.78	75.22
M/M	185	33.51	18,006	12.03	5,371	42.05	52,844	54.37	286	29.83	101,635	58.06	1.31	40.63	42.02	57.98
M/N	192	34.78	25,048	16.74	3,486	27.29	16,607	17.09	86	13.92	209,898	82.21	3.45	14.34	17.27	82.73
N/M	41	7.43	4,125	2.76	1,253	9.81	17,309	17.81	422	30.37	72,373	90.76	2.24	7.00	41.08	58.92
N/N	134	24.28	102,445	68.47	2,662	20.84	10,441	10.74	78	2.60	254,944	73.07	9.57	17.36	23.74	76.26

Note: See table 3.1 notes for definitions of value added, value-added ratio, and value-added productivity.

[a] The industry of the parent firm is given first, then the industry of the affiliate. M stands for manufacturing, and N stands for nonmanufacturing. E.g., "M/N" means that the parent firm is in the manufacturing sector and the affiliate in the nonmanufacturing sector.

nonmanufacturing (N) sectors. Sectors of a parent firm and its FAJF are reported separated by a slash.

Cases in which both the parent firm and the FAJF are in the manufacturing sector (M/M) have a particularly large share in East Asia; in terms of number of FAJFs, 660 out of 975 (68 percent) follow this pattern. The shares in North America and Western Europe are only 47 and 34 percent, respectively. M/M-type FAJFs in East Asia sell a large portion of their products to Japan and third countries (the sales shares to Japan and third countries are 19 and 31 percent, respectively). These are consistent with the fact that East Asia has a strong locational advantage for manufacturing activities. From this table, however, vertical linkage among FAJFs cannot be detected directly.

Cases in which the parent firm is in the manufacturing sector while the FAJF is in the nonmanufacturing sector (M/N) are pervasive in North America and Western Europe. M/N-type FAJFs account for 26 and 35 percent of FAJFs in these regions. They sell their products predominantly to local markets, which indicates that these regions are attractive as large, matured markets for their products and it is thus worth setting up wholesale trade affiliates there. Their extremely high value-added productivity would be a reflection of their good commerce. In Western Europe, sales to local markets by M/N-type FAJFs are 82 percent while those by M/M-type FAJFs are 58 percent. Sales to third countries by M/N-type FAJFs, on the other hand, are only 14 percent while those by M/M-type FAJFs are 41 percent. This means that manufacturing FAJFs are located only in selected countries in Europe, but wholesale trade FAJFs tend to be located in each country. There are only 67 M/N-type FAJFs in East Asia, of which 50 are located in Hong Kong and Singapore (not shown in the table). The large share of sales to third countries and the large share of imports from abroad suggest that these FAJFs work as global distribution centers. East Asia is not yet a market attractive enough for Japanese MNEs to establish wholesale trade affiliates for local sales.

Cases in which the parent firm is in the nonmanufacturing sector and the FAJF is in the manufacturing sector (N/M) are particularly important in East Asia, where 138 FAJFs out of 975 (14 percent) are of this type. Their share in terms of value added is as high as 31 percent. These FAJFs are characterized by large numbers of employees (799 persons on average), high value-added ratios (33 percent), and large proportions of sales to Japan (23 percent). N/M-type FAJFs make up only 7 percent of FAJFs in North America and Western Europe.

Last, cases in which both the parent firm and the FAJF are in the nonmanufacturing sector (N/N) have shares of 11, 20, and 24 percent in East Asia, North America, and Western Europe, respectively, in terms of number of affiliates. N/N-type FAJFs in North America and Western Europe have very high value-added productivity and low value-added ratios, which indicates that these FAJFs conduct pure trade intermediary functions with minimal storage functions. In addition, N/N-type FAJFs in East Asia and North America purchase a large portion of commodities from local markets and sell some of them to third countries and Japan. This suggests that some FAJFs of this type have purchasing functions. As for N/N-type FAJFs in Western Europe, their high local sales ratios and low ratios of sales to third countries suggest that FAJFs acting as distribution affiliates are located in each country, rather than selling from large-scale distribution centers for the whole of Europe.

In the usual location choice analysis, we simply check the industries and other characteristics of foreign affiliates and combine them with locational conditions. By introducing the industries of parent firms as we do here, the firms' strategies on location and internalization can be identified in a much richer manner.

3.4   Sector-Switching Analysis from the Parent Firm Side

Another way of looking at the same set of data is to analyze it from the parent firm side and to see what sort of foreign affiliates each parent firm has. Doing so, we can investigate the overall strategies of internalization and location of each firm group to a great extent. The MITI database provides precious information of this sort.

Table 3.4 presents the number of parent firms that have one or more than one foreign affiliates by industry of parent firm, together with the percentages of parent firms that have at least one nonmanufacturing foreign affiliate in the case of manufacturing parent firms and that have at least one manufacturing foreign affiliate in the case of nonmanufacturing parent firms. Out of 713 manufacturing parent firms, 408 have just one affiliate, only 13 percent of which have a nonmanufacturing affiliate. On the other hand, 47 percent of manufacturing parent firms with more than one affiliate have at least one nonmanufacturing affiliate. As for nonmanufacturing parent firms, 139 out of 232 have only one affiliate. The percentage having at least one manufacturing affiliate is 41 percent among parent firms with only one affiliate and 62 percent among parent firms with more than one affiliate.

We would like to emphasize that when a manufacturing parent firm has only one affiliate, sector switching hardly occurs. In addition, contrary to the conventional belief, parent firms in electric machinery (300) and transport equipment (310) do not show a particularly strong tendency to have nonmanufacturing foreign affiliates. These facts suggest that a considerable number of MNEs do not try to internalize wholesale trade activities but instead concentrate on production activities in affiliates in order to supply parts and components to other firms. Some parent firms, on the other hand, tend to have both manufacturing and wholesale trade affiliates

Table 3.4   **Foreign Affiliate Ownership Patterns of Japanese Parent Firms, 1994 (number of parent firms)**

Industry of Parent Firm	Total	With Only One Foreign Affiliate	With More Than One Foreign Affiliate
Manufacturing			
120	24 (16.67)	15 (0.00)	9 (44.44)
130	12 (41.67)	6 (16.67)	6 (66.67)
140	13 (7.69)	9 (0.00)	4 (25.00)
150	14 (28.57)	9 (11.11)	5 (60.00)
160	4 (0.00)	3 (0.00)	1 (0.00)
170	7 (14.29)	6 (0.00)	1 (100.00)
180	10 (20.00)	7 (14.29)	3 (33.33)
190	12 (25.00)	9 (22.22)	3 (33.33)
200	80 (25.00)	40 (10.00)	40 (40.00)
210	3 (66.67)	2 (50.00)	1 (100.00)
220	33 (6.06)	23 (8.70)	10 (0.00)
230	17 (35.29)	8 (25.00)	9 (44.44)
240	0 (n.a.)	0 (n.a.)	0 (n.a.)
250	22 (9.09)	18 (0.00)	4 (50.00)
260	17 (35.29)	14 (21.43)	3 (100.00)
270	29 (10.34)	13 (0.00)	16 (18.75)
280	36 (8.33)	20 (5.00)	16 (12.50)
290	91 (45.05)	47 (27.66)	44 (63.64)
300	145 (27.40)	84 (11.90)	61 (49.18)
310	91 (24.44)	50 (8.00)	41 (43.90)
320	28 (53.57)	13 (30.77)	15 (73.33)
330	1 (100.00)	0 (0.00)	1 (100.00)
340	24 (58.33)	12 (33.33)	12 (83.33)
Subtotal	713 (27.63)	408 (12.99)	305 (47.21)
Nonmanufacturing			
050	0 (n.a.)	0 (n.a.)	0 (n.a.)
481	190 (53.68)	105 (43.81)	85 (65.88)
540	32 (25.00)	26 (30.77)	6 (0.00)
Other	10 (50.00)	8 (37.50)	2 (100.00)
Subtotal	232 (49.57)	139 (41.01)	93 (62.37)
Total	945 (33.01)	547 (20.11)	398 (50.75)

Data source: MITI database.

Note: Numbers in parentheses are percentages of parent firms having affiliates in a different industry. "Different industry" means the nonmanufacturing sector for parents in the manufacturing sector and the manufacturing sector for parents in the nonmanufacturing sector.

and form global production-distribution networks. Internalization decisions are surely connected with the overall strategy of MNEs. For non-manufacturing parent firms, the high percentage having manufacturing affiliates indicates that upward internalization is pervasive in the international context.

Because the number of foreign affiliates is expected to depend on the size of the parent firm, we classify parent firms by number of regular workers. Table 3.5 presents the data for manufacturing parent firms. The percentage of having at least one nonmanufacturing affiliate is again shown in parentheses. The table indicates that small parent firms tend to have a small number of FAJFs and that parent firms tend not to have nonmanufacturing affiliates when their number of affiliates is small. At the bottom of the table, the percentage of nonmanufacturing FAJFs is also shown, which goes up from 13 percent to more than 50 percent and then comes down to 40 percent as the number of affiliates increases. These figures suggest that the location and internalization strategies of Japanese manufacturing parent firms may be classified into two categories. One is to concentrate on manufacturing activities to supply intermediate goods to other firms, and the other is to establish a global production-distribution network by internalizing wholesale trade activities. Parent firms in the former category may maintain long-term relationships with clients even after establishing affiliates abroad.

Table 3.6 presents the data for nonmanufacturing Japanese parent firms in the same format as table 3.5. Again, small parent firms tend to have small numbers of foreign affiliates. A sharp contrast from the manufacturing parent firms is found in the percentage having affiliates in a different industry. Even if parent firms are small or even if the number of affiliates is small, there is still a strong tendency to have manufacturing affiliates. N/M activities may still be underestimated here because the BS94 data include only majority-owned affiliates and large parent firms. On the other hand, there are GTCs with a large number of affiliates, both manufacturing and nonmanufacturing. The percentage of manufacturing affiliates comes down to 28 percent as the number of affiliates increases (shown at the bottom of the table).

Table 3.7 summarizes major characteristics of Japanese manufacturing firms. In the table, firms located in Japan are classified into three groups: (a) firms without foreign affiliates, (b) firms with only manufacturing foreign affiliates (no sector switching), and (c) firms with at least one nonmanufacturing foreign affiliate (sector switching). The table reports the mean and standard deviation of each indicator for firms in Japan. Because the microdata have fat tails and some of the variables cannot be normally distributed, the means and standard deviations must be interpreted with caution.

Table 3.7 reveals various features of Japanese manufacturing firms in the context of international operations. We would like to note the following four points in particular. First, groups a, b, and c clearly differ in firm size and capital-labor ratio. Manufacturing firms without foreign affiliates tend to have fewer regular workers, smaller total sales, and smaller ratios of tangible assets to regular workers than do those with foreign affiliates.

Table 3.5   Foreign Affiliate Ownership Patterns of Japanese Manufacturing Parent Firms, 1994 (number of parent firms)

Number of Regular Workers of Parent Firm	Number of Affiliates										
	1	2	3	4	5	6	7	8	9	10	More Than 10
50 to 99	28 (3.57)	2 (0.00)									
100 to 199	54 (3.70)	8 (12.50)		1 (0.00)							
200 to 299	66 (12.12)	2 (0.00)	2 (0.00)	2 (0.00)							
300 to 499	54 (9.26)	14 (7.14)	6 (16.67)								
500 to 999	87 (12.64)	27 (29.63)	15 (26.67)	5 (80.00)	3 (33.33)			1 (100.00)			
More than 1,000	119 (21.85)	71 (40.85)	41 (43.90)	29 (48.28)	18 (77.78)	14 (64.29)	6 (66.67)	7 (85.71)	3 (66.67)	5 (100.00)	23 (91.30)
Total	408 (12.99)	124 (31.45)	64 (35.94)	37 (48.65)	21 (71.43)	14 (64.29)	6 (66.67)	8 (87.50)	3 (66.67)	5 (100.00)	23 (91.30)
Percentage of nonmanufacturing affiliates	12.99	21.78	19.27	27.03	34.29	28.57	54.76	43.75	33.33	66.67	39.90

Data source: MITI database.

Note: Numbers in parentheses are numbers of manufacturing parent firms having at least one nonmanufacturing affiliate.

Table 3.6   Foreign Affiliate Ownership Patterns of Japanese Nonmanufacturing Parent Firms, 1994

Number of Regular Workers of Parent Firm	Number of Affiliates										
	1	2	3	4	5	6	7	8	9	10	More Than 10
50 to 99	19 (68.42)	4 (100.00)		3 (66.67)							
100 to 199	19 (58.89)		2 (50.00)								1 (0.00)
200 to 299	9 (44.44)	7 (85.71)									
300 to 499	21 (33.33)	6 (66.67)	2 (100.00)	2 (100.00)				1 (100.00)			
500 to 999	37 (37.84)	9 (55.56)	2 (0.00)	1 (0.00)	1 (100.00)		1 (100.00)				
More than 1,000	34 (23.53)	15 (53.33)	10 (50.00)	4 (50.00)	6 (50.00)	2 (50.00)	1 (100.00)	4 (75.00)		1 (0.00)	8 (75.00)
Total	139 (41.01)	41 (65.85)	16 (50.00)	10 (60.00)	7 (57.14)	2 (50.00)	2 (100.00)	5 (80.00)		1 (0.00)	9 (66.67)
Percentage of manufacturing affiliates	41.01	52.44	33.33	30.00	42.86	16.67	21.43	47.50		0.00	28.18

Data source: MITI database.

Note: Numbers in parentheses are numbers of nonmanufacturing parent firms having at least one manufacturing affiliate.

Table 3.7   **Characteristics of Japanese Manufacturing Firms, 1994**

Characteristic	Without Foreign Affiliates (a)	With Foreign Affiliates, No Sector Switching (b)	With Foreign Affiliates, At Least One Nonmanufacturing Foreign Affiliate (c)
Firm size			
Number of regular workers (number of persons)	311	1,452	6,060
	(1,073)	(2,277)	(11,270)
Total sales (million yen)	11,250	67,025	366,703
	(59,849)	(158,225)	(829,135)
Economic performance			
Ratio of tangible assets to regular workers (million yen per person)	9.16	12.09	16.57
	(13.06)	(10.47)	(19.20)
Ratio of operating surplus to total sales	0.0510	0.0494	0.0469
	(0.1368)	(0.0411)	(0.0420)
Foreign sales (1): 1 positive; 0 zero	0.2199	0.8152	0.9485
	(0.4142)	(0.3882)	(0.2211)
Foreign sales (2): ratio to total sales	0.0225	0.0891	0.2177
	(0.0811)	(0.1294)	(0.1967)

Product differentiation			
R&D expenditure (1): 1 positive; 0 zero	0.4851	0.8366	0.9742
	(0.4998)	(0.3700)	(0.1585)
R&D expenditure (2): ratio to total sales	0.0086	0.0195	0.0396
	(0.0207)	(0.0261)	(0.0301)
Ratio of advertisement expenditure to total sales	0.0045	0.0075	0.0110
	(0.0166)	(0.0202)	(0.0161)
Linkage			
Commissioning production: 1 yes; 0 no	0.7668	0.8774	0.9124
	(0.4229)	(0.3279)	(0.2828)
Using subcontractor(s): 1 yes; 0 no	0.5995	0.7393	0.7732
	(0.4900)	(0.4390)	(0.4188)
Working as a subcontractor: 1 yes; 0 no	0.3187	0.1907	0.0515
	(0.4660)	(0.3928)	(0.2211)
Number of foreign affiliates held	0.00	1.67	4.66
	(0.00)	(1.58)	(5.68)
N	12,473	514	194

Data source: MITI database.

Note: Figures are unweighted averages. Numbers in parentheses are standard deviations.

Firms with foreign affiliates, particularly with nonmanufacturing foreign affiliates, are large in size and capital intensive. The difference between groups b and c in size reflects the average number of foreign affiliates, too; group b has 1.67 foreign affiliates on average while group c has 4.66.

Second, R&D and advertisement expenditures also differ across the three groups. R&D expenditure (1) shows whether a firm has R&D expenditure or not. It assigns the value one if yes and zero otherwise. Hence, the mean of R&D expenditure (1) indicates the probability of having positive R&D expenditure. R&D expenditure (2), on the other hand, reports the ratio of R&D expenditure to total sales. The means of R&D expenditures (1) and (2) are smallest for firms without foreign affiliates and largest for firms with nonmanufacturing foreign affiliates. The ratio of advertisement expenditure to total sales shows the same pattern. These findings suggest that firms with foreign affiliates, particularly with nonmanufacturing foreign affiliates, think more about product differentiation than do firms without foreign affiliates. More product differentiation naturally generates more incentive for extensive internalization.

Third, foreign sales also reveal contrasts among groups a, b, and c. Again, foreign sales (1) indicates whether a firm has foreign sales or not, and thus the mean of foreign sales (1) is the probability of having positive foreign sales. Only 22 percent of firms without foreign affiliates have foreign sales, while 82 and 95 percent of firms with foreign affiliates (without and with nonmanufacturing foreign affiliates, respectively) have foreign sales. Foreign sales (2) reports the ratio of foreign sales to total sales, which shows a large difference between the no-sector-switching case (9 percent) and the sector-switching case (22 percent). Remember that these foreign sales include both arm's-length and intrafirm exports. Also note that the data are for just one time point and thus do not suggest any causal relation between exports and FDI. However, we can at least confirm that the tendency to export and the tendency to invest abroad are highly correlated.

Fourth, an interesting fact is that the mean ratios of operating surplus to total sales are almost the same for groups a, b, and c. This suggests that larger, more capital-intensive, more R&D- and advertisement-intensive, more foreign-exposed firms do not necessarily perform better. This observation may indicate a sharp contrast with U.S. MNEs. In the case of the United States, Doms and Jensen (1998) asserted that MNE establishments owned by U.S. nationals show superior performance, compared with both U.S. affiliates of foreign firms and indigenous establishments without foreign affiliates. Of course, here we check just one indicator of firm performance using a single year's data, so we must be careful in concluding anything definite. However, the finding at least suggests that the efficacy of small firms cannot be neglected. Firm size, capital intensity, degree of product differentiation, and foreign exposure are not direct indicators of firm performance but rather are choice variables indicating how firms adapt themselves to the economic environment. Both small and large firms adapt to survive, but in different ways. The key to understanding Japanese firms is the interfirm relationship and the degree of internalization.

Table 3.8 displays the data for Japanese nonmanufacturing (wholesale and retail trade and restaurants) firms using the same format as table 3.7. We can again find a clear contrast between firms with and without foreign affiliates. Firms without foreign affiliates are on average smaller in terms of number of regular workers and total sales and have smaller R&D expenditure and smaller foreign sales. The contrast between the sector-switching and no-sector-switching cases, however, is not very clear. Although R&D expenditure and foreign sales are larger in the sector-switching case than in the no-sector-switching case, average firm size is almost the same. Again, the mean ratios of operating surplus to total sales are almost the same for groups a, b, and c.

We do not claim any simple causal relation among the indicators shown in tables 3.7 and 3.8. A firm is supposed to decide whether to have foreign affiliates or not and whether to have foreign affiliates in a different industry or not, jointly with decisions about its size, R&D, foreign sales, and other things. However, just to see the controlled correlation among variables, some regression analysis is conducted. Table 3.9 reports the result of logit estimation for Japanese manufacturing firms.[7] The dependent variable of the first two regressions is whether a firm has foreign affiliates or not. As expected, firms with foreign affiliates are likely to have large employment size, capital-intensive technology, large foreign sales, and large R&D expenditure. The coefficient for the ratio of advertisement expenditure is less significant than those for other variables. The second two regressions have as dependent variable whether or not a firm has nonmanufacturing foreign affiliates. Firms tend to switch sectors when they have large employment size, large foreign sales, and large R&D expenditure. Overall, the regressions confirm our casual observations about table 3.7, even after putting these variables together.

Table 3.10 shows the result of logit estimation for Japanese nonmanufacturing firms. It is confirmed that firms are likely to have foreign affiliates when they are large in employment size, have capital-intensive technology, and have large foreign sales. Whether sector switching occurs is only weakly explained by the explanatory variables used here.

3.5   Conclusion

MNEs make location and internalization decisions jointly, and thus it is necessary to develop an empirical research strategy to treat them jointly. To approach this task, this paper concentrates on sector switching

---

7. The probit estimation provides similar results.

Table 3.8   Characteristics of Japanese Nonmanufacturing Firms, 1994

Characteristic	Without Foreign Affiliates (a)	With Foreign Affiliates, No Sector Switching (b)	With Foreign Affiliates, At Least One Manufacturing Foreign Affiliate (c)
Firm size			
Number of regular workers (number of persons)	331	1,814	1,876
	(976)	(2,663)	(5,421)
Total sales (million yen)	20,805	592,162	551,309
	(176,644)	(2,236,198)	(2,258,510)
Economic performance			
Ratio of tangible assets to regular workers (million yen per person)	8.77	17.58	12.43
	(19.36)	(31.51)	(10.36)
Ratio of operating surplus to total sales	0.0298	0.0338	0.0322
	(0.0568)	(0.0532)	(0.0331)
Foreign sales (1): 1 positive; 0 zero	0.1480	0.7813	0.7890
	(0.3551)	(0.4134)	(0.4080)
Foreign sales (2): ratio to total sales	0.0110	0.0639	0.1578
	(0.0629)	(0.1140)	(0.2160)

Product differentiation			
R&D expenditure (1): 1 positive; 0 zero	0.2036	0.4583	0.6697
	(0.4026)	(0.4983)	(0.4703)
R&D expenditure (2): ratio to total sales	0.0026	0.0058	0.0115
	(0.0800)	(0.0213)	(0.0197)
Ratio of advertisement expenditure to total sales	0.0083	0.0146	0.0085
	(0.0985)	(0.0320)	(0.0198)
Linkage			
Commissioning production: 1 yes; 0 no	0.3081	0.3646	0.6330
	(0.4617)	(0.4813)	(0.4820)
Using subcontractor(s): 1 yes; 0 no	0.2540	0.2292	0.5505
	(0.4353)	(0.4203)	(0.4974)
Working as a subcontractor: 1 yes; 0 no	0.1085	0.0313	0.1101
	(0.3110)	(0.1740)	(0.3130)
Number of foreign affiliates held	0.00	2.55	3.84
	(0.00)	(6.75)	(8.06)
N	7,468	95	109

Data source: MITI database.

Note: Figures are unweighted averages. Numbers in parentheses are standard deviations.

Table 3.9 **Logit Estimation: Japanese Manufacturing Parent Firms, 1994**

	Dependent Variables			
	Having Foreign Affiliates = 1; Not Having Foreign Affiliates = 0		With Sector Switching = 1; Without Sector Switching = 0	
Variable	(1)	(2)	(1)	(2)
Constant	-5.24037**	-3.65014**	-4.36070**	-2.81511**
	(-39.8323)	(-61.1530)	(-7.1547)	(-13.4923)
Number of regular workers	0.00318**	0.00443**	0.00203**	0.00182**
	(12.3862)	(15.0583)	(6.4591)	(5.5336)
Ratio of tangible assets to regular workers	0.07417**	0.07507**	0.01208	0.20337**
	(3.4920)	(3.2360)	(1.8227)	(3.0620)
Foreign sales (1): 1 positive; 0 zero	2.51558**		1.43142**	
	(21.7900)		(3.5637)	
Foreign sales (2): ratio to total sales		4.14423**		4.40818**
		(15.9442)		(7.2494)
R&D expenditure (1): 1 positive; 0 zero	0.91096**		1.43660**	
	(7.2658)		(2.9420)	
R&D expenditure (2): ratio to total sales		8.92044**		12.3372**
		(6.94679)		(3.6575)
Ratio of advertisement expenditure to total sales	1.89845	4.95214**	7.05935	10.2399*
	(1.0665)	(3.0122)	(1.6692)	(2.3329)
Log likelihood	-1,966.85	-2,282.44	-347.263	-319.061
N	13,181	13,181	708	708

Data source: MITI database.
Note: Numbers in parentheses are *t*-statistics.
*Significant at the 5 percent level.
**Significant at the 1 percent level.

Table 3.10   Logit Estimation: Japanese Nonmanufacturing Parent Firms, 1994

	Dependent Variables			
	Having Foreign Affiliates = 1; Not Having Foreign Affiliates = 0		With Sector Switching = 1; Without Sector Switching = 0	
	(1)	(2)	(1)	(2)
Constant	−5.50060** (−31.3683)	−4.06981** (−46.0116)	−0.06514 (−0.1633)	−0.05951 (−0.2462)
Number of regular workers	0.00304** (7.6964)	0.00331** (8.7640)	0.00002 (0.0533)	−0.0003 (−0.0826)
Ratio of tangible assets to regular workers	0.05230** (3.0821)	0.04856** (3.0754)	−0.01188 (−1.2608)	−0.01176 (−1.2479)
Foreign sales (1): 1 positive; 0 zero	2.85490** (15.3308)		−0.19957 (−0.0560)	
Foreign sales (2): ratio to total sales		5.32898** (12.8725)		3.23859** (2.9903)
R&D expenditure (1): 1 positive; 0 zero	0.86654** (5.5079)		0.87041** (2.9593)	
R&D expenditure (2): ratio to total sales		0.32472 (0.8022)		13.0254 (1.4897)
Ratio of advertisement expenditure to total sales	0.32509 (0.6674)	0.21017 (0.5242)	−11.1986 (−1.5971)	−7.05755 (−1.1088)
Log likelihood	−685.915	−826.71	−134.244	−130.727
N	7,673	7,673	205	205

Data source: MITI database.

Note: Numbers in parentheses are *t*-statistics.

*Significant at the 5 percent level.

**Significant at the 1 percent level.

of Japanese parent firms and foreign affiliates between manufacturing and nonmanufacturing. We find that the industries of parent firms and affiliates are often different and MNEs clearly choose internalization and location in a strategic manner. Large manufacturing parent firms tend to have both manufacturing and nonmanufacturing affiliates, the latter of which are mainly located in North America and Western Europe. Small manufacturing parent firms and firms with a small number of affiliates are apt to concentrate on production activities at their affiliates, particularly in East Asia. About half of nonmanufacturing parent firms have at least one manufacturing affiliate, usually located in East Asia. Large nonmanufacturing parent firms, mostly GTCs, have extensive networks of production and wholesale trade activities all over the world. Integrated studies of location and internalization decisions are essential to understanding the behavior of MNEs.

Although we must confront the limitations of statistical data, the MITI database at least allows us access to various characteristics of Japanese parent firms and interactions between parent firms and their related foreign affiliates. Further exploitation of this information is what we must work on in the future.

Appendix

Industry Classification of BS94

Manufacturing sector
120	Food processing
130	Beverages, tobacco, and animal feed
140	Textiles
150	Apparel
160	Wood and wood products
170	Furniture and fixtures
180	Pulp, paper, and paper products
190	Publishing and printing
200	Chemicals
210	Petroleum and coal products
220	Plastic products
230	Rubber products
240	Leather and leather products
250	Ceramics, clay, and stone products
260	Iron and steel
270	Nonferrous metal
280	Metal products

290   General machinery
300   Electric machinery
310   Transport equipment
320   Precision machinery
330   Arms
340   Other manufacturing

Nonmanufacturing sector
050   Mining
481   Wholesale trade
540   Retail trade
Other Services and other

References

Doms, Mark E., and J. Bradford Jensen. 1998. Comparing wages, skills, and productivity between domestically and foreign-owned manufacturing establishments in the United States. In *Geography and ownership as bases for economic accounting,* ed. Robert E. Baldwin, Robert E. Lipsey, and J. David Richardson. Chicago: University of Chicago Press.

Dunning, John H. 1993. *Multinational enterprises and the global economy.* Wokingham, England: Addison-Wesley.

Head, Keith, John Ries, and Deborah Swenson. 1995. Agglomeration benefits and location choice: Evidence from Japanese manufacturing investments in the United States. *Journal of International Economics* 38, no. 3/4 (May): 223–47.

Horstman, I., and J. Markusen. 1992. Endogenous market structures in international trade. *Journal of International Economics* 32:109–29.

Kimura, Fukunari, and Robert E. Baldwin. 1998. Application of a nationality-adjusted net sales and value added framework: The case of Japan. In *Geography and ownership as bases for economic accounting,* ed. Robert E. Baldwin, Robert E. Lipsey, and J. David Richardson. Chicago: University of Chicago Press.

Kimura, Fukunari, and Hirohisa Kohama. 1997. Nihon Kigyou no Kokusaika to Sougou Shousha (Globalization of Japanese firms and the role of general trading companies). *Kokusai Keizai* (International Economy) 48, no. 1 (September): 34–57.

Kimura, Fukunari, and Gabriel Talmain. 1994. International commerce, export networks, and general trading companies. Discussion Paper no. 94-02. Albany: State University of New York, April.

Ministry of International Trade and Industry (MITI). Minister's Secretariat. Research and Statistics Department. 1996. *Results of the Basic Survey of Business Structure and Activity, 1995.* Vol. 3, Report by subsidiary companies. Tokyo: Shadan Houjin Tsuusan Toukei Kyoukai. (BS94)

Smith, Donald F., and Richard Florida. 1994. Agglomeration and industrial location: An econometric analysis of Japanese-affiliated manufacturing establishments in automotive-related industries. *Journal of Urban Economics* 36, no. 1 (July): 23–41.

U.S. Department of Commerce. Economics and Statistics Administration. Bureau of Economic Analysis. 1997. *U.S. direct investment abroad: 1994 Benchmark survey, preliminary results.* Washington, D.C.: Government Printing Office. (FAUSF94)

Yamawaki, Hideki. 1991. Exports and foreign distributional activities: Evidence on Japanese firms in the United States. *Review of Economics and Statistics* 73 (May): 294–300.

————. 1998. Procurement, production, and distribution by foreign multinational enterprises in Japanese manufacturing industries. Los Angeles: University of California, John E. Anderson Graduate School of Management, March. Mimeograph.

Yoshino, M. Y., and Thomas B. Lifson. 1986. *The invisible link: Japan's sogo shosha and the organization of trade.* Cambridge, Mass.: MIT Press.

Comment   Eiji Ogawa

Kimura uses microdata from MITI's Basic Survey of Business Structure and Activity to study empirically the location and internalization decisions made by Japanese multinational enterprises. He focuses on the sectoral choices of parent firms and foreign affiliates between manufacturing and nonmanufacturing including wholesale and retail trade.

Kimura points out some "stylized facts" about Japanese multinational enterprises in this paper. First, many Japanese manufacturers have wholesale trade foreign affiliates. This is downward internalization, that is, sector switching from manufacturing to nonmanufacturing (M/N type). Second, Japanese multinational enterprises keep subcontracting relationships as loose internalization arrangements. This is a no-sector-switching case (M/M type). Third, a number of Japanese wholesale and retail trade companies establish manufacturing plants, particularly in East Asia. This is upward internalization, that is, sector switching from nonmanufacturing to manufacturing (N/M type). Finally, GTCs are one of the major components of the Japanese economic system. The author points out that GTCs work as a device through which other, client companies can avoid internalization of the distribution function, that is, switching to nonmanufacturing.

These stylized facts suggest that Japanese multinational enterprises could display all types of sector switching. Kimura uses the microdata to analyze formally these stylized facts.

He obtains four findings. First, for the M/M type, both large and small manufacturing firms tend to have manufacturing affiliates, mainly located in East Asia. Second, for the M/N type of sector switching, large manufacturing parent firms tend to have nonmanufacturing affiliates, mainly located in North America and Western Europe. Third, for the N/M type,

Eiji Ogawa is professor of commerce at Hitotsubashi University.

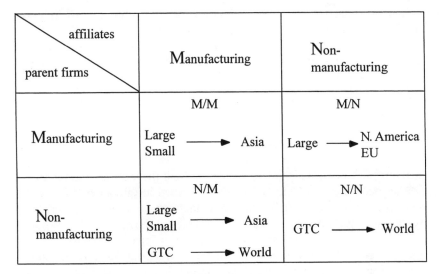

Fig. 3C.1   Patterns of sector switching

about half of large and small nonmanufacturing parent firms have manufacturing affiliates, mainly located in East Asia. Last, GTCs have extensive networks of production and wholesale activities all over the world (N/N and N/M types). Thus the pattern of sector switching depends on the size of the parent firm and the location of affiliates. I summarize Kimura's findings in figure 3C.1.

I have two comments. The first is about the relation between parent firm size and sector switching. Figure 3C.1 shows that no small manufacturing firms have nonmanufacturing affiliates. Large manufacturing firms enjoy economies of scale and scope and can afford to take the risk of sector switching by diversifying the risk. Small manufacturing firms cannot take the risk of sector switching. Small manufacturing firms avoid taking the risk by using GTC networks. How does Kimura interpret the finding that small manufacturing firms have manufacturing affiliates but do not have any nonmanufacturing affiliates?

My second comment is related to the location of foreign affiliates. Both manufacturing and nonmanufacturing parent firms have manufacturing affiliates, mainly located in East Asia. In contrast, nonmanufacturing affiliates held by manufacturing parent firms are mainly located in North America and Western Europe. How do we explain the asymmetric location patterns of sector switching?

I will explain the asymmetry from the viewpoint of the fixed and sunk costs of setting up a wholesale and retail network or distribution network in a foreign country. These fixed and sunk costs give firms more incentive to invest in wholesale and retail affiliates in larger markets. Therefore, manufacturing parent firms hold their own trading affiliates only in large markets such as North America and Western Europe. In small markets, such as in the Asian countries, they do not hold their own trading affiliates and use the wholesale networks of GTCs instead. How does Kimura explain the asymmetry?

Comment   Hock Guan Ng

Kimura puts forward a challenging idea to treat the location and internalization decisions of MNEs jointly. It is claimed in the paper that sector switching or nonswitching between manufacturing and nonmanufacturing reveals such joint decision making by Japanese MNEs.

The data presented on the sector switching of Japanese MNEs that are grouped according to the location of their foreign affiliates reveal some interesting patterns. Of note is the observation that the M/N type of FAJFs are pervasive in the United States and Western Europe but are scarce in East Asia, with the exception of Hong Kong and Singapore. This suggests that manufacturing parents find it worthwhile to set up trade affiliates only in economies with strong purchasing power. Perhaps a breakdown according to countries sorted by per capita GNP will confirm this. Similarly, the N/M type of FAJFs are highly represented in East Asia but are hardly found in the United States and Western Europe. This indicates that nonmanufacturing parents seek to locate their manufacturing affiliates in countries with cheap labor, so sorting the locations by labor cost might be useful.

While it is obvious to expect larger parent firms to have more foreign affiliates, the strength of this relation is hard to gauge without any formal statistical test. Regressing the number of foreign affiliates on parent firm size (while controlling for other determinants) would be useful in this respect.

The relation between the number of foreign affiliates and the incidence of sector switching is also not investigated fully. The numbers in the last rows of tables 3.5 and 3.6 give the impression that any such relation is probably weak, but further statistical modeling is needed to confirm this.

In presenting the results of logit regressions in tables 3.9 and 3.10, the author concedes that he is not claiming any causal relation among the variables. The estimation equations as modeled, however, have to be interpreted as showing the determinants of parent firm decisions on whether to have foreign affiliates and whether to switch sectors. As such, it cannot be claimed that "firms with foreign affiliates are likely to have large em-

Hock Guan Ng is senior lecturer of finance at the University of Western Australia.

ployment size, capital-intensive technology, large foreign sales, and large R&D expenditure." The estimated equation has assumed causality in the opposite direction.

To correctly model a joint decision about switching, firm size, R&D expenditure, and the like, a simultaneous-equation framework is required. Estimating a single-equation model does not allow any meaningful conclusions about the behavior of MNEs that make location and internalization decisions jointly.

4

Foreign Direct Investment and R&D Spillovers
Is There a Connection?

Lee Branstetter

4.1 Introduction

The surge of Japanese foreign direct investment (FDI) after the 1985 Plaza Accords has been well documented and extensively studied. Direct investment by Japanese firms in the U.S. manufacturing sector was an important part of this total movement of capital abroad, as figure 4.1 indicates. While Japanese aggregate FDI statistics contain some well-known flaws, these figures nevertheless indicate that in 1989 some $33.9 billion of total FDI flowed into the United States from Japan, representing about 50 percent of total Japanese FDI.[1] Of this total inflow into the United States, approximately $24.3 billion consisted of direct investment outside of the manufacturing sector (much of it in finance and real estate), while the remaining $9.6 billion consisted of direct investment in manufacturing. While such high-profile nonmanufacturing acquisitions as Rockefeller Center, Pebble Beach, and Columbia Pictures received much media attention, it is worth pointing out that, in aggregate, Japanese firms' total manufacturing investments in the United States exceeded, in dollar terms, their

Lee Branstetter is assistant professor of economics and director of the East Asian Studies Program at the University of California, Davis, and a faculty research fellow of the National Bureau of Economic Research.

The author thanks Thomas Pugel of New York University's Stern School of Business for generously providing his Japanese FDI data in computerized form. The author is grateful to Yoko Kusaka, Kentaro Minato, and especially Kaoru Nabeshima for excellent research assistance. The author thanks Robert Feenstra, Takatoshi Ito, Mariko Sakakibara, Deborah Swenson, and Akiko Tamura for valuable comments. Funding was provided by a University of California Faculty Research Grant. Parts of this paper borrow heavily from Branstetter (forthcoming) and Branstetter and Sakakibara (1998). The author is solely responsible for any errors.

1. See, e.g., Weinstein (1996) and Ramstetter (1996) on the flaws of statistics on FDI in Japan.

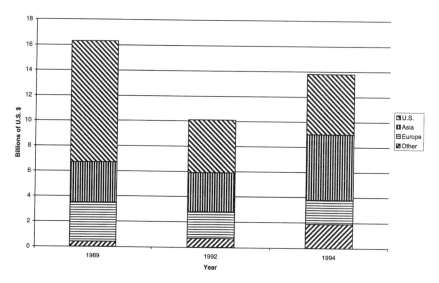

Fig. 4.1   Japanese manufacturing FDI
Source: Ministry of International Trade and Industry, *Tsusho Hakusho* (Tokyo, various is-sues).

direct investments in manufacturing in Asia until 1994. Both kinds of FDI raised concerns in the United States, where, prior to the 1980s, foreign-owned firms had played a relatively small role in the economy. Neverthe-less, even at the height of Japanese investment in the United States, Japa-nese purchases of "trophy" real estate properties raised less concern than Japanese investments in U.S. manufacturing, particularly the acquisition of existing U.S. firms in industries where the United States was perceived to maintain a competitive advantage.

These concerns were partly motivated by the perception, correct or not, that U.S. investment in Japan was more difficult than Japanese investment in the United States. However, for many in and out of government who worried about the "competitiveness" of U.S. industries in the late 1980s, the real source of unease was the belief that by being more geographically proximate to the headquarters, manufacturing plants, and R&D facilities of their U.S. competitors (and, in some cases, owning these assets outright through acquisition) Japanese firms would be able to "tap into" U.S. sources of technological strength, further eroding U.S. competitive advan-tages in the few industries and industry segments where the United States was perceived to maintain such strength.[2]

While the subsequent revival of American high-tech manufacturing and

2. The anxious mood of the times was well captured in the title of one academic volume published in 1989 by the Society for Japanese Studies, *Japanese Investment in the United States: Should We Be Concerned?*

the well-publicized problems of Japanese companies have taken these issues off the policy agenda, it is still an open empirical question whether Japanese FDI increased the ability of Japanese firms to learn from the research activities and technological strengths of U.S. firms. The idea that tapping foreign sources of technological strength through FDI and acquisition could be a profitable corporate strategy has received strong support from one of the world's best-known corporate strategy experts, Michael Porter, in his best-selling 1990 book, *The Competitive Advantage of Nations*. Porter provides little in the way of quantitative empirical evidence to support his claim that foreign knowledge and expertise can be effectively "siphoned" through judicious FDI. However, he buttresses his plausible argument with some fascinating "case studies."[3]

This idea has also received both renewed interest and qualified support from the expanding theoretical and empirical economic literature on international R&D spillovers and the channels by which they are mediated. Since the theoretical work of Grossman and Helpman emphasized the potential importance of both intranational and international R&D spillovers in models of trade and growth, a number of researchers have attempted to both quantify the importance of international R&D spillovers and investigate the means by which they are mediated. Early work by Coe and Helpman (1995), using aggregate data for a set of advanced economies, claimed that R&D spillovers were mediated through trade and that the effects were quite strong. Eaton and Kortum (1996), examining the related concept of technology transfer, found suggestive evidence of significant knowledge flows across countries. More recent work by Keller (1998) at the aggregated industry level qualified both the importance of these spillovers and the extent to which they are actually mediated through trade. Branstetter (forthcoming), who examined international and intranational spillovers at the firm level in the United States and Japan, found striking evidence that R&D spillovers are primarily an intranational phenomenon. Despite its obvious potential importance as a means of mediating knowledge flows, comparatively little empirical analysis has been conducted on FDI and the role it may play as a channel of R&D spillovers.

This gap in the literature is mirrored by a similar gap in the now rather voluminous literature on the benefits of "outward-oriented" economic policies. Many scholars have asserted that exports are likely to have important effects on economic growth due to the "knowledge spillovers" indigenous firms receive when they export to advanced country markets.[4] Much of the dynamic growth in the East Asian region has been ascribed to the spillover benefits allegedly received by East Asian firms through

---

3. See the section of Porter (1990) entitled "Tapping Selective Advantages in Other Nations" (606–13).

4. The emphasis placed by this literature on exports differs from that of the literature described in the previous paragraph, which emphasizes the role of *imports* as a channel of technology spillovers.

exports.[5] In fact, several well-executed microeconometric studies have found essentially *no* link between productivity growth at the firm level and the percentage of firm output that is exported.[6] However, many of these papers have not introduced an explicit channel whereby exporting might lead to higher levels of knowledge spillover. This paper introduces such a channel and explicitly tests its significance.

Thus this paper attempts to fill the gap in the literature by investigating the extent to which the stocks of foreign investment of Japanese firms in the United States are correlated with increased capacity to obtain useful technological spillovers from the research activities of U.S.-based firms. I also examine the extent to which Japanese firms' levels of exports to the U.S. market are correlated with increased capacity to obtain such spillovers from U.S. firms. To that end, I use microlevel data on the technological activities of Japanese firms, their FDI activities in the United States, and their exports to the U.S. market. The paper presents estimates of the impact of FDI on the R&D spillovers that these Japanese firms receive from U.S. firms. I find that firms with large stocks of FDI do tend to obtain slightly greater benefits from research conducted in the United States. However, this effect, while quite robust, is also small in magnitude. On the other hand, I find a much stronger relationship (in terms of magnitude of the estimated coefficients) between knowledge spillovers and higher levels of exports to the U.S. market, though these effects are less robust. I conclude with a number of caveats concerning these results and some suggestions for further research.

4.2 Prior Literature

The Japanese surge in FDI after 1985 has attracted the attention of economists, and a large number of well-executed studies have appeared in the literature. Studies have tended to focus on three different sets of questions. The first is as follows: What determines when and where Japanese firms invest? Important contributions to the resolution of this question in the English-language literature include the work of Caves (1993) and Drake and Caves (1992) at the industry level and of Kyoji Fukao et al. (1994) and Belderbos and Sleuwaegen (1996) at the firm level. Eaton and Tamura (1996) presented an interesting study using Japanese and U.S. data at the aggregate level.[7]

The second set of questions addressed by the literature is this: What are the effects of Japanese firm FDI on the host country and host country

---

5. See, e.g., chap. 6 of the World Bank (1993) study *The East Asian Miracle,* particularly the section "How Manufactured Exports Increased Productivity."
6. These studies include Bernard and Jensen (1999), Clerides, Lach, and Tybout (1998), and Aw, Chen, and Roberts (1997).
7. There are, of course, many other interesting studies that I do not have time or space to review.

firms in the targeted industry? One can make the argument that inward FDI allows the transfer to the host country of firm-specific intangible assets, including the "knowledge capital" of the firm, that might not be available through arm's-length market transactions such as licensing or exports and imports of goods embodying firm-specific knowledge capital. It is further believed that the impact of this technology transfer may spread beyond the multinational subsidiary, diffusing to local indigenous producers. Tax concessions for multinationals and other policies designed to attract foreign investment seem to be predicated on this belief.[8] However, past empirical analyses of FDI at the firm level have generally failed to find any strong statistical relations at the micro level between FDI or tie-ups to foreign firms and productivity growth of indigenous firms at the firm or plant level.[9] Rather, the evidence suggests that the positive effect of the presence of FDI comes through its impact on domestic competition, raising the allocative efficiency of the host country industry by driving out less efficient producers.[10]

This paper focuses on a different question: What are the effects of Japanese firm FDI on the *honsha*—that is, the impact on the operations of the parent firm in Japan? Again, the most important contributions to this line of research have come from Japan, where there is widespread concern that Japanese firms are substituting foreign for domestic production, lowering the demand for domestic production workers. To get at this issue most directly, a number of papers have focused on the extent to which FDI substitutes for or, alternatively, complements exports from the parent firm. I do not have space to review all of the papers that deserve mention, but I will note a few that are most relevant to the research conducted in this paper.

One of the most provocative contributions is by Fukao and Toru (1995). These authors found strong substitution effects between domestic and foreign production labor. These findings are corroborated by Blonigen (1996), but not by Head and Ries (1997). As far as I know, no one has

---

8. E.g., China's regulatory regime for FDI heavily favors multinationals who bring in "advanced technology."

9. The papers to which I am referring here do not focus exclusively on FDI by Japanese firms. Some of the best known work along these lines are papers by Columbia University economist Ann Harrison and a group of coauthors that fail to find evidence at the firm level of technology spillovers from the local subsidiaries of multinationals to indigenous producers in either Morocco or Venezuela. See Haddad and Harrison (1993) and Aitken and Harrison (1999). On the other hand, the survey by Blomström and Kokko (1996) cited studies at the industry level that do suggest the existence of such spillover effects. Aitken, Hanson, and Harrison (1997) find evidence of indigenous firms learning about export opportunities from the local affiliates of multinational firms, but this can be distinguished from flows of technology, per se.

10. Chung, Mitchell, and Yeung (1996) studied the productivity impact of Japanese FDI in the North American auto component industry. They found that U.S. parts suppliers with links to Japanese assembly plants actually registered *lower* rates of productivity growth than unaffiliated parts suppliers in the 1980s. Their evidence suggests that Japanese FDI did have a positive effect on productivity in the American industry but that this effect was almost entirely due to the increased competition the Japanese plants brought to the U.S. market.

analyzed at the firm level the impact of FDI on the ability of parent firms to "learn from" R&D conducted abroad. However, previous papers in the literature on Japanese FDI provide some indirect evidence on the importance of technology acquisition as a motive for Japanese FDI. A number of empirical studies, including those of Kogut and Chang (1991, 1996), Yamawaki (1991), and Blonigen (1997) have all found that Japanese U.S. acquisitions, in particular, are motivated by the desire to access technology.[11]

Almeida (1996) undertook research that bears some similarity to the work conducted in this paper.[12] He examined the patterns of citations of patents produced by U.S.-based subsidiaries of foreign multinational firms in the semiconductor industry. Almeida found that the patents generated by these subsidiaries cite other local patents more intensively than does a control group of "domestic" patents. He also found that the patents generated by these subsidiaries are cited more intensively by other local firms than are the control group. However, this study said nothing about how the presence of a subsidiary affects the research operations *of the parent firm.* This is an important omission because, even in high-tech sectors, multinationals tend to conduct the overwhelming majority of their total R&D effort in the home country. The innovative activities of foreign subsidiaries are only a small part of total firm R&D effort. An additional shortcoming of Almeida's research is that it was based on an analysis of only 114 patents generated by the subsidiaries of only twenty-two firms in a single industry. To put these numbers in perspective, since the early 1980s Hitachi Seisakushou (Hitachi Ltd.) has received more than six times as many patent grants in the United States as that 114 patent sample *every single year.*

This paper, then, takes a first look at the impact of FDI on the parent firms' ability to benefit from R&D undertaken abroad. It complements this analysis with a similar investigation of the relationship between exports to the U.S. market and the ability to receive R&D spillovers. In order to conduct such a study, one first has to establish an empirical framework for measuring R&D spillovers. This framework, based on work by Jaffe (1986), is developed below.

4.3 Empirical Methodology

4.3.1 A Framework for Measuring Knowledge Spillovers

This section borrows heavily from Branstetter (forthcoming), which, in turn, builds on the methodologies suggested by Zvi Griliches (1979) and

---

11. Wesson (1998) also found evidence of the importance of this motivation for FDI in the United States.

12. I thank Mariko Sakakibara for bringing this paper to my attention.

first implemented by Adam Jaffe (1986). The typical firm conducts R&D in a number of technological fields simultaneously. Let firm i's R&D program be described by the vector F, where

(1) $$F_i = (f_1, \ldots, f_k)$$

and each of the k elements of F represents the firm's research resources and expertise in the kth technological area.[13] We can infer from the number of patents taken out in different technological areas what the distribution of R&D investment and technological expertise across different technical fields has been. In other words, by counting the number of patents held by a firm in a narrowly defined technological field, we can obtain a quantitative measure of the firm's level of technological expertise in that field.[14] Thus the F-vector provides us with a measure of the firm's location in technology space. Over time, of course, a firm can change its location by building technological expertise in new areas, but this takes time and the adjustment costs associated with this kind of change can be high. For this reason, I calculate for each firm in my sample a single location vector based on its patenting behavior over the entire sample period.

Griliches and Jaffe have reasoned that R&D spillovers between firms should be proportional to the similarity of their research programs. Given that firms working on the same technologies will tend to patent in the same technological areas, a measure of technological proximity can be constructed from the F-vectors defined in equation (1). The "distance" in technology space between two firms i and j can be approximated by T_{ij}, where T_{ij} is the uncentered correlation coefficient of the F-vectors of the two firms, or

(2) $$T_{ij} = \frac{F_i F_j'}{[(F_i F_i')(F_j F_j')]^{1/2}}.$$

Other things being equal, firm i will receive more R&D spillovers from firm j if firm j is doing a substantial amount of R&D. Firm i will also receive more R&D spillovers if its research program is very similar to that of firm j. Thus the total potential pool of international R&D spillovers for a firm can be proxied by calculating the weighted sum of the R&D performed by all other foreign-based firms with the "similarity coefficients" for each pair of firms, T_{ij}, used as weights. The potential international, or

13. The k areas represent technological areas (based on the technology classification scheme of the U.S. patent office) rather than industry classifications. We do control for industry effects elsewhere, but here we aim to measure *technological proximity* rather than proximity in a "product market" sense.

14. Obviously, advances in some technological fields are more easily codified into and protected by patents than advances in others. However, the F-vector can still function as a reasonable measure of "relative" position in technology space as long as the "ease of codification" varies across fields in a common way across firms.

"foreign," spillover pool for the ith firm in the tth year is K_{fit}, where

(3)
$$K_{fit} = \sum_{i \neq j} T_{ij} R_{jt}.$$

Here R_{jt} is the R&D spending of the jth firm (j not equal to i) in the tth year and T_{ij} is the similarity coefficient.[15] Similarly, the potential intranational, or "domestic," spillover pool is computed as

(4)
$$K_{dit} = \sum_{i \neq j} T_{ij} R_{jt},$$

where, in this equation, R_{jt} is the R&D performed in the tth year by firms based in the *domestic* country, again weighted by the T_{ij}'s. Assume that innovation is a function of own R&D and external knowledge. Then the "innovation production function" for the ith firm in the tth year is

(5)
$$N_{it} = R_{it}^{\beta} K_{dit}^{\gamma_1} K_{fit}^{\gamma_2} \Phi_{it},$$

where

(6)
$$\Phi_{it} = e^{\sum_c \delta_c D_{ic}} e^{\varepsilon_{it}}$$

is a set of industry dummy variables and a multiplicative error term. Here the δ's can be thought of as exogenous differences in the "technological opportunity" of c different industries.

Taking the logs of both sides of equation (5) yields the following loglinear equation

(7)
$$n_{it} = \beta r_{it} + \gamma_1 k_{dit} + \gamma_2 k_{fit} + \sum_c \delta_c D_{ic} + \varepsilon_{it}.$$

In equation (7), n_{it} is innovation, r_{it} is the firm's own R&D investment, k_{dit} is the domestic spillover pool, k_{fit} is the international spillover pool, the D's are dummy variables to control for differences in the propensity to generate new knowledge across industries (indicated by the subscript c), and ε is an error term. The γ coefficients measure the "innovative output elasticity" of the domestic and international spillover pools.[16]

Unfortunately, there are no direct measures of innovation. However, if

15. Note that T_{ij} is not indexed by time because it is constructed from the time-invariant F-vectors.

16. One might suppose that external R&D only enters into the knowledge production function with a long and variable lag. Unfortunately, due to the features of the data, the precise lag structure of external R&D is likely to be difficult to identify. However, it is worth noting that empirical research suggests that the time required for new innovation to "leak out" is quite short. Mansfield's celebrated 1985 paper found that 70 percent of new product innovations leak out within one year and only 17 percent take more than eighteen months. Caballero and Jaffe (1993) found that diffusion of new knowledge as measured by patent citations is about as rapid.

some fraction of new knowledge is patented, such that the number of new patents generated by the ith firm is an exponential function of its new knowledge, as given by

$$(8) \qquad\qquad P_{it} = e^{\sum_c \alpha_c D_{ic}} e^{\xi_i} N_{it},$$

then the production of new knowledge can be proxied by examining the generation of new patents.[17] We take the logs of both sides of equation (8), and substituting into equation (7), we get

$$(9) \qquad\qquad p_{it} = \beta r_{it} + \gamma_1 k_{dit} + \gamma_2 k_{fit} + \sum_c \delta_c D_{ic} + \mu_{it},$$

where p_{it} is the log of the number of new patents and the other variables are as before, except for the error term, which is defined below.[18] With this substitution, the interpretation of the coefficients on the D's has changed. They now represent industry-level differences in the propensity to patent, which are a function of both the technological opportunity in the cth industry, as in equation (6), *and* the usefulness of patents as a tool of appropriation in the cth industry. It is known that strong differences in both factors exist across industries.

Note, however, that because of this substitution, the interpretation of the γ's has also necessarily changed. We do not observe the "pure effects" of knowledge spillovers on firm innovation because we do not directly observe innovation. We instead observe the effects of knowledge spillovers on economic manifestations of the firm's innovation, its patents. If technological rivalry with other firms is intense enough and the scope of intellectual property rights conferred by patents is broad enough, firms may sometimes find themselves competing for a limited pool of available patents—a patent race. For this reason, the positive technological externality of other firms' R&D is potentially confounded with a *negative* effect of other firms' research *due to competition.*[19] Thus, if actual flows of knowl-

---

17. Note that this formulation allows for both industry and firm differences in the propensity to patent. This flexibility is important given the observed differences in patenting behavior across firms and industries.

18. One advantage of using patents as an indicator of innovative output is the demonstrated immediate, tight link between R&D and patent generation. Survey evidence from the United States and Germany indicates that the time lag from initial conception of an idea to the filing of a patent application is about nine months (Scherer 1984)! Careful econometric evidence also suggests that the link between patenting and R&D is largely contemporaneous. On the other hand, the link between R&D and changes in revenue (and revenue-based measures such as total factor productivity), which result from the successful introduction of new products, is subject to long, variable lags.

19. To make this explicit, we can decompose the γ's in the following fashion: $\gamma = (\partial n/\partial k)$ $(k/n) - (\partial p/\partial k)(k/p)$. In other words, the γ's that we observe are the net result of two opposite effects—the "true" positive technological externality of external knowledge on firm i's innovation, $\partial n/\partial k$, and a negative "patent race effect," $\partial p/\partial k$, in which the ith firm's ability to patent new innovation is crowded out by the previous patenting of competitive firms. Adam Jaffe (1986) and others have also made this point.

edge are limited or weak and rivalry is strong, our estimates of the γ's may be negative even though the underlying knowledge externality is positive.[20] Unfortunately, it is not possible to disentangle these two effects in the data, though my empirical results suggest that both are present.[21]

In Branstetter (forthcoming), regressions along the lines of equation (9) were run for both U.S. and Japanese R&D-intensive firms. The somewhat surprising results of these regressions suggest that R&D spillovers are primarily an *intranational* phenomenon. Controlling for the presence of intranational R&D spillovers, I found little evidence of positive, significant international R&D spillovers. This result was robust to the use of data from either the United States or Japan and robust to changes in the functional form of the estimating equation. Similar results were obtained when an index of total factor productivity (levels) was used as the dependent variable. These results should be kept in mind in interpreting the empirical results presented in this paper. I find that in this paper, the impact of foreign spillovers tends to be "overwhelmed" by the impact of domestic knowledge spillovers when both terms are included in the regression. This is consistent with my own earlier results and with other recent evidence on the geographic localization of knowledge spillovers.[22]

However, these results should be interpreted as measuring the *average* "innovative output elasticities" of international and intranational R&D spillovers obtained by pooling data on both small and large corporations, some of which have substantial connections to markets and technological developments abroad through exports and FDI. Is it possible that the impact of international R&D spillovers is substantially higher for firms with a high level of exports to or FDI in the foreign market? It is ultimately this question that motivates the following empirical work in this paper.

4.3.2   The Impact of FDI and Exports on International Knowledge Spillovers

Because the effects of intranational R&D spillovers were found to so completely overwhelm the effects of international spillovers in previous work, the following empirical work will focus on international spillovers. Beginning with an "innovation production function," as in equation (7),

20. This can arise because only a small fraction of the constructed spillover "pool"—all of which is presumed to be technologically relevant external R&D—actually has a positive impact on the research output of the firm.

21. See Jaffe (1986), who found direct evidence of negative "competitive" externalities in a framework similar to the one used in this paper.

22. Jaffe and Trajtenberg (1996) and Francis Narin (1995) attempted to measure the extent to which knowledge spillovers are intranational in scope by analyzing patterns of patent citations and citations in the scientific literature, respectively. Both studies found that innovators are much more likely to cite innovators located in the same country than one would expect given the distribution of scientific resources across countries, technological fields, and time. Goto and Nagata (1997) presented survey evidence that indicates Japanese R&D managers perceive other domestic firms to be more important sources of technology spillovers than foreign firms.

we drop the intranational spillover variable to yield the following log-linear equation:

$$(10) \qquad n_{it} = \beta r_{it} + \gamma(\mathrm{FDI}_{if})k_{fit} + \sum_{d} \delta_d D_{id} + \varepsilon_{it}.$$

Here n_{it} is innovation, r_{it} is the firm's own R&D investment, k_{fit} is the potential foreign spillover pool, the D's are dummy variables to control for differences in the propensity to generate new knowledge across industries (indicated by the subscript d), and ε is an error term. However, we hypothesize that the impact of international spillovers on innovative output, γ, is an increasing function of the stock of FDI firm i has set up in the foreign market ($\gamma'(\mathrm{FDI}_{it}) > 0$), such that Japanese firms with high levels of FDI enjoy a higher innovation output elasticity for a given level of potential knowledge spillovers. The reasoning behind this is straightforward: spillovers are not automatic. To monitor and understand other firms' R&D can be a difficult task. It may be facilitated enormously by the geographical proximity attained through FDI, through which the cost of accessing foreign firms' knowledge assets is reduced. This increase in a firm's ability to receive spillovers may occur whether or not the subsidiary is set up explicitly or entirely for the purposes of following research trends in the United States, and it may occur whether or not the FDI by the Japanese firm takes the form of greenfield new investment or acquisition of existing U.S. firms.

However, there are also both theoretical and empirical reasons for thinking that the spillover-enhancing effects of acquisition FDI and greenfield FDI are different. The possibility exists that Japanese firms establishing new production facilities abroad may have relatively little to learn from their U.S. counterparts, being more technologically advanced than these counterpart firms at the time they undertake the actual investment. On the other hand, empirical work by a number of authors has suggested that acquisition FDI is at least partly motivated by the desire to obtain the technological assets of the purchased firms. In light of this, we break down Japanese FDI into acquisition FDI and greenfield FDI and present results based on total FDI as well as acquisition FDI only. Note that we are taking a broader view of the potential spillover benefits of acquisition than others have taken in this literature. We hypothesize that by purchasing a firm in the United States, a Japanese firm not only acquires the proprietary knowledge assets of the purchased firm but is also able to use the acquisition to tap into the informal technological networks and knowledge-sharing relationships possessed by the research personnel of the acquired firm.[23]

As in previous equations, we substitute observed patents for unobserved innovation, so that we are left with

23. Porter (1990) also stressed these "access" benefits as an important component of the potential strategic benefits of acquisition.

(11) $$p_{it} = \beta r_{it} + \gamma(FDI_{it})k_{fit} + \sum_d \delta_d D_{id} + \mu_{it}.$$

Again, we allow μ to contain an individual effect as well as a truly random error component.

We do not have enough degrees of freedom to allow γ to vary with either the number of subsidiaries in the United States or the number of employees in those subsidiaries. Instead, we divide our sample into firms with a "substantial" FDI presence in the United States and firms without such a presence and allow the parameter γ to vary across the two sub-samples. In practice, this is done by running a regression including an inter-action term in which the spillover term is multiplied by a dummy variable signifying whether the firm has "substantial" FDI in the United States. Thus we estimate

(12) $$p_{it} = \beta_1 + \beta_2 r_{it} + \gamma_0 k_{fit} + \gamma_1 k_{fit} * fdi_{it} + \sum_d \delta_d D_{id} + \mu_{it},$$

which is the econometric analogue of equation (11). Here fdi is a dummy variable equal to one if the firm has undertaken substantial FDI in the United States by year t, and zero otherwise.[24]

In a similar fashion, we can allow the strength of the spillover term to vary with the level of exports by firm i to the U.S. market as well as the level of its FDI in the United States. In this paper, I use data on the per-centage of firm sales exported to the United States as the measure of "U.S. export intensity." As in equation (12), I create an interaction term between this level of export intensity and the foreign spillover term. Here the mea-sure of export intensity is a percentage rather than a dummy variable equal to one if the export intensity is above some threshold level. Thus I estimate

(13) $$p_{it} = \beta_1 + \beta_2 r_{it} + \gamma_0 k_{fit} + \gamma_1 k_{fit} * exint_i + \gamma_2 k_{fit} * fdi_{it}$$
$$+ \sum_d \delta_d D_{id} + \mu_{it},$$

where exint is the measure of U.S. export intensity. This provides us with a crude but potentially useful framework for comparing the spillover-enhancing effects of FDI with the comparable effects of exports.[25]

Some attention needs to be devoted to the assumed properties of the

---

24. FDI is measured as a cumulative count of either numbers of subsidiaries in the United States or number of U.S. employees. The FDI dummy variable is set equal to one if this cumulative count is in the upper quartile of all observations in the sample. I present results using measures based on both counts of subsidiaries and counts of employees. In results not reported in this paper, I also tried constructing an interaction term of the cumulative counts (of subsidiaries or employees) multiplied by the foreign spillover term. I obtained qualita-tively similar, but statistically slightly weaker, results with this alternative formulation.

25. Note that there is no time subscript on the exint variable—we will rely on data from a single year.

new error term. Allowing the propensity to patent to vary across firms in a way not correlated with the other regressors creates a systematic component to the error—an individual effect, ξ, such that

$$(14) \qquad\qquad \mu_{it} = \xi_i + u_{it},$$

where the u is assumed to be a normal i.i.d. disturbance. If ξ_i is uncorrelated with the right-hand-side regressors, then this effect can be estimated using the random-effects framework.

One can imagine, though, that this individual effect in the propensity to patent may be correlated with a firm's own research levels. If we assume unobservable but permanent differences in the productivity of firms' research, owing perhaps to the unequal distribution of high-quality research personnel across firms, we can easily imagine that firms with high-quality research personnel will do more research and that this will lead to more patents. One can also imagine that more productive research teams might be able to more effectively monitor research developments outside the firm. More to the point, higher levels of research productivity might also lead firms to engage in more FDI. This could generate a spurious statistical relationship between high levels of FDI and higher measured output elasticities of international spillovers. In this case, estimates are biased unless we correct for the correlation between firm-specific research productivity and our other independent variables. We can do this using a fixed-effects estimator.[26] Results from both a random-effects specification and a fixed-effects specification are provided for our estimates of equation (12).

Unfortunately, the fixed-effects approach may create problems of its own. First of all, fixed-effects models effectively throw away the cross-sectional dimension of the data, obtaining identification from changes within firms over time. In this data set, most of the variance is in the cross-sectional dimension, so the cost of the fixed-effects approach is quite high. Furthermore, to the extent that measurement error is present in the data, using fixed-effects models can actually exacerbate the measurement error bias, leading to a downward bias in all estimated coefficients. Our results, presented in the next section, suggest that such measurement error bias is present.[27]

---

26. The obvious alternative would be some sort of instrumental variables approach. Unfortunately, the only instrumental variables available at the firm level are lagged values of the included variables. If research quality evolves slowly over time, these lagged values are likely to be no less endogenous than the variables for which we instrument. As for general method of moments "dynamic" panel estimators, which use lagged levels as instruments for current differences, Blundell and Bond (1995), among others, have found that in short, moderately sized panels with autoregressive explanatory variables (such as my data set), these estimators can behave quite badly.

27. The classic reference on this problem is Griliches and Hausman (1986).

4.4   Empirical Estimates of the Spillover-Augmenting Impact
of Foreign Direct Investment and Exports

I use microdata on publicly traded high-technology manufacturing firms in the United States and Japan. Considerable anecdotal evidence suggests that Japanese firms are particularly good at monitoring R&D developments abroad. In addition, some of these Japanese firms engaged in FDI on a large scale in the United States, at least some of which was explicitly motivated by the desire to "tap into" sources of U.S. technological strength. Fortunately, there also exists broadly comparable, publicly available data at the micro level on the innovative activities of publicly traded firms in both countries.[28]

I chose to examine the five industries in the United States and Japan for which the average ratio of R&D to sales is highest, for the simple reason that one is less likely to identify the sources and effects of spillovers in industries with little technological innovation. Since I rely on patents both as indicators of innovative activity and as a means of locating firms in technology space, I restricted my sample to U.S. and Japanese firms with more than ten patents granted in the United States during my initial sample period, 1977–89. Prior to 1985, the publicly available data on Japanese firm-level R&D spending are of uneven quality, with gaps and large jumps in the time series of individual firms. Thus, in most of my regressions, I am forced to further restrict the sample period to the years 1986–89.

The Japanese panel consists of 208 firms from the chemical, machinery, electronics, transportation, and precision instrument manufacturing industries. For each firm, we have data by year for the years 1986–89. For each year, we have the number of patents granted to these firms in the United States (classified by date of application), their R&D expenditures in that year, a domestic spillover term consisting of the weighted sum of external R&D performed by technologically related Japanese firms computed for each year, and a foreign spillover term consisting of external R&D performed by technologically related U.S. firms.[29] The FDI data, originally taken from volumes of *Japan's Expanding U.S. Manufacturing Presence,* published by the Japan Economic Institute (MacKnight 1987–91), include both cumulative counts of subsidiaries and numbers of U.S.

---

28. Note that the data are further described in the data appendix.

29. Here I use the U.S. patents of Japanese firms to locate them in technology space and to measure their innovation. The patent classification schemes and screening processes used in the two countries are different enough that, to ensure the comparability of patents for both sets of firms, I decided to use U.S. patents. It should be noted that Japanese firms are extremely aggressive about patenting their inventions in the United States as well as Japan. Japanese firms now account for about 25 percent of new patents in the United States, by far the most important foreign users of the American patent system. Finally, it is also true that detailed data on the Japanese patents held by these firms is difficult to obtain and extraordinarily expensive. To date, I have been unable to obtain a useful quantity of such data.

Table 4.1   **Sample Statistics for Japanese Firms with U.S. FDI**

Variable	Mean	Standard Deviation	Minimum	Maximum
Patents	95	179.3	0	966
R&D[a]	33,728.24	59,553.57	0	316,148
R&D/sales	.046	.025	0	.16
U.S. employees	1,069	1,870.3	0	12,233

[a] Unit is millions of 1985 Japanese yen.

Table 4.2   **Sample Statistics for Japanese Firms without U.S. FDI**

Variable	Mean	Standard Deviation	Minimum	Maximum
Patents	11	26	0	386
R&D[a]	4,844.65	7,969.15	100	82,152.65
R&D/sales	.043	.030	.002	.16

[a] Unit is millions of 1985 Japanese yen.

employees.[30] Tables 4.1 and 4.2 give some summary statistics for the Japanese sample.[31]

The foreign spillover term is based on firm-level data from a panel of 209 U.S. firms in the same five industries covering the same years. The construction of this U.S. data set is further described in the data appendix. Complete documentation of the data and original sources can be found in Branstetter (1996).

4.4.1   Sample Statistics

Tables 4.1 and 4.2 show that firms with FDI in the United States tend to be larger, obtain more patents, and have higher levels of R&D spending, both in absolute terms and as a percentage of sales.[32] The difference in

30. I am grateful to Thomas Pugel for providing me with these data in electronic form.

31. The use of U.S. patents to infer the R&D activities of Japanese firms raises the possibility that I am systematically undermeasuring Japanese research productivity. To the extent that the Japanese patent only a fraction of their inventions in the United States but this fraction is constant across firms and across time, it will fall into the constant term (since I estimate separate knowledge production functions for U.S. and Japanese firms). To the extent that it is constant across firms but not across time, it will fall out in the time dummies. To the extent that it is not constant across firms but is constant across time, this differential will be absorbed into the fixed effect. In the absence of more detailed information about the Japanese patents of Japanese firms, little more can be said on this issue, though I acknowledge that it may cloud my interpretation of the empirical results.

32. I note here that FDI is measured as a "cumulative" count of both subsidiaries and U.S. employees. Firms with a "significant presence" are those that obtain a level in the upper quartile of total observations. A number of firms moved from positions of no U.S. FDI to significant amounts over the course of the sample period, so there is substantial time variation in the fdi/foreign-spillover interaction term.

patenting is especially pronounced. In addition, not surprisingly, industry mix differs across the two subsamples, though this is not shown in the tables. Because the two groups of firms differ in many ways other than their levels of FDI, it may be necessary to use a fixed-effects approach in order to avoid erroneously attributing differences in the impact of spillovers to FDI because of omitted-variables bias.

4.4.2   Regressions Using Total Foreign Direct Investment

Table 4.3 gives the results of a number of alternative specifications of equation (12), where FDI is measured as the sum of greenfield investment, joint ventures, and acquisitions. The first two columns of table 4.3 show the results of OLS regressions on own R&D, the foreign spillover term, and the interaction term of the FDI dummy variable together with the foreign spillover term.[33] The first column gives results from a regression run without time dummies. The second column includes time dummies. The results, which are essentially confirmed in all other specifications, indicate that possession of an "FDI presence" in the United States does increase the innovative output of foreign spillovers, but only by a small amount. The coefficients can be interpreted as elasticities, so the reported numbers imply that if the amount of foreign spillovers were to increase by 10 percent, the innovative output of Japanese firms would go up by 2 percent, but the additional impact obtained by Japanese firms with a substantial FDI presence would only be 0.4 percent.

The third and fourth columns of table 4.3 illustrate the results from a random-effects specification. The coefficient on the fdi/foreign-spillover interaction term remains essentially unchanged in both columns. The fourth column reveals, however, that the estimated impact of foreign spillovers is quite sensitive to the inclusion of a domestic spillover term. When domestic spillovers are controlled for, the estimated coefficient on the overall foreign spillover term becomes negative, though it also is no longer statistically significant at the traditional 5 percent level. However, the fdi/foreign-spillover interaction term remains positive and significant.

Given our earlier concerns about the likelihood of firm-specific differences in research productivity, however, it may be that the random-effects coefficients are affected by the omitted-variables bias arising from the correlation of this unmeasured firm-specific research productivity with R&D inputs, innovative outputs, and FDI. If we assume that these firm-specific variables change slowly over time—so slowly that they can be assumed to be fixed over the 1986–89 four-year span of our data—then fixed-effects models will yield consistent estimates. Unfortunately, to the extent that

---

33. In these regressions, the foreign spillover term is lagged one period, partly to control for differences in fiscal years between U.S. and Japanese firms and partly to allow foreign knowledge more time to spill over.

Table 4.3   **Linear Regressions Based on Total Japanese FDI Data Measured by Counts of U.S. Subsidiaries**

Variable	OLS (Foreign)	OLS (Foreign)	Random Effects (1)	Random Effects (2)	Fixed Effects (1)	Fixed Effects (2)
log R&D	.6760 (.0286)	.6752 (.0288)	.5842 (.0435)	.5544 (.0436)	.1315 (.0894)	.1292 (.0893)
log Domestic spillovers				1.074 (.2702)		.5353 (.3282)
log Foreign spillovers	.2057 (.0952)	.2094 (.0961)	.3991 (.1695)	−.5341 (.2868)	.7755 (.3196)	.2126 (.4701)
log Foreign spillovers *fdi	.0401 (.0059)	.0403 (.0060)	.0309 (.0058)	.0311 (.0057)	.0225 (.0064)	.0220 (.0064)
Chemicals	−.6610 (.1499)	−.6602 (.1501)	−.6410 (.2732)	−.2488 (.2857)	n.a.	n.a.
Machinery	−.2959 (.1597)	−.2958 (.1599)	−.2923 (.2911)	−.2004 (.2865)	n.a.	n.a.
Electronics	−.5347 (.1522)	−.5355 (.1525)	−.5234 (.2784)	−.5762 (.2735)	n.a.	n.a.
Transportation	−.6952 (.1590)	−.6964 (.1593)	−.6567 (.2896)	−.5855 (.2847)	n.a.	n.a.
Year 2		−.0071 (.0966)	−.0534 (.1054)	.0879 (.0572)		
Year 3		.0332 (.0973)	.0365 (.1028)	.0422 (.0544)		
Year 4		−.0405 (.0985)	.0648 (.1025)	−.0632 (.0593)		

Note: Dependent variable is the log of the number of patents. $N = 832$. Numbers in parentheses are standard errors.

measurement error is present in the data, using a fixed-effects model could actually exacerbate the measurement error bias.

The fifth and sixth columns reveal the results obtained when one uses fixed-effects models. It is noted that the magnitude and significance of the own R&D term drops substantially, suggesting that measurement error is indeed present and the resulting bias is considerably worsened by using the fixed-effects approach. Again, the estimated impact of the foreign spillover term is quite sensitive to inclusion of domestic spillovers. When domestic spillovers are controlled for in the fixed-effects specifications, the overall foreign spillover term is no longer significant. However, the fdi/foreign-spillover interaction term remains positive and significant in all specifications.

4.4.3   The Negative Binomial Estimator

Linear estimators have the two considerable advantages of ease of estimation and interpretation and relative robustness to misspecification of

Table 4.4   **Negative Binomial Model Based on Total Japanese FDI Data Measured by Counts of U.S. Subsidiaries**

Variable	Negative Binomial
log R&D	.7420
	(.0291)
log Domestic spillovers	1.245
	(.1811)
log Foreign spillovers	−.8232
	(.1753)
log Foreign spillovers *fdi	.0295
	.0062
Chemicals	−.4713
	(.1769)
Machinery	−.2083
	(.1666)
Electronics	−.8794
	(.1555)
Transportation	−.5833
	(.1645)
Time dummies	Yes
α	.8978
Log likelihood	−2,988.69

Note: Dependent variable is the number of patents. $N = 832$. The negative binomial regressions follow Hausman, Hall, and Griliches (1984). Numbers in parentheses are standard errors, computed from the analytic second derivatives.

the nature of the error term. However, patent data are intrinsically "count" data, for which the normal distribution is likely to be an inappropriate approximation.[34] Over the past ten years, econometricians have developed a number of count data models to deal with such data. Among the most commonly used is the negative binomial estimator. The negative binomial estimator is a generalization of the familiar Poisson estimator.[35] Provided the assumption that the error term follows a negative binomial distribution is met, consistent estimates of the parameters of interest can be obtained through maximum likelihood estimation. Of course, if the distributional assumption is incorrect, then consistency is not assured, even in theory. Therefore, evidence from a negative binomial regression is offered in table 4.4 as a reality check on the linear results rather than as a superior alternative to linear estimation.

34. An additional problem arises from the fact that some Japanese firms take out no patents in some years—and the log of zero is undefined. In this analysis, this problem is addressed by simply setting the dependent variable equal to zero in such cases. Concerns that this transformation might affect results constitute an additional reason for using the negative binomial specification as a "robustness" check.

35. See Hausman, Hall, and Griliches (1984) for a derivation of these models and a discussion of their relative merits.

Fortunately, the results broadly corroborate those of the linear models. In this specification, as in others, there is no evidence of positive, significant foreign spillovers overall, but the fdi/foreign-spillover interaction term remains positive and significant.

4.4.4 Results from Acquisition Foreign Direct Investment and Other Robustness Checks

A number of theoretical and empirical papers on Japanese FDI have suggested the importance of breaking down Japanese FDI by category into greenfield investment and acquisition FDI. It has been suggested by some authors, including Blonigen (1997), that greenfield investment is likely to be motivated by the technological strengths of the investing Japanese firms rather than the relative technological strengths of the U.S.-based competitors. In fact, one could make a loose, heuristic argument on the basis of internalization theory that Japanese firms would be motivated to undertake the most greenfield FDI precisely where their U.S. counterparts were technologically weakest, in a relative sense. Therefore, there is little relevant technological innovation that could be expected to spill over to the more advanced Japanese firms.

On the other hand, as we have mentioned previously, there is some evidence that acquisition FDI is at least partly motivated by the desire to tap into sources of U.S. relative technological strength. For that reason, we constructed alternative measures of Japanese FDI using only data on acquired subsidiaries. The results of linear regressions using these data are given in table 4.5.

The layout of this table is similar to that of table 4.3, and the empirical

Table 4.5   **Linear Regressions Based on Japanese Acquisition FDI Data Measured by Counts of U.S. Subsidiaries**

Variable	OLS (1)	OLS (2)	Random Effects (1)	Random Effects (2)	Fixed Effects (1)	Fixed Effects (2)
log R&D	.7280 (.0277)	.7288 (.0279)	.6092 (.0437)	.5808 (.0437)	.1461 (.0902)	.1429 (.0901)
log Domestic spillovers				1.057 (.2755)		.5146 (.3304)
log Foreign spillovers	.2510 (.0967)	.2474 (.0978)	.4336 (.1733)	−.4831 (.2925)	.8807 (.3175)	.3448 (.4679)
log Foreign spillovers *fdi	.0235 (.0067)	.0230 (.0068)	.0249 (.0064)	.0244 (.0064)	.0199 (.0070)	.0189 (.0071)
Industry dummies	Yes	Yes	Yes	Yes	n.a.	n.a.
Time dummies	No	Yes	Yes	Yes	No	No

Note: Dependent variable is the log of the number of patents. $N = 832$. Numbers in parentheses are standard errors.

Table 4.6   **Negative Binomial Model Based on Japanese Acquisition FDI Data Measured by Counts of U.S. Subsidiaries**

Variable	Negative Binomial
log R&D	.7921
	(.0285)
log Domestic spillovers	1.258
	(.1809)
log Foreign spillovers	−.7954
	(.1768)
log Foreign spillovers *fdi	.001
	(.0027)
Industry dummies	Yes
Time dummies	Yes
α	.9211
Log likelihood	−3,000.1

Note: Dependent variable is the number of patents. $N = 832$. Numbers in parentheses are standard errors.

specifications are the same. By and large, the results are qualitatively identical to those in table 4.3, although the impact of acquisition FDI seems slightly smaller in estimated elasticity terms. The first two columns show the results of OLS regressions of patent output on own R&D, foreign spillovers, the interaction term, and industry dummies, with and without time dummies. The second two columns give the results of the random-effects models. Again, the foreign spillover term is quite sensitive to the inclusion of information on domestic spillovers, whereas the fdi/foreign-spillover term remains quite robust to it. Finally, the fixed-effects models demonstrate the same patterns as the fixed-effects models of table 4.3.

Table 4.6 gives the results of a negative binomial regression using the acquisition FDI data. As the reader can easily see, here too the results are broadly consistent with those obtained from the negative binomial specification that employed total FDI numbers. However, the estimated impact of FDI on spillovers is not statistically significant at conventional levels. Finally, table 4.7 gives the results of linear regressions using total FDI data where the FDI variable is based on numbers of U.S. employees rather than counts of subsidiaries.[36] The results are quite similar to those obtained using counts of subsidiaries as the measure of FDI.

36. Again, the FDI variable is a dummy variable, but here it is set equal to one where a firm lies in the upper quartile in terms of its number of U.S. employees rather than its number of U.S. subsidiaries.

Table 4.7   **Linear Regressions Based on Japanese Total FDI Data Measured by Total Number of U.S. Employees**

Variable	OLS (2)	Random Effects (1)	Fixed Effects (1)	Fixed Effects (2)
log R&D	.6760	.5852	.1542	.1514
	(.0297)	(.0437)	(.0904)	(.0903)
log Domestic spillovers				.5654
				(.3289)
log Foreign spillovers	.2385	.4046	.8740	.2747
	(.0966)	(.1707)	(.3166)	(.4710)
log Foreign spillovers∗fdi	.0395	.0336	.0221	.0217
	(.0069)	(.0066)	(.0074)	(.0075)
Industry dummies	Yes	Yes	n.a.	n.a.
Time dummies	Yes	Yes	No	No

Note: Dependent variable is the log of the number of patents. $N = 832$. Numbers in parentheses are standard errors.

4.4.5   The Impact of Export Intensity versus Foreign Direct Investment on Knowledge Spillovers

In this subsection, we present the results of a preliminary investigation of the impact of export intensity on a firm's ability to absorb R&D spillovers from U.S. firms. This effect is compared to that obtained from FDI. Our analysis here is limited by the fact that data at the firm level on exports broken down by region of export destination are only available for a subsample of our firms.[37] These data are taken from reports filed by Japanese firms that are listed on the Tokyo Stock Exchange, and they are currently only available for firms in the electronics sector.[38] Furthermore, these data record export levels in the year 1992.

In the regressions, shown in table 4.8, we create an interaction term in which our international spillover measure is multiplied by the percentage of total sales of the company that was exported to the U.S. market in 1992, as we specified in equation (13). We are implicitly assuming that this percentage of sales exported to the United States in 1992 is a reasonable proxy for the company's exports to the United States in the years of our sample period, 1986–89. To the extent that this assumption fails to hold, our export/spillover interaction term is measured with error.

In table 4.8, we run a number of versions of equation (13), using both OLS and random-effects regressions. The results are not robust to the use of fixed effects. Given the small sample size used in this regression, that

37. I thank René Belderbos for generously providing me these data in electronic form.
38. The data are originally taken from the *Yuka Shouken Hokokushou* filed by individual companies.

Table 4.8   **Exports versus FDI as Channels of R&D Spillovers**

Variable	OLS	Random Effects	Random Effects	Random Effects
log R&D	.844	.625	.588	.503
	(.067)	(.100)	(.101)	(.043)
log Foreign spillovers	−.229	.181	−.947	
	(.181)	(.325)	(.649)	
log Foreign spillovers from FDI	.075	.077	.077	.030
	(.013)	(.014)	(.013)	(.006)
log Foreign spillovers from exporting	.252	.329	.130	.359
	(.069)	(.129)	(.160)	(.072)
log Domestic spillovers			1.59	.545
			(.763)	(.152)
Industry dummies	Yes	Yes	Yes	Yes
Time dummies	Yes	Yes	Yes	Yes

Note: Dependent variable is the log of the number of patents. $N = 188$. Numbers in parentheses are standard errors.

result does not surprise us. In future research, with a larger sample of firms with both export and FDI data, we expect to find more robust results of the impact of export intensity on spillovers. As can be clearly seen from these preliminary results, in all cases the coefficient on the export-intensity/spillover interaction term is quite large relative to that of the fdi/spillover interaction term. Of course, in the form in which they are given in table 4.8, the two sets of coefficients are not strictly comparable. However, the estimated export-intensity/spillover interaction terms imply that evaluated at the mean of the data, the elasticity of patent output with respect to the foreign knowledge spillover term increases by 2 to 5 percentage points for every percentage point increase in U.S. export intensity. This suggests that exports *may* be a more important channel of R&D spillover than is FDI for Japanese firms.[39] Alternatively, one can argue that having already achieved a high degree of "contact" with the U.S. market, Japanese firms found little additional value in terms of increased "spillover absorption capacity" from their U.S. foreign investments.

4.5   Conclusions and Extensions

The primary results of the regressions undertaken in this paper can be simply stated. Having an FDI presence in the United States seems to augment the R&D spillovers Japanese firms are able to obtain from the research efforts of U.S. firms. However, the estimated effects, while quite

39. This needs to be tempered with the observation that the construction of the two interaction terms differs. Thus some care must be taken in the interpretation of these coefficients.

robust to alternative empirical specifications and alternative measures of FDI, tend to be quite small. In particular, they do not seem to be large enough to provide evidence in favor of the alarmist position of some American observers that Japanese firms have been able to secure competitive advantages by tapping into U.S. technological strengths. Instead, the evidence presented in this paper suggests that even those Japanese firms with a comparatively large stock of FDI in the United States tend to learn more from other Japanese firms than they do from their U.S. counterparts.

The much more preliminary results presented here on the impact of exports suggest that firms with high levels of exports to the U.S. market seem to receive more in the way of knowledge spillovers than firms without such high levels of exports. These results are based on information from a much smaller sample drawn from a single industry. Nevertheless, they could help us to interpret the results in the previous paragraph. It may be that Japanese firms were already well aware of developments in U.S. markets through their extensive exports to the United States. The additional learning obtained through actual establishment of manufacturing facilities may have contributed little to a level of sophistication concerning U.S. markets that was already high by the time the investment wave began in the late 1980s.[40] Redoing the export regressions with a larger data sample is the subject of current research.

Of course, all of these results need to be assessed in light of a number of important caveats. First, I do not possess R&D and patenting data on all Japanese firms that engaged in substantial FDI in the United States. To the extent that the missing Japanese investors were able to obtain substantially greater spillover benefits than the firms in my data set, I may be systematically undermeasuring the effects. I am currently gathering data in order to expand the cross-sectional dimension of this data set and hope to include that data in future work. Second, the data on foreign spillovers come from a panel of large U.S. R&D-performing firms, not the firms wholly acquired by Japanese purchasers. It is possible that acquiring Japanese firms obtained substantial benefits from their acquisitions but that the more indirect spillover-enhancing benefits I am looking for were not present. In principle, data on the patent portfolios and R&D spending of firms that were publicly traded prior to their acquisition by Japanese firms could be obtained from Compustat and other sources. I hope to investigate this possibility in future research. Third, the data series used in this paper ends in 1989, the year in which investment peaked. It is reasonable to think that the spillover benefits from investment or acquisition may not begin to affect the parent firm's innovative activity until several years after the investment or acquisition. If this is the case, then my time-series di-

---

40. In light of the relative paucity of data, these conclusions must remain tentative.

mension may be too short to capture the impact of the data. I am currently gathering data that will allow me to extend this analysis through the mid-1990s.

Of course, any extension of the data series into the 1990s will have to deal with the effects of the *Heisei* recession, which may swamp any of the positive effects of FDI on domestic innovation. As an additional caveat, it may be that the spillover-augmenting benefits obtained through foreign production plants are small, but the spillover-augmenting benefits obtained through research centers set up in other countries might be quite substantial. In the 1990s, leading Japanese corporations set up research centers in Silicon Valley and other areas expressly for the purpose of more closely following research trends in American high-technology industries. I am currently attempting to obtain data on these research subsidiaries in order to separate out their effects in future research.[41]

A number of extensions could be made to the work presented here. One particularly useful extension would be to use a more direct measure of knowledge spillovers. While Jaffe's (1986) framework has a number of desirable and useful features, spillovers are inferred rather than measured directly. In principle, it is possible to measure knowledge spillovers directly by observing the extent to which the patents of Japanese firms cite the patents of U.S. firms, both those they have acquired and those that remain independent competitors.[42] If we find that Japanese firms with a substantial FDI presence cite U.S. patents more frequently, this would be far more direct evidence of "spillover augmentation through FDI" than could be possibly obtained through the use of Jaffe's (1986) framework. I hope to pursue this alternative approach in future work.

An important omission in this paper was any consideration of the extent to which Japanese FDI served as a means by which technology spillovers flowed from Japanese firms to indigenous U.S. producers. Anecdotal evidence suggests that this effect may have been important in the auto industry, though empirical research has not given strong support to this view. In principle, the data and the empirical techniques used in this paper could be used to investigate this point. I hope to explore this question in future work as well.

Many countries and some subnational regions are actively soliciting foreign investment, offering tax incentives and other economic inducements, often in search of spillover benefits of technology from foreign investors. However, the real extent to which FDI functions as a channel of technology spillovers, either from investor to the host country or from host country firms back to the parent company of the investor, remains undeter-

41. R&D affiliates established abroad are the subject of a recent study by Kuemmerle (1997).

42. Analysis of knowledge spillovers using patent citations was undertaken by Jaffe and Trajtenberg (1996), among others.

mined. In spite of the formidable measurement challenges, it is important that economists attempt to quantify these benefits. I hope that this paper might stimulate other economists to use the kinds of data and the empirical techniques employed here to attempt to answer these extremely important questions.

Data Appendix

Data on U.S. firm sales, capital stock, R&D spending, and other factors were taken from the NBER Productivity Data Base created by Bronwyn Hall and others. Documentation for the NBER database is available online or in written form, and I will not reproduce it here. The patent data for U.S. firms were collected in the same manner as that for Japanese firms, which is described below. I identified the subsidiaries of the U.S. firms in my database using multiple editions of the *Directory of Corporate Affiliations.*

Data on Japanese firm sales, capital stock, employment, and other inputs were taken from the Japan Development Bank Corporate Finance Data Base. This proprietary database, collected and maintained by the Japan Development Bank, is an extremely rich firm-level panel data set containing information on hundreds of variables for thousands of firms from all sectors of the Japanese economy. Due to the well-known problems of output and productivity measurement in many service sector industries as well as the fact that most private R&D is concentrated in the manufacturing sector in both the United States and Japan, I chose to focus solely on manufacturing firms.

Data on Japanese R&D spending are taken from Japanese-language primary sources, namely, the *Kaisha Shiki Ho,* published by Toyo Keizai, and the *Nikkei Kaisha Joho,* published by the Nihon Keizai Shimbunsha. Both are quarterly published books of statistics on Japanese publicly traded firms. Responding to interest in the investor community in the R&D spending of Japanese firms, both books began publishing the results of annual surveys on R&D spending, in the early 1980s and late 1970s, respectively. Response to the surveys is voluntary, so coverage varies from year to year. Furthermore, firms are not legally required to submit precisely accurate figures when they do choose to respond. Nevertheless, knowledgeable Japanese sources contend that these books do provide reasonably accurate information.

Data on the U.S. patents of Japanese firms were obtained in electronic form from the U.S. Patent Office. Patents were obtained using the CASSIS CD-ROM. These patents were later reclassified by date of application, using application data supplied by Adam Jaffe. These data had to be matched to the other microdata firm by firm, since patents are classified by the English name of the Japanese firm (and occasionally the English translit-eration of the Japanese name) or by that of one of its subsidiaries, while my other data are classified by the Tokyo Stock Exchange code, which is the Japanese equivalent of the Compustat code. In identifying subsidiar-ies, I relied on the information from *Kigyo Keiretsu Soran,* published by Toyo Keizai, as well as the source *Kigyo Keiretsu to Gyokai Chizu* and the book *Industrial Groups in Japan,* published by Dodwell Marketing Consul-tants. The problem of matching patents to firms was simplified since a number of large research-intensive subsidiary firms were listed separately in my relatively disaggregated data.

Data on Japanese FDI in the United States were graciously provided to me in electronic form by Thomas A. Pugel of the Stern School of Business at New York University. The original source of Pugel's data is the publica-tion *Japan's Expanding U.S. Manufacturing Presence: 1990 Update,* which was produced by the Japan Economic Institute. Despite its title, this book also provides some data on Japanese subsidiaries that were *planned* by 1990 but not actually established until later. This source provides much useful data on Japanese subsidiaries, including the name of the Japanese parent firm, the address of the subsidiary, the date of establishment of the subsidiary, the number of employees of the subsidiary, and a brief description of the subsidiary's primary businesses.[43] Unfortunately, infor-mation on all of these variables is not always available for all subsidiaries. Data on subsidiaries were matched to other data for Japanese companies based on the name of the firm. This matching was done using a computer algorithm that keyed in on fragments of firm names. Where necessary, the matching was corrected by hand. As these data focus on Japanese direct investment in U.S. manufacturing, it is not a comprehensive data source. It is possible that some nonmanufacturing investments by Japanese manu-facturing firms were missed in these data.

References

Aitken, Brian, Gordon Hanson, and Ann Harrison. 1997. Spillovers, foreign in-vestment, and export behavior. *Journal of International Economics* 43:103–32.
Aitken, Brian, and Ann Harrison. 1999. Do domestic firms benefit from foreign direct investment? Evidence from Venezuela. *American Economic Review* 89 (3): 605–18.
Almeida, Paul. 1996. Knowledge sourcing by foreign multinationals: Patent cita-

---

43. A slightly different version of these data were used in Pugel, Kragas, and Kimura (1996).

tion analysis in the U.S. semiconductor industry. *Strategic Management Journal* 17:155–65.

Aw, Bee, Xiaomin Chen, and Mark Roberts. 1997. Firm-level evidence on productivity differentials, turnover, and exports in Taiwanese manufacturing. NBER Working Paper no. 6235. Cambridge, Mass.: National Bureau of Economic Research.

Belderbos, René, and Leo Sleuwaegen. 1996. Japanese firms and the decision to invest abroad: Business groups and regional core networks. *Review of Economics and Statistics* 78:214–20.

Bernard, Andrew, and J. Bradford Jensen. 1999. Exceptional exporter performance: Cause, effect, or both? *Journal of International Economics* 47 (1): 1–25.

Blomström, Magnus, and Ari Kokko. 1996. Multinational corporations and spillovers. Discussion Paper no. 1356. London: Centre for Economic Policy Research.

Blonigen, Bruce. 1996. In search of substitution between foreign production and exports: The case of Japanese auto parts. Eugene: University of Oregon. Working paper.

———. 1997. Firm-specific assets and the link between exchange rates and foreign direct investment. *American Economic Review* 87 (3): 447–65.

Blundell, Richard, and Stephen Bond. 1995. On the use of initial conditions in dynamic panel data models. Working Paper no. 95/11, Institute for Fiscal Studies, London.

Branstetter, Lee. 1996. Innovation, knowledge spillovers, and dynamic comparative advantage: Evidence from Japan and the United States. Ph.D. diss., Harvard University, Cambridge, Mass.

Branstetter, Lee. Forthcoming. Are knowledge spillovers intranational or international in scope? Microeconometric evidence from the United States and Japan. *Journal of International Economics.*

Branstetter, Lee, and Mariko Sakakibara. 1998. Japanese research consortia: A microeconometric analysis of industrial policy. *Journal of Industrial Economics* 46 (2): 207–33.

Caballero, Ricardo, and Adam Jaffe. 1993. How high are the giants' shoulders? In *NBER Macroeconomics Annual 1993,* ed. Olivier Blanchard and Stanley Fischer. Cambridge, Mass.: MIT Press.

Caves, Richard. 1993. Japanese investment in the United States: Lessons for the economic analysis of foreign investment. *World Economy* 16:279–300.

Chung, Wilbur, Will Mitchell, and Bernard Yeung. 1996. Foreign direct investment and host country productivity: The case of the American automotive components industry. Ann Arbor: University of Michigan School of Business Administration. Manuscript.

Clerides, Sofronis, Saul Lach, and James Tybout. 1998. Is learning by exporting important? Micro-dynamic evidence from Columbia, Mexico, and Morocco. *Quarterly Journal of Economics* 113 (3): 903–48.

Coe, David, and Elhanan Helpman. 1995. International R&D spillovers. *European Economic Review* 39:859–87.

Drake, Tracey, and Richard Caves. 1992. Changing determinants of Japanese foreign investment in the United States. *Journal of the Japanese and International Economies* 6:228–46.

Eaton, Jonathan, and Samuel Kortum. 1996. Trade in ideas: Patenting and productivity in the OECD. *Journal of International Economics* 40:251–78.

Eaton, Jonathan, and Akiko Tamura. 1996. Japanese and U.S. exports and investment as conduits of growth. In *Financial deregulation and integration in East*

Asia, ed. Takatoshi Ito and Anne O. Krueger. Chicago: University of Chicago Press.

Fukao, Kyoji, Toshiyasu Izawa, Morio Kuninori, and Toru Nakakita. 1994. R&D investment and overseas production: An empirical analysis of Japan's electric machinery industry based on corporate data. *BOJ Monetary and Economic Studies* 12 (2): 1–60.

Fukao, Kyoji, and Nakakita Toru. 1995. Genchi Hojin no Seisan Katsudou ga Honsha Kigyou no Yuushutsu, Gyaku Yuunyuu ni Ataeru Eikyou Ni Tsuite: Denki Sangyou Kigyou Paneru Deeta ni Yoru Jisshou Bunseki. Discussion Paper no. 95-DOJ-59. Tokyo: Ministry of International Trade and Industry, Research Institute of International Trade and Industry.

Goto, Akira, and Akiya Nagata. 1997. Innovation no Senyusei to Gijutsu Kikai: Survey Data ni yoru Nichibei Hikaku Kenkyu. NISTEP Report no. 48. Tokyo: Science and Technology Agency of Japan.

Griliches, Zvi. 1979. Issues in assessing the contribution of R&D to productivity growth. *Bell Journal of Economics* 10 (1): 92–116.

Griliches, Zvi, and Jerry Hausman. 1986. Errors in variables in panel data. *Journal of Econometrics* 31 (1): 93–118.

Haddad, Mona, and Ann Harrison. 1993. Are there positive spillovers from direct foreign investment? Evidence from panel data for Morocco. *Journal of Development Economics* 42:51–74.

Hausman, Jerry, Bronwyn Hall, and Zvi Griliches. 1984. Econometric models for count data with an application to the patents-R&D relationship. *Econometrica* 52 (4): 909–38.

Head, Keith, and John Ries. 1997. Overseas investments and firm level exports. Vancouver: University of British Columbia, Faculty of Commerce. Manuscript.

Jaffe, Adam. 1986. Technological opportunity and spillover of R&D: Evidence from firms' patents, profits, and market value. *American Economic Review* 76: 984–1001.

Jaffe, Adam, and Manuel Trajtenberg. 1996. Flows of knowledge spillovers from universities and federal labs: Modeling the flow of patent citations across institutional and geographic boundaries. NBER Working Paper no. 5712. Cambridge, Mass.: National Bureau of Economic Research.

Keller, Wolfgang. 1998. Are international R&D spillovers trade-related? Analyzing spillovers among randomly matched trade partners. *European Economic Review* 42 (8): 1469–81.

Kogut, Bruce, and Sea Jin Chang. 1991. Technological capabilities and Japanese foreign direct investment in the United States. *Review of Economics and Statistics* 73:401–13.

———. 1996. Platform investments and volatile exchange rates: Direct investment in the U.S. by Japanese electronics companies. *Review of Economics and Statistics* 78:221–31.

Kuemmerle, Walter. 1997. Building effective R&D capabilities abroad. *Harvard Business Review,* March–April, 61–70.

MacKnight, Susan. 1987–91. *Japan's expanding U.S. manufacturing presence.* Washington, D.C.: Japan Economic Institute.

Ministry of International Trade and Industry. 1996. *Tsushou Hakusho* (White paper on commerce and industry). Tokyo: MITI.

Narin, Francis. 1995. Linking biomedical research to outcomes: The role of bibliometrics and patent analysis. Haddon Heights, N.J.: CHI Research, Inc. Working paper.

Porter, Michael E. 1990. *The competitive advantage of nations.* New York: Free Press.

Pugel, Thomas, Erik Kragas, and Yui Kimura. 1996. Further evidence on Japanese direct investment in U.S. manufacturing. *Review of Economics and Statistics* 78:208–13.

Ramstetter, Eric. 1996. Estimating economic activities by Japanese transnational corporations: How to make sense of the data. *Transnational Corporations* 5 (2): 107–43.

Scherer, F. M. 1984. Using linked patent and R&D data to measure interindustry technology flows. In *R&D, patents, and productivity,* ed. Z. Griliches. Chicago: University of Chicago Press.

Weinstein, David. 1996. Foreign direct investment and keiretsu: Rethinking U.S. and Japanese policy. In *The effects of U.S. trade protection and promotion policies,* ed. R. Feenstra. Chicago: University of Chicago Press.

Wesson, Tom. 1998. Asset-seeking foreign direct investment. York: York University. Working paper.

World Bank. 1993. *The East Asian miracle.* New York: Oxford University Press.

Yamawaki, Hideki. 1991. Exports and foreign distributional activities: Evidence on Japanese firms in the United States. *Review of Economics and Statistics* 73: 294–300.

Comment   Akiko Tamura

In this paper, Branstetter presents a very interesting and powerful treatment of empirical facts that invites the reader to extend to other data sets or samples.

The most interesting finding in this paper is that the effects of international R&D spillover are greater on the innovative output of Japanese firms with FDI in the United States than for other Japanese firms. This can be seen clearly from the empirical results; the coefficient on the fdi/foreign-spillover interaction term is significantly positive and very robust for all regressions. The coefficient estimate is surprisingly unchanged for all regressions except in table 4.6, which reports a much smaller number for the coefficient estimate in the negative binomial model based on Japanese acquisition FDI data. However, the amount of fdi/foreign-spillover impact is quite small; the coefficient estimates are around 0.02 to 0.04.

The FDI function as a channel for spillovers is very important. In this paper, the technology spillovers from host country to parent company, from U.S. firms to Japanese firms, is examined. I agree that this channel is significant in acquisition FDI cases. Japanese firms will purchase American firms for the purpose of getting their technology. On the other hand, technology spillovers from investors to host country firms will be significant in greenfield FDI cases. When we research Japanese FDI in other countries, especially East Asian countries, the channel of technology spillovers from Japanese investor firms to host country firms is considered

Akiko Tamura is associate professor of economics at Hosei University.

more essential. Thus technology spillover from Japanese firms to U.S. affiliate firms should be also examined when Japanese firms establish new production facilities in the United States. However, the impact of acquisition FDI on foreign spillover is smaller than that of greenfield FDI, as can be seen by comparing the regression results in table 4.5 and table 4.3. It would be interesting to investigate why the empirical results conflict with the above intuitive understanding of the differences between the roles of greenfield and acquisition FDI.

It might also improve our understanding of the empirical results to consider domestic spillover and foreign spillover. When domestic spillovers enter the regressions, the coefficient of foreign spillover becomes negative or insignificant. This may suggest that domestic spillovers overwhelm foreign spillovers. When the R&D spending patterns of Japanese firms and U.S. firms are very similar, domestic spillover and foreign spillover will be correlated and the multicollinearity will affect the regressions.

I would like to comment on the use of data on the number of patents granted as the dependent variable. For reasons of availability, the data consist of U.S. patents held by Japanese firms instead of Japanese patents. From the aggregate 1991 data supplied by the Japanese Patent Office, Japanese patents granted in Japan numbered 30,453,000 and Japanese patents granted in the United States numbered 21,027,000. These numbers are close enough to allow us to assume that Japanese firms patent most of their inventions in the United States as well as in Japan.

However, it is possible that the number of patent *applications* would be a better measure of innovation than the number of patents granted. One reason why patent applications might present a clearer picture is the time lag between the invention and the granting of its patent. In addition, many Japanese patent applications never request examination for a grant because it is felt that the application already supplies some protection by simply having been submitted and does not need to be granted. According to data supplied by the Japanese Patent Office (1994), only 9 percent of applications filed in 1991 requested examination for a grant by 1993. Some patent applications may be useless, but it is difficult to determine the quality of patent applications. The number of Japanese patent applications in Japan, 335,933,000, is much larger than Japanese patent applications in the United States, 38,609,000. The number of Japanese patent applications is so large partly because Japanese patents contain fewer claims per patent. As the author mentioned in the paper, the differences between the Japanese and U.S. patent systems should be considered carefully.

Branstetter carefully constructs a measure of knowledge spillovers, which itself can be considered an excellent contribution of this paper. Although it will be less impressive, I would like to present some facts concerning the relation between knowledge spillover and FDI from a much simpler, more straightforward perspective. If Japanese firms with FDI in the United States cite U.S. patents more frequently, knowledge spillovers from the United States to Japan are augmented. Correspondingly, if U.S. affiliates of Japanese firms license Japanese patents, the knowledge spillover is from Japan to the United States. A survey by Japan's Science and Technology Agency (1997) reports on Japanese technology imports and exports, mostly giving the payment amounts from patent licensing, including initial payments and ongoing royalties. From the data for 1995, about 30 percent of Japanese technology exports to the United States were directed toward affiliates. On the other hand, most Japanese technology imports, more than 95 percent, are from nonaffiliate firms. These surveys are much less complete than the data Branstetter has. However, the technology import data puzzle me a little in terms of technology transfer from U.S. affiliates to Japanese parent firms. (More complete data for Japanese technology exports and imports are available from Japan's Management and Coordination Agency [1997], but the data do not show whether the firms export/import technology from affiliate or nonaffiliate firms.)

Since Branstetter gets remarkable results from his empirical work, extending his analytical tools to other data sets, such as data on Japanese firms with FDI in other countries, would be fascinating. Can the findings in this paper, the relations between technology spillover and FDI, apply to Japanese firms with FDI in East Asian countries? Collecting such data as Branstetter used in the paper would be extremely difficult, so we may have to begin with industry-level aggregate data instead of data on individual firms.

References

Japan. Management and Coordination Agency. Statistics Bureau. 1997. *Report on the Survey of Research and Development*. Tokyo: Management and Coordination Agency.
Japan. Science and Technology Agency. National Institute of Science and Technology Policy. 1997. *Nippon no gijutsu yushutsu no jittai* (Fact-finding study of Japanese technology exports). Tokyo: Science and Technology Agency.
Japanese Patent Office. 1994. *Tokkyo-cho koho* (Patent office annual). Tokyo: Japanese Patent Office.

Comment   Mariko Sakakibara

This paper begins by distinguishing between two types of FDI: the first is home-base-exploiting FDI, based on the internalization theory first devel-

Mariko Sakakibara is assistant professor at the Anderson Graduate School of Management of the University of California, Los Angeles.

oped by Hymer (1960). In this type of FDI, the formation of multinational enterprises (MNEs) is tied to the existence of firm-specific advantages, which provide these firms with offsetting cost advantages and market power over foreign producers. Intangible assets such as sales and marketing or technological resources are subject to market imperfections, and the creation of internal markets across national boundaries for the exploitation of these assets gives rise to MNEs (Caves 1971; Buckley and Casson 1976). The second type of FDI is home-base-augmenting FDI, proposed by Porter (1990). In this type, the objective of FDI is to tap superior host country knowledge and learn from it. This distinction has been examined by Wesson (1993) and others.

Based on this distinction, Branstetter intends to measure the home-base-augmenting effect of FDI. Assumptions made here are that acquisitions might be a more effective means for home-base-augmenting FDI, while home-base-exploiting FDI is more likely to be conducted through greenfield investments. Branstetter finds that for both aggregate FDI and acquisition FDI, FDI-intensive firms benefit more from foreign spillovers. Though this effect is small, it is robust. In this analysis, foreign spillovers are measured as the sum of R&D efforts conducted by U.S. firms, weighted by the technological proximity to a "receiving" Japanese firm.

I would like to pose a fundamental question: Why do Japanese firms want to learn from U.S. firms through acquisitions? Branstetter's implicit assumption here, indicated by his construction of technological proximity measures, is that U.S. firms have more advanced technological knowledge in the same technological areas as the Japanese acquiring firms. This assumption might imply that technologically inferior firms want to acquire superior firms or, more realistically, larger firms want to acquire small but technologically competent firms. A more plausible and perhaps more prevalent scenario, however, is that U.S. firms have knowledge in different technological areas from Japanese acquiring firms. If this scenario is indeed more prevalent, it is necessary to add another dimension to the analysis.

The distinction between acquisition of a firm in the same business as the acquiring firm (the existing business case) and acquisition of a firm in a different business from the acquiring firm (the diversification case) provides additional insight into the process of knowledge transfer through acquisitions. Table 4C.1 illustrates the importance of this distinction.

If a firm possesses a firm-specific advantage (i.e., the home-base-exploiting FDI case), it may invest in a U.S. firm in the same business, as with the NKK–National Steel acquisition, in order to utilize its expertise in its business. In this case of home-base-exploiting FDI, it is unlikely that a Japanese firm will invest in a different business unless it wants to conduct portfolio investment.

On the other hand, in the case of home-base-augmenting FDI, Japanese

Table 4C.1	**Existing Business versus Diversification**	
FDI Type	Existing Business	Diversification
Home-base-augmenting FDI	Yamanouchi–Roberts Pharmaceutical (perhaps limited cases?)	Sony–Columbia Pictures Kubota–Akashic Memories (hard disk drives)
Home-base-exploiting FDI	NKK–National Steel	∅

investment in the same business in the United States would be limited, as with Yamanouchi Pharmaceutical's acquisition of a smaller pharmaceutical firm. What might be more prevalent is acquisition for diversification, as with the Sony–Columbia Pictures case or the farm equipment company Kubota's acquisition of a hard disk drive company. In these cases, the Japanese firms will learn R&D capabilities different from those they already have, and so the technological distance between a Japanese firm and the U.S. spillover pool should be calculated as the distance between a U.S. subsidiary and the spillover pool it is tapping. Since Branstetter does not make a distinction between the existing business and diversification cases, technological distance is measured from the Japanese headquarters in both cases. This can be a source of measurement error.

As for the small but robust effect of foreign spillovers on Japanese FDI-intensive firms, Branstetter interprets the presence of subsidiaries in the United States as contributing to the R&D productivity of a Japanese firm through learning. Given the possible measurement error explained above, this analysis might capture the effect that foreign presence brings firms greater revenue or profit; further, if economies of scale in R&D are present, the greater R&D input will increase R&D productivity. If this is true, it is not a learning effect, as interpreted.

My suggestion is to modify the current model to reflect the actual learning process. Perhaps Branstetter can assign different weights to the distance between a Japanese firm and the U.S. spillover pool by the type of U.S. subsidiary. Alternatively, he can use another measure of spillovers: patent citation, which might be a more direct measure of spillovers.

There already exists a literature that measures the learning effect of FDI by using patent citations. Almeida (1996) examined the U.S. semiconductor industry and found that foreign subsidiaries in the United States cite more local knowledge than would be expected given the geographic distribution of innovative activities and also cite more locally than U.S. firms. He also found evidence that foreign subsidiaries in the United States contribute to local knowledge; that is, foreign subsidiaries are cited more locally than would be expected. Frost (1995) conducted a similar analysis for broader industries.

In addition to the issue of the learning process, I would like to point out a minor issue. Branstetter deals with technological proximity between

Japanese and U.S. firms. There is another proximity issue: geographical proximity in the United States, or the geographical distance between a Japanese subsidiary and the U.S. spillover pool. This would be a larger issue in the United States than in Japan, given the large size of the country. For example, if a Japanese firm wants to learn semiconductor technology, it will benefit more from establishing a subsidiary in Silicon Valley than in Kentucky. Different geographical locations of Japanese subsidiaries might have differential effects on learning.

References

Almeida, P. 1996. Knowledge sourcing by foreign multinationals: Patent citation analysis in the U.S. semiconductor industry. *Strategic Management Journal* 17:155–65.

Buckley, P. J., and M. Casson. 1976. *The future of the multinational enterprise.* London: Macmillan.

Caves, R. E. 1971. International corporations: The industrial economics of foreign investment. *Economica* 38:1–27.

Frost, T. 1995. Multinationals and spillovers of technical knowledge: A comparative institutional analysis. Cambridge: Massachusetts Institute of Technology. Working paper.

Hymer, S. H. 1960. The international operations of national firms: A study of direct investment. Ph.D. diss., Massachusetts Institute of Technology, Cambridge.

Porter, M. E. 1990. *The competitive advantage of nations.* New York: Free Press.

Wesson, T. J. 1993. An alternative motivation for foreign direct investment. Ph.D. diss., Harvard University, Cambridge, Mass.

5

Affiliates of U.S. and Japanese Multinationals in East Asian Production and Trade

Robert E. Lipsey

Foreign direct investment (FDI) is one of the main avenues for the movement of technology and modern business methods across national borders. FDI from more developed countries is presumably more likely to carry advanced technology than that from developing countries. Among the developing countries, those in Asia have been more receptive to inward direct investment than those in other regions.

Of all the direct investment by developed countries in the developing countries of Asia, the United States and Japan account for by far the largest shares. Together they were responsible for over 80 percent of the outward FDI stock from developed countries at the end of 1996 (OECD 1998). This combination of the importance of FDI to Asian host countries and the importance of the United States and Japan in FDI in Asia is the motivation for the focus in this paper on the roles of U.S. and Japanese multinational enterprises (MNEs), in particular the affiliates of these MNEs, in the growth and composition of production and trade in the countries of East Asia.

There are two basic types of data with which one can study the role of multinational firms in the host countries where they operate. One type is home country data on the foreign activities of the multinational firms based there. The other is host country data on the activities of foreign-

Robert E. Lipsey is professor emeritus of economics at Queens College and the Graduate Center, City University of New York, and a research associate of the National Bureau of Economic Research.

The author is indebted to his discussants, Hong-Tack Chun of Korea Development Institute and Yuzo Honda of Osaka University, and to other conference participants for many useful suggestions. The study could not have been carried out without the excellent research and computer assistance of Shachi Chopra-Nangia and Li Xu.

owned firms within their borders. Each type of data has advantages and drawbacks. The home country data have the advantage of comparability across host countries and coverage of all host countries, although not always in published form for each of them individually. The U.S. data have a high degree of coverage of U.S. investing firms and extensive published descriptions of the data. Unfortunately, few home countries collect such data and among those few, Japan issues data that are deficient in many respects (Ramstetter 1996; Lipsey, Blomström, and Ramstetter 1998). The U.S. data, despite their high quality, suffer from the extensive suppression of information for confidentiality reasons, especially for individual countries, industries, and industries within countries. Because of the suppressions, we alternate here between two definitions of "developing Asia." One is called by that name and covers all Asia and Oceania except the Middle East, Japan, Australia, and New Zealand. The other consists of eight individual entities, Hong Kong, Indonesia, Korea (South), Malaysia, the Philippines, Singapore, Taiwan, and Thailand. These account for over 85 percent of sales of U.S. affiliates in developing Asia.

Host country data have the advantage of comparability within each country. There is comparability between information on foreign-owned firms or establishments and on domestically owned ones and among data for establishments owned by different home countries. They are presumably comparable with respect to definitions, such as those for sales, employment, wages, value added, and other variables, and also with respect to industry definitions. However, there are differences from host country to host country in industry coverage, size or type of firm coverage, and definitions of concepts and industries, so that regional summations are questionable. For that reason, this paper, with its concentration on the region, is based mainly on home country data, but some comparisons with host country data are added in the discussions of individual countries.

This paper focuses on the role of MNEs in the development of the exports of their host countries, with some attention also to their role in the development of host country production. One reason for this focus is that MNEs play a particularly large role in trade, larger than in host country production, at least in manufacturing and mining, and especially larger than in employment. Another reason is that there exists, in comprehensive and long-term series on the trade of individual countries, classified by product, a natural basis for comparison between the activities of MNEs and those of other firms within host countries. Some much less detailed data are available on production in some host countries, covering shorter time periods than those of the trade data.

An additional difference between production for export and production for host country domestic sale is that export production is probably more footloose and less under the influence of host country government restrictions than production for local sale, although export production can be influenced by host country incentives. Given that incentives are expensive for host governments, the pattern of exports may reflect the comparative advantages of the host countries better than the more easily influenced production for domestic use.

An earlier examination of the role of multinational firms in developing country trade concluded that in the late 1960s and the 1970s, when exports of manufactured goods by developing Asian countries grew by almost 800 percent, U.S. affiliates were the sources of about 6.5 percent of that growth, and of an increasing share of exports. Up to 1983, the export growth of these countries was to almost twenty times the 1966 level, and U.S. firms accounted for a little over 6 percent of the increase. Over a shorter period, from 1974 to 1983, Japanese firms' affiliates were responsible for another 7 percent, so that the two sets of foreign firms together may have been responsible for about 13 percent of the export growth, not an insignificant share but certainly not a dominant one (Blomström, Kravis, and Lipsey 1988).

The roles of the two countries' MNEs in developing Asia in these early years become clearer if we look at the industry distribution of manufactured exports. Between 1966 and 1977, for example, the Asian developing countries remained predominantly exporters in "other manufacturing," mainly textiles and apparel, which made up half of the enormous growth in their manufactured exports. U.S. firms' manufacturing affiliates in these countries played no role in this export growth, and if we judge by their 1977 share, discussed below, Japanese affiliates could not have been very important either. There were two major changes in export composition. One was a shift out of food products, an industry in which U.S. affiliates were unimportant, and by 1977, so were Japanese affiliates. The other was a move into machinery, which grew from 4 to 14 percent of exports. More than a quarter of the growth in machinery exports, and a higher proportion of that in electrical machinery, was in exports by U.S. affiliates in these countries (Lipsey and Kravis 1985, table A-6). The 1977 data suggest that Japanese affiliates played a negligible role in nonelectrical machinery, but a larger one in the growth of exports of electrical machinery.

5.1   Developing Asia as a Whole in 1977

The export pattern of developing Asia in manufacturing as of 1977 and the position of U.S. and Japanese affiliates in manufactured exports at that point are summarized in table 5.1. The Japanese affiliate data are subject to major problems, worse for the industry distribution than for the total, but serious for the total too, as is explained in Ramstetter (1996) and in Lipsey et al. (1998). However, the general outlines of the picture are probably correct.

The developing Asian countries were, within manufacturing, still

Table 5.1 Industry Distribution of Manufactured Exports from Developing Asia, 1977

Industry	Total Manufacturing Exports:[a] Distribution (%)	Exports By			Affiliate Shares in Total Exports		Industry Share in Affiliate Exports as Percentage of Share in Region's Total Exports	
		Japanese Manufacturing Affiliates		U.S. MOFAs: Distribution (%)	Japanese (%)	U.S. (%)	Japanese (%)	U.S. (%)
		Amount (million $)	Distribution (%)					
Foods	14.2	245	9.1	6.1	4.2	3.1	64.3	43.2
Chemicals	3.5	77	2.9	4.8	5.4	9.8	82.8	137.5
Metals	7.6	76	2.8	2.4	2.4	2.2	37.0	30.9
Nonelectrical machinery	3.9	45	1.7	5.9	2.8	10.6	42.4	149.3
Electrical machinery	13.3	787	29.3	67.7–69.3	14.4	36.3–37.2	220.5	509–521
Transport equipment	3.5	137	5.1	0.9	9.6	1.8	146.3	25.6
Other manufacturing	54.0	1,322	49.2	10.6–12.3	6.0	1.4–1.6	91.0	3.0
Textiles and apparel	26.0	803	29.9	n.a.	7.5		115.0	
Other	28.0	519	19.3	n.a.	4.5		68.9	
Total[b]	100.0	2,689	100.0	100.0	6.5	7.1	100.0	100.0

Sources: NBER World Trade Database (1997), Lipsey and Kravis (1985), Ramstetter (1993), and appendix tables 5A.1 and 5A.2.

Note: Developing Asia excludes the Middle East and includes the Asia and Pacific regions except for Australia, New Zealand, and Japan. MOFA = majority-owned foreign affiliate.

[a] Eight East Asian exporters: Hong Kong, Indonesia, Korea, Malaysia, Philippines, Singapore, Taiwan, and Thailand. Manufactured exports by other countries of developing Asia outside the Middle East, including Bangladesh, China, India, Myanmar, and Pakistan, were $9,902,502 in 1977.

[b] Excludes petroleum and coal products.

predominantly exporters of foods and "other manufactures" in 1977. These industries were the source of over two-thirds of their manufactured exports and, with metals, three-quarters of the total. Electrical machinery had already reached some importance, at 13 percent of the total. The specializations of Japanese and U.S. manufacturing affiliates in this group of countries were different from those of the countries and from each other. Japanese affiliate exports were relatively larger than U.S. affiliate exports in transport equipment, and particularly in "other manufacturing," mainly textiles and apparel, almost half of Japanese affiliate exports. U.S. affiliate exports were more concentrated in electrical machinery, which made up two-thirds of U.S. affiliate exports, and to a smaller extent in chemicals and nonelectrical machinery.

With relatively large shares in foods and especially in textiles and apparel and the rest of "other manufacturing," the export pattern of the Japanese affiliates was much closer than that of the U.S. affiliates to the comparative advantages of the host countries. Relative to the exports of the host countries, those of U.S. affiliates were extremely high in electrical machinery, and a little high also in chemicals and in nonelectrical machinery, all industry groups of U.S. home-country-export comparative advantage, and also relatively R&D-intensive industries. Thus one could say that as of the mid-1970s, both U.S. and Japanese affiliates, but especially the U.S. affiliates, were pushing Asian host countries toward specialization in electrical machinery. Japanese affiliates differed from U.S. affiliates in being much more involved in exploiting the traditional comparative advantages of these host countries.

U.S. and Japanese affiliates together were responsible for 14 percent of the region's manufactured exports, but the share varied widely across industries. Despite the concentration of Japanese affiliate exports in "other manufacturing," they were a minor part of total exports in this industry group. In electrical machinery, however, the two countries' affiliates were responsible for over half of their host countries' exports, and affiliates accounted for between 10 and 15 percent of total exports in chemicals, nonelectrical machinery, and transport equipment.

The comparative advantages of U.S. and Japanese affiliates relative to their host countries are described by the ratios in the last two columns of table 5.1. Both countries' affiliates had large comparative advantages relative to their host countries in electrical machinery. U.S. affiliates, but not Japanese affiliates, also had them in chemicals and nonelectrical machinery, and Japanese, but not U.S. affiliates, in transport equipment and, more surprisingly, in textiles and apparel.

The industry distributions of production, as measured by gross product for U.S. majority-owned foreign affiliates (MOFAs) and by sales for U.S. and Japanese affiliates, are shown in table 5.2. There are no comparable data for production and sales in the region. As was the case for exports,

Table 5.2   Industry Distribution of Gross Product and Sales of U.S. and Japanese Manufacturing Affiliates in Developing Asia, 1977

| | U.S. MOFAs | | | | Japanese Affiliates: Sales | |
| | Amount (million $) | | Distribution (%) | | | |
Industry	Gross Product	Sales	Gross Product	Sales	Amount (million $)	Distribution (%)
Foods	121–364[a]	548–612	8.1–24.3	10.7–11.9	480	5.9
Chemicals	270	911	18.1	17.8	546	6.8
Metals	38	104	2.5	2.0	691	8.6
Nonelectrical machinery	154[b]	243	10.3	4.7	132	1.6
Electrical machinery	586	2,306	39.2	45.0	1,988	24.6
Transport equipment	≤190[c]	195–212	≤12.7	3.8–4.1	930	11.5
Other manufacturing	324	754–801	21.7	14.7–15.6	3,308	41.0
Textiles and apparel	n.a.	66	n.a.	1.3	2,154	26.7
Other	n.a.	688–735	n.a.	13.4–14.3	1,154	14.3
Total	1,495	5,125	100.0	100.0	8,074	100.0

Sources: Ramstetter (1993), appendix table 5A.2, U.S. Department of Commerce (1981, table III.F5), and Mataloni and Goldberg (1994).

Note: Developing Asia excludes the Middle East and includes the Asia and Pacific regions except for Australia, New Zealand, and Japan.

[a] Includes Japan and New Zealand.

[b] Assumes all the excess of individual industries over the total (2,433 − 1,495 = 938) is exports of nonelectrical machinery by U.S. affiliates in Japan.

[c] Includes New Zealand.

U.S. affiliate sales were more concentrated in foods, chemicals, and machinery, and Japanese affiliate sales in metals, transport equipment, and "other manufacturing," particularly textiles and apparel. The most extreme concentrations in industry distribution that were seen for exports, such as for U.S. and Japanese affiliates in electrical machinery and for Japanese affiliates in "other manufacturing," are somewhat muted in production and sales, although they are still visible.

The difference between the industry distributions for exports and for sales implies that export-sales ratios, or export orientation, differ among the industries. As can be seen by comparing tables 5.1 and 5.2, U.S. affiliates were far more export oriented than Japanese affiliates in metals and in both machinery groups, with electrical machinery the least focused on its host country markets, selling only 15 percent or less there. In the food industry, Japanese affiliates exported a little more than half of their sales, considerably more than U.S. affiliates did, and in chemicals, transport equipment, and "other manufacturing," the export ratios of the two countries' affiliates were similar. For the most part (six out of eight industries), higher shares of an industry in exports by one country's affiliates were associated with higher export-sales ratios in that country's affiliates. U.S. firms' machinery affiliates were the only group exporting far more than they sold in their host countries. Other high export ratios were found in foods, Japanese electrical and nonelectrical machinery affiliates, and both countries' affiliates in "other manufacturing."

Thus, by 1977, a group of foreign-owned affiliates had been drawn to developing Asia to produce for export, and another, smaller group, mainly in chemicals and transport equipment, had been drawn there by the prospect of selling to the host countries themselves. The exporting activities of the affiliates that did export accounted for only about 14 percent of the region's exports because most of the region's exports were in foods, metals, and "other manufacturing," where foreign firms seemed to have little advantage over local firms.

5.2   The Trade of Individual Countries in 1977

The export patterns of the eight East Asian countries had one common feature in the mid-1970s, as is shown in table 5.3. Exports of food products and "other manufacturing" were more than half of total manufactured exports in every country except Singapore. But there were also some sharp differences. In the four newly industrialized economies (NIEs), Hong Kong, Korea, Singapore, and Taiwan, led by Singapore, electrical machinery accounted for at least 10 percent of exports. Malaysia was not far behind, but in the other three countries, electrical machinery exports were a minor part of the total, less than 4 percent. Nonelectrical machinery was much less important than electrical machinery, but the comparative

Table 5.3   Industry Distributions of Manufactured Exports by Eight East Asian Countries, 1977

Industry	Hong Kong	Indonesia	Korea	Malaysia	Philippines	Singapore	Taiwan	Thailand
Foods	2.7	22.6	9.9	26.2	44.7	11.5	12.0	54.5
Chemicals	3.7	3.6	2.5	2.4	3.9	7.2	3.3	1.4
Metals	2.7	9.2	9.9	20.4	6.6	5.4	4.8	13.4
Nonelectrical machinery	5.2	0.8	1.3	1.5	0.8	11.1	5.0	1.0
Electrical machinery	12.8	1.6	11.4	9.3	2.1	28.8	16.9	3.5
Transport equipment	0.8	0.5	7.3	1.0	1.0	9.7	2.2	0.2
Other manufacturing (total)	72.1	61.7	57.7	39.1	41.1	26.3	55.9	25.9
Textiles and apparel	41.4	11.2	33.7	3.7	10.9	9.8	26.2	14.4
Other	30.7	50.5	24.0	35.4	30.2	16.5	29.7	11.5
Total[a]	100.0	100.0	100.0	100.0	100.0	100.0	100.0	100.0

Source: NBER World Trade Database (1997).

[a]Excludes petroleum and coal products.

advantages seemed to be related. Three of the four countries in which electrical machinery made up a large part of exports were also the ones with the largest shares of their exports in nonelectrical machinery. However, comparative advantage in chemicals, the other group in which R&D is relatively high, appears to be unrelated to that in machinery.

Thus, even by 1977, the region was dividing into two groups of countries. One, consisting of four or five countries, was, with the participation of foreign affiliates, moving into the export of machinery and chemicals. The other group showed little indication of moving away from their traditional export specializations.

5.3   The Growth of the Region's Production and Exports, 1977–95

The story of developing Asia's growth over the fifteen or twenty years after 1977 is a familiar one. The eight countries of table 5.3 grew more than twice as fast, in terms of their GDP, as the world as a whole. Their exports of manufactured goods grew to sixteen times the 1977 level by 1995 and their share of world manufactured exports from 6 to 15 percent (18 percent if China is added). The composition of the eight countries' exports changed drastically, with foods and "other manufacturing" declining from 68 to 38 percent and machinery rising from 17 to 44 percent (appendix table 5A.1). While 41 percent of the increase in exports was in the older sectors, foods, metals, and "other manufacturing," more than half of the growth came from the chemical and machinery sectors.

Another way of describing the export patterns is by the extent to which exports are the product of industries characterized by high, medium, or low ratios of R&D expenditure to output, recognizing that the particular products that make up a country's exports in one of these industries may not themselves be the ones resulting from the R&D. U.S. parent companies investing in developing Asia, even in 1977, were not only in relatively high R&D industries but, within those industries, were R&D intensive relative to other firms. Parents in the nonelectrical machinery industry with direct investments in developing Asia in 1977 were over 50 percent more R&D intensive than those with investments in Europe, the next highest area in this respect. Parents in the electrical machinery industry with direct investments in developing Asia were almost 40 percent more R&D intensive than those with European investments (Lipsey, Blomström, and Kravis 1990).

The exports of the eight developing East Asian countries in 1977 were mostly from industries of low R&D intensity. The main ones were foods, metals, and, within the broad "other manufacturing" group, textiles and apparel, lumber and furniture, and leather and leather products. By 1995, the export distributions, especially those of Singapore, Malaysia, and Taiwan, were much more tilted toward high-R&D industries. The shares of high-R&D industries in the manufacturing exports of Singapore and Malaysia were far above those in the exports of the United States and Japan, and their share in Taiwan's exports was a little above the shares for those two high-tech leaders. In all the East Asian countries, except Indonesia, the share of high-R&D-intensity industries in manufactured exports was higher than in such advanced countries in Europe as France and Germany (table 5.4).

What role, if any, did the affiliates of U.S. and Japanese companies play in these transformations? From 1977 to 1995, the region's dependence on U.S. affiliates for exporting, never large, declined. The share of U.S. affiliates in total manufactured exports declined from 7 to about 5.5 percent. In 1977, U.S. affiliates accounted for more than 4 percent of East Asian exports only in chemicals and machinery, concentrated in a share of more than a third in electrical machinery. By 1995, the two machinery industries were the only ones with U.S. affiliate shares over 4 percent (table 5.5). The role of U.S. affiliates in the region's exports shrank substantially in both chemicals and electrical machinery, but grew in nonelectrical machinery to 18 to 20 percent. These changes can also be seen in the shares of U.S. affiliates in the growth of exports, large in both machinery industries in the first period, from 1977 to 1982, around 15 and 25 percent, but after that concentrated in the nonelectrical machinery sector. In that industry,

Table 5.4   **R&D Intensities of Manufacturing Export Industries: Developing Countries in East Asia, the United States, Japan, and Europe**

Country	1977			1995		
	Low[a]	Medium	High[b]	Low[a]	Medium	High[b]
Hong Kong	53	34	14	40	33	27
Indonesia	93	5	3	74	17	9
Korea	69	20	11	32	40	28
Malaysia	82	6	12	26	27	47
Philippines	88	10	2	53	18	29
Singapore	36	35	28	13	25	62
Taiwan	60	27	12	31	33	36
Thailand	88	7	5	45	27	28
Japan	28	57	15	11	54	35
United States	25	56	19	23	44	33
Germany	27	61	12	25	56	19
France	38	50	12	36	41	23
United Kingdom	29	57	14	26	47	27

Source: NBER World Trade Database (1997).

[a]Food; metals; textiles and apparel; leather and leather products; paper, pulp, etc.; other paper and allied products; printing and publishing; lumber, wood, and furniture; glass products; and stone and clay products.

[b]Drugs; office machinery and computers; communication equipment except radio and TV; electronic components; other electrical machinery; aircraft; and instruments.

Table 5.5   **Share of U.S. MOFA Exports[a] in Total Exports from Eight East Asian Countries,[b] 1977–95 (percent)**

Industry	1977	1982	1989	1995
Foods	3.1	0.7–1.6	1.8	3.1[c]
Chemicals	9.8	4.1	6.2	3.2
Metals	2.2	0.7	1.7	1.4
Nonelectrical machinery	10.6	12.2	19.2	19.5
Electrical machinery	36.3–37.2	29.3	11.9	5.6
Transport equipment	1.8	3.9	3.1	1.2
Other manufacturing	1.4–1.6	0.7	0.8	1.0[c]
Total[c]	7.1	6.3–6.4	5.6	5.6

Source: Appendix tables 5A.1 and 5A.2.

[a] From developing Asia as a whole, excluding the Middle East.

[b] Excludes petroleum and coal products.

[c] 1995 MOFA export data include New Zealand.

U.S. affiliates still accounted for about 20 percent of export growth in 1989–95, but the U.S. affiliate share was below 6 percent in the other broad industry groups.

These broad industry group categories and aggregations of countries conceal differences among individual industries and individual countries. Many of these are hidden in the published data by suppression rules, but for a few industries we can compare total sales, including both exports and local sales, by U.S. affiliates in Asian countries other than Japan and Australia, but including New Zealand, with total exports by the eight East Asian countries. A high ratio of affiliate sales to exports could mean that the industry is dominated by the U.S. affiliates or it could mean that the U.S. affiliates are producing for sale in the host country rather than for export. The available information on these affiliate sales ratios by industry is shown in table 5.6. The high ratio for soaps, cleansers, and toilet goods, far over 100 percent, indicates that U.S. affiliates in this industry focus on host country markets rather than export markets. Within electrical machinery, the U.S. affiliates' importance is concentrated in electronic components and accessories.

Japanese affiliates accounted for a little less of Southeast Asia's exports than U.S. affiliates in each of the years for which we can make a comparison, through 1989, and their share of the region's exports also declined. After that, however, their exports and their shares of the region's exports rose sharply through 1995, considerably surpassing those of U.S. MOFAs (table 5.7). The major differences among industries were that Japanese affiliates were a negligible factor in exports of nonelectrical machinery, the industry in which U.S. affiliates were most important as exporters in 1995, but were more important than U.S. affiliates in exports of every other

Table 5.6 **United States MOFA Sales and Sales Relative to Region Exports of Developing Asian Countries in Eleven Individual Industries, 1995**

Industry	Affiliate Sales (million $)	Affiliate Sales as Share of Region Exports[a] (%)
Chemicals		
Industrial chemicals	2,245	6.9
Drugs	1,693	77.7
Soaps, cleansers, and toilet goods	3,167	174.0
Agricultural and other chemicals	1,511	14.5
Electrical machinery		
Household appliances, audio, video, etc.	≤6,333	≤7.5
Electronic components and accessories	15,910	21.7
Electronic and other electrical equipment n.e.c.	≥361	≥1.3
Other manufacturing		
Lumber, wood, and furniture	418	2.6
Printing and publishing	554	26.2
Misc. plastic products	1,060	9.7
Instruments and related products	648	3.0

Sources: Appendix table 5A.1 and U.S. Department of Commerce (1998, table III.E.4).
[a]Region exports are the total of eight East Asian developing countries.

Table 5.7 **Share of Japanese Manufacturing Affiliate Exports in Total Exports from East Asian Countries (percent)**

	Ramstetter			MITI: NIE-4 and ASEAN-4	
	Asia		ASEAN-5[a] and NIEs:		
Industry Group	1977	1989	1989	1989	1995[b]
Foods	4.2	1.3	1.5	1.7	4.8
Chemicals	5.4	4.1	4.1	4.7	6.0
Metals	2.4	3.6	3.5	4.0	3.0
Nonelectrical machinery	2.8	1.7	1.7	1.9	2.2
Electrical machinery	14.4	12.5	12.3	14.1	16.7
Transport equipment	9.6	4.5	5.3	6.1	7.4
Other manufacturing	6.0	0.9	1.0	1.5	3.6
Textiles and apparel	7.5	0.8	0.8	0.9	1.9
Instruments	4.5	1.0	1.1	6.6	10.1
Other manufacturing				1.2	3.6
Total	6.5	4.0	4.0	4.8	7.2

Sources: Ramstetter (1993, table 4) and appendix tables 5A.1 and 5A.5.
[a]Includes Brunei.
[b]Excludes petroleum and coal products.

industry group, particularly transport equipment and electrical machinery. The original Japanese share in textile and apparel exports almost vanished between 1977 and 1989.

The region's dependence on U.S. and Japanese affiliates together as sources of exports declined between 1977 and 1989 from about 13.5 to 10.5 percent and then rose again to almost 13 percent with the large growth in exporting by Japanese affiliates. The combined U.S. and Japanese affiliate shares fell in four or five of the seven industry groups, most notably in electrical machinery, where the affiliates were responsible for over half of exports in 1977 but only 22 percent in the mid-1990s, indicating some maturing of the domestic industry. The outstanding exception was nonelectrical machinery, where the affiliate share grew to over 20 percent by 1989 and remained close to that level in the next six years. Thus, at the regional level, there seems to have been some growing out of dependence on foreign affiliates, except in the case of U.S. affiliates in nonelectrical machinery, mainly involved in computer-related products.

5.4   Production and Exports in Individual Countries

Although East Asia has been treated here so far mainly as a unit, there are large differences among the countries. A separation by country gives a picture of the differences and also provides a larger number of observations.

Singapore has been the country most dependent on U.S. affiliates as exporters, with their share close to 20 percent in 1977 and 1995 (appendix tables 5A.6–5A.10). The Philippines are next, still at about 7 percent, and in Malaysia these shares were high in 1982 but fell sharply after that. In Hong Kong and Taiwan, and even more in Indonesia and Korea, U.S. affiliate shares in manufactured exports were low and falling, although U.S. affiliates were important as exporters in Indonesia's petroleum industry, not included in the manufacturing totals here.

The great importance of U.S. affiliates in the electronics industry, especially in the early stages of development of the industry, stands out in the comparison of tables 5A.7 through 5A.10 with table 5A.6. At the first appearance of the industry in the data here, which does not mean the beginning of the industry itself for the earlier entrants, the shares of U.S. affiliates are very high. They range from 97 percent in the Philippines (ignoring the anomalous 1982 ratio, which shows the affiliates exporting almost twice the national total), to three-quarters in Malaysia and Thailand in 1982 and over half in Singapore and close to 30 percent in Hong Kong and Taiwan in 1977. Only Indonesia and Korea show no such high ratios, and Indonesia hardly entered the industry. After those initial high ratios, which suggest that U.S. firms were the initiators of the industries in these countries, the role of U.S. affiliates diminished sharply in the most successful exporting countries, to 3 percent in Hong Kong, 6 percent in Singapore, and 7 percent in Taiwan.

On a smaller scale, the chemical industry went through a similar evolution, although the U.S. affiliate shares of exports were never as high and the pattern was not as consistent. The shares did decline from 12 to 3.5 percent in Hong Kong, from 18 to 3 percent in Taiwan, from 27 to 1.5 percent in Indonesia, from 8 to 1.5 percent in Malaysia, and from 42 to 5 percent in the Philippines. In this case also, affiliates may have been teachers with apt students.

The major exception to the pattern of receding importance of U.S. affiliates as exporters is the nonelectrical machinery industry in Singapore. The industry was already an important exporter in 1977, and the share of U.S. affiliates in 1982, the first year we can calculate it, was over 30 percent. That share grew to 37 and 45 percent in 1989 and 1995 even as the industry's share in Singapore's exports grew steadily from 11 percent in 1977 to over a third in 1995. In the last period, U.S. affiliates accounted for almost half of Singapore's export growth in this industry.

The declining role of affiliates in the region's exports does not necessarily mean that there were similar declines in their role in production. As their export role was declining, U.S. affiliates were being naturalized, in the sense that they were selling more of their production in host country markets (appendix tables 5A.7–5A.10). The overall export-sales ratios for U.S. manufacturing affiliates fell in six out of the seven countries for which they could be calculated between 1977 and 1995 and also, more often than not, in individual industry groups within countries. Shifts toward host country markets over time were more common than shifts toward export markets in each industry in each period in each country, wherever data were available. That predominance suggests that production for export preceded production for host country markets on the part of U.S. MNEs. Perhaps the MNEs were more knowledgeable about export markets than about host country markets or perhaps host country markets did not develop until after production for export had begun. The export production itself may have stimulated the growth of host country markets in general or in the same industries.

Japanese manufacturing affiliates in East Asia have generally been less export oriented than U.S. affiliates. About a third of their sales were outside host countries in 1977 (tables 5.1 and 5.2), as compared with 57 percent for U.S. affiliates. In 1995, the export-sales ratio for U.S. affiliates was down to 54 percent (appendix table 5A.2), and those for Japanese affiliates were up to 43.5 percent in the NIEs and 38 percent in the ASEAN-4 (appendix table 5A.4). Thus Japanese affiliates have become a little more like U.S. affiliates as time has passed. Among the major industries, Japanese affiliates were much less export oriented in nonelectrical machinery than U.S. affiliates in 1995 but had become considerably more export oriented in electrical machinery.

Some of the country studies in Dobson and Chia (1997) offer a closer look at trade-investment relations in Southeast Asia, particularly in the two machinery industries. In Singapore, for example, in a category called "electronic products and accessories," which encompasses most of the two machinery groups in our tables, foreign affiliates accounted for almost 90 percent of the capital. Over 80 percent of sales were exports, and they constituted almost two-thirds of Singapore's domestic exports of manufactures in 1992; (Chia 1997). U.S. and European affiliates were particularly export oriented; each group sent about half its exports to its home region (Chia 1997, table 2.8). Japanese affiliates, more involved in consumer electronics, sold the highest proportion locally among all the foreign-owned operations. Chia concluded that the data demonstrate "differences in U.S. and Japanese corporate strategies for offshore production, the former to supply the home and third-country markets, the latter to supply largely the host and third-country markets" (1997, 449).

A study of a sample of foreign-owned firms in Taiwan by Tu (1997) covering electronics and chemical firms did not find such large differences in export behavior between U.S. and Japanese affiliates as in the Singapore study but did note two points that help to explain aggregate behavior. One is the effect of the age of an affiliate. Younger affiliates relied much more than older affiliates on their home markets; as an affiliate matured, and perhaps as the local market matured at the same time, it tended to sell more in its local market. This process could be one explanation for the similar tendency visible in the aggregate data. A more disturbing finding in this study is that affiliates reported as sales to parents products that were actually shipped to third countries. Such a practice would put into question the reliability of the division between exports to home countries and exports to third countries (Tu 1997, 75).

The study of foreign firms in Hong Kong in the same volume, also based on a nonrandom sample survey, suggested large differences between U.S. and Japanese firm behavior, as was reported for Singapore (Chen and Wong 1997). Japanese affiliates were more tightly tied to their parents in the sense that more of their exports went to them, while U.S. affiliates sold somewhat more to other affiliates and much more to unrelated firms. Japanese affiliates were also more dependent on their parents for "the supply of capital, machinery, components, and parts" (Chen and Wong 1997, 91). One gets the impression that U.S. firms have gone further than Japanese firms in the division of labor among affiliates.

In Thailand, the differences between U.S. and Japanese firms do not appear as large (Ramstetter 1997). Both are focused substantially on their home markets, although that dependence has been rising for Japanese firms and declining for U.S. affiliates. Japanese affiliates are much more important than U.S. affiliates, accounting for 22 percent of Thai exports of nonpetroleum manufactured exports, as compared with 8 percent for U.S. affiliates. Exports are concentrated in electrical and computing machinery (nonelectrical machinery in the aggregate data), especially on the part of U.S. affiliates (Ramstetter 1997, 122–23).

Japanese affiliates in the electrical and electronics industries in Malaysia differed from U.S. and European affiliates in being to a larger extent producers of final products, and much less exporters to home markets (Sieh and Yew 1997, 138–39). U.S. affiliates purchased few inputs from unrelated suppliers in third countries but much more from affiliates in those countries, the main reason being that "U.S. affiliates as semiconductor producers were higher up on the value-added chain and could use imports only from their proprietary sources whereas Japanese firms turning out intermediate products half way down the value-added chain had more procurement options" (140). One U.S. firm was described as having "a no duplication policy, which divided production activities among affiliates in different locations to avoid duplicating the output of another affiliate" (140).

In a study of the location of export production by U.S. and Japanese MNEs Kumar (1997) distinguished between production for export to the MNEs' home markets and production for export to the rest of the world and found some differences in determinants for the two types and between Japanese and U.S. firm practices. Although the study is not specific to FDI in Asia, Kumar attempted to measure the attractiveness of the "first generation of NIEs" and of a "second tier," the ASEAN-4 countries and China. One conclusion is that the first-generation NIEs were favored by U.S. MNEs over other locations for production for the U.S. market in 1982 and 1989 but that they had lost their advantage by 1994. "Favored" in that study means favored beyond the degree expected from the measured determinants of export production location. These same countries were attractive to Japanese MNEs in 1989, but not before, and they had lost that advantage by 1994. The explanation offered was that export-oriented investment was discouraged by the combination of "rising wages, appreciating currencies, loss of GSP [Generalized System of Preferences] benefits and MFA [Multi-Fiber Arrangement] quotas." At the same time, coefficients representing membership in the "second tier" in equations explaining exports to U.S. and Japanese markets were increasing over time. Among industry groups, these trends were clearest, and the coefficients most frequently statistically significant, for U.S. affiliates in the electrical machinery industry, confirming the impression from the data reported here.

Kumar also suggested that there are differences in the behavior of U.S. and Japanese affiliates, as appears to be the case in our data here. His interpretation was that "U.S. MNEs tend to relocate production of intermediate products for home consumption, whereas Japanese MNEs seem to shift production of more finished goods in relatively simpler technology industries. The offshore production by U.S. MNEs would seem from this more of 'globalized production' which links subsidiaries in home and host countries vertically" (Kumar 1997, 33–34). This picture of the close relationships between parents and affiliates within U.S. firms fits with the finding in Lipsey (1998) that exports to individual markets from U.S. affiliates in Asian countries are larger when parent exports to affiliates in those markets are also large. This phenomenon was particularly noticeable in the electronic component and accessory industry, part of the electrical machinery industry reported on here.

5.5   Conclusions

The composition of manufacturing production and of the manufactured exports of East Asian countries has been completely transformed over the past twenty years or so. To varying degrees, these countries went from a pattern of exports within manufacturing fairly typical of developing countries to one much more like that of highly developed countries. In some cases they have moved quite far up the scale into R&D-intensive industries, although not necessarily in the more sophisticated sectors of these industries. Foods, textiles and apparel, and "other manufacturing," mainly labor-intensive products of industries of low R&D intensity, declined from almost 68 percent of exports to 38 percent, and exports from the chemical and machinery industries rose from 21 percent to more than half of exports. In all the countries, the share of exports from R&D-intensive industries at least doubled and in most cases grew much more than that.

It would be hard to explain these changes by the initial comparative advantages of these countries in the late 1960s and early 1970s. The decisions to welcome foreign firms as direct investors, taken at different times and to different degrees among the countries, seem to have been a crucial element in these developments. Foreign firms, particularly American firms at the beginning, saw a way to integrate these countries into worldwide networks of production, first in electronics and then in aspects of the computer industry. Foreign firms supplied the technology and the links to other parts of the production networks that completed the set of resources necessary for the growth of these industries. The most typical pattern seemed to be the establishment of affiliates almost completely for export production, followed by the development of these affiliates over time to produce more for domestic sale and by the growth of production by non-affiliated host country firms in the same or related industries.

Although this is a general description, each country has its own story. Indonesia does not fit the pattern except a bit for chemicals. Korea looks to be a country that transformed almost entirely without inward FDI, although chapter 9 in this volume, by Kim and Hwang, suggests that this source was more influential than is visible from our data. The smallest countries have been, as we would expect, most dependent on trade for the growth of these industries.

U.S. and Japanese firms seem to have played somewhat different roles. U.S. firms were earlier major investors, and their investments and affiliate exports were distributed across industries along the lines of U.S. comparative advantage, while the industry distribution of Japanese affiliate production and exports was closer to that of the host countries. Thus U.S. investments initially did more to drive changes in the composition of their host countries' production and trade. Over time, however, U.S. and Japanese affiliates have become more alike in transmitting home country technologies and comparative advantages, U.S. firms more in computer equipment, Japanese firms more in motor vehicles, and both in electronics.

It is a little difficult to match the growth of exports by foreign-owned affiliates in these countries with total export growth. Of the two fast-growing machinery sectors, in electrical machinery, U.S. and Japanese affiliates alone were responsible for half of exports in 1977 and their share diminished in the next twenty years. In nonelectrical machinery, mainly computers and accessories and parts, the share of the two home countries' affiliates, chiefly U.S. affiliates, increased substantially between 1977 and 1995.

By 1995, the two machinery industries' exports were 30 percent or more of total manufactured exports in seven out of the eight countries we cover here. The exception is Indonesia, where "investments in export-oriented electronic components by multinational enterprises (MNEs) failed to take off . . . because of the lack of a conducive investment climate between 1973 and 1985" (Pangestu 1997, 204). Two semiconductor investments that had been established by major American firms were closed in 1985–86. In the seven other countries, except for Korea, which seems to have managed without much inward FDI, the earliest data for the electrical machinery industry show large initial shares in exports for U.S. affiliates alone (we do not have individual country data for Japanese affiliates). The large early affiliate shares of exports were followed by declines in every case. The data seem to say that U.S. affiliates were extremely important in the initial stages of this now major industry for the region but have been replaced to some extent, at least in their export roles, by firms from other home countries, especially Japan, and by local firms. While their role in exports was declining, U.S. affiliates were shifting their sales to their host country markets to some extent.

A somewhat similar pattern of initially high U.S. affiliate shares in exports, declining in later years, can be observed in the chemical industry, although the shares were never as high as in electrical machinery, and U.S.

affiliates in chemicals were always much more oriented toward their host country markets than those in electrical machinery.

The major exception to this trend was the nonelectrical machinery industry, mainly computers and parts. In this case, the share of U.S. affiliates in the region's exports grew over time. The industry was particularly important as an exporter in Taiwan, where it was a larger exporter than electrical machinery, and in Singapore, where it was a little smaller. U.S. and Japanese data are not available in sufficient industry detail to test whether what appear to be differences in behavior are explainable by the detailed industry composition of their investments, and the data that do exist are undermined by differences in consolidation rules, by the extent of transshipments with little value added, and by many other problems. Detailed industry composition does seem to be the explanation in many individual cases, as in the distinction between consumer electronics and semiconductor specializations in individual countries within the electrical machinery industry, which seems to explain the extent of exporting relative to host country sales.

The declining share of U.S. and Japanese affiliates in exports of most manufacturing industries in East Asia does not reflect any withdrawal from the region or decline in affiliate activity. Exports by U.S.-owned affiliates grew by almost twelve times their original level between 1977 and 1995 and by 20 percent in 1995 alone. Local sales in host countries grew even faster. Exports by Japanese affiliates grew by seventeen times their original value during the same period and more than tripled between 1989 and 1995. The declines in affiliate shares of exports over time reflect the enormous growth of local firms and of other countries' affiliates, particularly the former, and local firm growth may itself have been partly a result of the growth of U.S. and Japanese affiliates.

Appendix

Table 5A.1   Total Manufacturing Exports from Eight East Asian Developing Countries, by BEA Industry (thousand dollars)

| BEA Industry | Eight East Asian Countries | | | | China |
	1977	1982	1989	1995	1995
Foods, beverages	5,821,264	9,148,580	18,842,283	32,302,726	8,382,957
Grain and bakery products	973,120	1,325,249	2,550,353	3,294,523	242,055
Beverages	56,719	147,902	521,524	1,640,030	377,354
Other foods	4,791,425	7,675,429	15,770,406	27,368,173	7,763,548
Metals	3,134,546	7,931,640	19,235,083	41,959,157	11,487,855
Primary ferrous metals	522,892	2,945,840	6,397,892	12,016,614	5,150,802
Primary nonferrous metals	696,045	2,486,644	6,982,512	17,013,441	2,629,008
Fabricated metals	1,915,609	2,499,156	5,854,679	12,929,102	3,708,045
Chemicals	1,420,428	4,662,246	14,378,199	46,840,356	9,038,614
Drugs	238,851	435,684	851,535	2,179,272	1,576,508
Soaps etc.	100,061	193,635	715,352	1,820,308	255,190
Agricultural chemicals	148,795	421,328	678,032	1,116,177	324,808
Industrial chemicals	657,697	2,879,271	9,119,940	32,441,071	5,673,745
Other chemicals	275,024	732,328	3,013,340	9,283,528	1,208,363
Nonelectrical machinery	1,619,786	4,543,134	33,371,652	109,901,639	8,517,448
Farm machinery	7,274	20,322	62,257	105,436	30,894
Construction machinery	170,857	622,518	1,550,159	4,539,509	615,859
Office machinery and computers	287,088	1,289,448	20,421,918	75,304,945	4,314,138
Other nonelectrical machinery	1,154,567	2,610,846	11,337,318	29,951,749	3,556,557

Electrical machinery	5,449,590	15,308,265	62,903,273	186,338,138	19,918,362
Household appliances	379,354	1,473,990	5,113,634	8,920,646	2,449,297
Communication equipment	2,690,290	6,748,263	28,890,560	75,412,819	10,109,288
Electronic components	1,496,885	4,642,779	19,029,095	73,297,736	1,290,004
Other electrical machinery	883,061	2,443,233	9,869,984	28,706,937	6,069,773
Transport equipment	1,429,584	6,046,633	10,786,016	30,201,357	4,019,598
Motor vehicles and equipment	275,738	854,101	4,119,487	13,879,435	770,761
Other transport equipment	1,153,846	5,192,532	6,666,529	16,321,922	3,248,837
Other manufacturing	22,181,030	46,434,273	129,468,588	219,145,317	73,991,027
Tobacco	31,602	141,180	1,123,437	2,710,042	881,111
Textiles and apparel	10,681,181	21,990,140	58,399,709	88,139,101	37,756,419
Leather and leather goods	1,938,555	4,992,661	15,034,178	26,440,852	9,951,212
Pulp and paper	104,362	272,341	1,352,956	4,955,717	398,102
Paper products	163,703	229,285	943,937	2,329,828	544,110
Printing and publishing	141,183	264,745	863,964	2,112,456	174,366
Rubber products	283,286	669,848	1,933,883	4,012,348	693,181
Plastic products	381,948	1,037,387	4,815,120	10,955,936	2,850,202
Lumber, wood, and furniture	3,607,149	5,027,258	11,905,881	16,192,271	2,309,235
Glass products	114,405	304,852	959,950	2,256,762	651,440
Nonmetallic minerals	496,230	1,241,159	2,594,052	3,889,019	2,308,794
Instruments	1,517,636	3,398,382	9,641,167	21,875,646	4,337,914
Other manufacturing	2,719,790	6,865,035	19,900,354	33,275,339	11,134,941
Total	41,056,228	94,074,771	288,985,094	666,687,690	135,355,861

Source: NBER World Trade Database (1997).

Note: BEA = U.S. Bureau of Economic Analysis.

Table 5A.2   Estimate of U.S. Manufacturing MOFA Sales and Exports in Developing Asia (million dollars)

Industry Group	1977	1982	1989	1995
Sales				
Foods	548–612	873	1,330	3,866[a]
Chemicals	911	1,578	3,020	8,297
Metals	104	177	448[a]	1,273
Nonelectrical machinery	243	796	7,082	25,996
Electrical machinery	2,306	5,099	9,658	21,472
Transport equipment	195–212	417–589	1,718	2,056
Other manufacturing	754–801	821–1,026	2,354	7,362[a]
Total	5,125	9,933	26,008	69,230
Exports				
Foods	179	65–150	340	996[a]
Chemicals	139	189	891	1,518
Metals	69	53	67–397	581
Nonelectrical machinery	172	552–629	6,412	21,479
Electrical machinery	1,978–2,025	4,478	7,495	10,470
Transport equipment	26	234	333	357
Other manufacturing	311–358	326	990	2,126[a]
Total	2,921	5,954–6,024	16,095	37,493

Sources: U.S. Department of Commerce (1981, tables III.F5, III.H3, III.H4, III.H5; 1985, tables III.D3, III.E3, III.E4, III.E5; 1992, tables III.E3, III.F4, III.E7, III.F8; 1998, tables III.E3, III.F7).

[a]Includes New Zealand.

Table 5A.3   Estimate of Exports by Japanese Manufacturing Affiliates in NIE-4 and ASEAN-4, 1989 (million yen)

Country Group and Industry	In Local Markets	Sales Reported by Destination — Exports to			Total Sales	Estimated Exports[a]
		Japan	Other	Total		
NIE-4						
Foods	55,737	9,101	6,268	71,106	72,423	15,654
Chemicals	163,039	27,453	31,897	222,389	258,903	69,095
Metals						
Iron and steel	30,505	3,150	6,725	40,380	46,600	11,396
Nonferrous metals	196,465	1,975	26,109	224,549	231,924	29,006
Nonelectrical machinery	65,431	34,656	47,484	147,571	156,549	87,137
Electrical machinery	404,331	331,133	355,522	1,090,986	1,563,046	983,765
Transport equipment	191,890	8,569	36,156	236,615	367,415	69,449
Other manufacturing (total excl. petroleum and coal products)	290,172	66,029	52,059	408,260		159,573
Textiles	79,016	14,301	11,701	105,018	115,464	28,588
Pulp, paper, and products	3,303	128	1,494	4,925	4,925	1,622
Instruments	71,299	27,991	14,664	113,954	176,482	66,060
Petroleum and coal products	607			607	607	0
Miscellaneous	136,554	23,609	24,200	184,363	244,107	63,302
Total manufacturing	1,398,177	482,066	562,220	2,442,463	3,238,445	1,425,074
Excl. petroleum and coal products	1,397,570	482,066	562,220	2,441,856	3,237,838	1,425,074

(*continued*)

Table 5A.3 (continued)

Country Group and Industry	In Local Markets	Sales Reported by Destination				Total Sales	Estimated Exports[a]
		Exports to					
		Japan	Other	Total			
ASEAN-4							
Foods	5,585	5,882	9,451	20,918		39,342	28,838
Chemicals	108,655	9,049	9,609	127,313		161,471	23,664
Metals							
Iron and steel	44,258	387	234	44,879		83,083	1,150
Nonferrous metals	41,797	37,207	21,433	100,437		112,135	65,470
Nonelectrical machinery	42,361	301	543	43,205		45,154	882
Electrical machinery	106,628	53,508	145,217	305,353		366,308	238,395
Transport equipment	544,685	4,829	15,604	565,118		584,118	21,120
Other manufacturing (total excl. petroleum and coal products)	241,122	48,368	50,554	390,044			103,312
Textiles	84,086	18,268	22,021	124,375		130,312	42,212
Pulp, paper, and products	1,155	4,528	2,350	8,033		8,033	6,878
Instruments	1,383	4,334	15,487	21,204		22,945	21,448
Petroleum and coal products	84			84		84	0
Miscellaneous	154,498	21,238	10,696	186,432		191,334	32,774
Total manufacturing	1,135,175	159,531	252,645	1,547,351		1,744,319	482,830
Excl. petroleum and coal products	1,135,091	159,531	252,645	1,547,267		1,744,235	482,830

Source: Data supplied by Ministry of International Trade and Industry from its *Overseas Business Activities of Japanese Companies: The 1996 Basic Survey of Overseas Business Activities,* no. 6 (Tokyo, 1998).

Note: NIE-4 comprises Hong Kong, Korea, Singapore, and Taiwan. ASEAN-4 comprises Indonesia, Malaysia, the Philippines, and Thailand.

[a]Estimated by multiplying reported exports by the ratio of sales by all firms reporting sales to sales by firms reporting exports.

Table 5A.4 Estimate of Exports by Japanese Manufacturing Affiliates in NIE-4 and ASEAN-4, 1995 (million yen)

Country Group and Industry	In Local Markets	Exports to			Total Sales	Estimated Exports[a]
		Japan	Other	Total		
NIE-4						
Foods	140,143	11,193	16,722	168,058	259,870	43,165
Chemicals	105,792	7,568	89,986	203,346	391,538	187,838
Metals						
Iron and steel	61,165	2,692	10,155	74,012	82,088	14,249
Nonferrous metals	45,827	5,119	19,446	70,392	97,059	33,871
Nonelectrical machinery	130,972	67,811	62,505	261,288	369,535	184,304
Electrical machinery	817,658	406,712	578,192	1,802,562	2,792,722	1,525,919
Transport equipment	540,678	10,821	31,060	582,559	757,806	54,480
Other manufacturing (total excl. petroleum and coal products)	269,796	140,858	120,794	531,448		343,922
Textiles	64,335	10,084	17,126	91,545	197,248	58,628
Pulp, paper, and products	4,261	133	32	4,426	4,426	165
Instruments	46,141	102,509	37,739	186,389	219,808	165,394
Petroleum and coal products	7,270	49,400	45,392	102,062	124,851	115,958
Miscellaneous	155,059	28,132	65,897	249,088	317,184	119,735
Total manufacturing	2,119,301	702,174	974,252	3,795,727	5,614,135	2,503,705
Excl. petroleum and coal products	2,112,031	652,774	928,860	3,693,665	5,489,284	2,387,747

(*continued*)

Table 5A.4 (continued)

Country Group and Industry	In Local Markets	Exports to				Total Sales	Estimated Exports[a]
		Japan	Other	Total			
		Sales Reported by Destination					
ASEAN-4							
Foods	34,150	22,762	52,471	109,383	151,179	103,980	
Chemicals	229,804	11,854	40,229	281,887	402,790	74,422	
Metals							
Iron and steel	135,886	2,745	4,407	143,038	206,840	10,342	
Nonferrous metals	97,779	24,872	32,317	154,968	166,417	61,414	
Nonelectrical machinery	54,072	22,081	8,925	85,078	118,811	43,300	
Electrical machinery	446,731	551,024	523,113	1,520,868	1,984,968	1,401,915	
Transport equipment	1,104,801	30,190	67,336	1,202,327	1,920,034	155,742	
Other manufacturing (total excl. petroleum and coal products)	355,778	108,349	132,266	596,393		273,038	
Textiles	116,377	19,253	69,984	205,614	225,886	98,035	
Pulp, paper, and products	27,161	5,500	2,626	35,287	39,110	9,006	
Instruments	24,533	24,923	6,979	56,435	76,481	43,234	
Petroleum and coal products	3,702		20	3,722	3,722	20	
Miscellaneous	187,707	58,673	52,677	299,057	329,709	122,763	
Total manufacturing	2,462,703	773,877	861,084	4,097,664	5,625,947	2,124,173	
Excl. petroleum and coal products	2,459,001	773,877	861,064	4,093,942	5,622,225	2,124,153	

Source: See table 5A.3 source.

[a]Estimated by multiplying reported exports by the ratio of sales by all firms reporting sales to sales by firms reporting exports.

Table 5A.5   **Estimated Exports by Japanese Manufacturing Affiliates in Asia, 1977–95 (million dollars)**

| | Ramstetter | | | MITI: NIE-4 and ASEAN-4 | |
| | Asia | | ASEAN-5[a] and NIEs: | | |
Industry Group	1977	1989	1989	1989	1995
Foods	245	237	282	322.5	1,564.4
Chemicals	77	595	585	672.4	2,788.2
Metals	76	684	677	775.7	1,274.5
Nonelectrical machinery	45	555	558	638.0	2,419.8
Electrical machinery	787	7,873	7,741	8,858.8	31,127.3
Transport equipment	137	490	577	656.5	2,235.0
Other manufacturing (total)	1,322	1,207	1,250	1,905.5	6,559.2
Textiles and apparel	803	465	448	513.2	1,665.6
Instruments	519	742	802	634.3	2,218.0
Other manufacturing				758.0	2,675.6
Total	2,689	11,640	11,669	13,829.4	47,968.3

Sources: Ramstetter (1993) and tables 5A.3 and 5A.4.

[a] Includes Brunei.

Table 5A.6   **Exports of Manufactures[a] from Eight East Asian Countries by Industry Group, 1977–95 (thousand dollars)**

Country and Industry Group	1977	1982	1989	1995
Hong Kong				
Foods	256,802	662,472	1,882,668	3,582,198
Chemicals	348,964	828,680	4,026,423	11,383,580
Metals	255,766	693,988	2,609,562	8,053,573
Nonelectrical machinery	495,528	1,057,120	5,474,508	15,210,030
Electrical machinery	1,213,898	3,291,700	13,863,662	38,805,902
Transport equipment	74,193	481,051	654,222	2,646,318
Other manufacturing	6,835,003	14,235,886	42,949,392	88,915,715
Total	9,480,154	21,250,897	71,460,437	168,597,316
Indonesia				
Foods	465,239	482,282	1,480,611	3,186,468
Chemicals	73,437	102,084	594,328	1,964,915
Metals	190,621	271,415	1,327,256	1,497,760
Nonelectrical machinery	17,243	23,681	40,079	854,940
Electrical machinery	32,577	152,287	184,387	2,582,789
Transport equipment	10,836	49,998	50,953	498,228
Other manufacturing	1,271,806	1,852,418	8,385,785	18,638,042
Total	2,061,759	2,934,165	12,063,399	29,223,142
Korea				
Foods	951,604	1,093,836	2,154,627	2,615,023
Chemicals	237,418	775,222	2,421,485	10,017,341
Metals	955,248	3,426,428	6,379,956	12,926,587
Nonelectrical machinery	124,994	519,754	4,774,447	11,676,193
Electrical machinery	1,092,561	2,415,386	14,556,488	38,111,603
Transport equipment	699,307	3,429,626	5,737,720	16,281,059
Other manufacturing	5,544,306	10,512,615	26,642,572	29,879,132
Total	9,605,438	22,172,867	62,667,295	121,506,938
Malaysia				
Foods	958,905	1,710,206	2,585,565	5,219,501
Chemicals	89,057	191,460	964,498	3,351,459
Metals	743,853	705,840	1,006,563	2,339,194
Nonelectrical machinery	54,727	181,462	905,575	9,457,032
Electrical machinery	341,482	1,730,515	7,015,158	28,958,402
Transport equipment	36,139	92,722	459,995	2,098,706
Other manufacturing	1,429,386	2,850,005	6,363,782	13,334,417
Total	3,653,549	7,462,210	19,301,136	64,758,711

Table 5A.6 (continued)

Country and Industry Group	1977	1982	1989	1995
Philippines				
Foods	627,074	907,574	1,224,237	1,674,770
Chemicals	54,255	112,721	301,423	352,365
Metals	92,676	97,254	557,107	1,231,200
Nonelectrical machinery	10,787	24,787	287,288	503,733
Electrical machinery	28,986	132,519	1,509,044	2,644,959
Transport equipment	13,809	23,907	46,267	239,913
Other manufacturing	576,554	1,099,154	2,867,666	2,705,713
Total	1,404,141	2,397,916	6,793,032	9,352,653
Singapore				
Foods	465,869	879,931	1,393,198	2,498,570
Chemicals	293,950	1,773,415	3,175,826	6,993,314
Metals	218,151	900,026	1,894,330	4,390,085
Nonelectrical machinery	453,116	1,446,278	9,825,956	35,410,739
Electrical machinery	1,171,020	3,312,026	11,191,121	39,716,887
Transport equipment	395,719	789,503	1,545,859	2,517,585
Other manufacturing	1,069,305	2,364,878	6,393,573	12,871,241
Total	4,067,130	11,466,057	35,419,863	104,398,421
Thailand				
Foods	1,033,687	2,012,206	5,123,919	9,357,212
Chemicals	26,303	73,802	403,013	2,348,829
Metals	255,076	431,551	716,735	1,837,748
Nonelectrical machinery	19,571	33,687	1,435,820	7,560,101
Electrical machinery	66,745	349,718	1,883,851	9,616,727
Transport equipment	4,232	56,632	200,448	1,447,577
Other manufacturing	491,010	1,376,276	7,212,798	18,880,388
Total	1,896,624	4,333,872	16,976,584	51,048,582
Taiwan				
Foods	1,062,084	1,400,073	2,997,458	4,168,984
Chemicals	297,044	804,862	2,491,203	10,428,553
Metals	423,155	1,405,138	4,743,574	9,683,010
Nonelectrical machinery	443,820	1,256,365	10,627,979	29,228,871
Electrical machinery	1,502,321	3,924,114	12,699,562	25,900,869
Transport equipment	195,349	1,123,194	2,090,552	4,471,971
Other manufacturing	4,963,660	12,143,041	28,653,020	33,919,669
Total	8,887,433	22,056,787	64,303,348	117,801,927

Source: NBER World Trade Database (1997).

[a]Excludes petroleum and coal products.

Table 5A.7   Sales, Local Sales, and Exports by U.S. Manufacturing[a] MOFAs in Eight East Asian Countries by Industry Group and Country, 1977 (million dollars)

Industry Group	Hong Kong	Korea	Singapore	Taiwan	Indonesia	Malaysia	Philippines	Thailand
Sales								
Foods	D	44	5	D	5	D	379	33
Chemicals	122	4	D	78	58	58	270	53
Metals	D	0	50	0	4	3	D	D
Nonelectrical machinery	53	D	104	D	0	D	0	0
Electrical machinery	400	111	670	482	58	316	76	D
Transport equipment	0	0	D	D	0	D	D	0
Other manufacturing	141	D	27	48	136	D	171	67
Total	745	187	882	782	262	445	1,010	234
Local sales								
Foods	D	D	0	D	5	0	213	32
Chemicals	80	3	D	25	38	51	247	48
Metals	2	0	D	0	4	3	D	D
Nonelectrical machinery	D	2	D	1	0	0	0	0
Electrical machinery	40	D	20	40	D	D	48	D

Transport equipment	0	0	D	D	0	D	D	0
Other manufacturing	D	D	D	D	D	D	141	65
Total	145	59	60	224	155	106	750	D
Exports[b]								
Foods	0[c]	D	5	D	0	1[c]	166	1
Chemicals	42	1	2[c]	53	20	7	23	5
Metals	D	0	D	0	0	0	D	0[c]
Nonelectrical machinery	D	D	D	D	0	D	D	0
Electrical machinery	360	D	650	442	D	262–316	28	D
Transport equipment	0	0	D	D	0	1[c]	2[c]	0
Other manufacturing	D	D	D	D	D	D	30	2
Total	600	128	822	558	104	339	260	D

Source: U.S. Department of Commerce (1981, tables III.F5, III.H3, III.H4, III.H5).

Note: D = suppressed in source.

[a] Excludes petroleum and coal products.

[b] Sales minus local sales unless otherwise indicated.

[c] Sum of tables III.H4 and III.H5.

Table 5A.8   Sales, Local Sales, and Exports by U.S. Manufacturing[a] MOFAs in Eight East Asian Countries by Industry Group and Country, 1982 (million dollars)

Industry Group	Hong Kong	Korea	Singapore	Taiwan	Indonesia	Malaysia	Philippines	Thailand
Sales								
Foods	D	D	11	D	D	D	510	26
Chemicals	210	D	58	114	130	88	478	155
Metals	D	0	10	D	D	D	D	D
Nonelectrical machinery	92	0	536	D	3	D	D	0
Electrical machinery	641	267	1,034	820	159	1,335	335	297
Transport equipment	0	0	212	D	0	0	D	0
Other manufacturing	155	D	16	116	D	98	181	D
Total	1,135	414	1,877	1,496	484	1,618	1,678	521
Local sales								
Foods	D	D	3	D	D	D	411	D
Chemicals	145	D	16	102	D	75	454	D
Metals	D	0	2	D	D	D	D	D
Nonelectrical machinery	20	0	78	D	3	D	D	D
Electrical machinery	57	≤35[b]	43	93	50	52	92	35

Transport equipment	0	0	4	D	0	0	D	0
Other manufacturing	D	D	7	D	D	84	D	D
Total	256	148–180	154	608	306–375	299	1,233	D
Exports[c]								
Foods	0	1[d]	8	0[d]	0[d]	2[d]	99	D
Chemicals	65	0	42	12	D	13	24	D
Metals	D	0	8	D	0[d]	0[d]	D	0[d]
Nonelectrical machinery	72	0	458	D	0	8[d]	D	0
Electrical machinery	584	232[d]–264	991	727	109	1,283	243	262
Transport equipment	0	0	208	D	0	0	D	0
Other manufacturing	D	1[d]	9	D	D	14	D	6
Total	879	234[d]–266	1,723	888	109–178[d]	1,319	445	268–486

Source: U.S. Department of Commerce (1985, tables III.D3, III.E3, III.E4, III.E5).

Note: D = suppressed in source.

[a] Excludes petroleum and coal products.
[b] Total sales minus exports.
[c] Sales minus local sales unless otherwise indicated.
[d] Sum of tables III.E4 and III.E5.

Table 5A.9   Sales, Local Sales, and Exports by U.S. Manufacturing[a] MOFAs in Eight East Asian Countries by Industry Group and Country, 1989 (million dollars)

Industry Group	Hong Kong	Korea	Singapore	Taiwan	Indonesia	Malaysia	Philippines	Thailand
Sales								
Foods	D	289	109	245	D	D	461	89
Chemicals	250	167	523	494	156	189	590	342
Metals	D	D	89	D	4	D	0	D
Nonelectrical machinery	610	33	3,800	1,094	D	50	D	D
Electrical machinery	1,382	644	2,832	1,641	≤42	2,090	404	633
Transport equipment	D	D	} 226	D	0	0	0	0
Other manufacturing	1,139	338	}	314	D	D	D	100
Total	3,543	1,518	7,579	4,879	341	2,681	1,664	2,132
Local sales								
Foods	D	286	30	D	D	D	284	30
Chemicals	163	154	119	421	150	165	576	337
Metals	D	D	31	8	4	D	0	D

Nonelectrical machinery	142	D	171	≤365[b]	D	D	0	≤247[b]
Electrical machinery	457	130	562	605	D	286	89	D
Transport equipment	0	D	3	D	0	0	0	0
Other manufacturing	230	311	54	203	D	166	154	77
Total	1,111	933	970	2,615	≥154	678	1,103	570
Exports[c]								
Foods	D	3	79	D	1[d]	2[d]	177	59
Chemicals	87	13	404	73	6	24	14	5
Metals	D	D	68	D	0	D	0	6[d]
Nonelectrical machinery	468	D	3,629	≥729	0[d]	D	D	D
Electrical machinery	925	514	2,270	1,036	D	1,804	315	≥386
Transport equipment	D	0[d]	169	0[d]	0	0	0	0
Other manufacturing	909	27		111	D	D	D	23
Total	2,432	585	6,609	2,264	≤187	2,003	561	1,558

Source: U.S. Department of Commerce (1992, tables III.E3, III.F4, III.F7, III.F8).

Note: D = suppressed in source.

[a] Excludes petroleum and coal products.

[b] Total sales minus exports.

[c] Sales minus local sales unless otherwise indicated.

[d] Sum of tables III.F4 and III.F8.

Table 5A.10 Sales, Local Sales, and Exports by U.S. Manufacturing[a] MOFAs in Eight East Asian Countries by Industry Group and Country, 1995 (million dollars)

Industry Group	Hong Kong	Korea	Singapore	Taiwan	Indonesia	Malaysia	Philippines	Thailand
Sales								
Foods	106	460	110	422	90	D	909	373
Chemicals	1,025	566	1,152	1,304	405	400	1,127	826
Metals	337	28	311	56	25	116	0	183
Nonelectrical machinery	974	514	18,233	1,157	144	D	32	D
Electrical machinery	3,271	1,311	5,792	2,513	89	4,970	1,389	726
Transport equipment	86	113	300	D	D	0	0	0
Other manufacturing	1,855	1,050	512	D	D	D	436	D
Total	7,654	4,042	26,410	7,948	999	8,288	3,893	5,086
Local sales								
Foods	D	459	13	371	87	D	613	199
Chemicals	625	543	545	1,021	377	345	1,110	778
Metals	189	27	60	4	23	47	0	177
Nonelectrical machinery	252	264	2,455	125	138	D	28	D
Electrical machinery	1,995	1,022	3,238	865	45	2,230	197	226

	1	2	3	4	5	6	7	8
Transport equipment	5	113	28	D	D	0	0	0
Other manufacturing	D	969	262	D	D	D	361	D
Total	4,399	3,398	6,602	4,637	829	3,389	2,309	2,157
Exports[b]								
Foods	D	1	97	51	3	D	296	174
Chemicals	400	23	607	283	28	55	17	48
Metals	148	1	251	52	2	69	0	6
Nonelectrical machinery	722	250	15,778	1,032	6	1,407[c]	4	D
Electrical machinery	1,276	289	2,554	1,648	44	2,740	1,192	500
Transport equipment	81	0	272	3[c]	0	0	0	0
Other manufacturing	D	81	250	≥207[c]	D	D	75	≥43[c]
Total	3,255	644	19,808	3,311	170	4,899	1,584	2,929

Source: U.S. Department of Commerce (1998, tables III.E3, III.F4, III.F7, III.F8).

Note: D = suppressed in source.

[a] Excludes petroleum and coal products.
[b] Sales minus local sales unless otherwise indicated.
[c] Sum of tables III.F4 and III.F8.

References

Blomström, Magnus, Irving B. Kravis, and Robert E. Lipsey. 1988. Multinational firms and manufactured exports from developing countries. NBER Working Paper no. 2493. Cambridge, Mass.: National Bureau of Economic Research, January.

Chen, Edward K. Y., and Teresa Y. C. Wong. 1997. Hong Kong: Foreign direct investment and trade linkages in manufacturing. In *Multinationals and East Asian integration,* ed. Wendy Dobson and Chia Siow Yue. Ottawa: International Development Research Centre; Singapore: Institute of Southeast Asian Studies.

Chia Siow Yue. 1997. Singapore: Advanced production base and smart hub of the electronics industry. In *Multinationals and East Asian integration,* ed. Wendy Dobson and Chia Siow Yue. Ottawa: International Development Research Centre; Singapore: Institute of Southeast Asian Studies.

Dobson, Wendy, and Chia Siow Yue, eds. 1997. *Multinationals and East Asian integration.* Ottawa: International Development Research Centre; Singapore: Institute of Southeast Asian Studies.

Kumar, Nagesh. 1997. Multinational enterprises and export-oriented industrialization in the host countries: An empirical analysis for the U.S. and Japanese affiliates. UNU/INTECH Discussion Paper no. 9704. Maastricht: United Nations University Institute for New Technologies, September.

Lipsey, Robert E. 1998. Trade and production networks of U.S. MNEs and exports by their Asian affiliates. In *Globalization, trade, and foreign direct investment,* ed. John H. Dunning. Oxford: Elsevier.

Lipsey, Robert E., Magnus Blomström, and Irving B. Kravis. 1990. R&D by multinational firms and host country exports. In *Science and technology: Lessons for development policy,* ed. Robert E. Evenson and Gustav Ranis, 271–300. Boulder, Colo.: Westview.

Lipsey, Robert E., Magnus Blomström, and Eric D. Ramstetter. 1998. Internationalized production in world output. In *Geography and ownership as bases for economic accounting,* Studies in Income and Wealth, vol. 59, ed. Robert E. Baldwin, Robert E. Lipsey, and J. David Richardson. Chicago: University of Chicago Press.

Lipsey, Robert E., and Irving B. Kravis. 1985. The competitive position of U.S. manufacturing firms. *Banca Nazionale del Lavoro Quarterly Review,* no. 153 (June): 127–54.

Mataloni, Raymond J., Jr., and Lee Goldberg. 1994. Gross product of U.S. multinational companies, 1977–91. *Survey of Current Business* 74, no. 2 (February): 42–65.

NBER World Trade Database. 1997. Cambridge, Mass.: National Bureau of Economic Research. CD-ROM.

OECD (Organization for Economic Cooperation and Development). 1998. *International direct investment statistics yearbook.* Paris: Organization for Economic Cooperation and Development.

Pangestu, Mari. 1997. Indonesia: Trade and foreign investment linkages. In *Multinationals and East Asian integration,* ed. Wendy Dobson and Chia Siow Yue. Ottawa: International Development Research Centre; Singapore: Institute of Southeast Asian Studies.

Ramstetter, Eric D. 1993. Prospects for foreign firms in developing economies of the Asian and Pacific region. *Asian Development Review* 11 (1): 151–85.

———. 1996. Estimating economic activities by Japanese transnational corporations: How to make sense of the data? *Transnational Corporations* 5 (2): 107–43.

————. 1997. Thailand: International trade, multinational firms, and regional integration. In *Multinationals and East Asian integration,* ed. Wendy Dobson and Chia Siow Yue. Ottawa: International Development Research Centre; Singapore: Institute of Southeast Asian Studies.

Sieh Lee Mei Ling and Yew Siew Yong. 1997. Malaysia: Electronics, autos, and the trade-investment nexus. In *Multinationals and East Asian integration,* ed. Wendy Dobson and Chia Siow Yue. Ottawa: International Development Centre; Singapore: Institute of Southeast Asian Studies.

Tu Jenn-hwa. 1997. Taiwan: A solid manufacturing base and emerging regional source of investment. In *Multinationals and East Asian integration,* ed. Wendy Dobson and Chia Siow Yue. Ottawa: International Development Centre; Singapore: Institute of Southeast Asian Studies.

U.S. Department of Commerce. 1981. *U.S. direct investment abroad, 1977.* Washington, D.C.: Department of Commerce, Bureau of Economic Analysis, April.

————. 1985. *U.S. direct investment abroad: 1982 Benchmark survey data.* Washington, D.C.: Department of Commerce, Bureau of Economic Analysis, December.

————. 1992. *U.S. direct investment abroad: 1989 Benchmark survey, final results.* Washington, D.C.: Department of Commerce, Bureau of Economic Analysis, October.

————. 1998. *U.S. direct investment abroad: Operations of U.S. parent companies and their foreign affiliates, revised 1995 estimates.* Washington, D.C.: Department of Commerce, Bureau of Economic Analysis, October.

Comment   Hong-Tack Chun

Lipsey examines the role of U.S. and Japanese manufacturing affiliates in the production and exports of eight developing Asian countries between 1977 and 1995. He obtains several interesting findings.

First, Japanese and U.S. manufacturing affiliates in this region had different specializations in 1977. Japanese affiliate exports were relatively larger in foods, electrical machinery, and particularly other manufacturing, mainly textiles and apparel, whereas U.S. affiliate exports were more concentrated in machinery, particularly electrical machinery. The difference in specialization between U.S. and Japanese affiliates is in large part due to the difference between home country comparative advantages of the two countries, as Lipsey points out. Electrical machinery, chemicals, and nonelectrical machinery are all industries in which the United States possessed comparative advantages, while the Japanese had comparative advantages in the electrical machinery and transport equipment industries. Japanese MNEs also must have had a comparative advantage in textiles and apparel, at least until 1977.

Second, by 1977, U.S. and Japanese MNEs were drawn to developing Asian countries mainly to produce for export, and in some industries, such

Hong-Tack Chun is a senior fellow at Korea Development Institute.

as chemicals and transport equipment, to produce for sale to the host countries. It would be interesting to compare the effects on host countries of direct investment with the different objectives of producing for export and for sale to host countries.

Another interesting finding is the drastic changes in the R&D intensities of major export industries in developing Asian countries over the fifteen to twenty years after 1977. The exports of developing Asian countries in 1977 were mostly from industries of low R&D intensity such as foods, metals, textiles and apparel, lumber and furniture, and leather products. However, the 1995 export distributions of developing Asian countries, especially those of Singapore, Malaysia, and Taiwan, were much more tilted toward high-R&D industries. In fact, in all the developing Asian countries except Indonesia, the share of high-R&D industries in manufactured exports was significantly greater than in such advanced countries in Europe as France and Germany.

Lipsey investigates the role of U.S. and Japanese affiliate companies in this transformation. In terms of source of exports, the importance of U.S. and Japanese affiliates declined in most industry groups, as the share of U.S. and Japanese affiliate exports fell from 14 to 9 percent between 1977 and 1995. However, the R&D intensity of parent companies suggests that direct investment by U.S. and Japanese affiliates might have played some role in this transformation. This is because the parent companies investing in developing Asian countries, even in 1977, were not only in relatively high R&D industries but, within those industries, were very R&D intensive relative to other firms. Parent companies in the nonelectrical machinery and electrical machinery industries with direct investments in developing Asian countries in 1977 were 40 to 50 percent more R&D intensive than those with investments in Europe. This difference may be due to the special treatment of foreign investment in high-R&D industries by developing Asian countries or to industrial policies that favor these industries in the region.

At any rate, the fact that foreign direct investment in this region was highly R&D intensive relative to other regions in 1977 must have had a positive effect on the drastic changes in the R&D intensity of exports by developing Asian countries between 1977 and 1995, particularly in the late 1970s and early 1980s. Supporting evidence might be found in a microlevel study that focuses on a few selected industries such as electrical and nonelectrical machinery for the period covering the late 1970s and early 1980s.

Interestingly, there seems to be a difference between the roles of U.S. and Japanese affiliates in the drastic change in R&D intensity of manufactured exports by developing Asian countries. U.S. manufacturing affiliates in developing Asian countries have generally been more export oriented than Japanese affiliates. The importance of U.S. affiliate exports of electrical machinery, especially in the early stages of development of the industry, stands out. Why were U.S. affiliates more export oriented than Japanese affiliates, especially in the earlier years?

The author does not give a direct answer himself and cites the interpretation of the data suggested by Kumar: "U.S. MNEs tend to relocate production of intermediate products for home consumption, whereas Japanese MNEs seem to shift production of more finished goods in relatively simpler technology industries. The offshore production by U.S. MNEs would seem from this more of 'globalized production' which links subsidiaries in home and host countries vertically."

However, the difference in the behavior of U.S. and Japanese affiliates after 1977, especially until the early 1980s, may reflect a difference in the stages of development of U.S. and Japanese MNEs. Japanese MNEs are newcomers relative to their U.S. counterparts. During the early stage of outward direct investment, the major objective of direct investment by Japanese MNEs might have been to sell to the host countries. This is partly confirmed by Kumar's finding that developing Asian countries were not attractive to Japanese MNEs as locations for export-oriented investment before 1989. Japanese outward direct investment increased rapidly after the mid-1980s, and Japanese MNEs became mature, more like their U.S. and European counterparts. This explanation is also consistent with the data that show Japanese affiliates becoming more export oriented as time passed.

Comment   Yuzo Honda

Exports or Foreign Direct Investment as a Strategic Variable

Both exports and foreign direct investment generate income to host country people. This is an obvious fact, but it has a strategic meaning in economic development. People cannot purchase valuable goods or services when they are poor. They can buy these goods only when they have sufficient income. With little income, however, they may still be able to purchase valuable goods if they can export their own goods abroad and earn income. Alternatively, if multinational corporations happen to start their businesses in host countries, they might hire local people and provide them with income. Therefore, exports or foreign direct investment can be a good starting point from which low-income countries can take off.

At an early stage after the Second World War, Japan adopted the same strategy. The Japanese government took various measures to promote exports. For example, it provided various tax exemptions and larger allowances for depreciation for export-related industries. The government chan-

Yuzo Honda is professor of economics at Osaka University.

neled necessary funds for these industries through government financial institutions with interest rates lower than the market rate. Also recall that the Export-Import Bank of Japan, a Japanese government financial institution, originally started operation as the Export Bank of Japan in 1951 and extended its operations to imports as well only in 1952.

In short, exports and foreign direct investment are sources of income to host country people and may play crucial roles in the take-off of an economy. Two comments pertain to this point.

First, the paper by Lipsey mainly discusses foreign direct investment or export structures in Southeast Asian countries, as well as the role played by affiliates of U.S. and Japanese multinationals in the region. Why is it interesting to examine these? The above discussion provides motivation for the paper. It is interesting simply because foreign direct investment and exports are important strategic variables in the take-off of an economy.

Second, the paper points out that the share of U.S. multinational sales to local markets relative to export markets tends to increase as time elapses. Two interpretations are possible. First, U.S. multinationals know more about export markets than host country markets at the start, but as time passes, they come to know local markets as well. Second, host country markets do not develop until after production for export starts.

Here again, however, I want to emphasize the role of the income that multinationals generate. When multinational companies start to operate, most newly employed workers are local people. The income they earn is just like an exogenous increase in endowment to the country. A rise in income increases the purchasing power of the local people and gradually increases sales to local markets. It is the income that host country people earn at multinational corporations that increases sales to host countries.

I have not empirically investigated yet, but I suspect that multinational enterprises can be kick-off players that create the series of income generation in a region.

Relative Values or Absolute Values?

The paper discusses whether the region's dependence on U.S. and Japanese affiliates together as sources of exports declined for some time periods. However, it is important to make clear whether we are discussing the issue in *relative* terms or in *absolute* terms. Both U.S. and Japanese affiliates have consistently expanded their activities in the region in absolute terms, even if their relative shares might have shrunk for some periods.

Look at the case of Japanese affiliates, for example. The paper compares exports by Japanese affiliates between 1989 and 1995 in table 5.7. Now figure 5C.1 plots the average exchange rate of U.S. dollars against yen on the vertical axis versus the annual Japanese current account measured in yen

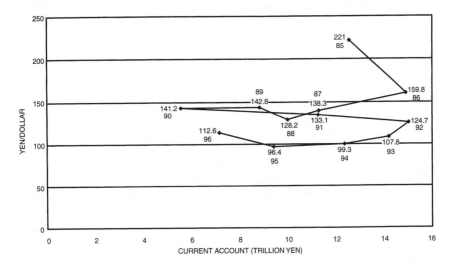

Fig. 5C.1   Japanese foreign exchange rate and current account

on the horizontal axis. During the six-year period 1989–95, the yen appreciated from about 142 to 96 yen per U.S. dollar, as shown in the figure.

During that period, the grand total of sales by Japanese affiliates both in the NIE-4 (Hong Kong, Korea, Singapore, and Taiwan) and in the ASEAN-4 (Indonesia, Malaysia, the Philippines, and Thailand) has increased by 2.3 times, and the grand total of the corresponding estimated exports by 2.4 times. (Compare appendix tables 5A.3 and 5A.4.) In particular, total sales and exports by Japanese affiliates in the ASEAN-4 have increased by 5.4 times and 5.9 times, respectively, in the electrical machinery industry.

In fact, around the end of 1994, many Japanese manufacturers established affiliates in Southeast Asian countries due to the deepening of appreciation of yen at that time. Incidentally, I believe this is one very important reason why we are having such a serious and lingering recession in Japan today.

The second point I want to emphasize is that both U.S. and Japanese affiliates vigorously expanded their activities in the region in absolute terms at least up until 1995.

International Joint Ventures, Economic Integration, and Government Policy

Kenzo Abe and Laixun Zhao

6.1 Introduction

Since the end of the cold war, the world economy has become more integrated. Cooperation between firms in different countries is the new trend. In particular, direct investment is one of the main strategies firms use to gain access to foreign markets. The Organization for Economic Cooperation and Development reports: "International direct investment grew rapidly and from more countries during the 1980s. . . . Mergers and acquisitions and strategic alliances became important investment vehicles as companies tried to increase sales quickly and cheaply. Steady economic growth, market integration, the globalization of business, the growth of regional economies, and technological innovation were behind FDI's (foreign direct investment) growth in the 80s. What happens in the 90s will depend largely on these factors" (OECD 1992).

Indeed, one of the chief arguments against the North American Free Trade Agreement was that a large portion of manufacturing activities in the United States and Canada would be relocated to Mexico, producing the alleged "giant sucking sound." It was also reported that a major reason behind the initiation of APEC was U.S. fears that Japanese firms would move in and have a headstart in the East Asian market, building their own networks and excluding outside competitors.

Kenzo Abe is professor of economics at Osaka University. Laixun Zhao is associate professor of economics at Hokkaido University.

The authors are grateful to their discussants, Shin-ichi Fukuda and Mahani Zainal-Abidin, and to an anonymous referee. For helpful comments the authors also thank Wilfred Ethier, Takatoshi Ito, Anne Krueger, and other conference participants. Suggestions by Jota Ishikawa, Koji Shimomura, and seminar participants at Niigata University also improved the paper.

Thus the effects of economic integration cannot be fully understood if we do not take FDI into consideration. In this paper, we focus on economic integration in the presence of international joint ventures (JVs). We have in mind the case of Japanese firms. They export to other Asian countries. But facing restrictions on trade and investment, they also directly produce in these countries. According to Japan's Ministry of International Trade and Industry (MITI 1994), nearly 70 percent of Japanese FDI in manufacturing to other Asian countries is in the form of JVs, probably due to legal limits on local ownership by foreign firms. Most of the production by these Japanese firms is sold in local markets.

International JVs are one type of strategic alliance between firms in different countries. As explained in Harrigan (1985) and Contractor and Lorange (1988), they are formed for various reasons. A project may be carried out jointly by more than one firm when the cost of the project is enormous. Restrictions on foreign ownership of local firms or trade barriers may facilitate the formation of international JVs, as in the case of Japanese firms.

In spite of the increase in international JVs in the real world, there have been few developments in their theoretical analysis. Svejnar and Smith (1984) introduced the Nash bargaining approach to study JV profit sharing in less developed countries. Abe and Zhao (1994) extended their framework to include competition between parent firms and examined the effects of trade barriers on resource allocation and welfare.

In the present paper, we model an international JV that aims to overcome trade barriers and to take advantage of low wage costs. We use this model to investigate the effects of economic integration on output, profits, and welfare. The international JV is located in a developing country. It is operated by a local firm and a firm from a developed country, both located in the integrated region. The product of the international JV is sold locally. The developed country also exports both an intermediate input and the final product to the developing country, subject to import tariffs in the latter country.

Economic integration in this paper is defined as a reduction of tariff rates within the integrated region. Jovanović (1992) identifies five types of international economic integration: free trade area, customs union, common market, economic union, and total economic union. "Economic integration" in this paper means a free trade area (FTA). The goal of an FTA is to remove tariffs and quotas on trade within the integrated region, but it allows each member country to keep its own original trade restrictions against nonmember countries. An example is the North American Free Trade Area, whose member countries will remove internal trade barriers in several steps.[1]

---

1. De Melo and Panagariya (1993) included more detailed studies of regional integration.

Our main results show the following: (1) Economic integration has two major effects. First, it reduces the tariff on the final output imported from the developed country, which in turn increases the exports and profits of the parent firm in the developed country and decreases the output of the international JV located in the developing country and the profits of the local firm. Second, economic integration also reduces the tariff on the intermediate input imported into the developing country, which in turn reduces the output of the parent firm in the developed country but raises that of the international JV in the developing country. However, the profits of the parent firms in both countries increase, and the welfare in the developing country may also rise. (2) A subsidy to the JV reduces the output of the foreign firm but raises that of the JV and the total supply in the developing country. (3) A subsidy to the JV raises the profits of both parent firms and the welfare of the developing country if the level of JV output is low enough.

The results above imply that economic integration may increase or decrease the welfare of the developing country, depending on whether the developing country imports the intermediate input from the developed country or not. The subsidy to the JV is a policy that is acceptable to both countries because it raises profits in both countries. This is perhaps why subsidies are adopted in various forms by many developing countries in order to attract FDI.

Viner (1950) first showed that economic integration could lead to trade creation and trade diversion. The former occurs because member countries eliminate internal tariffs, which leads to an expansion of trade; the latter occurs because member countries still keep positive tariffs against nonmember countries, which "diverts" trade to the member countries. Trade creation improves welfare because it results in efficient allocation of resources, while trade diversion could reduce welfare because it discriminates against the most efficient producers—the nonmember countries.

Viner's classical results are derived under perfect competition. In the present paper, we consider economic integration in an oligopolistic market structure. Furthermore, we allow the exporting country to produce directly in the importing country in the form of an international JV. A reduction in the import tariff raises imports from the developed country. However, the parent firms of the JV adjust JV output to maximize their joint profits. Thus changes in tariff rates affect the allocation of production in the two countries, but not total production, under a technology of constant marginal cost. As a consequence, economic integration in the present model does not lead to trade diversion through the change in the import tariff on the final output, even though trade creation occurs (in the sense that trade volume expands). In addition, the welfare of the developing country may be lowered by the reduction in the tariff on the final output.

Section 6.2 develops the basic model. Section 6.3 investigates the conditions needed for the JV to be formed. Section 6.4 examines the effects of economic integration. Section 6.5 analyzes the impact of the subsidy. Section 6.6 explains how our model works if the subsidy appears in other forms and provides some concluding remarks.

6.2   The Model

Consider a firm X located in a developed country A (e.g., Japan), which exports output of its final good, x, to a developing country B (e.g., a certain country in Southeast Asia). The exports are subject to a tariff, t. To evade the tariff and to take advantage of a lower wage rate, firm X offers to form an international JV with a firm Y in country B. The international JV produces the final good also. Its output is denoted by y. For analytical simplicity, we assume firm Y does not produce alone.[2] The production of final goods in both countries requires an intermediate input, which is produced in country A only. Country B imposes a tariff, τ, on the imported intermediate input from country A. In order to attract FDI, the host country offers a subsidy to the international JV. For each unit of its output, the JV receives a subsidy of s, which is eventually divided between the parent firms X and Y.

In addition to countries A and B, there is a collection of other countries, which is called country C. Because we want to focus on the effects of economic integration on the JV and firm X, we assume that firms in the other countries behave competitively and that they produce the final good using their own intermediate inputs. Let firm Z be a representative of these firms. Firm Z also exports its final product to country B, subject to a tariff, t^z. Then the export supply function of country C can be written as

$$(1) \qquad z = F(P - t^z),$$

where P is the price in country B, taken as given by firm Z, and $F' > 0$.[3] The price P (also the inverse demand function in country B) is derived as follows. Let the demand function in country B be

$$(2) \qquad D(P) = x + y + z.$$

Then from equations (1) and (2) we obtain[4]

$$(3) \qquad v = x + y = D(P) - F(P - t^z) \equiv d(P).$$

---

2. Our model can be extended to include independent production by firm Y straightforwardly.

3. If $F' = 0$, then our model corresponds to one without the third country. Our main results remain valid, though the formation of the FTA or the subsidy does not affect output z.

4. Since we do not change t^z throughout this paper, we suppress it in the inverse demand function.

Thus $P = P(v) \equiv d^{-1}(v)$ is the inverse demand function for firm X and the international JV. We assume $P'(v) = dP(v)/dv < 0$ and $2P'(v) + vP''(v) = 2P'(v) + vdP'(v)/dv < 0$.

We consider a two-stage problem. In the first stage, firm X decides how much to export to country B, given the tariffs and the subsidy to the international JV. In the second stage, firms X and Y negotiate to form and operate the JV. This sequential structure can be justified on the grounds that in practice, many developed countries first export to developing countries. Faced with trade restrictions or production cost disadvantages at home, they begin to undertake FDI in the form of wholly owned subsidiaries or JVs.

For consistency, let us first consider the second stage. The formation of the JV is determined by a Nash bargaining process between parent firms X and Y. If bargaining is successful, the JV is formed and it produces output y. While the JV uses labor in country B and an intermediate input imported from country A, firm X uses labor and an intermediate input obtained in a competitive market in country A to produce the final output.

The unit production cost functions for firm X and the JV are, respectively,

(4a) $$c^X = h^X(w^X, m),$$

(4b) $$c^J = h^J(w^Y, m + \tau),$$

where w^X and w^Y are the exogenous wage rates in countries A and B, respectively, m is the exogenous price of the intermediate input in country A, and τ is the tariff on the imported intermediate input.

The JV's profit function is then written as

(5) $$\pi^J(x, y, \tau, s) = [P(v) + s]y - c^J y,$$

where s is the unit subsidy to the JV. Thus the profit functions of firms X and Y are obtained:

(6) $$\pi^X(x, y, \alpha, t, \tau, s) = [P(v) - t]x - c^X x + \alpha \pi^J(x, y, \tau, s),$$

(7) $$\pi^Y(x, y, \alpha, \tau, s) = (1 - \alpha)\pi^J(x, y, \tau, s),$$

where α is firm X's share of JV profits and t is the tariff rate on the imported final good x. All profit functions are assumed to be concave in x, y, and α.[5]

If bargaining breaks down, the international JV does not produce. Then the profits of firms X and Y become

(8a) $$\Pi^X(x, t) = [P(x) - t]x - c^X x,$$

---

5. We suppress w^X, w^Y, and m in the profit functions because we do not change them in the comparative statics analysis.

(8b) $$\Pi^Y = 0.$$

The combination of these profits is the threat point of this bargaining game.

Parent firms X and Y bargain over the output level and their shares of the profits of the international JV, given the other variables. We define the Nash product as

(9) $$H(x, y, \alpha, t, \tau, s) \equiv [\pi^X(x, y, \alpha, t, \tau, s) - \Pi^X(x, t)]^\beta$$
$$\times [\pi^Y(x, y, \alpha, \tau, s)]^{1-\beta},$$

where β is the relative bargaining power of parent firm X.

The solution to this game is obtained by maximizing the Nash product with respect to y and α. Then the first-order conditions can be written as

$$\partial H/\partial y = H[\beta(\pi^X - \Pi^X)^{-1}\pi_y^X + (1 - \beta)(\pi^Y)^{-1}\pi_y^Y] = 0,$$

$$\partial H/\partial \alpha = H[\beta(\pi^X - \Pi^X)^{-1} - (1 - \beta)(\pi^Y)^{-1}]\pi^J = 0,$$

where a subscript on a function represents the partial derivative of the function with respect to the subscripted variable throughout this paper; for example, $\pi_y^X = \partial \pi^X(x,y,\alpha,t,\tau,s)/\partial y$, and $\pi_y^Y = \partial \pi^Y(x,y,\alpha,\tau,s)/\partial y$. Rearranging these equations, we obtain

(10a) $$\pi_y^X + \pi_y^Y = P(v) + vP'(v) + s - c^J = 0,$$

(10b) $(1 - \beta)[\pi^X(x, y, \alpha, t, \tau, s) - \Pi^X(x, t)] - \beta\pi^Y(x, y, \alpha, \tau, s) = 0.$

Equation (10a) implies that the parent firms maximize their joint profits through the JV by choosing output; while equation (10b) states that the two parents should divide the profits of the JV in such a way that the net gains from running the JV are equal for both parties, adjusted according to their relative bargaining power. These two conditions determine JV output and profit shares as functions of output x; that is, $y(\cdot) = y(x;t,\tau,s,\beta)$ and $\alpha(\cdot) = \alpha(x;t,\tau,s,\beta)$.

Now we turn to the first stage, in which firm X maximizes its own profits given in equation (6) by choosing the level of output, taking into consideration that y and α are functions of x. Substituting $y(\cdot)$ and $\alpha(\cdot)$ into equation (6), we obtain the first-stage profit function of firm X as

(6′) $$\hat{\pi}^X(x, t, \tau, s, \beta) \equiv \pi^X(x, y(\cdot), \alpha(\cdot), t, \tau, s)$$
$$= [P(x + y(\cdot)) - t]x - c^Xx + \alpha(\cdot)\hat{\pi}^J(x, y(\cdot), \tau, s),$$

where $\hat{\pi}^J(x,y(\cdot),\tau,s) \equiv [P(x + y(\cdot)) + s]y(\cdot) - c^Jy(\cdot)$. It is important to note the difference between the profit function in the first stage (in eq. [6′]) and that defined by equation (6). The former function includes solutions of y and α as functions of x, obtained by solving the second-stage game, that is, bargaining for the international JV.

The first-order condition to equation (6′) is given by

(11) $$\hat{\pi}_x^X \equiv \partial\hat{\pi}^X(\cdot)/\partial x = 0,$$

which can be expressed in the following expanded form, from the appendix:

(11′) $P(v) - t + vP'(v) - c^X = -[(1 - \beta)/\beta][P(x) - t + xP'(x) - c^X].$

The right-hand side of equation (11′) is negative (as shown in conditions [12] and [13] in the next section). The left-hand side of equation (11′) would be the marginal profit if firms X and Y merged to become a monopolist. Thus condition (11′) implies that the own production of firm X is larger than the level of output if firms X and Y merged and acted as a monopolist. This occurs because firm X can improve its threat point payoff in the second-stage bargaining game if its output is increased (condition [13]).

6.3   The Equilibrium

The equilibrium for this economy is determined by conditions (10a), (10b), and (11′). Given the policy variables t, τ, and s, these three equations determine y, α, and x.

We first investigate the conditions for the JV to be formed; that is, the JV produces positive output and is jointly operated by the two parent firms: $y > 0$ and $0 < \beta < 1$. Differentiating equation (8a) with respect to x, we obtain

(12) $\Pi_x^X = P(x) - t + xP'(x) - c^X > P(v) - t + vP'(v) - c^X$

$$= -[(1 - \beta)/\beta]\Pi_x^X.$$

The inequality arises because $v > x$, $y > 0$, and $P(v) + vP'(v)$ is decreasing by assumption; that is, $2P'(v) + vP''(v) < 0$. The second equality in equation (12) is the same as condition (11′). Condition (12) then implies

(13) $$\Pi_x^X > 0,$$

given that $0 < \beta < 1$. Thus, by comparing conditions (10a) and (A5) in the appendix, we must have

(14) $$\pi_x^X + \pi_x^Y < \pi_y^X + \pi_y^Y,$$

which expands as

$$P(v) - t + vP'(v) - c^X < P(v) + s + vP'(v) - c^J.$$

Using conditions (4a) and (4b), it finally boils down to

(14′) $$h^J(w^Y, m + \tau) < h^X(w^X, m) + s + t.$$

Expression (14') is the necessary condition for the JV to be formed. It implies that in equilibrium, given the combination of the government policy variables t, τ, and s, the wage rate in country B must be low enough to satisfy condition (14'). Otherwise, the JV is not formed. This result is supported by the fact that, in practice, many developed countries undertake FDI in developing countries to take advantage of low wages.[6]

A related question is when the JV degenerates to full-ownership FDI by firm X. So far we have assumed the bargaining powers of both parent firms to be exogenously given. But suppose both governments can impose some policy to affect the bargaining powers, then as $\beta \to 1$, that is, as parent firm X's bargaining power approaches 100 percent, from equations (10b) and (7) we have

(15) $\pi^Y(x, y, \alpha, \tau, s) = 0 = (1 - \alpha)\pi^J(x, y, \tau, s)$.

If the subsidiary in country B produces positive output, then $\pi^J(x, y, \tau, s) > 0$. It follows that $\alpha = 1$ by condition (15); that is, the JV approaches to full-ownership FDI by the foreign parent firm.

Note that besides legal limits on foreign ownership in host countries, in practice JVs are preferred to full-ownership FDI for various reasons. For either partner, the JV lowers total production costs relative to going it alone; the JV also enables each partner to benefit from the comparative advantage of the other. The foreign parent may bring better technology, while the local parent knows the domestic market and culture.

6.4   The Effects of Economic Integration

In this section, we analyze the impact of economic integration. When countries A and B form an FTA, import tariffs on both the final output and the intermediate input from country A are reduced. The two cases are analyzed sequentially. We consider the equilibrium with an internal solution, that is, $x > 0$, $y > 0$, $z > 0$, and $0 < \alpha < 1$.

Since α does not appear in equations (10a) and (11'), these two equations determine the outputs of firm X and the international JV. By total differentiation, we obtain

(16) $\begin{bmatrix} M & M \\ M + (1 - \beta)M_0/\beta & M \end{bmatrix} \begin{bmatrix} dx \\ dy \end{bmatrix} = \begin{bmatrix} 0 \\ 1/\beta \end{bmatrix} dt + \begin{bmatrix} k \\ 0 \end{bmatrix} d\tau + \begin{bmatrix} -1 \\ 0 \end{bmatrix} ds,$

where $M = 2P'(v) + vP''(v) < 0$, $M_0 = 2P'(x) + xP''(x) < 0$, and k is the amount of the imported intermediate input required to produce one unit of JV output. The determinant is

$\Delta = -(1 - \beta)MM_0/\beta < 0,$ if $\beta \neq 1$.

---

6. As will be shown in later sections, the tariff on the final good and the subsidy to the JV facilitate the formation of the JV.

6.4.1   The Tariff on Final Good Imports

Using condition (16), we obtain the effects of the tariff on final output:

(17a) $dx/dt = -\Delta^{-1}M/\beta < 0,$

(17b) $dy/dt = \Delta^{-1}M/\beta > 0,$

(17c) $dv/dt = 0,$

(17d) $dz/dt = F'P'(dv/dt) = 0.$

From conditions (17a) and (17b), a decrease in the import tariff on the final good raises the output of firm X but reduces that of the JV by the same amount. This occurs because, for any tariff rate and any level of output x determined in the first stage, the parent firms adjust JV output in the second stage to maximize their joint profits. Under the constant marginal cost of the JV, the total output of countries A and B remains constant. As a consequence, imports from country C to country B are not affected. In turn, total supply from the three countries remains unchanged. Hence, neither the price nor the consumer surplus is affected by the tariff on the final good.

The effects of t on the profits of the parent firms are examined next. Substituting $y(\cdot)$ and $\alpha(\cdot)$ into condition (10b), and differentiating with respect to a policy variable $i\ (= t, \tau, s,$ respectively), we obtain

$$[(1 - \beta)(\pi_x^X - \Pi_x^X) - \beta\pi_x^Y]dx/di + [(1 - \beta)\pi_y^X - \beta\pi_y^Y]dy/di$$
$$+ \pi^J d\alpha/di + (1 - \beta)(\pi_i^X - \Pi_i^X) - \beta\pi_i^Y = 0,$$

which can be rearranged to yield (for $i = t, \tau, s,$ respectively)

(18) $\pi^J d\alpha/di = -[(1 - \beta)(\pi_x^X - \Pi_x^X) - \beta\pi_x^Y]dx/di$
$$+ [\beta\pi_y^Y - (1 - \beta)\pi_y^X]dy/di - (1 - \beta)(\pi_i^X - \Pi_i^X) + \beta\pi_i^Y.$$

Using equations (6), (7), and (18) with $i = t,$ we can establish

(19) $d\pi^X/dt = \pi_x^X dx/dt + \pi_y^X dy/dt + \pi^J d\alpha/dt + \pi_t^X$
$$= [\beta(\pi_x^X + \pi_x^Y) + (1-\beta)\Pi_x^X]dx/dt + \beta(\pi_y^X + \pi_y^Y)dy/dt + \pi_t^X$$
$$= -x < 0,$$

(20) $d\pi^Y/dt = \pi_x^Y dx/dt + \pi_y^Y dy/dt - \pi^J d\alpha/dt$
$$= (1 - \beta)(\pi_x^X + \pi_x^Y - \Pi_x^X)dx/dt$$
$$+ (1 - \beta)(\pi_y^X + \pi_y^Y)dy/dt$$
$$= -[(1 - \beta)/\beta]\Pi_x^X dx/dt > 0.$$

In deriving the above, we have used conditions (10a), (13), and (A5) in the appendix. As expected, a drop in t reduces the profits of the JV but raises those of firm X, even though firm X owns a share of the JV. The reason is that firm X is producing less than the optimal level for exporting to country B, due to the tariff.

Now we turn to the more important question—welfare implications. The welfare function in country B is the sum of the consumer surplus, $U^Y(x + y + z)$, firm Y's profits, tariff revenues on imports from countries C and A (including both the final output and the intermediate input), minus the subsidy:

$$(21) \quad W^Y = U^Y(x + y + z) + \pi^Y + tx + \tau ky + t^Z z - s^J y.$$

We assume that the tariff revenue is transferred to consumers directly and the subsidy to the JV is financed by a lump-sum tax on consumers.[7] Thus the government budget is balanced.

Differentiating equation (21) with respect to t yields

$$(22) \quad dW^Y/dt = PD'dP/dt + d\pi^Y/dt + x + tdx/dt$$
$$+ (\tau k - s)dy/dt + t^Z dz/dt$$
$$= d\pi^Y/dt + x + tdx/dt + (\tau k - s)dy/dt,$$

where $D(P) = x + y + z$, $dU^Y/dt = PD'dP/dt = 0$, and $dz/dt = 0$ by conditions (17c) and (17d). The first term on the right-hand side of equation (22) is the effect on firm Y's profits, which is positive. The last three terms are the effect on government revenue in country B. If t and s are sufficiently small, this effect is positive because $dy/dt > 0$. Thus a reduction in t will reduce welfare in country B if t and s are sufficiently small.

Economic integration results in lower internal import tariffs in the integrated region. From the above, we can state one effect of economic integration, which is the effect brought about by the reduction of the import tariff on the final output of firm X.

PROPOSITION 1. *In the presence of the international JV, the formation of the FTA leads to trade creation in that it raises the exports of the developed country to the developing country, while it reduces the output of the JV. It increases the profits of the parent firm in the developed country but reduces those of the parent firm in the developing country. Finally, it reduces the welfare of the developing country if the tariff and the subsidy to the JV are sufficiently small.*

The profits of firm X increase because economic integration reduces production distortions in country A by lowering tariffs imposed on its

---

7. Note that we call $U^Y(x + y + z)$ the consumer surplus, although we assume that the government surplus is transferred to consumers.

exports to country B. This causes JV output to decrease, which reduces parent firm Y's profits. Because total supply of the good and in turn consumer surplus in country B are not affected, welfare in country B decreases.

6.4.2   The Tariff on Intermediate Input Imports

Economic integration also reduces the tariff on the imported intermediate input. From condition (16), we obtain the effects of the tariff on the intermediate input as

$$(23a) \qquad dx/d\tau \; = \; k\Delta^{-1}M \; > \; 0,$$

$$(23b) \qquad dy/d\tau \; = \; -k\Delta^{-1}[M + (1 - \beta)M_0/\beta] \; < \; 0,$$

$$(23c) \qquad dv/d\tau \; = \; -k\Delta^{-1}(1 - \beta)M_0/\beta \; < \; 0,$$

$$(23d) \qquad dz/d\tau \; = \; F'P'dv/d\tau \; > \; 0.$$

Thus a decrease in the import tariff on the intermediate input used by the JV raises the output of the JV but reduces those of firms X and Z. This occurs because firm X reduces its output in expectation of the increase of y. In addition, condition (13) shows that the decrease in x also reduces firm X's threat point payoff, which raises firm X's net gains in the bargaining game for the JV (i.e., the difference between the regular profit and the threat point payoff decreases). This makes firm X less aggressive in negotiations. As a consequence, the reduction in x is less than the increase in y, which causes the price to decrease and in turn raises the output of country C. It follows that the net effect is an increase in the total supply of final output from the three countries. As a result, consumer surplus rises.

The effects of τ on the profits of the parent firms can be obtained by using equations (6), (7), and (18) with $i = \tau$:

$$(24) \qquad d\pi^X/d\tau \; = \; \pi_x^X dx/d\tau + \pi_y^X dy/d\tau + \pi^1 d\alpha/d\tau + \pi_\tau^X$$

$$= \; \beta(\pi_\tau^X + \pi_\tau^Y)$$

$$= \; -\beta ky \; < \; 0,$$

$$(25) \qquad d\pi^Y/d\tau \; = \; \pi_x^Y dx/d\tau + \pi_y^Y dy/d\tau - \pi^1 d\alpha/d\tau$$

$$= \; (1 - \beta)(\pi_\tau^X + \pi_\tau^Y) - \{[(1 - \beta)/\beta]\Pi_x^X\}dx/d\tau$$

$$= \; -[(1 - \beta)/\beta]\Pi_x^X dx/d\tau - (1 - \beta)ky \; < \; 0.$$

Conditions (24) and (25) imply that a decrease in τ will raise the profits of the JV as well as those of firm X. Even though firm X's exports fall, its total profits rise because its revenue from the JV is increased due to the reduction in τ.

Next, using equation (21), we obtain the welfare effect of τ:

(26) $dW^Y/d\tau = PD'dP/d\tau + d\pi^Y/d\tau + tdx/d\tau + ky$

$$+ (\tau k - s)dy/d\tau + t^z dz/d\tau.$$

The sign of equation (26) is ambiguous. But if t, t^z, s, and y are sufficiently small, then $dW/d\tau$ approximates the expression $PD'dP/d\tau + d\pi^Y/d\tau + \tau k dy/d\tau$. Thus it is negatively signed; that is, a reduction in τ will raise welfare in country B.

Summarizing the above, we can state a second effect of economic integration.

PROPOSITION 2. *Economic integration between the developed country and the developing country also reduces the tariff rate on the imported intermediate input. In the presence of the international JV, it reduces the final good exports of the former to the latter, while it raises the output of the JV. It increases the profits of the parent firms in both countries. For small values of the policy variables, it also raises welfare in the developing country if JV output is small initially.*

From propositions 1 and 2, economic integration as modeled in the present paper has two (somewhat) opposing effects: On the one hand, it reduces the tariff on the final good imported from the developed country, which in turn increases the exports and profits of the parent firm in the developed country and decreases the output of the international JV located in the developing country, the profits of the local firm, and welfare in the developing country. On the other hand, it also reduces the tariff on the intermediate input imported into the developing country, which in turn reduces the output of the parent firm in the developed country but raises that of the international JV in the developing country. However, the profits of the parent firms in both countries increase, and welfare in the developing country may also rise.

6.5   The Government Subsidy to the Joint Venture

In this section, we investigate the impact of the government subsidy to the international JV. From condition (16), we obtain

(27a) $dx/ds = -\Delta^{-1}M < 0,$

(27b) $dy/ds = \Delta^{-1}[M + (1 - \beta)M_0/\beta] > 0,$

(27c) $dv/ds = \Delta^{-1}(1 - \beta)M_0/\beta > 0,$

(27d) $dz/ds = F'P'dv/ds < 0.$

As expected, a subsidy to the JV raises the output of the JV and reduces those of the foreign firms. But the increase outweighs the reduction, and the net effect is an increase in the total supply and a reduction in the price.

The effects of the subsidy on the profits of the parent firms can be obtained by using equations (16) and (18):

(28) $d\pi^X/ds = \pi_x^X dx/ds + \pi_y^X dy/ds + \pi^J d\alpha/ds + \pi_s^X$

$= \beta y > 0,$

(29) $d\pi^Y/ds = \pi_x^Y dx/ds + \pi_y^Y dy/ds - \pi^J d\alpha/ds + \pi_s^Y$

$= -[(1 - \beta)/\beta]\Pi_x^X dx/ds + (1 - \beta)y > 0.$

Thus the profits of both parent firms are increased by the subsidy to the JV, even though parent firm X's output is reduced. Firm X is more than compensated by the increase in its profits from the JV.

Using equation (21), we obtain the welfare effect of the subsidy as

(30) $dW^Y/ds = PD'dP/ds + d\pi^Y/ds + tdx/ds - y$

$+ (\tau k - s)dy/ds + t^z dz/ds.$

The sign of expression (30) is ambiguous. But if t, t^z, s, and y are sufficiently small, the welfare change can be approximately expressed as $PD'dP/ds + d\pi^Y/ds + \tau k dy/ds$. Then it is positively signed; that is, an increase in s will raise welfare in country B. Thus the subsidy to the JV works almost exactly like a reduction in the import tariff on the intermediate input the JV uses.

We are now in a position to state the impact of the subsidy to the JV.

PROPOSITION 3. *A subsidy to the international JV reduces the outputs of the foreign firms but raises that of the JV and the total supply of the good in the developing country and reduces the price. It increases the profits of the parent firms in both countries. For small values of the policy variables, it also raises welfare in the developing country if JV output is small initially.*

Note the above restrictive conditions for welfare to increase in country B. If the values of the policy variables are large, the welfare effect of the subsidy is ambiguous; and if JV output is large, the cost of the subsidy outweighs the gain in country B, resulting in a welfare loss because a portion of JV profits goes to firm X while country B bears the whole cost of the subsidy.[8]

8. Also, in a more general framework, a subsidy to one sector is a cost to other sectors, which may bring inefficient allocation of resources and result in a welfare loss in the whole economy.

6.6   Concluding Remarks

This paper used a simple model to analyze economic integration and other trade policies in the presence of an international JV in a developing country. We showed that while economic integration benefits the firm in the developed country, it may increase or decrease the welfare of the developing country, depending on whether the developing country imports an intermediate input from the developed country or not. A policy beneficial to both countries is a subsidy to the international JV.

In practice, the subsidy posited in the present paper can appear in various forms (see Slemrod 1995; Sumantoro 1984; China, Ministry of Foreign Relations 1987). For instance, many developing countries (e.g., China and the ASEAN countries) provide tax concessions to attract FDI, based on JV output, or on the volume of foreign capital attracted, or on the amount of local content used by the JV. In such cases, our model and results would remain the same if we assume fixed-coefficient production technology; that is, subsidies or tax credits to outputs work the same way as those on inputs. Some countries also allow accelerated depreciation in JVs. As can be seen in equation (5), accelerated depreciation is similar to a reduction in unit cost, c^J, by some proportion, which brings the same effects as the subsidy s. Another common form of tax holiday is a reduction of the corporate tax paid by the JV. Such a policy is qualitatively similar to a subsidy to JV output, which would not alter the results of the present paper.

The purpose of the paper has been to construct a model addressing the major pattern of FDI in East Asia, that is, shared ownership, and policies related to economic integration. In doing so, we have abstracted from modeling FDI from countries outside of the integrated region. Our model can be extended to include the situation in which the outside country C also forms a JV in the developing country. The developing country may gain by "playing off" the two foreign countries against each other, that is, making simultaneous but independent offers to form JVs with both countries. If bargaining in one game breaks down, the threat point payoff for the developing country is positive because it can form a JV with the other foreign country.

Often a developed country undertakes FDI in a developing country and sells the final product in a third country. If outputs are sold in a country outside of the integrated region, our results on output and profits remain valid but those on welfare may change. In particular, because consumer surplus disappears in country B, the level of welfare falls in country B for each of the policies we have analyzed.

Suppose instead of forming an FTA, country B conducts unilateral tariff reduction for all imports, then the effects on resource allocation and welfare can be studied by letting $dt^Z = dt < 0$. Certainly a reduction in t raises x and reduces y, but by equation (3), a reduction in t^Z may reduce both x and y. The total effects depend on the elasticity of the inverse demand curve and are generally ambiguous.

Many Japanese firms produce in Southeast Asian countries (e.g., Thailand) and import back to Japan, to take advantage of low wages. Although the structure of our model is a little different, our paper can still shed light on such cases. Suppose Thailand imposes a tariff on intermediate inputs imported from Japan and Japan imposes a tariff on final outputs imported from Thailand, then economic integration reduces both types of tariffs, which increases both Thailand's imports of inputs and its exports of final outputs. As a result, welfare in both countries may rise.

Some developing countries encourage local firms to form JVs with foreign firms in order to obtain better technology. In this paper we have abstracted from analyzing endogenous technology transfer. We conjecture that a subsidy to the JV would increase such technology transfer.

Appendix

This appendix derives an explicit expression for condition (11). Note that

(A1)
$$
\begin{aligned}
\hat{\pi}_x^X + \hat{\pi}_x^Y &= (\pi_x^X + \pi_y^X y_x + \pi_\alpha^X \alpha_x) + (\pi_x^Y + \pi_y^Y y_x + \pi_\alpha^Y \alpha_x) \\
&= (\pi_x^X + \pi_x^Y) + (\pi_y^X + \pi_y^Y)y_x + (\pi_\alpha^X + \pi_\alpha^Y)\alpha_x \\
&= \pi_x^X + \pi_x^Y,
\end{aligned}
$$

because $\pi_y^X + \pi_y^Y = 0$ by condition (10a) and $\pi_\alpha^X + \pi_\alpha^Y = 0$ by differentiating equations (6) and (7) with respect to α. Then condition (11) can be expressed as

(A2)
$$
\hat{\pi}_x^X = (\pi_x^X + \pi_x^Y) - \hat{\pi}_x^Y = 0.
$$

Moreover, equation (10b) is satisfied for any x and s when $y = y(\cdot)$ and $\alpha = \alpha(\cdot)$. Differentiating equation (10b) with respect to x, we obtain

(A3)
$$
(1 - \beta)(\hat{\pi}_x^X - \Pi_x^X) - \beta\hat{\pi}_x^Y = 0.
$$

From equations (11) and (A3), we establish

(A4)
$$
\begin{aligned}
\hat{\pi}_x^Y &= -[(1 - \beta)/\beta]\Pi_x^X \\
&= -[(1 - \beta)/\beta][P(x) - t^X + xP'(x) - c_x^X(x)].
\end{aligned}
$$

Therefore, from equations (A2) and (A4), we obtain

(A5) $$\pi_x^X + \pi_x^Y = -[(1 - \beta)/\beta]\Pi_x^X,$$

which can be expanded as in equation (11′).

References

Abe, K., and L. Zhao. 1994. International joint ventures and trade policy. Unpublished manuscript.

China. Ministry of Foreign Economic Relations. 1987. *Guide to China's foreign economic relations and trade: Investment special, 1987–1988.* Beijing: Policy Research Department and Foreign Investment Administration.

Contractor, F. J., and P. Lorange. 1988. *Cooperative strategies in international business.* Lexington, Mass.: Lexington Books.

De Melo, J., and A. Panagariya. 1993. *New dimensions in regional integration.* Cambridge, New York, and Melbourne: Cambridge University Press.

Harrigan, K. R. 1985. *Strategies for joint venture.* Lexington, Mass.: Lexington Books.

Japan. Ministry of International Trade and Industry (MITI). 1994. *White papers,* 282–84.

Jovanović, M. N. 1992. *International economic integration.* London: Routledge.

Nash, J. 1950. The bargaining problem. *Econometrica* 28:155–62.

Organization for Economic Cooperation and Development (OECD). 1992. *International direct investment: Policies and trends in the 1980s.* Paris: Organization for Economic Cooperation and Development.

Slemrod, J. 1995. Tax policy toward foreign direct investment in developing countries in light of recent international tax changes. In *Fiscal incentives for investment and innovation,* ed. A. Shah. Oxford and New York: Oxford University Press.

Sumantoro. 1984. *MNCs and the host country: The Indonesian case.* Singapore: Institute of Southeast Asian Studies.

Svejnar, J., and S. C. Smith. 1984. The economics of joint ventures in less developed countries. *Quarterly Journal of Economics* 199:149–67.

Viner, J. 1950. *The customs union issue.* New York: Carnegie Endowment for International Peace.

Comment   Shin-ichi Fukuda

This paper presents a simple but interesting model to analyze economic integration and trade policy in the presence of an international joint venture in a developing country. A key characteristic of the paper is its theoretical analysis of FDI by focusing on trade restrictions, especially tariffs and subsidies. The approach is quite different from that of other papers in this volume, most of which analyze issues related to FDI empirically by

Shin-ichi Fukuda is associate professor of economics at the University of Tokyo.

allowing various possible factors but paying relatively little attention to their theoretical background. Thus the contribution made by this paper is unique and important for this conference. In addition, although the model structure is complicated, most of the derived propositions are unambiguous, so their policy implications are clear.

However, most of the propositions in the paper hold only under the restrictive assumptions of the model. This type of criticism may not be appropriate when the purpose of this paper is only intended to satisfy theoretical curiosity. But when pursuing some practical policy implications, we need to think about the more general "role of foreign direct investment in economic development" that provides the title of this conference. Therefore, from more practical points of view, I will mainly comment on what restrictive assumptions this theoretical paper may have imposed.

My first comment is on the welfare effects of international joint ventures or FDI in a developing country. In addition to the low wage rates in a developing country, there are two reasons why international joint ventures are profitable for a developed country in this model. One is the existence of trade restrictions, more specifically the existence of a tariff. Because the developed country can avoid tariff payments by undertaking joint ventures, it obviously has an incentive to begin joint ventures with the developing country. The other reason is a government subsidy to joint venture firms. Because exporters cannot obtain this subsidy, it produces another incentive to start joint ventures. Needless to say, both are important factors in making joint ventures profitable. However, in explaining the welfare effects of FDI, the paper did not mention several important welfare gains that the developing country may enjoy.

Among the possible welfare gains, at least the following two factors are important. One is the technological spillover effects that joint ventures may have on local companies. Several papers in this volume explore extensively what technological spillover effects FDI can have. But these effects are completely neglected in this theoretical model. Modeling technological spillover effects is difficult because we need to extend the static model to a dynamic one. But even without a formal theoretical analysis, we can easily imagine that FDI will have various technological spillover effects and may benefit the developing country a lot. The other important factor is the creation of new employment in the developing country. Usually, before joint ventures start, most workers are employed in traditional sectors, such as agriculture, whose returns are very low. Therefore, putting aside welfare gains from tariffs and subsidies, joint ventures can bring an important welfare gain to the developing country.

My second comment is on the definition of "economic integration." In this paper, economic integration is defined as a reduction of tariff rates within the integrated region. Given this definition, the propositions derived in the paper are plausible. However, the definition is a narrow one, applicable in an early stage of economic integration. In fact, when we think of economic integration, we usually expect wider effects than those that tariff rate reduction will have.

One possible effect is the scale effect from integration. Although economic integration can have several types of scale effects, most previous theoretical and empirical studies have pointed out that it would have positive impact on the integrated region. Allowing additional factors such as increasing returns to scale in production, it is desirable to incorporate scale effects into the model for practical considerations. Another important effect of economic integration is that of monetary integration such as the European Monetary System. Monetary integration is usually considered desirable because it reduces the effects of exchange rate volatility on intraregional trade. Since it is not standard to introduce money into this type of trade model, this may not be an appropriate criticism of the theoretical analysis. However, in considering economic integration practically, monetary aspects are also far from negligible.

My final comment is on the policy implications of this paper. Given the various assumptions, the derived propositions are correct and clear-cut. However, even if we accept the assumptions, the propositions indicate only the direction of changes and say little about the quantitative changes that tariff cuts or subsidies would cause. In considering practical policy implications, it is more important to see how large the effects of a tariff cut or subsidy will be. I think that this would be possible by specifying profit functions in the model. In addition, various comparative statics analyses were done in order to discuss the second-best welfare implications of each policy. But it would be more desirable to discuss which policy is better than the others in terms of welfare more rigorously.

Comment   Mahani Zainal-Abidin

The paper by Abe and Zhao investigates profit allocation among joint venture partners in an economic integration. The joint venture is between a firm in a developed country (A) and another firm in a developing country (B). The production of the joint venture and its output are sold in the developing country. The paper starts with the premise that because of the imposition of tariffs on imports into the developing country, a firm that exports final goods into that developing country would go into a joint venture with a firm from the developing country to avoid the high tariff.

Mahani Zainal-Abidin is associate professor in the faculty of economics and administration at the University of Malaya, Malaysia, and associate fellow of the Malaysian Institute of Economic Research.

Besides avoiding the high tariff, the joint venture was formed to take advantage of the low labor costs in the developing country. The viability of the joint venture rests on the assumption that it receives a subsidy from the developing country's government. The developing country also imports the same final goods from another country, C, and these goods are subjected to the same level of import duties. The model is then expanded to allow for the use of an intermediate input imported from the developed country in the production of the final good. The ensuing economic integration in the form of a customs union lowers the tariffs on both final and intermediate goods. This leads to the reallocation of production level between the parent company in the developed country and its joint venture as well as affecting the level of welfare in the developing country.

With the advent of an economic integration, the unchanged level of imports from country C and the output combination between the joint venture and its parent company in the developed country as proposed in this paper need to be examined more closely. Imports from country C will have a distinct price disadvantage when the tariff on similar imports from country A, which has now formed a customs union with country B, is lowered. The reallocation of output must then involve all three producers, and country C's output cannot remain unaffected. Faced with higher prices, imports from country C will decline. This leaves the total supply to be shared between the joint venture and the parent companies. A lower tariff in the developing country does not necessarily mean that production of the joint venture will decrease while that of the parent company in the developed country will increase. This proposition is true if the tariff is the only reason why the joint venture was established. However, in the model, high wages in the developed country were assumed to be one of the push factors, and one of the equilibrium conditions is that the wage rate in the developing country must be low enough for the joint venture to take place. In addition, the joint venture was given an incentive in the form of a subsidy that will lower its cost of production or increase its profits. Therefore, when the tariff is reduced, the output of the joint venture may not drop because of these other two factors (wage rate and subsidy) that sustain profitability.

The paper uses a Nash bargaining position to represent the interest and returns to both the joint venture partners and includes a parameter to represent this variable. However, the bargaining position is largely seen from the point of view of the parent company in the developed country. The government of the developing country, which gives the subsidy, has quite a strong bargaining position to ensure that its interest is also protected. Thus, rather than taking a passive role as implied by the model, the government of the developing country will want to influence the outcome of the game. In fact, it can set conditions on the joint venture, especially if there are political pressures from domestic constituencies, since the benefit of incentives will be mainly enjoyed by a foreign company, assuming that the local partner is neither involved in the production process nor in possession of the technological capability. The conditions imposed may be in the form of a tax on the profits accruing to the joint venture (direct condition) or indirect ones such as employment objectives (usually a requirement that a certain number of local staff members be hired), transfer of technology, or a local content target. The imposition of these conditions is more likely if the local joint venture partner is a public sector company, in the sense that it has to meet government requirements. Therefore, the bargaining position should reflect the more active position of the developing country government.

Another aspect that has not been considered in the paper is that if the developed country also imposes a tariff on imports of similar goods, economic integration (customs union) will require this tariff also to be reduced. The commonly cited advantage of economic integration is that it results in trade creation and not trade diversion; with lower tariffs, production will be reallocated to the lowest cost producer. In this model, if the developing country has lower labor costs, the joint venture's output should increase, not otherwise. In a customs union all members have to reduce their tariffs. In this case, if the developed country had previously protected its market for the product that it exports to the developing country, this product now can be produced much more cheaply in the latter because of lower labor costs. Production will be then be relocated from the developed to the developing country. A good example is the increase in output of the automotive industry in Turkey. Prior to Turkey's entry into a customs union with the European Union, some EU automotive producers had established joint ventures to penetrate the Turkish market. But since Turkey's entry into the customs union with the European Union, these European producers have made Turkey their production base because the output, which is now produced much more cheaply, can be exported back into other EU developed member economies with lower tariffs.

Proposition 2 in this paper needs to be analyzed carefully. It says that economic integration, for small values of the policy variables, raises welfare in the developing country if joint venture output is small initially. This proposition is contrary to the aim of the joint venture, which is to increase output in order to augment the welfare of the population. If output is limited and a subsidy has to be given to produce the output, there is then no justification for the existence of the joint venture. The issue of welfare can be related to two aspects—the assumption about the subsidy and the definition of welfare. Although the paper has covered various forms of subsidy, their inclusion in the joint venture profit equation could be varied. In particular, the most important kind of subsidy, exemption from payment of income tax given on the basis of the amount of capital invested, could not be assumed to be proportionally constant to units produced. This subsidy is normally valid for a limited period of time. The benefit of the subsidy decreases as output increases, assuming that output performance partly reflects time period. Thus the cost of the subsidy to the government diminishes as output expands, and consequently, welfare will also increase.

The definition of welfare should be expanded to include employment generated and export revenue. It is acknowledged that a high proportion of international joint ventures in developing countries do not create as much benefit as expected. Studies have shown that about 30 percent of foreign investment costs the host country more in terms of the opportunity cost of its resources than it earns from the investment (Helleiner 1989). The benefits are especially questionable for foreign investment located in free trade areas where these companies are given exemptions from export and import taxes. Why then do developing countries still encourage foreign joint ventures even though they seem to reduce welfare and can only increase profits to the private sector? Welfare is viewed in a wider context where employment creation is considered a vital spillover in developing countries usually faced with the problem of high unemployment. When joint venture products are exported, the welfare effect becomes even more important because of the large employment potential as well as export revenue contribution. Many developing countries suffer from balance-of-payments constraints that can hinder economic growth, and hence the ability to generate export revenue features prominently in the government decision to grant a subsidy to joint ventures. Thus the welfare effects of a foreign joint venture extend beyond consumer surplus, private sector profits, and tariff revenues.

This paper constructs a general model to elucidate the effects of economic integration on international joint ventures, but it cannot fully meet its objective of explaining the major pattern of FDI in East Asia. First, East Asia has not followed the route of customs union toward economic integration. Most countries in the region opt for unilateral trade liberalization or multilateral trading arrangements. In these types of liberalization, tariff levels are usually low and direct benefits that can be given by developing countries to joint ventures are minimal because companies from outside the integration region can enter and compete effectively in the domestic markets. In the case of ASEAN, a free trade area has been proposed, but ASEAN members' external tariff rates, on average, are quite low. Meanwhile, many ASEAN members have introduced tariff reductions, and the liberalization is offered to all trading partners. For existing joint ventures in ASEAN, even though they now have a tariff advantage, the surplus is getting smaller as a result of the tariff liberalization.

Second, most joint ventures do not produce final products for domestic markets but are instead part of the production chains of multinational companies. Initially, joint ventures in ASEAN assembled intermediate goods that were later exported. Then joint ventures became almost fully integrated manufacturers, having taken over from their parent companies some of the R&D work, production of the intermediate goods, assembly of the products, and marketing to third countries. Joint ventures gained more autonomy and became more independent from their parent companies. In other words, joint ventures matured while economic integration (in the form of tariff reduction) was taking place.

This paper makes a commendable effort to analyze the existence of a joint venture in the context of economic integration. The authors may want to consider expanding the model to include other features of the joint venture relationship, such as transfer pricing. Since the joint venture partner from the developed country is the source and producer of the product while the other partner (from the developing country) is assumed to be inactive in the production process, the former has an incentive to engage in transfer pricing. As a consequence, the profits of the joint venture partner from the developed country may be higher than stated because of inflated transfer prices. In this case, the implicit bargaining position of the joint venture partner from the developed country is stronger, as evidenced by its ability to achieve higher profits than the other partner. Thus its desire to form the joint venture is far stronger than the other partner's, and this implies a weaker bargaining position.

The specification of products is critical in this model because the implications of output level and share and profits depend on it. Most joint ventures, particularly in the ASEAN countries, are not aimed at serving domestic markets. If a joint venture is part of an international production chain and it processes intermediate goods that will be sent back to its parent company in a developed country, a lower tariff rate will increase both the exports of intermediate goods by the parent company and the output of the joint venture because the production cost of the latter is now lower. A similar conclusion holds if the product is exported to a third country. In such a situation, the subsidy consideration is secondary to labor cost, which is the main reason why firms undertaking FDI locate their production in East Asia.

In conclusion, the model offers interesting propositions about a joint venture under economic integration, which rest heavily on the provision of a subsidy. Under the restrictive conditions stated, the model provides propositions about how a joint venture between firms from developed and developing countries could be mutually beneficial. However, the test of its validity lies very much with the empirical conditions prevailing and the variations of its assumptions.

Reference

Helleiner, G. K. 1989. Transnational corporation. In *Handbook of development economics,* vol. 2, ed. H. Chenery and T. N. Srinivasan. Amsterdam: North Holland.

The Location of Foreign Direct Investment in Chinese Regions
Further Analysis of Labor Quality

Leonard K. Cheng and Yum K. Kwan

7.1 Introduction

Cross-border investment by multinational firms is one of the most salient features of today's global economy, and many countries see attracting foreign direct investment (FDI) as an important element in their strategy for economic development. In this paper, we extend our earlier work (Cheng and Kwan 1999b), which attempted to uncover the factors that attract FDI based on the Chinese experience, by using a set of different proxies for labor quality. The Chinese experience with FDI is interesting for several reasons. First, China emerged as the largest recipient of FDI among developing countries beginning in 1992, and it has been the second largest recipient in the world (after the United States) since 1993. Second, unlike the United States and other developed economies, China has explicit policies to encourage the "export processing"–type FDI and has set up different economic zones for foreign investors.[1] Third, the most important source economies investing in China (i.e., Hong Kong and Taiwan) are close to some provinces but not to others. In contrast, Western Europe and Japan, the most important sources of FDI for the United States, are not particularly close to any of the American states.

Leonard K. Cheng is professor of economics at the Hong Kong University of Science and Technology. Yum K. Kwan is associate professor of economics and finance at the City University of Hong Kong.

The authors thank Gregory Chow for suggesting the partial stock adjustment approach adopted in this paper, and Anne Krueger, Shang-Jin Wei, Laixun Zhao, and an anonymous referee for their helpful comments and suggestions. The work described in this paper was substantially supported by a grant from the Research Grant Council of the Hong Kong Special Administrative Region, China (Project no. HKUST484/94H).

1. Until the early 1990s, the Chinese domestic market was not open to foreign firms in China.

The Chinese experience is an important case in the study of FDI, partly because of the sheer magnitude and fast growth of FDI the country has received in such a short period of time, but more importantly because of the diversity of the data. Due to changes in policies toward FDI and the occurrence of major economic and political events that caused changes in FDI flows, the Chinese case also serves as a natural experiment for us to test hypotheses about the incidence of FDI. We believe that the test results are not only relevant to China but also important in understanding the determinants of the location of FDI in general.

Figure 7.1 summarizes the Chinese data on regional FDI stocks by box plots.[2] Each box presents succinctly the regional distribution of the stocks in a given year; and the chronologically juxtaposed boxes reveal the time-series aspects of the data, in particular, the persistence of the median stock and the temporal variations of the regional distribution. The figure clearly shows that the location of FDI in China is characterized by enormous spatial as well as temporal diversity. A satisfactory empirical model must be able to explain these salient features in a consistent framework.

Potential determinants of FDI location have been extensively studied in the literature.[3] The typical approach is to regress the chosen dependent variable, such as the probability of locating FDI in a location or the amount of investment in a location, on a set of independent variables that on theoretical grounds would likely affect the profitability of investment. These variables typically reflect or affect local market potential, cost of production, cost of transport, taxes, and the general business environment faced by foreign firms. In contrast with the bulk of the existing literature that is based on a comparative statics theory of FDI location, some recent papers have emphasized the importance of the self-perpetuating growth of FDI over time (including the agglomeration effect). They include Smith and Florida (1994), Head et al. (1995), O Huallachain and Reid (1997), and Cheng and Kwan (1999a, 1999b).

As an extension of our earlier work (1999b), the present paper distin-

---

2. As will be explained in section 7.3 below, the stock of FDI is taken to be the sum of FDI flows since 1979, where FDI flows are measured in constant U.S. dollars. The box plot summarizes a distribution by the median (the horizontal line within the box), the lower and upper quartiles (the two edges of the box), the extreme values (the two whiskers extending from the box), and outliers (points beyond the whiskers).

3. Reflecting U.S. leadership in both inward and outward FDI, the existing literature has focused on the geographical distribution of FDI in the United States as well as the location of U.S. direct investment in other countries. Recent studies include Coughlin, Terza, and Arromdee (1991), Friedman, Gerlowski, and Silberman (1992), Wheeler and Mody (1992), Woodward (1992), Smith and Florida (1994), Head, Ries, and Swenson (1995), Friedman et al. (1996), Hines (1996), and O Huallachain and Reid (1997). Hill and Munday (1995) studied the locational determinants of FDI in France and the United Kingdom. Rozelle, Ying, and Barlow (n.d.), Cheng and Zhao (1995), Chen (1996), Head and Ries (1996), and Cheng and Kwan (1999a, 1999b) examined the case of China.

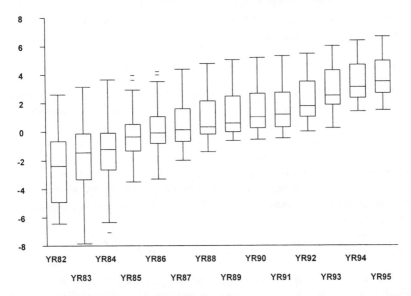

Fig. 7.1   Realized FDI stock (logarithmic scale)

guishes itself from existing studies by explicitly recognizing that (1) invest-ment flow takes time to adjust toward the target stock of FDI, (2) invest-ment flow depends on the actual stock, and (3) the target stock itself changes with the environment. Conceptually, the observed FDI stock re-flects the interplay of two forces. First, a "self-reinforcing" effect propels the stock toward an equilibrium level even without the inducement of pol-icy and other determinants of FDI. Second, in the meantime, these deter-minants do change over time, so that the equilibrium level is being contin-uously altered.

A partial adjustment model of FDI is specified in section 7.2. The data and estimation procedures are described in section 7.3, and the estimation results are reported in section 7.4. Section 7.5 compares these results with existing findings in the literature, while section 7.6 compares the actual and equilibrium stocks of FDI. Section 7.7 concludes the paper.

7.2   A Partial Stock Adjustment Model

Let Y_{it} be the stock of FDI in region i at time t and Y_{it}^* the correspond-ing equilibrium or desired stock. The variable to be studied is capital stock rather than investment flow because the profitability of investment de-pends on the marginal return to capital, which is generally a decreasing function of the stock of capital. Following Chow (1967) and Cheng and

Kwan (1999b), we assume that the flow of investment serves to adjust Y_{it} toward Y_{it}^* according to the following process:

(1) $$d\ln Y_{it}/dt = \alpha(\ln Y_{it}^* - \ln Y_{it}), \quad 0 < \alpha < 1.$$

Equation (1) provides a simple way of capturing the interaction between actual and equilibrium stocks. Besides its analytical simplicity, it is chosen because of its proven success in helping us to understand the evolution of and interaction between actual and equilibrium stocks of certain consumer durables. The equation says that the percentage change in the FDI stock is proportional to the gap between $\ln Y_{it}$ and $\ln Y_{it}^*$. Since $d \ln Y_{it} = dY_{it}/Y_{it}$, the equation posits that the rate of change of the FDI stock is proportional to the existing stock, holding the gap constant, and vice versa; that is,

(2) $$dY_{it}/dt = \alpha Y_{it}(\ln Y_{it}^* - \ln Y_{it}).$$

The term Y_{it} on the right-hand side of equation (2) represents a self-reinforcing effect. This effect is consistent with the agglomeration effect—positive externalities generated by concentration of industry in a locality—emphasized by Smith and Florida (1994), Head et al. (1995), and O Huallachain and Reid (1997) in their studies of FDI location in the United States, and Head and Ries (1996) in the case of China. It says that FDI attracts further FDI. However, in our model there is no agglomeration effect in the sense that Y_{it}^* is a positive function of Y_{it}.

The term $\ln Y_{it}^* - \ln Y_{it}$ implies that the self-reinforcing effect of Y_{it} on itself diminishes as the actual stock approaches the equilibrium stock. It captures a process of gradual adjustment toward the equilibrium stock and is in line with the investment literature, which argues that convex adjustment costs for changing the stock of productive capacity imply that the desired capital stock is attained gradually rather than instantaneously.

Thus, conditional on a particular level of the equilibrium stock Y_{it}^*, equation (1) specifies how the self-reinforcing effect (Y_{it}) and gradual adjustment process ($\ln Y_{it}^* - \ln Y_{it}$) interact to determine the actual path of adjustment. Because they both point in the same direction through a product term, it is impossible to decompose their individual contributions to the actual investment flow.

If $Y_{it}^* = Y_i^*$ for all t, equation (1) can be solved as a differential equation to yield the Gompertz growth curve

(3) $$Y_{it} = \exp(\ln Y_i^* - \exp(-\alpha t)).$$

Equation (3) describes the natural growth of the FDI stock that would have prevailed had there been no change in factors that shift the equilibrium stock. Therefore, equation (1) combines two elements that account for the observed accumulation of FDI. First, the self-reinforcing effect and the adjustment effect drive the FDI stock to an equilibrium level, and second, the equilibrium level itself shifts as a result of changes in the environment.

In empirical applications, equation (1) is replaced by its discrete version (where lowercase letters stand for logarithmic values, e.g., $y_{it} = \ln Y_{it}$),

$$(4) \qquad\qquad y_{it} - y_{it-1} = \alpha(y_{it}^* - y_{it-1}),$$

which, after collecting terms, becomes

$$(5) \qquad\qquad y_{it} = (1 - \alpha)y_{it-1} + \alpha y_{it}^*.$$

For the adjustment process described by equation (5) to be nonexplosive and nonfluctuating, $1 - \alpha$ must be a positive fraction. To estimate the above equation, we need to specify the determinants of y_{it}^*. Theoretically, the location choice of FDI is determined by relative profitability. If a location is chosen as the destination of FDI, then from the investor's point of view, it must be more profitable to produce in that location than in others, given the location choice of other investors. If the goods are produced for export, the costs of producing the goods and the costs and reliability of transporting them to the world market are most crucial. If the goods and services are produced for the local market, then local demand factors would also matter. In both cases, government policies such as preferential tax treatment, the time and effort needed to gain government approval, the environment for doing business, and so forth, would affect a location's attractiveness to foreign investors.[4] Depending on the relative importance of export-oriented and domestic-market-oriented FDI, however, the importance of the same determinants of FDI may vary.

Since FDI in China was primarily in the form of new plants, we focus on the statistical analysis of the location choice of greenfield FDI in the literature. Consistent with the theoretical considerations and empirical observations mentioned above, the existing literature has pointed to the importance of five sets of variables:[5]

---

4. A general empirical observation is that export-oriented FDI is more responsive to preferential tax treatment, but FDI that is aimed at the local market is more responsive to policies on market access and policies that affect domestic demand. The Organization for Economic Cooperation and Development has stated that "one factor influencing the role played by investment incentives is whether the foreign investment is intended to replace imports by local production or is geared to production for export. In the former case, it is likely that the effect of incentives will be relatively limited. The existence of a specific and often protected market is often the major determinant of the investment, as market protection is a powerful incentive. In the second case, on the other hand, incentives are probably more important" (OECD 1992, 81).

5. See the references cited in n. 3.

Access to national and regional markets

Wage costs adjusted for the quality of workers or labor productivity, and other labor market conditions such as unemployment and degree of unionization

Policy toward FDI including tax rates

Availability and quality of infrastructure

Economies of agglomeration

On the basis of the existing statistical analyses of the location of FDI in China, the United States, the United Kingdom, and France, we postulate that the desired stock of FDI in region i in period t, y_{it}^*, is a function of region i's infrastructure, labor quality, wage rate, regional income, and policies designed to attract FDI. Since our dependent variable is the per capita stock of FDI, we use per capita regional income to capture the regional market potential.

In Cheng and Kwan (1999b), three alternative proxies for labor quality were used, namely, the percentages of the population with at least primary school education, junior secondary school education, and senior secondary school education, respectively. None of these variables turned out to be statistically significant. Because they were generated by linear interpolation and extrapolation of actual census data for four years dispersed between 1982 and 1993, it would be desirable to see if alternative proxies might not perform better. Thus, in this analysis, we adopt three new proxies for labor quality. They are the number of teachers and staff in universities per 10,000 population (to be referred to as *university education*), the number of teachers and staff in secondary schools per 10,000 population (to be referred to as *secondary education*), and the *ratio of farming to non-farming population*.

As in Cheng and Kwan (1999b), we use three alternative proxies for the infrastructure variable. They are the *total length of road* per unit of land mass, the *total length of high-grade paved road* per unit of land mass, and the *total length of railway* per unit of land mass. A region's *real wage cost* is given by its average wage cost divided by its retail price index, and as explained above *per capita regional real income* captures the attractiveness of the regional market.[6]

The policy variables include the number of Special Economic Zones, Open Coastal Cities, Economic and Technological Development Zones, and Open Coastal Areas. Special Economic Zones and Open Coastal Cities were the two most important policy designations for attracting FDI to China, but they were confined to a small subset of regions along the coast. To a large extent, Economic and Technological Development Zones were an extension of the Open Coastal Cities. In contrast with these three

---

6. The use of per capita regional real income to capture the regional market and of road and railway density to capture infrastructure follows Coughlin et al. (1991) and Chen (1996).

policy designations, Open Coastal Areas were introduced later, were far more numerous, and were geographically the most dispersed. In terms of the benefits provided by these policy designations, Special Economic Zones were clearly at the top, followed by Open Coastal Cities and Economic and Technological Development Zones, and Open Coastal Areas would be at the bottom.[7] Given the positive and significant correlation of the policy variables Open Coastal Cities, Economic and Technological Development Zones, and Open Coastal Areas, we enter their sum as an aggregate policy variable (called ZONES) in our empirical model. In contrast, we leave Special Economic Zones (SEZ) as a separate explanatory variable. To allow a time lag for the policy variables to have an impact, their lagged values are used in the econometric analysis.

Collecting the above-mentioned explanatory variables in a vector x_{it}, we postulate a two-factor panel formulation for the equilibrium stock

$$(6) \qquad y_{it}^* = \pi' x_{it} + \lambda_i + \gamma_t + \varepsilon_{it},$$

where π is a vector of parameters; λ_i and γ_t are unobserved region-specific and time-specific effects, respectively; and ε_{it} is a random disturbance. That is, λ_i captures time-invariant regional effects such as geographic location and culture, whereas γ_t represents factors that affect all regions at the same time (national policy toward FDI, foreign demand for goods produced by foreign-invested enterprises, etc.).

Substituting equation (6) into equation (5), we arrive at a dynamic panel regression model ready for empirical implementation,

$$(7) \qquad y_{it} = (1 - \alpha)y_{it-1} + \beta' x_{it} + u_{it},$$

$$u_{it} = \eta_i + \omega_t + v_{it}, \qquad i = 1, 2, \ldots, N, \qquad t = 2, \ldots, T,$$

where $\beta = \alpha\pi$, $\eta_i = \alpha\lambda_i$, $\omega_t = \alpha\gamma_t$, and $v_{it} = \alpha\varepsilon_{it}$.

7.3   Data and Estimation Procedure

The exact definitions of the variables discussed above is given in appendix A. All real variables are measured in 1990 prices. Additional explanations of the data are given in appendix B. In our sample, a region is either a province, a centrally administered municipality, or an autonomous region. The stock of FDI in year t is defined as the amount of cumulative FDI from 1979 (the year China's open door policy began) to the end of the year. That is to say, we have not allowed for depreciation, but annual FDI was measured in constant U.S. dollars. While FDI stock figures were

7. See Cheng (1994) for a detailed description of the evolution of the policy. For our purpose, Shanghai's Pudong New Zone is treated as equivalent to a Special Economic Zone.

available beginning in 1982, most regions started to have positive stocks only in 1983, and some did not have positive stocks as late as 1985. Because of data availability, we confine our analysis to a balanced panel of twenty-nine regions over an eleven-year period from 1985 to 1995. The thirtieth region, Xizang (Tibet), had no FDI at all during this period and is thus excluded.

Equation (7) is a dynamic panel regression with a lagged dependent variable on the right-hand side.[8] We treat the time-specific effects as fixed but unknown constants, which is equivalent to putting time dummies in the regression. The treatment of the region-specific effects requires extra care. It is known that in a dynamic panel regression, the choice between a fixed-effects and a random-effects formulation has implications for estimation that are of a different nature than those associated with the static model (Anderson and Hsiao 1981, 1982; Hsiao 1986, chap. 4). Further, it is important to ascertain the serial correlation property of the disturbances in the context of our dynamic model because that is crucial for formulating an appropriate estimation procedure. Finally, the issue of reverse causality will have to be addressed. We have to deal with the potential endogeneity of the explanatory variables (notably wages and per capita income) arising from the feedback effects of FDI on the local economy.

Following Holtz-Eakin, Newey, and Rosen (1988), Arellano and Bond (1991), Ahn and Schmidt (1995, 1997), Arellano and Bover (1995), and, more recently, Blundell and Bond (1998), we address the above-mentioned econometric issues under a generalized method of moments (GMM) framework. The details are described in appendix C. It suffices to point out that we mainly rely on the system GMM approach of Blundell and Bond (1998), which uses not only the moment conditions for the first-differenced version of equation (7) but also the moment conditions for equation (7) itself, for the purpose of enhancing estimation efficiency. We have also performed extensive specification tests to ascertain the validity of our estimation procedure.

7.4   Estimation Results

Tables 7.1 and 7.2 report results for system GMM estimation and the associated specification tests for various combinations of explanatory variables. The selection of instruments and other econometric issues is first discussed with reference to table 7.2. One issue is the endogeneity of the explanatory variables. In the first-differenced equations we consider $\Delta x =$ (wage, income, education, infrastructure) as potential instruments. The assumption of weak exogeneity for wage, income, and infrastructure, under which the first differences of these variables lagged two periods serve as

---

8. See Sevestre and Trognon (1996) for a survey.

Table 7.1   **Estimation Results**

Variable	(1)	(2)	(3)	(4)	(5)	(6)
Lagged FDI stock $(1 - \alpha)$	0.5005	0.4343	0.4541	0.4938	0.5077	0.5427
	(10.28)	(8.97)	(9.27)	(10.50)	(10.07)	(11.84)
Wage	−0.3463	−0.5886	−0.5256	−0.4788	−0.6781	−0.3681
	(−1.62)	(−2.26)	(−2.07)	(−1.83)	(−2.44)	(−1.64)
Per capita income	0.6950	0.6587	0.5677	0.6598	0.8596	0.5954
	(2.60)	(2.45)	(1.91)	(2.48)	(2.83)	(2.25)
Labor quality						
University education	−0.1791					−0.0782
	(−1.18)					(−0.53)
Secondary education		0.1473		0.0124	0.0441	
		(0.40)		(0.04)	(0.12)	
Farm/nonfarm			−0.0112			
			(−0.07)			
Infrastructure						
All roads	0.2493	0.2345	0.2978			
	(1.96)	(1.89)	(2.52)			
High-grade paved roads				0.0180		0.0859
				(0.16)		(0.82)
Railway					−0.0600	
					(−0.64)	
Policy variables						
Lagged SEZ	0.3923	0.4825	0.4045	0.3070	0.7892	0.4118
	(2.19)	(2.61)	(2.28)	(1.96)	(3.42)	(2.62)
Lagged ZONES	0.0353	0.0989	0.0650	0.1292	0.1322	0.0800
	(0.79)	(2.11)	(1.38)	(2.75)	(2.65)	(1.98)

Note: Numbers in parentheses are *t*-statistics.

valid instruments, is not rejected by the Sargan overidentification tests in row "INST 1." In contrast, the assumption of strict exogeneity for all four variables, under which current values serve as valid instruments, is rejected by the overidentification test in row "INST 2." To ascertain which variables are responsible for the rejection, we experiment with various hybrid cases by augmenting the basic instrument set INST 1 with subsets of INST 2. INST 3 is such a hybrid case in which the current values of wage and income are included. The Sargan-difference test in row "INST 3 vs. 1" strongly rejects the strict exogeneity of wage and income, although the overidentification test in row "INST 3" is barely significant. In contrast, the hybrid case INST 4, in which the current values of labor quality and infrastructure are included, is not rejected by the Sargan-difference test in row "INST 4 vs. 1." These test results reveal the endogeneity of wage and income in explaining FDI, while confirming the strict exogeneity of labor quality and infrastructure. In view of the specification test results, we adopt INST 4 as our instrument set for the first-differenced equations.

Table 7.2 **Specification Tests**

Instrument Set	(1)	(2)	(3)	(4)	(5)	(6)
First differenced						
INST 1	71.749 (65)	71.605 (65)	73.107 (65)	66.266 (65)	55.553 (65)	64.548 (65)
	[0.2641]	[0.2680]	[0.2292]	[0.4329]	[0.7919]	[0.4924]
INST 2	94.542 (74)	90.073 (74)	93.839 (74)	95.192 (74)	92.711 (74)	96.424 (74)
	[0.0540]	[0.0985]	[0.0596]	[0.0492]	[0.0696]	[0.0411]
INST 3	103.54 (83)	99.367 (83)	103.02 (83)	99.589 (83)	98.337 (83)	98.664 (83)
	[0.0630]	[0.1063]	[0.0674]	[0.1035]	[0.1199]	[0.1155]
INST 3 vs. 1	31.787 (18)	27.761 (18)	29.913 (18)	33.323 (18)	42.784 (18)	34.115 (18)
	[0.0232]	[0.0657]	[0.0383]	[0.0152]	[0.0008]	[0.0121]
INST 4	90.217 (83)	81.358 (83)	93.193 (83)	81.838 (83)	72.446 (83)	81.530 (83)
	[0.2755]	[0.5304]	[0.2083]	[0.5154]	[0.7894]	[0.5250]
INST 4 vs. 1	18.468 (18)	9.7528 (18)	20.086 (18)	15.571 (18)	16.893 (18)	16.982 (18)
	[0.4252]	[0.9396]	[0.3279]	[0.6224]	[0.5304]	[0.5243]
m_1	−3.7521	−3.3826	−3.9165	−3.4613	−3.1908	−3.7882
m_2	−0.5761	−0.6183	−0.4434	−0.8365	−1.0977	−0.7813

System (first differenced + level)						
INST 5	96.612 (98) [0.5206]	91.246 (98) [0.6722]	104.77 (98) [0.3014]	92.476 (98) [0.6384]	82.899 (98) [0.8624]	90.580 (98) [0.6900]
INST 5 vs. 4	6.3958 (15) [0.9723]	9.8874 (15) [0.8267]	11.576 (15) [0.7108]	10.638 (15) [0.7778]	10.453 (15) [0.7903]	9.0498 (15) [0.8749]

Note: INST 1 to INST 4 refer to different instrument sets for the first-differenced equations. $(y_1, y_2, \ldots, y_{t-2})$ is common to all sets. The four sets differ by including explanatory variables of different periods as summarized in the following:

	Δx_{t-2}	Δx_t
INST 1	Wage, income, infrastructure	Wage, income, labor quality, infra-structure
INST 2		
INST 3	Wage, income, infrastructure	Wage, income
INST 4	Wage, income, infrastructure	Labor quality, infrastructure

INST 5 includes INST 4 for the first-differenced equations, plus $(\Delta y_{t-1}, \Delta x_t, \Delta x_{t-1})$ for the level equations, where $\Delta x_t =$ (labor quality, infrastructure) and $\Delta x_{t-1} =$ (wage, income, SEZ, ZONES).
Rows labeled "INST 1" to "INST 5" report Sargan overidentification tests corresponding to moment conditions implied by the relevant instrument sets. Each cell contains the value of the test statistic, the degrees of freedom (*parentheses*) of the χ^2 distribution, and the p-value (*brackets*) of the test.
The three rows labeled "INST a vs. b" report Sargan-difference tests for comparing two sets of moment conditions implied by INST a and INST b.
The statistics m_1 and m_2 test the first-differenced residuals for zero first-order and second-order autocorrelation, respectively. Both statistics are asymptotically $N(0,1)$ under the null.

The Arellano-Bond m_1 and m_2 serial correlation statistics from the INST 4 case are also reported in table 7.2. The significant m_1 and insignificant m_2 statistics indicate that there is no serial correlation in the level residuals, justifying the use of y lagged two periods or more as instruments for the first-differenced equations and lagged Δy for the level equations; that is, the moment conditions (C2) and (C5) in appendix C are valid. The system GMM estimates reported in table 7.1 are obtained by using the enlarged instrument set INST 5, which contains INST 4 for the first-differenced equations, plus $(\Delta y_{t-1}, \Delta x_t, \Delta x_{t-1})$ for the level equations, where Δx_t = (labor quality, infrastructure) and Δx_{t-1} = (wage, income, SEZ, ZONES). As can be seen from the last two rows of table 7.2, neither the overidentification test nor the Sargan-difference test rejects the additional level moment conditions, and this justifies the extra assumptions needed for the more efficient system GMM approach.

Table 7.1 shows that all the explanatory variables except university education have the expected sign. The coefficient for the lagged dependent variable is highly significant and quite stable. It is on average about 0.5, indicating a strong but not overwhelming self-reinforcing effect of the dependent variable's past value on its current value. The coefficient for real wage is also quite significant and stable, ranging from -0.35 to -0.68, indicating that a 1 percent increase in a region's wage costs would tend to reduce its FDI by about half a percent. The coefficient of per capita income is significant and lies in the vicinity of 0.7 across different specifications.

Using the density of all roads as a proxy for infrastructure, columns (1), (2), and (3) of table 7.1 report estimation results for three alternative indicators of labor quality. The first two are university education and secondary education, and the third is the ratio of farming to nonfarming population, which is negatively correlated with the educational level of the population. None of the coefficients for these labor quality indicators is statistically significant, and university education is even of the wrong sign. We shall come back later to the role of labor quality as a determinant of FDI in China in section 7.5.

To consider other combinations of the proxies, we use secondary school for labor quality and the density of high-grade paved roads and that of railways for infrastructure. The coefficient estimates for these two infrastructure variables (cols. [4] and [5], respectively) were both insignificant, and even with the wrong sign in the case of railways. One explanation for the last result is that railways were mostly built in the past to support a planned economy and are not a very good indicator of the infrastructure that is needed to attract FDI.

The results for the combination of university education and high-grade paved roads are given in column (6). The coefficient for university education is still negative but getting smaller in magnitude as well as statistical significance.

The coefficient for the density of all roads is between 0.2 and 0.3, indicating that a 1 percent increase in a region's roads would increase its FDI by 0.2 to 0.3 percent. The policy variable SEZ is statistically significant in all cases, and the policy variable equal to the sum of the other three zones (ZONES) is significant in all cases but two (cols. [1] and [3]). A comparison of the magnitude of the coefficients for SEZ and ZONES suggests that a Special Economic Zone was on average as effective as three to eleven other zones. Such a difference in the relative magnitude of their impact on FDI is consistent with the fact that Special Economic Zones gave much more favorable treatment to FDI than did the other policy designations.

7.5 Comparison with Other Studies

As in Cheng and Kwan (1999b), we have found a strong positive self-reinforcing effect of FDI on itself, which is consistent with the agglomeration effect identified by Head and Ries (1996). In addition, both regional income and good infrastructure (roads) contributed to FDI, although high-grade paved roads did not perform any better than all roads. In contrast with Chen's (1996) finding that wages did not affect FDI and Head and Ries's (1996) finding that the effect of wages was negligible, wage cost had a negative effect on FDI.

As expected, the coefficients for SEZ and ZONES are both significantly positive. The evidence reaffirms the well-known fact that the Special Economic Zones, which are close to Hong Kong and Taiwan, were more successful than the other zones in attracting FDI to China.

None of the education variables serving as proxies for labor quality had a significant impact on FDI, as first found by Cheng and Zhao (1995) and later in Cheng and Kwan (1999b). Together with our earlier work, a total of six proxies for labor quality have failed to show any significantly positive effect on FDI stock, indicating that the negative finding might not be explained away by the poor choice of any particular proxy. However, FDI from Japan and the United States tended to be concentrated in major cities known for their labor quality (namely, Beijing, Shanghai, and Tianjin).[9] Thus, even though labor quality is not a significant determinant of the total FDI received by each of the regions, it might be significant for FDI originating from the developed economies.

A related explanation is that much of the FDI was in labor-intensive manufacturing industries and in real estate. Labor quality is not particularly crucial in these industries, suggesting that lumping FDI in different industries may have the effect of confounding their differential underlying determinants.

---

9. See Cheng (1994, table 15). FDI from Hong Kong and Taiwan tended to concentrate in the coastal regions, in particular, Guangdong, Fujian, Zhejiang, and Jiangsu.

7.6   Actual and Equilibrium Stocks of Foreign Direct Investment

Using the estimated equation, we can recover the unobserved equilibrium stock of FDI, y_{it}^*, and compare it with the actual (i.e., realized) stock of FDI, y_{it}. The equilibrium stock is interesting not only because it measures a region's potential for absorbing FDI but also because its movement reflects the comparative static effect of changes in policy and other exogenous variables without the interference of the self-reinforcing effect and adjustment cost effect.

To highlight the difference between the equilibrium and realized stocks, we focus on the series of medians and quartiles computed from the regional distributions over the years. Figure 7.2 reports the paths of the actual and equilibrium median stock growth rates, whereas figure 7.3 highlights the regional distributions of the deviation of actual FDI stock from equilibrium, where the equilibrium entities are calculated using the coefficients reported in column (2) of table 7.1.[10] The equilibrium stock growth rates reveal the impacts of a few well-known events. The big dip in 1986 was due to a deterioration in the overall investment environment that prompted the government to introduce the "Twenty-Two Articles" in October of that year in order to stimulate FDI. The Tiananmen event in 1989 had a strong negative impact on the equilibrium growth rate, but the impact on the realized growth rate was hardly discernible. Deng Xiaoping's tour of south China in spring 1992 helped push the country's open door policy back on track, resulting in a significant increase in the equilibrium growth rate. To cool the national economy and to discourage FDI in real estate, macroeconomic controls in 1994 brought down both the equilibrium and actual growth rates of FDI stock.

We calculate the deviation of the realized stock from the equilibrium stock to obtain a region's potential for absorbing further FDI. This is the potential FDI that can be achieved under the assumption that the equilibrium stock stays at the existing level forever. Figure 7.3 summarizes the panel data of such deviations from equilibrium by the paths of the median and the lower and upper quartiles. As can be seen, over the years, the realized stock tends to converge to the equilibrium, but the convergence is occasionally disturbed by major policy shifts such as the Twenty-Two Articles and Deng's south China tour, mentioned above. Interestingly, there is also a tendency toward convergence among the regions, as indicated by the shrinking dispersions over the years. Notice that the convergence is not in the stock of FDI a region will eventually achieve; rather, the convergence is in terms of the deviation of a region's actual FDI stock from its equilibrium stock, which has little tendency to converge. That is

---

10. Using the coefficients given in col. (1) of table 7.1 would not make much difference in the equilibrium stocks and growth rates.

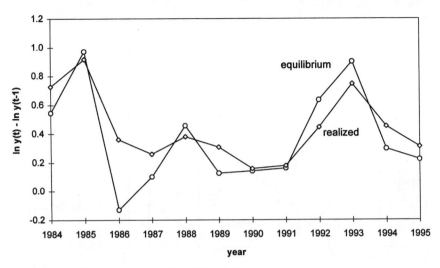

Fig. 7.2   Median annual growth of FDI stock

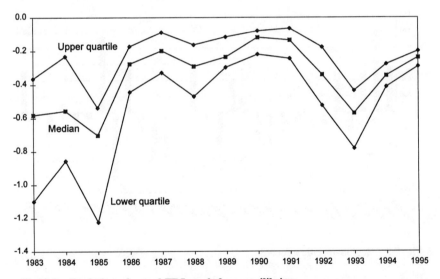

Fig. 7.3   Deviation of actual FDI stock from equilibrium

to say, there is only convergence in the ratio of actual to potential FDI stocks but not convergence in the FDI stocks themselves.

The time-specific effects are depicted in figure 7.4, which clearly shows the effects of the 4 June event in 1989, Deng's tour in 1992, and the macroeconomic controls in 1994 and 1995. The region-specific effects are depicted in figure 7.5, where the regions are ordered by distance from Hong

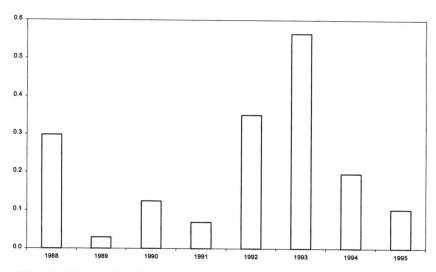

Fig. 7.4   Time-specific effects (annual increment)

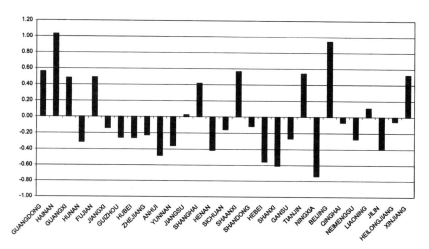

Fig. 7.5   Region-specific effects

Kong. As can be seen, the three regions closest to Hong Kong, namely, Guangdong, Guangxi, and Hainan, exhibit very strong positive effects. But proximity to Hong Kong does not explain everything, because Shanghai, Tianjin, Beijing, and even Xinjiang also had strong region-specific factors that attracted FDI. Moreover, Guangdong, Hainan, and Fujian not only are close to Hong Kong and Taiwan but also possess Special Economic Zones. In the case of Shanghai, Tianjin, and Beijing, they were

China's three most advanced cities. In addition, Shanghai began to have its own version of the Special Economic Zone (the Pudong New Zone) in 1990. These findings are consistent with the general observation that the determinants of export-oriented FDI are quite different from those of domestic-market-oriented FDI.

7.7   Concluding Remarks

With minor quantitative variations, our findings are very similar to those obtained in Cheng and Kwan (1999b). They not only are broadly consistent with the comparative statics results obtained in the literature on the location of FDI in the United States, China, and other countries but also provide support to existing studies that have empirically identified the self-reinforcing effect of FDI.

By integrating the traditional comparative statics theory of FDI location choice into a model of natural growth, our model has provided a better vantage point for understanding the potential determinants of FDI. The size of a region's market as approximated by regional income has a positive effect, but wage cost has a negative effect on FDI. Good infrastructure as measured by the density of all roads attracts FDI, but the effect of the labor quality variables is insignificant. In fact, the coefficient for university education had the wrong sign. The positive impact of Special Economic Zones is far greater than that of the other key policy designations, including Open Coastal Cities, Economic and Technological Development Zones, and Open Coastal Areas. There was no convergence in the equilibrium FDI stocks of the regions between 1985 and 1995; there was, however, convergence in the deviation of actual from equilibrium FDI.

Despite the use of six different proxies, we have not found any significantly positive effect of labor quality on FDI in China. Nevertheless, regions with high-quality labor (i.e., the centrally administered municipalities) were indeed successful in attracting FDI from Japan and the United States. Together these two facts suggest that it would be interesting for future research to analyze the determinants of FDI by source economy.

Appendix A

Table 7A.1   **Definition of Variables**

1. FDI stock	Cumulative per capita real FDI at the end of year t
2. University education	Number of teachers and staff in institutions of higher education (universities, colleges, and graduate schools) per 10,000 population
3. Secondary education	Number of teachers and staff in secondary schools (specialized and regular) per 10,000 population
4. Farm/nonfarm	Ratio of population employed in the farming sector to nonfarming sector
5. All roads	Roads (km/km² of land mass)
6. High-grade paved roads	High-grade paved roads (km/km² of land mass)
7. Railway	Railway (km/km² of land mass)
8. Wage	Real wage
9. Per capita income	Per capita real regional income
10. SEZ	Number of Special Economic Zones + 1, where 1 is added to allow for zero SEZ in many regions
11. ZONES	1 + Sum of numbers of Open Coastal Cities, Economic and Technological Development Zones, and Open Coastal Areas

Appendix B
Additional Explanations

The FDI data were obtained from China's Ministry of Foreign Trade and Economic Cooperation, and most of the other data are from various issues of *China Statistical Yearbook.*

Price Deflators. The deflator for FDI is the U.S. producer price index of capital equipment published by the U.S. Bureau of Labor Statistics. The deflator for per capita real income is the consumer price index of each region.

Regional Income (RI). Regional income data are only available up to 1992; figures for 1993–95 are interpolated from the corresponding regional GDP data that replace the national income data starting from 1993. We first estimate a fixed-effects model, $\ln RI_{it} = \alpha_i + \beta \ln GDP_{it} + \varepsilon_{it}$, using data for the interim period 1990–92 during which both RI and GDP are available. RI figures for 1993–95 are then interpolated from the estimated equation using the available GDP data.

Appendix C
The GMM Estimation Procedure

Under the assumption of regional fixed effects, the usual least squares dummy variable estimator is biased in the order of $1/T$, even assuming strictly exogenous explanatory variables. The bias is caused by having to eliminate the fixed effects from each observation, an operation that creates a correlation between the lagged dependent variable and the residuals in the transformed model. In contrast, the GMM approach starts with the first-differenced version of equation (7) in the text:

$$(C1) \quad \Delta y_{it} = (1 - \alpha)\Delta y_{it-1} + \beta'\Delta x_{it} + \Delta u_{it}, \quad i = 1, 2, \ldots, N,$$

$$t = 3, \ldots, T,$$

in which the region-specific effects are eliminated by the differencing operation. Under the assumptions of serially uncorrelated residuals v_{it} and $E(y_{i1}v_{it}) = 0$ for $t = 2, \ldots, T$, values of y lagged two periods or more qualify as valid instruments in the first-differenced system, implying the following $(T - 1)(T - 2)/2$ moment conditions:

$$(C2) \qquad E(y_{it-s}\Delta u_{it}) = 0, \quad t = 3, \ldots, T, \quad s \geq 2.$$

But GMM estimation based on equation (C2) alone can be highly inefficient. In most cases, it is necessary to make use of the explanatory variables as additional instruments. For strictly exogenous explanatory variables, that is, $E(x_{ir}v_{it}) = 0$ for all r, both past and future Δx are valid instruments:

$$(C3) \qquad E(\Delta x_{it-s}\Delta u_{it}) = 0, \quad t = 3, \ldots, T, \quad \text{all } s.$$

But using equation (C3) for $s < 2$ will lead to inconsistent estimates if reverse causality exists in the sense that $E(x_{ir}v_{it}) \neq 0$ for $r \geq t$. To allow for this possibility, one may assume x to be weakly exogenous, that is, $E(x_{is}v_{it}) = 0$ for $s < t$, which implies the following subset of equation (C3):

$$(C4) \qquad E(\Delta x_{it-s}\Delta u_{it}) = 0, \quad t = 3, \ldots, T, \quad s \geq 2.$$

Since $\Delta u_{it} = \Delta y_{it} - (1 - \alpha)\Delta y_{it-1} - \beta'\Delta x_{it}$ by equation (C1), equations (C2), (C3), and (C4) constitute a set of moment conditions linear in the unknown parameters (α, β). The consistency of the GMM estimator hinges on the validity of these moment conditions, which in turn depends on maintained hypotheses on the residuals v_{it} being serially uncorrelated and the exogeneity property of the explanatory variables. It is therefore essential to ensure that these assumptions are justified by conducting specification tests.

For the overidentified case in which the number of moment conditions q exceeds the number of unknown parameters k, the minimized GMM criterion function provides a specification test for the overall validity of the moment conditions (i.e., the Sargan test). The null hypothesis of no misspecification (i.e., all moment conditions valid) is rejected if the GMM criterion function registers a large value compared with a χ^2 distribution with $q - k$ degrees of freedom. Another useful diagnostic is the Sargan-difference specification test that evaluates the validity of extra moment conditions in a nested case. For example, strict exogeneity implies extra moment conditions over that of weak exogeneity (i.e., condition [C4] is nested in [C3]). Let the minimized GMM criterion function for the nested, weak exogeneity case be s_1 and that of the strict exogeneity case be s_2, with the numbers of moment conditions for the two cases being q_1 and q_2, respectively. By construction, $q_2 > q_1$ and $s_2 > s_1$. The null hypothesis of strict exogeneity can be tested against the alternative of weak exogeneity by testing the validity of the extra moment conditions, using the Sargan-difference statistic $s_2 - s_1$ compared with a χ_2 distribution of degrees of freedom $q_2 - q_1$.

We also report a residual-based specification test suggested by Arellano and Bond (1991). Based on the differenced residuals, the Arellano-Bond m_1 and m_2 serial correlation statistics, both distributed as $N(0,1)$ in large sample, test the null hypotheses of zero first-order and second-order autocorrelation, respectively. An insignificant m_1 and/or significant m_2 will issue warnings against the likely presence of invalid moment conditions due to serial correlation in the level *residuals*.[11]

The GMM approach discussed so far utilizes moment conditions (C2), (C3), and (C4) based on the first-differenced equation (C1). The first-differencing operation not only eliminates unobserved region-specific effects but also time-invariant explanatory variables for which only cross-sectional information is available. This is problematic in our application because the two policy variables of interest, SEZ (the number of Special Economic Zones in a region) and ZONES (the total number of Open Coastal Cities, Economic and Technological Development Zones, and Open Coastal Areas), are nearly time invariant so that their first differences are relatively uninformative, rendering the associated parameters close to being unidentified in the first-differenced system. Moreover, as demonstrated by Ahn and Schmidt (1995, 1997) and Blundell and Bond (1998), under a random-effects model, the first-differenced GMM estimator can suffer from serious efficiency loss, for potentially informative moment conditions are ignored in the first-difference approach. Following

---

11. See Arellano and Bond (1991) for the relevant formulas and proofs of the statistical distribution theory for various specification tests.

Blundell and Bond (1998), we augment the first-differenced moment conditions (C2), (C3), and (C4) by the level moment conditions

(C5) $$E(u_{it}\Delta y_{it-1}) = 0, \quad t = 3,\ldots,T,$$

which amounts to using lagged differences of y as instruments in the level equation (7). For strictly exogenous explanatory variables, there are level moment conditions

(C6) $$E(u_{it}\Delta x_{it-s}) = 0, \quad t = 2,\ldots,T, \quad \text{all } s;$$

and for weakly exogenous explanatory variables, the appropriate level moment conditions would be

(C7) $$E(u_{it}\Delta x_{it-s}) = 0, \quad t = 3,\ldots,T, \quad s \geq 1.$$

The Blundell-Bond system GMM estimator is obtained by imposing the enlarged set of moment conditions (C2) through (C7). By exploiting more moment conditions, the system GMM estimator has a smaller asymptotic variance (more efficient) than the first-differenced GMM estimator that uses only the subset (C2), (C3), and (C4). The validity of the level moment conditions (C5), (C6), and (C7) depends on a standard random-effects specification of equation (7) in which

(C8) $$E(\eta_i) = E(v_{it}) = E(v_{it}\eta_i) = 0, \quad \text{for } i = 1,\ldots,N \text{ and } t = 2,\ldots,T,$$

$$E(v_{it}v_{is}) = 0, \quad \text{for } i = 1,\ldots,N \text{ and } t \neq s,$$

$$E(y_{i1}v_{it}) = 0, \quad \text{for } i = 1,\ldots,N \text{ and } t = 2,\ldots,T,$$

plus two additional assumptions: (a) $E(u_{i3}\Delta y_{i2}) = 0$, a restriction on the initial value process generating y_{i1}, and (b) $E(\eta_i\Delta x_{it}) = 0$, which requires that the region-specific effects be uncorrelated with the explanatory variables in first difference.

The efficiency gain from imposing the level moment conditions certainly does not come free; we do make more assumptions the violation of which may lead to bias. Since the first-differenced moment conditions are nested within the augmented set, the additional level moment conditions can be tested by the Sargan-difference testing procedure described above, using the GMM criterion functions from the first-difference and the system approaches. In addition, invalid level moment conditions can also be detected by the Sargan overidentification test from the system GMM estimation.

References

Ahn, S. C., and P. Schmidt. 1995. Efficient estimation of models for dynamic panel data. *Journal of Econometrics* 68:5–27.

———. 1997. Efficient estimation of dynamic panel data models: Alternative assumptions and simplified estimation. *Journal of Econometrics* 76:309–21.

Anderson, T. W., and C. Hsiao. 1981. Estimation of dynamic models with error components. *Journal of the American Statistical Association* 76:598–606.

———. 1982. Formulation and estimation of dynamic models using panel data. *Journal of Econometrics* 18:47–82.

Arellano, M., and S. Bond. 1991. Some tests of specification for panel data: Monte Carlo evidence and an application to employment equation. *Review of Economic Studies* 58:277–97.

Arellano, M., and O. Bover. 1995. Another look at the instrumental variable estimation of error-components models. *Journal of Econometrics* 68:29–51.

Blundell, R., and S. Bond. 1998. Initial conditions and moment restrictions in dynamic panel data models. *Journal of Econometrics* 87:115–43.

Chen, C. 1996. Regional determinants of foreign direct investment in mainland China. *Journal of Economic Studies* 23:18–30.

Cheng, L. K. 1994. Foreign direct investment in China. OECD Report no. COM/DAFFE/IME/TD (94) 129. Paris: Organization for Economic Cooperation Development, November.

Cheng, L. K., and Y. Kwan. 1999a. FDI stock and its determinants. In *Foreign direct investment and economic growth in China,* ed. Y. Wu, 42–56. Cheltenham, England: Elgar.

———. 1999b. What are the determinants of the location of foreign direct investment? The Chinese experience. *Journal of International Economics.* Forthcoming.

Cheng, L. K., and H. Zhao. 1995. Geographical patterns of foreign direct investment in China: Location, factor endowments, and policy incentives. Hong Kong: Hong Kong University of Science and Technology, Department of Economics, February. Mimeograph.

Chow, G. C. 1967. Technological change and the demand for computers. *American Economic Review* 57:1117–30.

Coughlin, C., J. V. Terza, and V. Arromdee. 1991. State characteristics and the location of foreign direct investment within the United States. *Review of Economics and Statistics* 73:675–83.

Friedman, J., H. Fung, D. Gerlowski, and J. Silberman. 1996. A note on "State characteristics and the location of foreign direct investment within the United States." *Review of Economics and Statistics* 78:367–68.

Friedman, J., D. Gerlowski, and J. Silberman. 1992. What attracts foreign multinational corporations? Evidence from branch plant location in the United States. *Journal of Regional Science* 32:403–18.

Head, K., and J. Ries. 1996. Inter-city competition for foreign investment: Static and dynamic effects of China's incentive areas. *Journal of Urban Economics* 40:38–60.

Head, K., J. Ries, and D. Swenson. 1995. Agglomeration benefits and location choice: Evidence from Japanese manufacturing investment in the United States. *Journal of International Economics* 38:223–47.

Hill, S., and M. Munday. 1995. Foreign manufacturing investment in France and the U.K.: A regional analysis of locational determinants. *Tijdschrift voor Economische en Sociale Geografie* 86:311–27.

Hines, J. 1996. Altered states: Taxes and the location of foreign direct investment in America. *American Economic Review* 86:1076–94.

Holtz-Eakin, D., W. Newey, and H. Rosen. 1988. Estimating vector autoregressions with panel data. *Econometrica* 56:1371–95.

Hsiao, C. 1986. *Analysis of panel data.* Cambridge: Cambridge University Press.

O Huallachain, B., and N. Reid. 1997. Acquisition versus greenfield investment: The location and growth of Japanese manufacturers in the United States. *Regional Studies* 31:403–16.

Organization for Economic Cooperation and Development (OECD). 1992. The OECD declaration and decisions on international investment and multinational enterprises: 1991 review. Paris: Organization for Economic Cooperation and Development.

Rozelle, S., Y. Ying, and M. Barlow. N.d. Targeting transaction costs: An evaluation of investment incentive policies in China's foreign trade zones. Stanford, Calif.: Stanford University, Food Research Institute, Mimeograph.

Sevestre, P., and A. Trognon. 1996. Dynamic linear models. In *The econometrics of panel data: Handbook of theory and applications,* 2d rev. ed., ed. L. Matyas and P. Sevestre, 120–44. Dordrecht: Kluwer.

Smith, D., and R. Florida. 1994. Agglomeration and industrial location: An econometric analysis of Japanese affiliated manufacturing establishments in automotive-related industries. *Journal of Urban Economics* 36:23–41.

Wheeler, D., and A. Mody. 1992. International investment location decisions: The case of U.S. firms. *Journal of International Economics* 33:57–76.

Woodward, D. 1992. Locational determinants of Japanese manufacturing startups in the United States. *Southern Economic Journal* 58:690–708.

Comment   Yumiko Okamoto

I much appreciated the paper by Cheng and Kwan. In fact, I analyzed the capacity of noncoastal areas of China to utilize FDI as part of their development strategies last year. Since whether FDI could be part of a region's development strategy depends largely on the determinants of FDI location, this paper is clearly relevant to my research.

Cheng and Kwan examine the determinants of the location of FDI in China by combining the comparative statics theory of FDI location and Chow's partial adjustment model. The combination of the two is an innovative part of their paper. They find that the magnitude of national and regional markets, good infrastructure, and the number of Special Economic Zones have positive effects on FDI, while wage cost has a negative effect. Surprisingly, the education variable has no significant effect on FDI. They also find strong evidence for an agglomeration effect.

The separation of relative from absolute convergence among the regions in absorbing FDI is particularly interesting. In my study I also found that although there is no evidence whatsoever of convergence in the absolute

Yumiko Okamoto is associate professor of economics at Nagoya University.

amount of FDI inflow between coastal areas and inland China, inland China has also begun attracting FDI in the past couple of years. This phenomenon seems to be confirmed by Cheng and Kwan's regression results. If so, there is still room for inland China to attract more FDI by adopting appropriate policies regardless of whether there is convergence among regions in absorbing FDI in absolute terms.

About investigating the determinants of FDI location, I have one suggestion. It might be interesting to repeat the analysis separating FDI from Hong Kong and Taiwan and FDI from other industrialized countries such as the United States and Japan. I found the regional investment pattern between the two to be different. Also several past studies have seemed to suggest that the investment behavior of overseas Chinese differs from that of others. Therefore, the explicit introduction of FDI source into the research might enrich the study further.

I also found the inclusion of a variable to represent nationwide as well as regional markets interesting. This seemed to control for a demand factor that might influence the whole region simultaneously. If that is the case, it might also be interesting to introduce a variable that represents a regionwide supply-side factor for FDI as well.

Finally, the fact that no education variable shows any statistical significance as a determinant of FDI location bothers me. I wonder whether this is due to a statistical problem such as multicollinearity or, on the other hand, whether it suggests that investors do not care about the quality of the labor force in the case of China.

Comment   Shang-Jin Wei

This well-written paper investigates an important topic. A number of studies have looked into the consequences of FDI in China (e.g., Lardy 1992), including some that used Chinese city-level data (e.g., Wei 1995, 1996). This paper, following other papers that these authors have done (Cheng and Zhao 1995; Cheng and Kwan 1999), is among the first that studies the determinants of FDI locations within China.

The paper very sensibly applies a partial adjustment framework to the specification, and very properly uses a GMM method for estimation and specification tests. The version of the paper presented here also represents significant improvement over the first draft presented at the conference.

Shang-Jin Wei is associate professor of public policy at the Kennedy School of Government, Harvard University, and a faculty research fellow of the National Bureau of Economic Research. During 1999–2000, he serves as an advisor on anticorruption issues at the World Bank.

So I will confine my revised comments to a few points that I would bring to the reader's attention.

Interpretation of a Positive Coefficient on the Past FDI Stock

The main equation estimated in the paper is what is called a partial adjustment specification: the change in the log (FDI stock) is regressed on the difference between lagged log (FDI stock) and an equilibrium level of FDI stock, which is a function a vector of "state" variables. Several papers in the literature (including the earlier version of this paper) applied a framework like this and interpreted a positive coefficient on the lagged FDI stock as evidence of agglomeration. Agglomeration (which is motivated by some kind of externality) and partial adjustment (which is motivated by convex adjustment costs) are conceptually very different. But both can produce a positive coefficient on the lagged FDI stock. I am pleased to see that the revised paper takes into account my suggestion that the specification in the paper cannot disentangle the agglomeration effect versus partial adjustment. I would suggest that the authors make this point more clearly and forcefully, as it could help to correct a common impression one gets from several papers in the literature that adopt this interpretation.

Possible Missing Fixed Effects?

In an effort to estimate certain virtually time-invariant policy fixed effects (i.e., numbers of Special Economic Zones, Open Coastal Cities, etc.), the authors add what they call level moment conditions. This ability to estimate the policy fixed effects comes with a possible cost; namely, it may have reintroduced missing fixed effects that the first-difference is supposed to eliminate. Specifically, distance and linguistic connection between the source countries and host regions (countries) were found to be important determinants of bilateral FDI in the literature (see, e.g., Wei 1996, 1997) but are not included in the current paper. For example, the facts that Guangdong is the only province that shares a common dialect with Hong Kong and that it is closest in distance to Hong Kong, the biggest source of FDI into China, is most likely correlated with the fact that it is the biggest recipient of FDI among all provinces. That coastal provinces/municipalities have the largest number of English- (or Japanese-)speaking personnel is also likely correlated with the observation that there is substantially more FDI in coastal areas than inland.

Interpretation of the Policy Effect

The authors use two variables to capture what they term the policy effects: SEZ, the number of Special Economic Zones in a region; and ZONES, the total number of Open Coastal Cities, Economic and Technological Development Zones, and Open Coastal Areas. These variables are virtually time-invariant. They found that both variables produce positive coefficients, and the coefficient for SEZ is at least three times as large as the one on ZONES. They interpret this as the effect of special favorable treatment in these zones that were offered to foreign firms.

It is quite likely that the special policies do alter the locational choice of the foreign firms. However, the positive coefficients reported may very well also reflect the effects of other missing variables rather than exclusively the effects of either SEZs or other zones. This is, of course, related to the previous point. Specifically, three of the four initial Special Economic Zones are located in Guangdong Province alone (the other is in Fujian province, the closest province to Taiwan). Guangdong attracts more FDI than the model predicts, for whatever reason (some were speculated in the previous observation), so the SEZ dummy may simply capture this Guangdong effect, regardless of the true effect of the policies within the Special Economic Zones. Likewise, the so-called Open Coastal Cities or Open Coastal Areas are near the coast. Therefore, the positive coefficient on the ZONES variable could be just a relabeling of the fact that the coastal provinces receive more FDI on average.

Overall, reading this paper is a rewarding experience. None of the above comments should detract from the fact that this is a nice piece of work both for understanding locational decisions of multinational firms in general and for understanding FDI into China in particular.

References

Cheng, Leonard K., and Yum K. Kwan. 1999. FDI stock and its determinants. In *Foreign direct investment and economic growth in China,* ed. Y. Wu, 42–56. Cheltenham, England: Edward Elgar.

Cheng, Leonard K., and Haiying Zhao. 1995. Geographic patterns of foreign direct investment in China: Location, factor endowment, and policy incentives. Hong Kong University of Science and Technology, Department of Economics, February. Unpublished paper.

Lardy, Nicholas. 1992. *Foreign trade and economic reform in China, 1978–1990.* Cambridge: Cambridge University Press.

Wei, Shang-Jin. 1995. The open door policy and China's rapid growth: Evidence from city-level data. In *Growth theories in light of the East Asian experience,* ed. T. Ito and A. O. Krueger. Chicago: University of Chicago Press.

———. 1996. Foreign direct investment in China: Sources and consequences. In *Financial deregulation and integration in East Asia,* ed. T. Ito and A. O. Krueger. Chicago: University of Chicago Press.

———. 1997. How taxing is corruption on international investors? NBER Working Paper no. 6030. Cambridge, Mass.: National Bureau of Economic Research. (Forthcoming, *Review of Economics and Statistics*)

8

Why Does China Attract So Little Foreign Direct Investment?

Shang-Jin Wei

"China fever" has been a phenomenon of the 1990s. In 1995,
the last year for which definite figures are available, China
received more foreign direct investment than any country
except the United States.
—*Economist,* 1 March 1997, 38, U.S. edition

Headline: China Projects Another Record Investment Year;
European, Japanese, U.S. Firms Top List
The world's strongest magnet for overseas investment is pro-
jecting another record tally for 1996, even though the number of
project approvals will be lower than in the previous year.
—P. T. Bangserg, *Journal of Commerce,* 27 December 1996, 3A

8.1 Introduction

"China fever" and "the world's strongest magnet for overseas investment" are but two phrases one reads often in the media that describe
the supposed euphoria that international investors have about investing in
China. While the recent Asian financial crisis has reduced the official forecast somewhat on how much foreign direct investment (FDI) will go into
China in 1998, it remains an attractive host for FDI. Or so the press will
lead you to believe.

This paper has two objectives. First, it will show that contrary to the
impression one gets from the popular media, China continues to be an
underachiever, rather than an overachiever, as a host of direct investment
from the world's major source countries (e.g., the United States, Japan,

Shang-Jin Wei is associate professor of public policy at the Kennedy School of Govern-
ment, Harvard University, and a faculty research fellow of the National Bureau of Economic
Research. During 1999–2000, he serves as an advisor on anticorruption issues at the World
Bank.

The author thanks Akira Kohsaka, Mari Pangestu, Anne Krueger, and other conference
participants for very helpful comments; and Greg Dorchak and Deirdre Shanley for able
research and editorial assistance. The views in the paper are the author's and may not be
shared by any organization with which he is associated.

Germany, the United Kingdom, and France). Most of the high volume of inward FDI comes from unusual source economies such as Hong Kong, Taiwan, Macao, and Singapore.

Second, the paper will examine whether corruption by government officials, the excessive burden of regulation, and other institutional characteristics may have contributed to the relatively low volume of inward FDI from the major source countries.

In an earlier (1996) paper using data from the United Nations Council of Trade and Development, I fitted a linear regression on direct investment during the 1987–90 period from the world's five largest source countries to a number of host countries and compared China's actual reception of FDI with its potential as predicted by the regression. Based on that methodology, I found that FDI in China was significantly below its potential, in both an economic and a statistical sense.

A number of factors could explain that finding. First, given that China's opening to foreign investment started relatively late (from 1980) and that the Tiananmen Square incident temporarily diminished FDI over 1989–90, 1987–90 may not be a good period by which to judge China's appeal as a host country. FDI in China has grown exponentially recently. For example, total FDI in China in 1993 was between five to eight times that in 1990 (see table 8.1 below).

Second, the linear specification with the logarithm of FDI as the dependent variable excludes all source-host country pairs that have zero FDI. This could bias the results to exaggerate the potential amount of FDI that China could receive.

Third, while the earlier paper examined host country size, level of development, and relationship with the source country as determinants of FDI, it neglected the importance of business environment, particularly the extent of corruption by government officials in the host country. Recent papers by Hines (1995) and Wei (1997a, 1997b) have suggested that severe corruption in a host country could significantly deter foreign investors from investing in the country.

The current paper seeks to advance our understanding of FDI in China in a number of ways. We will use more recent data with more source countries, that is, bilateral stock of direct investment in 1993 from the OECD. We will employ a modified Tobit specification that takes into account possibly zero FDI in certain source-host country pairs. And we will explicitly examine whether corruption has deterred FDI.

The paper is organized in the following way. Section 8.2 reviews the recent trend in FDI in China and the source country composition of the FDI. Section 8.3 looks into the questions of whether China has attracted enough FDI from the world's major source countries and whether corruption has impeded the FDI in a significant way. Section 8.4 concludes.

8.2   Foreign, Quasi-Foreign, and False-Foreign Direct Investment

8.2.1   The Overall Picture

The transformation of China from a country with virtually no foreign investment before 1979 to "the world's strongest magnet for overseas investment" is remarkable and has been well documented.

In Chinese statistics, two notions of FDI are used: the contractual amount and the realized value. The contractual amount is the amount that investors plan to invest over a period of time at the time of applying for approval for investment. The actual or realized value is not bound by the contractual amount and indeed is typically much smaller. Because being able to attract foreign investment is often counted to the credit of local officials by their superiors, government officials have an incentive to encourage foreign investors to overstate the (not legally binding) contractual amount. For this reason, all data on FDI in this paper refer only to realized values.

Table 8.1 exhibits the trajectory of the realized flow of FDI going into China every year from 1983 to 1998 (estimated amount) as reported by the China State Statistics Bureau. The growth is truly exponential: total inward FDI flow was a mere $0.64 billion in 1983. It grew to $3.19 billion in 1988, to $27.52 billion in 1993, and to $41.7 billion in 1996. Every year

Table 8.1	Realized FDI in China: Annual Flows, 1983–98 (billion U.S. dollars)
Year	Annual Flow
1983	0.64
1984	1.26
1985	1.66
1986	1.88
1987	2.31
1988	3.19
1989	3.39
1990	3.49
1991	4.37
1992	11.00
1993	27.52
1994	33.77
1995	37.52
1996	41.73
1997	37.00[a]
1998	37.00[a]

Source: China State Statistics Bureau, *Zhongguo Tongji Nianjian* (China statistical yearbook; Beijing, 1998).

[a]Estimates by the China State Statistics Bureau.

since 1995, China received more FDI than any other country except the United States.

The recent Asian financial crisis has lowered the official estimate of the inward flow of FDI in 1997 to $37 billion (another estimate forecasts modest growth over the 1996 number, to $45.3 billion). The 1998 inward flow is forecast to stay at the 1997 level.

IMF estimates are generally $3 to $5 billion (roughly 10 percent of the total) less than Chinese official statistics. One Chinese official during an interview with the author in March 1998 suggested that the market value of the shares in Chinese companies floated in the international market (mainly on the Hong Kong and New York Stock Exchanges) are counted as part of FDI. This, if true, would be the first source of false-foreign direct investment in the official statistics. While equity investment may be counted as direct investment in other countries if the investment implies foreign control of the company, in the Chinese case no company floated in the international capital market transfers control rights to foreign shareholders. In fact, the state typically maintains 51 percent or more nontrading shares in the companies listed on domestic as well as foreign stock markets. Even the shares bought by domestic investors do not entail control rights over the management of the companies. So this amount should be subtracted from the official statistics on inward FDI, at least for recent years.

To put inward FDI in the context of China's overall participation in the international capital market, table 8.2 presents data on all forms of capital inflow into China over the period 1992–96. Two features are worth noting. First, during the sample period, FDI has consistently been a more important source of foreign capital inflow than portfolio investment. Second, within the category of portfolio investment, loans from international commercial banks tend to be a small fraction of overall external loans, dominated by loans from foreign governments, international financial institutions, and export credits. These are significant because recent studies have suggested that a low ratio of FDI to portfolio inflow and a high ratio of short-term debt to overall foreign borrowing tend to be associated with a higher probability of currency crisis (Frankel and Rose 1996; Radelet and Sachs 1998).

FDI takes one of the following four forms: joint ventures, contractual joint ventures, wholly owned foreign firms, and joint exploration (mainly for offshore oil). Joint ventures are by far the dominant form of FDI, accounting for roughly half of all FDI throughout the sample. Foreign wholly owned firms as a form of FDI are catching up fast, growing by 400 percent cumulatively over the 1992–96 period, as compared to the 279 percent growth rate for all FDI in the same period.

Chinese statistics contain a third category of foreign capital aside from

Table 8.2   **Realized Foreign Capital Going into China, Including Loans and Direct Investment, 1992–96 (million U.S. dollars)**

Inflow	1992	1993	1994	1995	1996
Total	19,202.33	38,959.72	43,212.84	48,132.69	54,804.16
External loans	7,910.71	11,188.85	9,267.00	10,327.00	12,669.00
Loans from foreign governments	2,566.38	3,040.81	2,400.00	2,773.00	3,451.00
Loans from international financial institutions	1,306.18	2,268.71	1,466.00	2,707.00	2,997.00
Export credit	989.11	1,220.66	2,190.00	2,669.00	1,328.00
Commercial bank loans	1,778.32	3,270.55	1,857.00	1,395.00	1,494.00
Bonds and equity shares issued abroad	1,270.72	1,388.12	1,354.00	783.00	3,399.00
FDI	11,007.51	27,514.95	33,766.50	37,520.53	41,725.52
Joint ventures	6,114.62	15,347.78	17,932.53	19,077.90	20,754.50
Contractual joint ventures	2,122.45	5,237.56	7,120.18	7,535.60	8,109.43
Wholly owned foreign firms	2,520.31	6,505.57	8,035.60	10,316.83	12,606.14
Joint exploration	250.13	424.04	678.19	590.20	255.45
Other foreign investment	284.11	255.92	179.34	285.16	409.64
International leasing	44.50	46.20	19.69	29.25	87.22
Compensation trade	172.31	89.70	88.91	211.49	158.32
Export processing or assembly	67.30	120.02	70.74	44.42	164.10

Source: China Ministry of Foreign Economic Relations and Trade (MOFTEC), *Almanac of China's Foreign Economic Relations and Trade* (various issues). See also MOFTEC's website: http://www.moftec. gov.cn/moftec/official/html/statistics_data/utilization_of_foreign_capital.html.

loans and direct investment. This category, labeled "other foreign investment" in table 8.2, includes three subcategories: leasing, compensation trade, and export processing or assembly. The biggest part of the three, compensation trade, in which foreign firms provide machines or product designs to Chinese firms and obtain part of the output as compensation, is no longer as popular as at the beginning of the reform in early 1980s. In fact, this other foreign investment is small relative to FDI and has become ever less important.

8.2.2   Source Country Composition of Foreign Direct Investment

FDI in China has a very unusual composition of source countries. According to the United Nations, the world's five most important source countries in terms of outflow during 1990–95 were the United States, Japan, Germany, the United Kingdom, and France. Collectively, they accounted for over 70 percent of all direct investment from developed countries.

If one looks at who invests in China (table 8.3), one finds that Hong Kong is the dominant direct investor. Hong Kong's annual inflow accounts

Table 8.3   **Source Country Distribution of FDI in China: Flow Data (million U.S. dollars)**

Country	1990	1991	1992	1993	1994	1995	1996
Total	3,487.11	4,366.34	11,007.51	27,514.95	33,766.50	37,520.53	41,725.52
Hong Kong	1,880.00	2,405.25	7,507.07	17,274.75	19,665.44	20,060.37	20,677.32
Japan	503.38	532.50	709.83	1,324.10	2,075.29	3,108.46	3,679.35
United States	455.99	323.20	511.05	2,063.12	2,490.80	3,083.01	3,443.33
Germany	64.25	161.12	88.57	56.25	258.99	386.35	518.31
Macao	33.42	81.62	202.00	586.50	509.37	439.82	580.39
Singapore	50.43	58.21	122.31	490.04	1,179.61	1,851.22	2,243.56
United Kingdom	13.33	35.39	38.33	220.51	688.84	914.14	1,300.73
Italy	4.10	28.21	20.69	99.89	206.16	263.31	166.94
Thailand	6.72	19.62	83.03	233.18	234.87	288.24	323.31
Australia	24.87	14.91	35.03	109.96	188.26	232.99	193.92
Switzerland	1.48	12.31	29.14	41.02	70.54	63.53	187.61
Canada	8.04	10.76	58.24	136.88	216.05	257.02	337.93
France	21.06	9.88	44.93	141.41	192.04	287.02	423.75
Bermuda	–	8.00	0.29	18.53	50.74	109.14	86.12
Netherlands	15.98	6.67	28.41	84.00	111.05	114.11	125.11
Norway	2.23	6.05	5.06	1.34	2.31	1.53	26.79
Philippines	1.67	5.85	16.28	122.50	140.40	105.78	55.51
Panama	6.76	3.56	8.19	14.84	18.30	15.66	15.47
Ireland	–	2.50	1.00	1.50	–	0.99	10.03
Indonesia	1.00	2.18	20.17	65.75	115.70	111.63	93.54
Malaysia	0.64	1.96	24.67	91.42	200.99	259.00	459.95

Source: See table 8.2 source.

for half or more of total FDI inflow into China for every year during the 1992–96 period. Hong Kong's dominance tends to be more important in earlier years. So if one looks at the stock of FDI, Hong Kong's share is close to 60 percent. Japan and the United States are the second and third largest investors in China (the relative ranking may switch between the two depending on the year examined). However, each invests significantly less than Hong Kong, typically less than a quarter of what Hong Kong invests. The United Kingdom, France, and Germany are important source countries. However, their investments not only lag distantly behind that of Hong Kong but sometimes also lag behind Singapore and Macao.

One may question whether Hong Kong's investment in mainland China should be counted as FDI. Ever since the founding of the People's Republic, the Chinese government consistently declared that it did not regard the various treaties that ceded or leased what is now the Hong Kong territory to Britain as valid and legally binding. It claimed that Hong Kong was always part of China. On 1 July 1997, Britain formally returned the territory to China. In that connection, one can at most treat investment coming from Hong Kong as quasi-foreign.[1]

Part of reported FDI from Hong Kong is in fact capital originating from the mainland and coming back to the mainland disguised as Hong Kong investment—sometimes labeled "round-tripping" capital—to take advantage of tax, tariff, and other benefits accorded to foreign-invested firms. One estimate puts round-tripping capital at 15 percent of total Hong Kong investment in China in the Chinese official statistics. Round-tripping capital is best described as "false-foreign" direct investment. Using the previous estimate, false-foreign investment was on the order of $3 billion in 1996, or over 7 percent of the total FDI flow into China, according to the official statistics.

To summarize, if one excludes false-foreign and quasi-foreign direct investment in China, true FDI would be 50 percent smaller in terms of the flows in recent years, and 60 percent smaller in terms of the stocks.

8.3 China as a Host of Direct Investment from the Major Source Countries

I now examine whether China is an underachiever as a host of investment from the world's major source countries, and whether corruption

---

1. Part of Hong Kong investment may be Taiwanese investment disguised to avoid political inconvenience with the Taiwanese government. If one adopts the view that Taiwan and China belong to the same country, which is the official position of the two governments on both sides of the Taiwan Strait, then this part of investment should also be treated as quasi-foreign.

Another part of Hong Kong investment may truly be investment from the world's major source countries such as the United States and United Kingdom. This portion is not likely to be big. We will return to this discussion later in the paper.

has deterred foreign investment. Let me first explain the data, and then the specification of the statistical framework, before presenting and discussing the results.

8.3.1   Data

Foreign Direct Investment

The dependent variable is the bilateral stock of FDI at the end of 1993 from seven major source countries to forty-two host countries. The data come from the OECD bilateral FDI database covering outward FDI by destination. They are based on reports by individual source countries. The source countries are the United States, Japan, Germany, the United Kingdom, France, Italy, and Norway. These seven countries are the only source countries that have nonmissing data on FDI in China. The number of host countries is constrained by availability of data on corruption and taxes.

From this database, table 8.4 presents the bilateral stock of FDI from these seven countries into China and Hong Kong in 1993, 1991, and 1989. Comparing tables 8.3 and 8.4, one notices discrepancies, sometimes quite large, in the bilateral FDI from the two reporting sources (also see appendix table 8A.1). The stock values of FDI in 1993 by the United States, Japan, and Italy according to source country reports in the OECD database were actually a lot smaller than the *flows* of FDI from these countries in the same year according to Chinese (host country) statistics, sometimes by a factor of three. The stock values of FDI in 1993 from the United Kingdom and France according to their reports to the OECD were close to the flow values reported by the Chinese. Stocks of FDI for Germany and Norway in 1993 were higher than the corresponding flows, and the two can plausibly be matched.

There are reasons why the Chinese data may be overstated (related to bureaucrats' incentives to exaggerate their ability to attract FDI and foreign investors' incentives to exaggerate their amount of investment in order to report lower taxable incomes). But there are also plausible reasons why the OECD numbers may be understated (e.g., reinvested dividends may not be properly counted). Given that the Chinese reported flow in 1993 was bigger for some countries than the entire stock in the same year, it seems likely that the Chinese figures contain much fat.

In any case, in the interest of using a consistent database, all subsequent regressions are run using the OECD data. I will, however, discuss the implications of measurement errors for the interpretation of the statistical results.

Corruption Measure

By its nature, corruption is very difficult if not infeasible to measure objectively. Researchers have relied on corruption perception indexes based on surveys of experts or firms. For example, the Business International

Table 8.4   Bilateral Stock of FDI in China and Hong Kong

Source Country	China			Hong Kong			Unit
	1993	1991	1989	1989	1991	1993	
France	827	536	337	2,727	2,166	8,607	Million francs
	140.3	103.5	58.2	471.1	418.1	1,459.9	Million US$
Germany	734	339	173	1,127	1,233	1,718	Million marks
	425.2	223.6	101.9	663.8	813.3	995.2	Million US$
Italy	88	48	n.a.	n.a.	90	218	Billion lira
	51.6	41.7	n.a.	n.a.	78.2	127.9	Million US$
Japan	6,163	3,402	2,474	8,065	10,775	12,748	Million US$
United Kingdom	183	80	n.a.	2,059	1,895	3,568	Million pounds
	217.1	149.7	n.a.	3,305.7	3,545.0	5,284.9	Million US$
United States	916.0	426.0	436.0	5,412.0	6,656.0	10,063.0	Million US$
Norway	43	n.a.	n.a.	189	68	364	Million kroners
	5.7	n.a.	n.a.	28.6	11.4	48.4	Million US$

Sources: Unless otherwise noted, data in units of source country currency are from table 8: "Direct Investment Abroad: Position at Year-End by Country" in each source country section of OECD, *International Direct Investment Statistics Yearbook* (Paris, 1996). U.S. dollar amounts for France, Germany, Italy, the United Kingdom, and Norway are converted using the end-of-year exchange rate from IMF, *International Financial Statistics* (Washington, D.C., various issues), line ae. Japanese outward FDI is reported in million U.S. dollars in the OECD book.

(BI) index, based on surveys conducted during 1980–83, asked experts or consultants to rank the countries with which they worked according to "the degree to which business transactions involve corruption or questionable payments." Mauro (1995) and Wei (1997a, 1997b) used it to examine the relations between economic growth and corruption and between FDI and corruption, respectively. Unfortunately, the BI index does not cover China in its sample.

The corruption measure that I use in this paper is the Transparency International (TI) index for 1988–92. Transparency International is an agency dedicated to fighting corruption worldwide. Its index is an average of four surveys of perception of corruption conducted during 1988–92.[2]

Other corruption indexes are available. The International Country Risk Group (ICRG) index is another index based on surveys of experts or consultants. The Global Competitiveness Report (GCR) 1997 index is based on a survey of about 2,400 firms in fifty-eight countries. The pairwise correlations among the BI, TI, and GCR indexes are very high. For example, the correlation coefficient between the BI and TI (or GCR) indexes is .88 (or .77). This gives one confidence that the statistical results I will present are not likely to be sensitive to the choice of index. To get a concrete idea of the corruption measure, table 8.5 reports the values of these corruption indexes for a selection of countries.

Other Data

For host country tax rate, I use the 1989 number because tax rates did not change very much over 1989–91. The actual measure is the minimum of two numbers: the statutory marginal tax rate on foreign corporations as reported by Price Waterhouse[3] (1990) and the actual average tax rate paid by foreign subsidiaries of American firms in that country. Data on twenty-eight of the host countries are taken from Desai and Hines (1996, app. 2). The rest were obtained using the Price Waterhouse source with the kind assistance of Mihir Desai.

GDP data come from the International Monetary Fund's (IMF's) *International Financial Statistics* database. In a few cases where GDP data are not available, GNP data are substituted. Wage data are obtained from the International Labor Organization (1995).

Bilateral distance data measure "greater circle distances" between economic centers in source-host pairs. The dummy on linguistic tie takes the value one if the source and host countries have a common language and zero otherwise. Both sets of data were used in Frankel, Stein, and Wei (1995).

---

2. The four surveys are Business International (1988); Political Risk Service, East Syracuse, New York (1988); World Competitiveness Report, Institute for Management Development, Lausanne (1992); and Political and Economic Consultancy, Hong Kong (1992).

3. See Price Waterhouse website on corporate taxes around the world: http://www.i-trade. com/infosrc/pw/corptax/toc.htm.

Table 8.5	Corruption Ratings for Selected Countries (0–10 scale)			
Country	TI 1988–92	TI 1997	BI 1980–83	GCR 1997
Asian countries				
China	5.29	7.12	n.a.	5.86
Singapore	0.84	1.34	1.00	1.77
Hong Kong	3.13	2.72	3.00	2.17
Japan	2.75	3.43	2.25	2.96
Taiwan	4.86	4.98	4.25	4.60
Malaysia	4.90	4.99	5.00	5.67
South Korea	6.50	5.71	5.25	6.20
Thailand	8.15	6.94	9.5	7.93
Philippines	8.04	6.95	6.5	7.94
India	7.11	7.25	5.75	7.30
Indonesia	9.43	7.28	9.50	7.94
Pakistan	8.10	9.20	7.00	n.a.
Non-Asian countries				
Canada	1.03	0.90	1.00	2.37
United Kingdom	1.74	1.72	1.75	1.93
Germany	1.87	1.77	1.50	2.61
United States	1.24	2.39	1.00	2.41
France	2.55	3.34	1.00	3.51
Mexico	7.77	7.34	7.75	6.24
Kenya	8.40	7.70	6.50	n.a.
Colombia	9.29	7.77	6.50	7.41
Russia	6.73	7.73	n.a.	7.61
Nigeria	9.33	8.24	8.00	n.a.

Note: In the original Business International (BI), Transparency International (TI), Global Competitiveness Report (GCR) indexes, small numbers imply more corruption. All the indexes in the table have been rescaled so that large numbers imply more corruption. For the BI and TI indexes, the values in the table are 11 minus the original scores; for the GCR index, the values in the table are 8 minus the original scores, times 10/7.

"Regulatory burden" is a subjective measure from Freedom House. Its relatively small country coverage would reduce the sample size significantly in regressions that include it as a regressor. "Easy access to domestic capital markets" and "infrastructure efficiency" are subjective measures from the *Global Competitiveness Report 1996.*

8.3.2   Econometric Specification

One could run an ordinary least squares (OLS) specification of the following sort:

$$\ln \text{FDI}_{ij} = X_{ij}\beta + u_{ij},$$

where FDI_{ij} is the stock of foreign investment from source country i to host country j and X is a vector of regressors including the host country's GDP in logarithm and the distance between the source and host countries in logarithm. Experience indicates that, in analogy to the gravity specification on trade flows, the logarithmic transformation of both sides of the equation (of the dependent variable and of most of the regressors), called the double-log linear specification, produces the best functional fit.

Many host countries receive no direct investment from some source countries. A serious drawback of the double-log linear specification is that zero-FDI observations are dropped by this specification. It is natural to think about using a Tobit specification to replace the OLS. The problem there is that the simple Tobit specification conflicts with the double-log transformation, because the log of zero is not defined. To deal with this problem, I will employ the following specification in this paper:

$$\ln(\text{FDI}_{ij} + A) = X\beta + u_{ij}, \qquad \text{if } X\beta + u_{ij} > \ln A,$$
$$= \ln A, \qquad \text{if } X\beta + u_{ij} \leq \ln A,$$

where A is a threshold parameter to be estimated and u is an i.i.d. normal variate with mean zero and variance σ^2. In this specification, if $X\beta + u$ exceeds a threshold value, $\ln A$, source country i accumulates a positive stock of investment in host country j; otherwise, the realized foreign investment is zero (and the desired level could be negative). I use the maximum likelihood method to estimate this equation. Eaton and Tamura (1996) pioneered a version of this specification. Wei (1997a) provided a derivation of the likelihood function.

In actual implementation, I will use a quasi-fixed-effects specification. That is, all regressions will include source country dummies, which take care of all source-country-specific characteristics such as size, level of development, propensity to invest abroad, and possibly idiosyncratic definition of outward FDI. Aside from source country dummies, the list of regressors will include various variables for host country characteristics and source-host pair characteristics.

8.3.3 Regression Results and Interpretation

Basic Findings

Column (1) of table 8.6 provides a benchmark regression. Aside from source country dummies, the list of regressors includes corruption, marginal tax rate, a dummy for the host country's being an OECD member, two measures of the size of the host country (namely, GDP and population, both in logarithmic form),[4] log distance between the economic centers of the source and host countries, and a dummy for whether the source and the host have a common linguistic tie and a historical colonial tie. On

---

4. One may prefer to include log GDP and log GDP per capita instead. The coefficients on these two variables would be a linear combination of the two coefficients on log GDP and log population.

Table 8.6   **China as a Host of FDI**

Variable	(1)	(2)	(3)	(4)	(5)
Corruption	−0.13*	−0.011	−0.14*	−0.12#	−0.13
	(0.04)	(0.108)	(0.06)	(0.07)	(0.15)
Corruption^2		−0.013			0.0025
		(0.009)			(0.0115)
Tax	−2.72*	2.55	−2.75*	−2.81*	−1.82
	(0.66)	(1.98)	(0.65)	(0.72)	(1.77)
Tax^2		−9.55*			−8.21*
		(4.03)			(3.61)
China	−1.15*	−1.59*	−0.74#	−1.30*	−1.25*
	(0.35)	(0.44)	(0.41)	(0.41)	(0.47)
East Asia				−0.21	
				(0.45)	
East Asia × Corruption				0.07	
				(0.06)	
OECD	0.26##	0.30#	0.27#	0.46#	0.39##
	(0.17)	(0.17)	(0.17)	(0.26)	(0.27)
log Wage				−0.24	−0.21
				(0.20)	(0.20)
OECD × log Wage				−0.09	−0.08
				(0.14)	(0.14)
	0.30*	0.21*	0.28*	0.50*	0.47*
	(0.11)	(0.09)	(0.14)	(0.20)	(0.19)
log Population	0.30*	0.40*	0.84	0.06	0.09
	(0.11)	(0.13)	(1.35)	(0.17)	(0.18)
(log Population)^2			−0.015		
			(0.037)		
log Distance	−0.11	−0.12##	−0.11	−0.16#	−0.15#
	(0.08)	(0.08)	(0.08)	(0.08)	(0.08)
Linguistic tie	0.72#	0.76#	0.71#	0.85*	0.89*
	(0.39)	(0.39)	(0.39)	(0.42)	(0.42)
A	8.6E+9*	8.6E+9*	8.6E+9*	9.3E+9*	9.1E+9*
	(1.1E+7)	(6.6E+6)	(7.6E+6)	(5.8E+6)	(4.8E+6)
σ	1.01*	1.00*	1.00*	0.98*	0.99*
	(0.17)	(0.17)	(0.17)	(0.17)	(0.17)
Source dummies	Yes	Yes	Yes	Yes	Yes
N	286	286	286	231	231
Log likelihood	1,288.5	1,292.1	1,288.9	1,124.2	1,121.6

Note: Numbers in parentheses are standard errors. All coefficients and standard errors have been multiplied by 1,000. All regressions include a constant and source country dummies whose coefficients are not reported.

*Significantly different from zero at the 5 percent level.
#Significantly different from zero at the 10 percent level.
##Significantly different from zero at the 15 percent level.

top of that, a dummy for China as host country is added to see whether China receives more or less FDI than predicted by the model.

The coefficients on both corruption and tax rate are negative and statistically significant, indicating that more corruption or higher taxes tend to discourage foreign investment. The coefficients on log GDP and log population are positive, significant, but less than one, suggesting that larger economies receive more FDI, although the increment in FDI is less than proportional to the increment in country size. The coefficient on log distance is negative but insignificant. That on the linguistic dummy is positive, significant, and quantitatively large.

The key variable of interest is the dummy for China as host country for FDI from these seven major source countries. The coefficient on this variable is -1.15 and statistically significant at the 5 percent level. In other words, controlling for these regressors, China is a significant underachiever as a host of FDI. The nonlinear nature of the specification prevents an intuitive interpretation of how much smaller FDI in China is relative to its potential. But the quantitative effect is large. Taking the point estimates on the China dummy and the tax variable literally, one needs to raise the tax rate by 42 percentage points ($= 1.15/0.0272$) in order to reduce FDI in a country that is otherwise identical to China (in terms of the values of the regressors) to the level that actually went into China in 1993.

The relative quantitative effect of corruption on FDI is also significant. A one-step worsening in the TI corruption rating would be equivalent to raising the marginal tax rate by 4.78 percentage points (see Wei 1997a). An increase in the host country corruption rating from the Singapore level (TI value $= 1$) to the China level (TI index $= 6$) has the same effect on inward FDI as raising the tax rate by 23.9 percentage points ($= 4.78 \times 5$). In other words, (perceived) corruption in China is likely to have significantly discouraged FDI.

The benchmark specification in column (1) of table 8.6 assumes that the effects of corruption and the tax rate are linear. In column (2), squared values of both corruption and the tax rate are added to check for the presence of nonlinearity. Neither corruption nor corruption squared is statistically significant, suggesting that there is no nonlinear effect from corruption. On the other hand, tax squared does have a negative and significant effect, although the level effect becomes insignificant. The estimated coefficient on the China dummy remains negative (-1.59) and statistically significant.

It is interesting to note that the coefficient on the host country population term is less than one. This suggests that while inward FDI increases with population size, it does so less than proportionally.

To see a possibly nonlinear effect from host country population size on inward FDI, in column (3) squared log population is included as an additional regressor. The coefficient on the China dummy does get smaller but remains negative and statistically significant at the 10 percent level. However, neither the log population variable nor its square has a statistically significant coefficient. So in subsequent regressions, I will drop the squared term.

In columns (4) and (5), log wage and an interactive term between log wage and the OECD dummy are added. Because wage data are missing for some host countries, this reduces the sample size quite a bit. In any case, the coefficient on log wage is negative, consistent with the idea that countries with low labor costs attract more FDI, but the effect is not statistically significant. In the regression reported in column (4), we also add a dummy for East Asian developing country host and an interactive term between the East Asia dummy and the corruption measure. The objective is to test the hypothesis that the effect of corruption on FDI is smaller for East Asian developing hosts. The coefficient on the interactive term is a small positive number but statistically insignificantly different from zero. Hence, East Asian exceptionalism with respect to the effect of corruption on FDI is not supported by the data.[5]

Are American and Japanese Investors Different?

I now look at whether American and the Japanese investors react to host country corruption in ways that may differ from the response of average OECD investors. Specifically, the United States has a unique law— the Foreign Corrupt Practices Act of 1977—that prohibits its firms from bribing foreign officials. Violators can be fined or put in jail. Until very recently, the United States was the only major source country in the world that criminalized the act of bribing a foreign official.[6] For many other major source countries, bribes paid to foreign officials not only are not illegal but in fact are tax deductible as legitimate business expenses. The uniqueness of the United States leads one to think that American firms may be particularly averse to corruption in foreign host countries.[7]

Japan, on the other hand, is said to have a culture of substantial "gift exchange" between firms and government officials even in the purely domestic context. This might translate into some comparative advantage for Japanese businesses in corrupt foreign countries. In other words, Japan may be less sensitive to foreign corruption than an average source country.

Column (1) in table 8.7 puts these hypotheses to the test. Two more variables are added to the basic specification: an interactive variable be-

5. This agrees with the finding of Wei (1997a) on an earlier data set.
6. Britain claims to have a law that specifies the same thing. The law is apparently not enforced.
7. Hines (1995) found a negative association between the size of U.S. direct investment in a country and that country's corruption rating according to the BI index. While finding that FDI in general is negatively related to host country corruption, Wei (1997a) did not find a statistically significant difference between American and other OECD investors.

Table 8.7   Are American and Japanese Firms Special?

Variable	(1)	(2)[a]
Corruption	−0.13*	−0.13*
	(0.05)	(0.04)
Tax	2.90	2.73
	(2.10)	(1.99)
Tax^2	−10.23*	−9.64*
	(4.15)	(3.93)
China	−1.38*	−1.20*
	(0.40)	(0.38)
U.S. × Corruption	−0.27*	−0.25*
	(0.10)	(0.10)
Japan × Corruption	0.04	0.04
	(0.05)	(0.05)
OECD	0.27	0.25##
	(0.18)	(0.17)
log GDP	0.25*	0.24*
	(0.11)	(0.11)
log Population	0.39*	0.36*
	(0.12)	(0.12)
log Distance	−0.15##	−0.14##
	(0.09)	(0.09)
Linguistic tie	0.77#	−0.72##
	(0.40)	(0.37)
A	8.1E+9*	8.6E+9*
	(7.7E+6)	(1.8E+7)
σ	1.03*	0.97*
	(0.17)	(0.16)
Source dummies	Yes	Yes
N	286	286
Log likelihood	1,284.8	1,284.8

Note: Numbers in parentheses are standard errors. All coefficients and standard errors have been multiplied by 1,000. All regressions include a constant and source country dummies whose coefficients are not reported.

[a]In col. (2), FDI into China has been multiplied by five.

*Significantly different from zero at the 5 percent level.

#Significantly different from zero at the 10 percent level.

##Significantly different from zero at the 15 percent level.

tween the U.S. source country dummy and the corruption measure, and a similar interactive variable between the Japan source country dummy and the host country corruption measure. If American investors are more averse to foreign corruption than investors from an average source country, the coefficient on the first interactive variable should be negative and statistically significant. If Japanese investors are less sensitive to foreign corruption than investors from an average source country, one expects to find a positive and significant coefficient on the second interactive variable.

The results reported in column (1) support the first hypothesis but not the second. In other words, American investors are more discouraged from investing in corrupt host countries than average investors.

While the coefficient on the China dummy is still negative and significant, it is noteworthy that its absolute value is smaller than the corresponding coefficient in column (2) of table 8.6. In other words, taking into account American investors' aversion to foreign corruption is a step toward understanding the gap between China's actual reception of FDI and its potential as predicted by the model in columns (1) and (2) of table 8.6.

Measurement Errors on FDI into China

We mentioned the possibility that FDI in China from the major source countries may be underreported in the OECD database (specifically, OECD numbers tend to be a lot smaller than the numbers China reports in its official statistics). Note that if a particular OECD country adopts a definition of FDI that merely underreports its FDI abroad, it would underreport FDI to all destination countries by the same or a similar factor, which would not explain the negative China coefficient here. Although there is no evidence to think so, let us assume that for some reason, FDI in China from the major source countries is underreported by a larger extent than is FDI in other countries. To see if China's underachievement as a host can be explained by this assumption, I conduct an entirely arbitrary exercise: I multiply all FDI in China by a factor of five while keeping FDI in other host countries intact and rerun the regression reported in column (1) of table 8.7. The results are reported in column (2) of table 8.7.

As one might expect, the absolute value of the coefficient on the China dummy—a measure of the gap between China's actual inward FDI and its potential—declines from 1.38 to 1.20. But multiplying actual FDI in China by five is not enough: the gap is still negative and statistically significant at the 5 percent level.

The Hong Kong Connection

It is often remarked that Hong Kong is a mecca for FDI. It seems possible that in part because investors from the major source countries loathe the corrupt situation on the mainland, they invest heavily in Hong Kong as a stepping stone toward or substitute for investing in mainland China. Indeed, part of Hong Kong investment in China may have been made on behalf of investors from the major source countries.

We examine this possibility. In column (1) of table 8.8, a dummy for Hong Kong as host country is added to the regression. As one expects, the coefficient is positive (0.46) and statistically significant, indicating that Hong Kong is an overachiever as a host of FDI.

To see if the Hong Kong connection helps to solve the puzzle of China's underachievement, I redefine all FDI in Hong Kong from the major

Table 8.8   **The Hong Kong Connection**

Variable	(1)	(2)[a]	(3)[b]	(4)[c]
Corruption	−0.13*	−0.13*	−0.13#	−0.14*
	(0.05)	(0.05)	(0.05)	(0.05)
Tax	3.24	3.03	3.01##	2.89*
	(2.15)	(2.05)	(2.05)	(2.00)
Tax^2	−10.63*	−10.01*	−10.06*	−9.78*
	(4.22)	(4.03)	(4.01)	(3.93)
China	−1.52*	−1.04*	−0.93*	−0.49*
	(0.40)	(0.42)	(0.44)	(0.50)
Hong Kong	0.46*			
	(0.18)			
U.S. × Corruption	−0.30*	−0.24*	−0.23*	−0.19#
	(0.12)	(0.10)	(0.10)	(0.11)
OECD	0.29##	0.30#	0.30#	0.30##
	(0.19)	(0.18)	(0.18)	(0.18)
log GDP	0.23*	0.22*	0.22*	0.22*
	(0.11)	(0.11)	(0.11)	(0.11)
log Population	0.41*	0.40*	0.40*	0.39*
	(0.13)	(0.12)	(0.12)	(0.12)
log Distance	−0.16#	−0.15#	−0.15#	−0.14#
	(0.09)	(0.08)	(0.08)	(0.08)
Linguistic tie	0.79#	0.74#	0.74#	0.71#
	(0.41)	(0.40)	(0.40)	(0.39)
A	8.1E+9*	8.5E+9*	8.5E+9*	8.7E+9*
	(5.9E+7)	(5.6E+6)	(3.5E+6)	(4.8E+6)
σ	1.01*	1.00*	1.00*	0.99*
	(0.16)	(0.16)	(0.17)	(0.16)
Source dummies	Yes	Yes	Yes	Yes
N	286	279	279	279
Log likelihood	1,286.4	1,252.4	1,259.0	1,254.8

Note: Numbers in parentheses are standard errors. All coefficients and standard errors have been multiplied by 1,000. All regressions include a constant and source country dummies whose coefficients are not reported.

[a]In col. (2), FDI in Hong Kong is counted as a part of FDI in China. Hong Kong as a host country is excluded from the sample.

[b]In col. (3), constructed FDI in China is FDI in Hong Kong, plus five times original FDI in China.

[c]In col. (4), constructed FDI in China is FDI in Hong Kong, plus twenty times original FDI in China.

*Significantly different from zero at the 5 percent level.

#Significantly different from zero at the 10 percent level.

##Significantly different from zero at the 15 percent level.

source countries as part of FDI in China from the same source countries and exclude from the regression those observations in which Hong Kong is a host. The results are presented in column (2) of table 8.8. While the coefficient on the China dummy drops substantially (from −1.52 to −1.04), it remains negative and significant.

In column (3) of table 8.8, I reconstruct bilateral FDI in China as original FDI in China as reported by the source countries multiplied by five, plus bilateral FDI in Hong Kong from the same source countries. The coefficient on the China dummy again drops (to −0.93) but is still significantly different from zero. In column (4), I reconstruct yet again bilateral FDI in China, as FDI reported by the source countries multiplied by twenty, plus actual FDI in Hong Kong. The coefficient on the China dummy this time is statistically insignificant (although still negative). All of these experiments are completely arbitrary. They serve to show that the gap between actual FDI in China and potential FDI as defined by these regressions is enormous.

Adding Regulatory Burdens and Other Factors to the Regressions

As a final exercise, we add host country labor cost, regulatory burden, ease of access to domestic capital markets by foreign-invested firms, and efficiency of infrastructure to the regressions. In this exercise, FDI in Hong Kong is counted as a part of FDI in China, but original FDI in China is not amplified. All four new variables have missing observations for some host countries, and therefore, the sample size is reduced. The results are presented in table 8.9.

When just log wage in the host country is added to the regression, in column (1), it has a negative coefficient that is statistically significant at the 10 percent level. When a measure of regulatory burden is added to the regression, reported in column (2), it has a statistically significant and negative coefficient (−0.34). It is noteworthy that the coefficient on the China dummy now becomes statistically insignificantly different from zero.

In column (3), an index for easy access to domestic capital markets by foreign-invested firms and another index for infrastructure efficiency are added. Neither is statistically significant. Indeed, both have wrong signs.

The measure of regulatory burden and the TI corruption index are positively correlated (with a correlation coefficient of .6). Shleifer and Vishny (1994) and Kaufmann and Wei (1999) have argued that the burden of regulation is often imposed or maintained by corruption-prone officials to facilitate the extraction of bribes. In that sense, the severity of the regulatory burden can be taken as an indirect measure of the severity of corruption.

8.4   Concluding Remarks

While the absolute value of FDI in China in recent years looks very impressive, it masks an unusual composition of source countries. A significant

Table 8.9   **Regulatory Burden and Other Obstacles to FDI**

Variable	(1)	(2)	(3)
Corruption	−0.07	0.07	0.04
	(0.05)	(0.07)	(0.09)
Tax	1.92	5.04#	6.29##
	(1.90)	(2.84)	(3.91)
Tax²	−8.40*	−14.32*	16.82
	(3.62)	(5.71)	(7.74)
China	−0.93*	−0.47	−0.84
	(0.44)	(0.48)	(0.86)
U.S. × Corruption	−0.20*	−0.30*	−0.31
	(0.09)	(0.13)	(0.13)
OECD	0.22	0.52#	0.66##
	(0.18)	(0.28)	(0.43)
log Wage	−0.34#	−0.23	−0.31
	(0.20)	(0.23)	(0.28)
Regulatory burden		−0.34*	−0.36#
		(0.17)	(0.20)
Easy access to domestic capital markets			−0.12
			(0.24)
Infrastructure efficiency			−0.09
			(0.27)
log GDP	0.56*	0.44#	0.48#
	(0.24)	(0.25)	(0.28)
log Population	−0.015*	0.11	0.07
	(0.215)	(0.27)	(0.30)
log Distance	−0.16*	−0.07	−0.07
	(0.08)	(0.10)	(0.10)
Linguistic tie	0.89*	1.08*	1.13*
	(0.44)	(0.48)	(0.50)
A	9.1E+9*	9.4E+9*	9.2E+9*
	(3.5E+6)	(9.6E+6)	(3.8E+6)
σ^2	0.97*	0.98*	1.01*
	(0.16)	(0.16)	(0.17)
Source dummies	Yes	Yes	Yes
N	224	170	170
Log likelihood	1,082.4	834.4	837.9

Note: Numbers in parentheses are standard errors. All coefficients and standard errors have been multiplied by 1,000. All regressions include a constant and source country dummies whose coefficients are not reported. Constructed FDI in China is FDI in Hong Kong plus original FDI in China.

*Significantly different from zero at the 5 percent level.

#Significantly different from zero at the 10 percent level.

##Significantly different from zero at the 15 percent level.

fraction (maybe 15 percent of Hong Kong investment in China can be round-tripping mainland capital in disguise. This should be counted as false-foreign direct investment and should be deleted from statistics on FDI in China.

The remaining part of Hong Kong investment in China should be regarded as quasi-foreign direct investment, for Hong Kong has always been a special extension of China even under British rule and has since 1 July 1997 been legally part of China. Taking out these two parts would reduce the annual flow of FDI into China in recent years by half, and the stock by 60 percent.

Using cross-country data on bilateral stocks of FDI from the seven most important source countries in the world, one can estimate the potential amount of inward FDI for a host country such as China. Compared with its model-predicted potential, China is found to be a significant underachiever as a host of FDI from the major source countries. The gap is huge. China's relatively high corruption discourages FDI by a significant amount. The regulatory burden in China may be another important impediment that discourages investors from the major source countries from investing more in China.

Appendix

Table 8A.1   FDI Flow into China: Chinese versus Source Country Statistics

Country	1990	1991	1992	1993	1994	1995	Units
United States							
OECD report	30	40	74	556	745	436	Million US$
Chinese report	455.99	323.20	511.05	2,063.12	2,490.80	3,083.01	Million US$
Japan							
OECD report	349	579	1,070	1,691	2,565	3,834	Million US$
Chinese report	503.38	532.50	709.83	1,324.10	2,075.29	3,108.46	Million US$
Germany							
OECD report	–	115	233	112	471	627	Million marks
OECD report (US$)	–	75.86	144	64.88	304.11	437.39	Million US$
Chinese report	64.25	161.12	88.57	56.25	258.99	386.35	Million US$
United Kingdom							
OECD report	–	17	20	21	8	54	Million pounds
OECD report (US$)	–	31.80	30.24	31.11	12.5	83.7	Million US$
Chinese report	13.33	35.39	38.33	220.51	688.84	914.14	Million US$
France							
OECD report	–11	463	296	505	607	693	Million francs
OECD report (US$)	–2.14	89.38	53.75	85.66	113.54	141.43	Million US$
Chinese report	21.06	9.88	44.93	141.41	192.04	287.02	Million US$
Australia							
OECD report	–	–	–	16	50	33	Million AU$
OECD report (US$)	–	–	–	10.83	38.84	24.59	Million US$
Chinese report	24.87	14.91	35.03	109.96	188.26	232.99	Million US$

References

Desai, Mihir, and James R. Hines Jr. 1996. "Basket" cases: International joint ventures after the Tax Reform Act of 1986. NBER Working Paper no. 5755. Cambridge, Mass.: National Bureau of Economic Research, September.

Eaton, Jonathan, and Akiko Tamura. 1996. Japanese and U.S. exports and investment as conduits of growth. In *Financial deregulation and integration in East Asia,* ed. Takatoshi Ito and Anne O. Krueger, 51–72. Chicago: University of Chicago Press.

Frankel, Jeffrey, and Andrew Rose. 1996. Currency crashes in emerging markets: An empirical treatment. *Journal of International Economics* 41 (November): 351–66.

Frankel, Jeffrey, Ernesto Stein, and Shang-Jin Wei. 1995. Trading blocs and the Americas: The natural, the unnatural, and the super-natural. *Journal of Development Economics* 47 (June): 61–95.

Hines, James, Jr. 1995. Forbidden payment: Foreign bribery and American business after 1977. NBER Working Paper no. 5266. Cambridge, Mass.: National Bureau of Economic Research, September.

International Labor Organization. 1995. *International labor yearbook.* Geneva: International Labor Organization.

Kaufmann, Daniel, and Shang-Jin Wei. 1999. Does "grease payment" speed up the wheels of commerce? NBER Working Paper no. 7093. Cambridge, Mass.: National Bureau of Economic Research.

Mauro, Paolo. 1995. Corruption and growth. *Quarterly Journal of Economics* 110:681–712.

Radelet, Steven, and Jeffrey D. Sachs. 1998. The East Asian financial crisis: Diagnosis, remedies, prospects. *Brookings Papers on Economic Activity,* no. 1:1–74.

Shleifer, Andrei, and Robert W. Vishny. 1994. Politicians and firms. *Quarterly Journal of Economics* 109 (November): 995–1025.

Wei, Shang-Jin. 1996. Foreign direct investment in China: Sources and consequences. In *Financial deregulation and integration in East Asia,* ed. Takatoshi Ito and Anne O. Krueger. Chicago: University of Chicago Press.

———. 1997a. How taxing is corruption on international investors? NBER Working Paper no. 6030. Cambridge, Mass.: National Bureau of Economic Research, May; *Review of Economics and Statistics,* forthcoming.

———. 1997b. Why is corruption so much more taxing than taxes? Arbitrariness kills. NBER Working Paper no. 6255. Cambridge, Mass.: National Bureau of Economic Research, November.

———. 1998. Corruption in Asian economies: Beneficial grease, minor annoyance, or major obstacle? Cambridge, Mass.: Harvard University, Kennedy School of Government. Working paper.

Comment   Mari Pangestu

This interesting paper enriches our understanding of the many facets of FDI in China and in particular questions the perception of China as a

Mari Pangestu is an economist at the Centre for Strategic and International Studies, Jakarta.

"magnet" for FDI. Wei aims to show that the gap between actual FDI in China and the potential amount from major source countries is large—or, contrary to what is perceived, that China is an "underachiever" as a host country of FDI from major source countries due to its corruption and regulatory burden.

However, the motivation for the paper, that is, why one should be concerned that China may be an underachiever with respect to FDI from source countries but an overachiever with respect to FDI from Hong Kong, Taiwan, Macao, and Singapore, is not obvious. One can postulate three possible reasons for concern. First is the quantity of FDI. The notion would be that China is not receiving enough FDI (after adjusting for Hong Kong investment that is "domestic"), whether measured as a shortfall between domestic savings and domestic investment or whether the quantity of FDI is small relative to the size of China.

Second is the diversity of FDI. If investment is dominated by Hong Kong, Macao, Taiwan, and Singapore, China may be too dependent on these sources. Such reasoning could be partly political and partly economic. Economically speaking, the type of investment from these source countries could differ from that from major source countries.

Related to the above point, a third reason is the notion that FDI from the major source countries is "different" from domestic investment and FDI from Hong Kong, Taiwan, Singapore, and Macao. FDI from major source countries could be preferable for various reasons normally argued to be the benefits of FDI: technology transfer, management and technology spillovers, demand for greater transparency, competition, and access to export markets. It is not clear whether the FDI numbers included in this study cover all FDI in China or whether they exclude certain sectors such as oil and gas. This distinction is important because it is likely that FDI from the major source countries dominates some sectors, such as oil and gas and mining, where these countries are likely to have firm-specific advantages.

The reason for investment from one set of source countries differing qualitatively from investment from another set is not self-evident. While the amount of domestic investment must be taken out of Hong Kong investment coming into China because of round-tripping and stop-tripping—or investment coming through Hong Kong to avoid corruption—should be subtracted, is the remaining pure Hong Kong investment qualitatively not desirable? After all, there has been a lot of synergy between Hong Kong and China, with the former having much higher technological capability and the latter providing lower cost labor, land, and infrastructure, as well as a large market. Furthermore, it is not self-evident that stop-tripping happens mainly because of corruption. FDI destined for China might go through Hong Kong because Hong Kong is a major financial and service center, and many firms have their regional headquarters in Hong Kong. So FDI entering China through Hong Kong could be based on synergy with existing activities in Hong Kong and proximity to the financial center and other infrastructure.

Once it is statistically established that FDI from major source countries in China is less than its potential, the results of the analysis could be improved by looking at which main factor explains the underachievement. Besides corruption and the other factors tested, it is possible that there are still other factors, such as lack of intellectual property protection and weak enforcement of contracts.

The data used in the study are for 1993. It is possible that updating the data to 1994–96 would yield different results because there was considerable outward investment from Japan in those years. Another way to push the analysis is to take China as a dummy compared with other countries as dummies—for example, Indonesia, one of China's main competitors for FDI from major source countries. Is Indonesia more or less of an underachiever, and what are the explanatory factors for its greater or lesser underachievement?

A final point: if the result is that underachievement is due to China's corruption and regulatory burden, then for the paper to be useful it should identify policy implications. For instance, China's attractiveness as a big market and source of low-cost labor is marred by its corruption and regulatory burden. Therefore, if the motivation is to increase FDI from major source countries for whatever reason, the priorities for policy would be to reduce corruption and the regulatory burden. Since it will take time for these policies to take effect, especially if corruption cannot be uprooted at once, it is also important to identify interim measures that can be introduced (e.g., one-stop administration of FDI and regulations facing foreign investors).

Comment   Akira Kohsaka

In this paper Wei examines the determinants of bilateral FDI stocks in 1993 from seven major OECD source countries to forty-two host economies, including China and Hong Kong. He concludes that China was an "underachiever" in attracting FDI from the seven countries within the framework of his empirical model. In 1994, Wei presented a paper at the NBER–East Asia Seminar on Economics in which he followed the same

Akira Kohsaka is professor of economics in the Osaka School of International Public Policy, Osaka University.

line of argument by examining the determinants of FDI flows in the years 1987–90 from five OECD countries (Wei 1996). What is the difference between the two papers?

First, he now uses a statistically more sophisticated estimation method with Tobit specification on the data set. Second, he scrutinizes more deeply the determinants of FDI by adding some explanatory variables related to the general business environment in the host economy; these include tax levels, degree of corruption, and other factors. Third, even though he starts his analysis with mainland China (table 8.6), he ends up consolidating China with Hong Kong as a host economy (tables 8.8 and 8.9).

I sympathize with Wei's goal of evaluating the accuracy of the popular view of China as a world magnet for FDI, and I find appealing the claim that China has in fact been an underachiever and can or will be a larger FDI absorber. As far as his analysis goes, however, I cannot help having a few reservations about his conclusion.

Let me begin my argument from within his data set as well as his analytical framework. To start, look at columns (2) and (3) of table 8.9. We find a significant negative effect of regulatory burden on FDI on one hand and insignificant (and wrongly signed) tax and corruption variables on the other. This is not surprising because all of them could be positively correlated one another, reflecting unfavorable general business environments in host economies. On top of that, we must note that the China dummy becomes insignificant, though negative, which suggests that FDI to "China" by the OECD-7 does not deviate from what the model predicts, or that China is not an underachiever contrary to the author's claim.

I am not necessarily saying that his claim is negated by his own results, but I would like to suggest we should be more careful in interpreting this series of his estimation results on two points.

One point concerns missing explanatory variables. In addition to ordinary determinants of FDI, such as those related to host economy size and physical and cultural distance between host and source countries, the author picks up variables related to general business environment in the host economy: taxation, corruption, wages, regulatory burden, access to domestic capital markets, and infrastructure efficiency. He could add others related to locational advantages and disadvantages. The problem is that these variables are more or less closely correlated with each other, and we generally cannot tell which of them matters most and is first to be tackled. Furthermore, this correlation problem is most serious with those variables based on subjective evaluations, such as corruption and regulatory burden.

The other point concerns his enlarged definition of China as a host economy that includes Hong Kong. The probable overstatement of FDI data on the Chinese side has been frequently mentioned and is well known. This is because of the *round-tripping* of Chinese capital as well as the *short-tripping* of other foreign capital, that is, because of the very nature of Hong Kong as an entrepôt not only in goods but in capital flows. So one idea is to focus only on "direct" FDI by the OECD countries to China. Yet once you add Hong Kong to greater China as a host of FDI, all the ambiguity and complexity revive. The business environments in the two economies were (and are) quite distinct. We cannot tell what portion of FDI by OECD countries was meant to reach China through Hong Kong and what portion was intended for Hong Kong on its own.

Now, I turn to general issues about Wei's framework as well as his data set. The deficiency or overstatement of FDI in China has been frequently mentioned. But it cannot be denied that Hong Kong has been the largest source economy for FDI in China. Although it would be difficult to identify the ultimate nationalities of Hong Kong capital invested in China, the fact that it does not matter is the raison d'être of Hong Kong. Above all (except for round-tripping Chinese capital motivated by domestic distortions), as correctly put by Deng Xiaoping, it does not matter who brings in capital but how. If this is the case, whether China is an under- or overachiever might have policy implications worth probing, and then the exclusion of Hong Kong as a source economy is not justified except for reasons of data availability.

As is well known, China became the largest FDI absorber among the developing economies as late as 1993. Until then, it had never been taken seriously as a significant absorber of FDI. Apparently, before 1993, no one spoke of "China fever" (*Economist,* 1 March 1997, 38, U.S. edition) or "The world's strongest magnet" (*Journal of Commerce,* 27 December 1996, 3A). What can we say about such comments with a data set of FDI stock figures in 1993? Probably not much. Rather, I would like to see what Wei will come up with on the basis of a more recent data set. If he finds again that China is underachieving as an FDI absorber, it would really be a surprise.

Reference

Wei, Shang-Jin. 1996. Foreign direct investment in China: Sources and consequences. In *Financial deregulation and integration in East Asia,* ed. Takatoshi Ito and Anne O. Krueger. Chicago: University of Chicago Press.

The Role of Foreign Direct Investment in Korea's Economic Development
Productivity Effects and Implications for the Currency Crisis

June-Dong Kim and Sang-In Hwang

9.1 Introduction

Since the 1960s, Korea has accomplished remarkable economic growth, allowing it to overcome the devastation caused by the Korean War. However, the currency crisis of 1997 brought Korea into the most severe hardship since the Korean War. One factor that could contribute to Korean recovery from the financial crisis is a stable flow of foreign direct investment (FDI) because FDI appears less prone to sudden swings than other forms of capital inflow. However, negative sentiment about foreign investment still exist, reflecting fears of foreign control over the domestic economy. In fact, the Korean government as well as the general public was in favor of indigenous industrialization rather than FDI-based development.

Now we need to investigate the role of FDI in economic development, as the Korean economy suffers a currency crisis. Specifically, with public sentiment running against the harsh conditions of the IMF financial arrangements, it is interesting to see whether FDI can in fact help Korea to avoid the IMF bailout loans. Multinational firms may help the crisis-ridden country to circumvent the IMF financial arrangements by providing local subsidiaries and business partners normal access to raw materials or trade financing.

As a longer term issue, we need to examine whether FDI enhances efficiency and thus contributes to sustainable growth. Despite the low realization of FDI, case study evidence shows that foreign firms helped to develop such strategic industries as semiconductors and to raise productivity through the transfer of technology and managerial know-how.

June-Dong Kim and Sang-In Hwang are research fellows of Korea Institute for International Economic Policy.

This paper investigates these two issues regarding the role of FDI in Korea's economic development. First, we examine whether the quantitative data supports anecdotal evidence of the productivity spillover effects of FDI in Korean manufacturing. Further, we investigate the role of FDI in a currency crisis by looking at the relation between the relative importance of FDI and the incidence of IMF bailout loans in developing countries.

The paper is organized as follows: Section 9.2 reviews the evolution of the Korean government's FDI policy. Section 9.3 presents the trends and patterns of FDI inflow into Korea. Section 9.4 estimates the effects of FDI on the productivity of Korean manufacturing industries. Section 9.5 investigates whether FDI can play a role in preventing IMF rescue loans using data for ninety developing countries. Concluding remarks are made in section 9.6.

9.2   Historical Overview of Foreign Direct Investment Policy in Korea

In order to investigate the role of FDI in Korea's economic development, it is helpful to review the government's policy on FDI. Korea is well known around the world as an "outward-oriented" country. Yet, as demonstrated below, the main orientation of Korea's investment policies has failed to embrace an open market strategy throughout its development stages.

9.2.1   Institutionalization, 1960–83

Following the import substitution drive of the 1950s, Korea shifted its development strategy toward a more outward-oriented system that emphasized export promotion. The new export-led growth strategy went hand in hand with policies aimed at introducing FDI. In 1960, the Korean government enacted the Foreign Capital Inducement Act (FCIA) and related decrees.

The government wanted to use FDI to ease balance-of-payments difficulties and as a supply of needed technology and expertise. FDI was welcomed into the light manufacturing export sector, especially in the two Free Export Zones at Masan and Iri. However, foreign investment continued to be discouraged in those sectors still protected by import substitution measures because the Korean government feared that otherwise the economy would become dominated by foreign firms. Moreover, the Korean government wanted to channel the limited amount of capital resources to industries vital to long-term economic growth. With this strategy in mind, the Korean government preferred foreign borrowing, which brought foreign resources under its control.

9.2.2   Liberalization of Foreign Direct Investment, 1984–97

A major change occurred in the early 1980s as the Korean economy began to experience serious difficulties due to the negative effects of the

Heavy and Chemical Industry Promotion Plan of the 1970s. A new industrial strategy was thus adopted in the early 1980s in an attempt to upgrade Korea's industrial structure into one embracing more technology- and skill-intensive sectors. A key component of this technological upgrade was the liberalization of FDI.

In 1984, the Korean government replaced the positive list system with a negative list system in which all industries not listed were open for FDI approval.

In December 1989, various performance requirements imposed on foreign-invested enterprises, such as export, local content, and technology transfer requirements, were abolished.

Starting in 1994, the Korean government liberalized restricted business categories according to the Five-Year Foreign Investment Liberalization Plan, which has been updated every year thereafter. Multilateral trade negotiations such as GATT and the government's aim to induce more competition in the domestic market fostered a gradual opening of the service sector.

In December 1996, when Korea joined the OECD, the Korean government furthered liberalization by amending the FCIA to create the Act on Foreign Direct Investment and Foreign Capital Inducement. Its main purpose was to bring Korea's FDI system in line with international norms and standards. For example, the concept of FDI was expanded to encompass long-term (five year or more) loans. Also, starting in February 1997, foreign investors were allowed to acquire outstanding shares of Korean companies through friendly mergers and acquisitions (M&As). Such friendly M&As required the consent of the board of directors of the targeted company.

Even though the Korean government made some real efforts to liberalize FDI, its overall stance toward FDI was passive. The government allowed FDI into liberalized business categories and activities but refused to remove various impediments and to promote FDI to the extent carried out in the Southeast Asian countries.

9.2.3 Promotion after Currency Crisis, 1998 and Afterward

At the end of 1997, Korea was throttled by a currency crisis when the won depreciated over 100 percent against the U.S. dollar. Loss of foreign reserves and the reluctance of foreign lenders to roll over loans brought Korea to the brink of default in late December 1997. To overcome the crisis in the most rapid and painless way possible, the Korean government is targeting more active promotion of FDI.

In November 1998, the Korean government enacted the Foreign Investment Promotion Act. This new legislation focuses on creating an investor-oriented policy environment by streamlining foreign investment procedures, expanding investment incentives, and establishing an institutional framework for investor relations, including one-stop service. The Korean government also undertook full-fledged liberalization in the area of hostile cross-border M&As and foreign land ownership.

9.3   Trends of Foreign Direct Investment in Korea

FDI in Korea was minimal during the initial liberalization that lasted from the 1960s until the mid-1980s (table 9.1). In the 1980s, however, annual average FDI in Korea increased from US$100 million to over $800 million. Following a contraction that lasted until 1993, FDI resumed an upward trend, reaching $3 billion in 1997 and a record $5.1 billion in 1998. This growth is in part explained by the fall in stock market and real estate prices and the depreciation of the won. It also reflects the Korean government's new policy measures to promote FDI and progress in restructuring the financial and corporate sectors.

For the sectoral distribution of FDI inflow into Korea, the manufacturing sector was the largest recipient during the early liberalization period, absorbing 67.4 percent of total inward FDI during 1962–86 (table 9.2). This trend continued until 1993, when the share of the manufacturing sector exceeded 65 percent of total FDI inflow. The share of manufacturing as a percentage of total FDI has remained at approximately 55 percent since 1996.

In the manufacturing sector, the composition of inward FDI changed toward more investment in the heavy and chemical industries. Since the mid-1980s, FDI in labor-intensive and low-technology industries, such as textiles and clothing, has fallen significantly because of the rise in labor costs. Instead, the electrical and electronics sector and transport equip-

Table 9.1   **Trends of FDI in Korea, 1962–98 (million U.S. dollars)**

Year	Notified	Actual
1962–81	1,886.1	1,477.8
1982–86	1,767.7	1,157.8
1987–88	2,347.1	1,519.7
1989	1,090.3	812.3
1990	802.6	895.4
1991	1,396.0	1,177.2
1992	894.5	803.3
1993	1,044.3	728.1
1994	1,316.5	991.5
1995	1,941.4	1,357.1
1996	3,202.6	2,308.3
1997	6,970.9	3,085.9
1998	8.852.4	5,155.6

Source: Ministry of Finance and Economy, *Trends in International Investment and Technology Inducement* (Seoul, 1999).

Table 9.2   Share of Selected Manufacturing Industries in Total FDI, 1962–98 (percent)

Industry	1962–86	1987–90	1991	1992	1993	1994	1995	1996	1997	1998	Cumulated
Manufacturing	67.4	63.3	80.0	75.3	67.6	35.4	43.2	56.2	59.4	54.9	59.4
Food	3.4	4.5	1.3	13.5	2.0	0.5	1.1	1.8	15.0	12.2	7.1
Chemicals	14.2	12.4	15.5	28.5	33.7	11.0	10.0	10.1	8.3	8.3	12.1
Medicine	2.8	3.6	4.8	3.8	1.8	3.2	2.9	1.1	1.3	2.3	2.5
Petroleum	3.3	1.5	33.5	0.2	2.8	0.5	3.3	9.3	0.1	0.0	3.8
Machinery	4.2	7.7	9.5	5.9	3.3	7.0	6.5	5.9	3.1	10.4	6.8
Electrical and electronics	14.7	17.9	9.1	7.1	3.6	3.7	10.2	12.2	7.1	4.5	9.6
Transport equipment	11.2	10.1	2.0	4.2	11.5	3.1	3.4	10.8	11.6	3.0	7.5
Other manufacturing	9.9	4.5	4.2	9.2	8.6	5.5	5.2	4.4	12.6	0.6	0.8

Source: Ministry of Finance and Economy, *Trends in International Investment and Technology Inducement* (Seoul, 1999).

Note: Based on actual investments. For 1962–86 and 1987–90, figures are annual averages.

ment and chemicals are receiving increased amounts of foreign investment. Since 1997, foreign food companies increased their investment in Korea by acquiring domestic food companies and their distribution networks.

The composition of FDI in the service sector has also changed. The hotel business used to be the largest subsector in terms of cumulated FDI up to the early 1990s. Since the mid-1990s, FDI in wholesale and retail trade as well as financing and insurance increased remarkably (table 9.3).

Since 1998, after the outbreak of the currency crisis, a number of domestic firms have been sold in order to alleviate debt burdens, as shown in table 9.4. Since the M&A market is not well developed in Korea, there are still wide gaps between the prices at which domestic firms are offered and the prices foreigners are willing to pay. Delay in the sale of such assets can also be attributed to the high debt ratios and lack of transparency of domestic firms, as well as the lack of improvement in labor market conditions.

9.4   Effect of Foreign Direct Investment in Korea on Productivity

Despite the small amount of FDI in Korea relative to the size of its economy, it was foreign firms that brought the key technology and constructed the basis for such industries as electronics and pharmaceuticals. For example, subsidiaries of foreign semiconductor firms contributed to the growth of domestic firms into major players in the world market by spinning out skilled workers and managers as well as through technical guidance to subcontractors. Also, multinational pharmaceutical firms helped the domestic pharmaceutical industry to develop new drugs by boosting local research capabilities.[1] More specifically, anecdotal evidence shows that foreign-invested firms may raise productivity by spinning out skilled workers, providing technical guidance to subcontractors, bringing in new capital goods and technology, introducing advanced management know-how, conducting in-house R&D, and enhancing competition.[2]

The purpose of this section is to examine whether the quantitative data support the qualitative case study evidence for productivity spillovers in Korea. Previous empirical studies of this issue present mixed evidence on productivity spillovers from foreign investment. Studies using sector-level data tend to show positive evidence for productivity spillovers from foreign presence (ownership) or level of FDI (Caves 1974; Globerman 1979; Blomström and Persson 1983; Choi and Hyun 1991; Hong 1997; Chan,

---

1. A more detailed description of the impact of foreign-invested firms on the development of the Korean semiconductor and pharmaceutical industries is given in Kim (1997).

2. Blomström and Kokko (1996) presented an overview of empirical studies on productivity spillovers by classifying them into backward and forward linkages, training of local employees, and demonstration and competition effects.

Table 9.3   Share of Selected Service Industries in Total FDI, 1962–98 (percent)

Industry	1962–86	1987–90	1991	1992	1993	1994	1995	1996	1997	1998	Cumulated
Service	31.9	36.3	20.0	24.4	32.4	64.6	56.8	43.8	39.0	41.5	39.3
Wholesale and retail	0.6	0.1	0.4	1.4	0.7	2.5	4.3	14.3	8.3	10.1	5.7
Trading	0.0	1.7	4.5	6.8	11.6	9.5	8.0	4.8	6.3	4.7	4.7
Hotel	18.7	20.7	3.1	1.1	7.1	20.8	4.3	5.0	3.1	0.0	8.1
Transport and storage	1.2	0.2	0.1	0.2	0.2	0.2	0.3	5.2	1.0	0.1	0.9
Financing	7.1	9.5	6.2	5.7	4.5	20.5	26.3	7.7	9.8	9.1	10.0
Insurance	0.1	2.4	3.7	5.4	1.2	0.8	4.0	0.7	0.2	1.4	1.6
Construction	1.6	0.3	0.2	0.0	0.1	0.7	0.9	1.4	1.6	0.1	0.7
Restaurant	0.0	0.1	0.3	1.3	4.7	0.6	0.5	0.1	0.1	0.1	0.4
Other service	2.5	1.2	1.6	2.5	2.4	9.0	8.3	4.5	8.5	15.8	7.1

Source: Ministry of Finance and Economy, Trends in International Investment and Technology Inducement (Seoul, 1999).

Note: Based on actual investment. For 1962–86 and 1987–90, figures are annual averages.

Table 9.4   **Major Cross-Border Mergers and Acquisitions since the Currency Crisis in Korea (1998)**

Korean Firm	Foreign Buyer	Contents
Hanwha	FAG OEM and Handel (Germany)	Sold bearing unit for 320 billion won (US$213 million)[a]
Hanwha	BASF (Germany)	Sold 50% stake in Hanwha BASF Urethane for 120 billion won ($80 million)[a]
Hyosung	BASF (Germany)	Sold 50% stake in Hyosung BASF for 64 billion won ($43 million)[a]
Daesang	BASF (Germany)	Sold Lysine unit for $600 million
Halla	Bowater (USA)	Sold Halla Pulp and Paper for $210 million
Shinho Paper Co.	Norske Skog (Norway)	Sold for $175 million
Sambo Computer	Seiko Epson (Japan)	Sold printer unit for $20 million
Korea Exchange Bank	Commerz Bank (Germany)	Sold 29.8% stake for $276 million
Korea Makro	Wal-Mart (USA)	Sold Makro's subsidiary for $181 million
Samsung Heavy Industries	Volvo (Sweden)	Sold construction equipment division for $750 million
Anam Semiconductor	ATI (USA)	Sold semiconductor manufacturing factory for $600 million
Samsung Electronics	Fairchild (USA)	Sold semiconductor manufacturing factory for $455 million

[a]Exchange rate of 1,500 won per dollar is applied.

chap. 12 in this volume).[3] However, studies using firm-level data find that FDI has a statistically insignificant impact on total factor productivity (TFP) growth (Haddad and Harrison 1993; Aitken and Harrison 1994; Djankov and Hoekman 1998).[4]

One reason for these differing results is that most studies using sector-level data did not cure the identification problem: if foreign investment tends to locate in more productive sectors, estimates of the impact of FDI on the productivity of domestic industries are biased upward (Aitken and Harrison 1994; Harrison 1996).

3. Using a cross-country data set for sixty-nine developing countries, Borensztein, de Gregorio, and Lee (1998) also found that FDI contributes more to growth than does domestic investment when sufficient capability to absorb advanced technologies, measured by human capital, is available in the host economy.

4. One exception is Chung, Mitchell, and Yeung (1994), which found, using firm-level panel data on U.S. automobile component manufacturers, that productivity gains among host country suppliers largely stem from the increase in competition created by FDI rather than from direct technology transfer.

Given the absence of appropriate firm-level data in Korea, we resort to industry aggregate data in six manufacturing subsectors; food, textiles and clothing, chemicals and petroleum, metals, machinery, and electrical and electronics.[5] This paper differs from previous studies using sector-level data by taking the endogeneity problem into consideration, estimating a random-effects model with instruments.

9.4.1 Empirical Framework

Constrained by the insufficient number of observations, we take the growth accounting approach for calculating TFP in each subsector. Although the growth accounting approach is subject to criticism, it can avoid such econometric problems as limited degrees of freedom that are expected to occur if the production function approach is used (Collins and Bosworth 1996, 139).[6]

The conventional growth accounting framework shows that the growth rate of value added in sector i can be decomposed into the contribution of increases in factor inputs plus a residual. That is, it assumes the underlying relation between output (Q) and the inputs capital (K), labor (L), and technology or TFP (A) as follows:

$$(1) \qquad Q_i = F(K_i, L_i, A_i), \qquad i = 1, \ldots, n.$$

Equation (1) yields an index of growth in TFP, denoted by a_i, which can be defined as the growth rate of output, q_i, less the share-weighted growth of the factor inputs, k_i and l_i:[7]

$$(2) \qquad a_i = q_i - \alpha_K k_i - \alpha_L l_i.$$

We use the Törnqvist approximation of the Divisia index for factor shares, which is the arithmetic average of the current and previous period's factor shares.[8]

For the impact of FDI on productivity, we use the following specification:

$$(3) \qquad a_{it} = \beta_0 + \beta_1 \text{fdi}_{i,t-1} + \beta_2 \text{roy}_{i,t-1} + \varepsilon_{it},$$

where fdi represents the growth rate of the FDI stock and roy stands for the growth rate of the royalty stock, which is used as a proxy for imported technology from foreign countries. Unlike the FDI stock, royalties paid

---

5. These are at the two-digit level.

6. Hong and Kim (1996) showed that estimates of TFP growth obtained by the growth accounting approach are similar to estimates obtained by the translog production function approach in Korean manufacturing industries during 1967–93.

7. Any deviations from constant returns to scale and unmeasured human capital are allocated to this residual of TFP (Lee 1995; Collins and Bosworth 1996).

8. Lee and Zang (1998) also used the Divisia-Törnqvist index for calculating regional productivity in Korea.

for imported technology may have offsetting effects on productivity. In other words, it may raise productivity through technology transfer or lower productivity by reducing the incentive to conduct R&D. We assume that it takes one year for foreign-invested firms to start operating after investment and also that technology imports affect productivity with a one-year lag. Hence, the explanatory variables fdi and roy are lagged one year to adjust for a time delay.[9]

9.4.2   Data

Annual data on real output (value added) and employment in the manufacturing industries were taken from the *Report on Mining and Manufacturing Survey,* published by the National Statistical Office, which contains very detailed microlevel industry data. The number of employees was multiplied by average man-hours to yield data on labor input. For real net capital input, we used industry-specific real net capital stock data calculated by Pyo (1997), who employed the polynomial benchmark estimation method.[10] We adjusted this net capital stock by operation ratio indexes from the *Korea Statistical Yearbook,* published by the National Statistical Office.[11]

For the real value of the FDI and royalty stocks, we used the data of Choi and Hyun (1991) for 1974–89, with the exception that we adjusted for 1990 constant gross fixed capital formation prices. For 1990–96, we updated these FDI and royalty stocks, by adding the new inflow of FDI and royalties to the depreciation-adjusted stocks.[12]

9.4.3   Estimation Results

Because of the possible endogeneity between productivity effects and the independent variables, estimating equation (3) by ordinary least squares (OLS) may give biased and inconsistent estimates. To deal with the possible endogeneity that FDI flows into the manufacturing subsectors with high productivity, we estimate a random-effects model. The random-effects model has an advantage over the fixed-effects estimation in that it avoids the imposition of constant productivity growth over time. To correct for the remaining endogeneity problem, we also estimate the random-effects model using instruments.[13]

---

9. Taking lags for the independent variables may also reduce the possible endogeneity.

10. Using net capital stock data (Nk) from the National Wealth Surveys for 1968, 1977, and 1987 and fixed capital formation data (I) in the polynomial benchmark-year equation, he estimated economic depreciation rates to calculate the real net capital stock for each year.

11. Basu (1995) found that cyclical factor utilization is very important for explaining procyclical productivity.

12. The assumed depreciation rates taken from Choi and Hyun (1991) are 12 percent for FDI and 15 percent for royalties.

13. Specifically, fitted values of the independent variables using instruments are inserted in the estimation of a random-effects model.

Table 9.5   **Regression Estimates of Productivity Effects of FDI in Korean Manufacturing, 1974–96**

Variable	OLS	Random Effects	Random Effects with Instruments[a]
Constant	0.049	0.050	0.066
	(3.413)	(3.123)	(3.106)
$fdi_{i,t-1}$	0.037	0.037	0.026
	(1.145)	(1.123)	(0.172)
$roy_{i,t-1}$	−0.054	−0.058	−0.138
	(−0.948)	(−0.980)	(−1.142)
N	138	138	138
LM test[b]		1.32	1.20
		[0.25]	[0.27]
Hausman test[c]		0.29	0.71
		[0.86]	[0.70]
R^2	0.014	0.014	0.014

Note: Equation is $a_{it} = \beta_0 + \beta_1 fdi_{i,t-1} + \beta_2 roy_{i,t-1} + \varepsilon_{it}$. Numbers in parentheses are *t*-statistics. Numbers in brackets are probability values of χ^2 tests.
[a]$fdi_{i,t-2}$, $fdi_{i,t-3}$, $roy_{i,t-2}$, and $roy_{i,t-3}$ are used as instruments.
[b]High values of the LM test favor a one-factor model over a classical regression model with no group specific effects.
[c]Low values of the Hausman test favor a random-effects model.

Table 9.5 reports the results of OLS and random-effects estimations with and without instruments.[14] For both the OLS and the random-effects models, the coefficient on the growth rate of FDI stock is positive but statistically insignificant.[15] Unlike the case study evidence, the industry aggregate data do not show that FDI has a positive effect on productivity. This might be due to aggregation of data at the sector level in that the experiences of individual firms are not sufficient to have an impact at the aggregate level. We expect a different result from a firm-level analysis, which we leave for future research.

The growth rate of the royalty stock has a negative but statistically insignificant effect for both the OLS model and the random-effects model with and without instruments. One possible explanation for the insignificant effect of royalties on productivity is that the negative effect of the importation of technology by reducing incentives to conduct in-house R&D may offset its positive effect on productivity through technology transfer.

14. We could not gain much using the random-effects model, as shown by the LM test results. This may be because growth rates of productivity across sectors do not differ much. The mean and variance of growth rates of productivity for each sector fall in the ranges −0.005 to 0.004 and 0.013 to 0.044, respectively.
15. The coefficient and *t*-ratio are smaller when the random-effects model is estimated using instruments.

9.5   The Role of Foreign Direct Investment in a Currency Crisis: Is It a Safety Net?

In 1997, Thailand, Indonesia, Malaysia, and Korea were hit by currency crises. There is a wide range of literature on the nature of the Asian crisis (Krugman 1998; Sachs 1997a; Fischer 1998; Frankel 1998).[16] According to this literature, the causes of the Asian crisis can be broadly summarized as two general factors: one is the moral hazard of domestic financial intermediaries, and the other is the bank run by foreign investors. From the midst of the crisis, we explain the causes as a combination of these two explanations—underlying structural problems and an abrupt loss of investor confidence.

In fact, the moral hazard of financial intermediaries whose liabilities were perceived as having an implicit government guarantee created bubbles in asset prices.[17] Asian-style corporate governance, which emphasizes growth rather than profitability, as well as the closed and underdeveloped domestic banking system, which lacks appropriate risk management, also contributed to these bubbles by allowing overinvestment.

The bursting of the bubbles touched off a downward spiral in which falling asset prices exposed the insolvency of intermediaries, forcing them to cease operations, leading to further asset deflation (Krugman 1998). The bank run or financial panic aggravated this vicious circle as foreign investors liquidated their investments early, thus making the crisis even more severe.

Frankel and Rose (1996) and Park and Lee (1998) showed that a low level of net FDI—that is, FDI inflow subtracted from FDI outflow—correlates closely with the incidence of currency crisis.

One argument in favor of FDI is that of stability. In the event of a crash, investors can suddenly dump securities and banks can refuse to roll over loans, but multinational corporations cannot quickly pack up their factories and go home (Frankel and Rose 1996, 355). In addition, the mere potential of FDI may act as a stabilizer against the risk of financial panic because the presence of potential foreign buyers would provide sufficient liquidity to make a liquidity crisis impossible (Krugman 2000).

Related to this argument, one can argue that even in a currency crisis, countries (such as Malaysia) where multinational firms have a dominant presence in the domestic economy may endure or overcome the crisis with-

---

16. The Asian currency crises were born in an environment marked by the globalization of financial and capital markets and the movement of massive capital flows across national borders. Thus they have distinct characteristics from the other currency crises in the past. See NBER (1998) for details.

17. The implicit government guarantee can be attributed to directed lending or connected lending, characteristic of "crony capitalism."

out being forced to resort to IMF bailout loans.[18] Thanks to their parent firms, subsidiaries of multinational firms in crisis-ridden countries do not suffer lowered credit ratings or such difficulties in importing raw materials or in trade financing as do other domestic firms.

The following subsections examine this last hypothesis, that FDI is associated with IMF rescue loans, by using cross-sectional data from 1994 to 1997 and pooled data from 1973 to 1994 for developing countries. Santaella (1995) provided a complementary work that analyzes the macroeconomic conditions surrounding IMF financial arrangements in developing countries but did not study the relation between IMF arrangements and FDI. For an empirical analysis, we adopt the probit estimation of Frankel and Rose (1996), which is a nonstructural exploration of the data.

9.5.1   Cross-Sectional Analysis of Currency Crashes and IMF Rescue Loans, 1994–97

We first use cross-sectional data on ninety developing countries to investigate whether countries experiencing currency crashes or IMF rescue loans during the period 1994–97 have lower levels of FDI than other countries.[19]

Variables and Data

As the dependent variable, we construct a binary variable, b9497, which takes a dichotomous value of one if the country received a bailout loan from the IMF during 1994–97 and zero otherwise. IMF Stand-By and Extended Fund Facility (EFF) Arrangements were used to proxy rescue loans. Stand-By Arrangements can be considered emergency loans for balance-of-payments support, and the EFF is intended to allow member countries

18. IMF bailout loans usually accompany painful macroeconomic adjustment. Sachs (1997b) criticized the IMF programs addressing the Asian crisis, pointing out that demanding too much austerity in the form of budget cuts and tight credit to countries with high savings and budget surpluses may transform a currency crisis into a rip-roaring economic downturn. Feldstein (1998) also argued that the IMF should have focused on providing technical advice and limited financial assistance as a supportive organization rather than as the agent of painful contractions in its dealing with the Asian crisis.

19. The ninety developing countries are Algeria, Argentina, Bangladesh, Barbados, Belize, Benin, Bolivia, Botswana, Brazil, Burkina Faso, Cameroon, Cape Verde, Central African Republic, Chad, Chile, China, Colombia, Comoros, Congo, Costa Rica, Côte D'Ivoire, Djibouti, Dominican Republic, Ecuador, Egypt, El Salvador, Equatorial Guinea, Ethiopia, Fiji, Gabon, Gambia, Ghana, Grenada, Guatemala, Guinea, Guinea-Bissau, Guyana, Haiti, Honduras, Hungary, India, Indonesia, Jamaica, Jordan, Kenya, Republic of Korea, Lesotho, Madagascar, Malawi, Malaysia, Maldives, Mali, Malta, Mauritania, Mauritius, Mexico, Morocco, Nepal, Nicaragua, Niger, Nigeria, Oman, Pakistan, Panama, Papua New Guinea, Paraguay, Peru, Philippines, Portugal, Romania, Rwanda, Saint Vincent, Senegal, Seychelles, Sierra Leone, Solomon Islands, Sri Lanka, Sudan, Swaziland, Syrian Arab Republic, Thailand, Togo, Trinidad and Tobago, Tunisia, Turkey, Uganda, Uruguay, Vanuatu, Venezuela, and Zimbabwe.

to adopt measures with a medium-term horizon for solving their balance-of-payments adjustment problems.

To compare the relation between FDI and IMF rescue loans with previous work on currency crisis, we also use a variable for currency crash, e9497, constructed as in Frankel and Rose (1996). The binary variable, e9497, takes the value one if the country experienced a nominal currency depreciation of at least 25 percent and an increase in the rate of depreciation of at least 10 percent during the period 1994–97 and zero otherwise.[20]

As independent variables, we use seven of the variables used in Frankel and Rose (1996), for which we use 1993 data due to availability.[21] As internal domestic macroeconomic variables, we use the growth rate of domestic credit (Domestic credit), which is a measure of monetary policy, and the growth rate of real GDP per capita (Growth rate). As measures of vulnerability to external shocks, we use the ratio of foreign exchange reserves to monthly import values (Reserves/imports), the current account as a percentage of GDP (Current account), and the ratio of total debt to GNP (Debt). For the composition of capital inflows and foreign debt, we use the ratio of short-term debt to total debt (Short-term debt), the ratio of net FDI inflow to total debt (FDI flow/debt), and the ratio of inward FDI stock to total debt (FDI stock/debt).

The variables of interest are FDI flow/debt and FDI stock/debt, denoting FDI inflow and inward FDI stock, respectively. FDI inflow represents the stability of the foreign capital inflow. It also incorporates the foreign investors' view of the policy regime or investment environment of the host country. Thus it is appropriate to test the first claim about the role of FDI in a currency crisis, that is, its role as a stabilizer. Meanwhile, inward FDI stock represents the presence of multinational firms in the host country. Hence, it is more suited for testing the other hypothesis, on the role of FDI in circumventing the need for IMF rescue loans in a crisis-ridden country.

Probit Estimation Results

Table 9.6 presents the probit estimation results of the cross-sectional analysis for the period 1994–97. For the currency crash case, only the coefficient on the growth rate of GDP per capita is significant. Its negative sign shows that countries with higher growth rates tend to have lower incidences of currency crash. Unlike previous studies, neither FDI flow nor FDI stock is associated with currency crash.

For IMF rescue loans, the coefficients on FDI flow and FDI stock, -0.1074 and -0.0209, respectively, are both significantly negative. This

20. In calculating the depreciation of currency, we use end-of-year exchange rates. The estimation results are not seriously affected by using the annual average of exchange rates, although the explanatory power in terms of log likelihood gets marginally smaller.
21. Definitions and data sources for the variables used are presented in appendix table 9A.3.

Table 9.6   **Probit Estimation of Currency Crashes and IMF Rescue Loans, 1994–97: Cross-Sectional Data for 90 Developing Countries**

Independent Variable	Dependent Variables			
	Currency Crash (e9497)		IMF Rescue Loan (b9497)	
Short-term debt	0.0039	0.0060	0.0125	0.0197
	(0.38)	(0.60)	(1.13)	(1.61)
Debt	−0.1214	−0.1085	−0.9743	−0.8793
	(−0.64)	(−0.66)	(−2.31)	(−2.56)
Growth rate	−0.0882	−0.0757	0.0038	−0.0140
	(−2.08)	(−2.23)	(0.09)	(−0.41)
Reserves/imports	0.0122	−0.0090	−0.0081	−0.0410
	(0.21)	(−0.17)	(−0.14)	(−0.59)
Domestic credit	−0.0005	−0.0005	−0.0010	−0.0015
	(−0.55)	(−0.55)	(−0.76)	(−0.30)
Current account	−0.0076	−0.0107	−0.0011	−0.0024
	(−0.47)	(−0.66)	(−0.06)	(−0.13)
FDI flow/debt	0.0186		−0.1074	
	(0.64)		(−2.53)	
FDI stock/debt		−0.0017		−0.0209
		(−0.51)		(−2.69)
N	84	90	84	90
N with dep. = 1	34	40	29	32
N with dep. = 0	50	50	55	58
Log likelihood	−53.57	−57.83	−46.34	−49.03

Note: Numbers in parentheses are *t*-values. For independent variables, 1993 data are used. Coefficients on the constant are not reported.

implies that countries with which the IMF made Stand-By and EFF Arrangements during 1994–97 tend to have lower FDI inflow and stock in 1993 than other countries. The coefficients on the other variables, except for the ratio of total debt to GNP (Debt), are not significant.

9.5.2 Analysis of Currency Crashes and IMF Rescue Loans Using Pooled Data, 1973–94

The cross-sectional analysis in subsection 9.5.1 has one drawback in that the number of total observations is small relative to the number of independent variables. In addition, the data in 1993 may not be able to sufficiently explain the incidence of currency crashes and IMF rescue loans in the four-year period ahead. To overcome this problem, we conduct the same analysis using pooled data for 1973–94 for eighty-four developing countries.[22]

22. Due to lack of data on IMF financial arrangements, seventeen countries are deleted from the list of ninety countries in subsection 9.5.1. They are Belize, Comoros, Djibouti, Equatorial Guinea, Grenada, Guinea-Bissau, Hungary, Maldives, Oman, Papua New Guinea, Portugal, Saint Vincent, São Tomé, Seychelles, Solomon Islands, Vanuatu, and Zim-

Variables and Data

The data descriptions are the same as in the cross-sectional analysis of subsection 9.5.1, except that for the dependent variable, ER, representing the event of currency crash, we adopt the three-year "windowing" of Frankel and Rose (1996).[23] That is, we exclude crashes that occurred within three years of each other to avoid counting the same crash twice. Similarly, for the other dependent variable, IMF, denoting the incidence of IMF Stand-By and EFF Arrangements, we exclude arrangements that were made in consecutive years to avoid double counting.[24] Among the independent variables, the ratio of inward FDI stock to total debt is deleted due to the absence of relevant data in the full sample period.

Probit Estimation Results

Table 9.7 reports the probit estimation results using pooled data for eighty-four countries during the twenty-two years from 1973 to 1994.[25] "Lagged t" means that the independent variables are those in the current year. In the "Lagged $t-1$" column, we tabulate the results in which all regressors are lagged one year to adjust for time lag in the relation between currency crashes or IMF rescue loans and macroeconomic conditions.

The estimated coefficient on our variable of interest, FDI flow/debt, is significantly negative in all cases, implying that FDI inflow relative to total debt is negatively associated with currency crashes and IMF rescue arrangements in both the current and lead periods.

For currency crashes, the coefficients on the other variables are similar to the results of Frankel and Rose (1996). Lower growth rates, higher growth of domestic credit, and higher portions of short-term debt all seem to raise the odds of a currency crash in the following year.

We saw roughly similar results for IMF rescue arrangements, except that the growth rate of domestic credit is not significantly associated with IMF arrangements and the coefficient on foreign reserves (Reserves/imports) is now significant. This is because the growth rate of domestic credit raises the inflation rate and hence has a direct effect on exchange rates or currency crashes. Meanwhile, a low level of foreign reserves relative to monthly imports indicates a country's inability to deal with a balance-of-payments problem without asking for rescue loans from the IMF. Otherwise, the results imply that the macroeconomic conditions behind cur-

---

babwe. Eleven countries are then added: Burundi, Lebanon, Liberia, Myanmar, Somalia, Tanzania, Western Samoa, Yemen, Yugoslavia, Zaire, and Zambia.

23. Here the annual average of the nominal exchange rate is used in calculating the depreciation rate.

24. For the case of arrangements made in more than three consecutive years, we count the first two years to take into account a delay or adjustment period in improving economic conditions.

25. For currency crash (ER), we reproduced the estimation results by Park and Lee (1998).

Table 9.7   **Probit Estimation of Currency Crashes and IMF Rescue Loans, 1973–94: Pooled Data for 84 Developing Countries**

	Dependent Variables			
	Currency Crash (ER)		IMF Rescue Loan (IMF)	
Independent Variable	Lagged t	Lagged $t - 1$	Lagged t	Lagged $t - 1$
Short-term debt	0.0030	0.0101	−0.0022	0.0069
	(0.61)	(2.22)	(−0.44)	(1.43)
Debt	0.5076	0.0594	0.3363	0.0981
	(3.96)	(0.46)	(3.24)	(0.92)
Growth rate	−0.0525	−0.0363	−0.0196	−0.0327
	(−4.96)	(−3.78)	(−2.00)	(−3.41)
Reserves/imports	−0.0087	−0.0377	−0.0525	−0.0786
	(−0.40)	(−1.73)	(−2.13)	(−3.03)
Government budget	0.0122	−0.0164	−0.0004	−0.0277
	(1.13)	(−1.74)	(−0.04)	(−3.00)
Domestic credit	0.0024	0.0005	0.0001	−0.0003
	(4.99)	(3.09)	(0.17)	(−0.75)
Current account	0.0241	0.0119	0.0179	0.0018
	(3.07)	(1.69)	(2.35)	(0.26)
FDI flow/debt	−0.0345	−0.0329	−0.0378	−0.0268
	(−3.43)	(−3.41)	(−3.51)	(−2.58)
N	1,080	1,111	964	996
N with dep. = 1	116	128	130	138
N with dep. = 0	964	983	834	858
Log likelihood	−306.27	−361.87	−354.56	−364.94

Note: Numbers in parentheses are t-values. Coefficients on the constant are not reported.

Table 9.8   **Probabilities of Currency Crashes and IMF Arrangements in Selected Countries, 1997**

	Korea	Indonesia	Thailand	Malaysia	Philippines	Mexico[a]
Currency crashes (ER)	0.195	0.065	0.093	0.064	0.100	0.119
IMF rescue loan (IMF)	0.168	0.050	0.071	0.065	0.097	0.119

Note: Based on estimated coefficients in "Lagged $t - 1$" columns of table 9.7 applied to the values of independent variables in appendix table 9A.8.
[a]For Mexico, probabilities are for the year 1994.

rency crashes and IMF rescue loans are similar. In particular, FDI inflow seems to lower the odds of both currency crashes and IMF rescue loans.

Using the estimated coefficients in the "Lagged $t - 1$" columns of table 9.7 and values of independent variables for 1996 (1993 for Mexico), we calculate in table 9.8 the predicted probabilities of currency crises and IMF arrangements in some crisis-ridden countries for 1997 (1994 for Mexico). According to the predictions, the probabilities of currency crisis and

IMF arrangements in Korea are the highest among the five crisis-ridden Asian countries. Furthermore, they are higher than the corresponding probabilities for Mexico for 1994. Appendix table 9A.8, which presents values for precrash macroeconomic variables, reveals that the high predicted probabilities of currency crisis and IMF arrangements for Korea can be attributed to the country's relatively high proportion of short-term debt and low ratio of FDI flow to total debt.

Meanwhile, the predicted probabilities for Indonesia are the lowest among these crisis-ridden countries, including Mexico. Indonesia, however, suffered a crisis no less severe than the other countries, so the above probit model may have failed to capture some political factors.

9.6   Concluding Remarks

Throughout Korea's economic development, FDI has played a negligible role. Even in 1996, FDI accounted for less than 1 percent of total domestic fixed capital formation in Korea, far less than in the Southeast Asian countries. Case study evidence shows, however, that despite its quantitative insignificance FDI has had a significant impact on the quality of Korean economic development by spinning out skilled workers and managers and through technical guidance of subcontractors.

However, industry aggregate data for six Korean manufacturing subsectors during 1974–96 fail to support the case study evidence. Estimation of a random-effects model using instruments shows that the productivity spillover effects of FDI are positive but statistically insignificant. We leave the analysis using firm-level data for future research.

Concerning the role of FDI in a currency crisis, the presence of multinational firms may help a crash-ridden country to overcome its crisis without resorting to bailout loans from the IMF. Probit estimation results using cross-sectional data reveal that inward FDI, in both flow and stock, in 1993 was negatively associated with the incidence of IMF Stand-By and EFF Arrangements during 1994–97. Probit analysis using pooled data for eighty-four developing countries during the twenty-two years from 1973 to 1994 also shows that FDI inflow tends to lower the odds of currency crash and IMF rescue loans.

Appendix

Table 9A.1   **Summary Statistics for Variables in Table 9.5**

Variable	Mean	Standard Deviation
a_{it}	0.042	0.116
$\mathrm{fdi}_{i,t-1}$	0.069	0.310
$\mathrm{roy}_{i,t-1}$	0.188	0.178

Table 9A.2   **Correlation Matrix for Variables in Table 9.5**

Variable	(1)	(2)	(3)
1. a_{it}	1.00		
2. $\mathrm{fdi}_{i,t-1}$	0.09	1.00	
3. $\mathrm{roy}_{i,t-1}$	−0.07	0.16	1.00

Table 9A.3   **Definitions and Data Sources for Variables in Section 9.5**

Variable	Definition	Source
IMF (b9497)	One if a country received IMF Stand-By or EFF Arrangements (in 1994–97), zero otherwise	1,2
ER (e9497)	One if a country suffered a depreciation by more than 25% in a year and an increase in the rate of depreciation of at least 10% (during 1994–97), zero otherwise	3
Short-term debt	Ratio of short-term debt to total debt (%)	4
Debt	Ratio of total debt to GNP	4
Growth rate	Growth rate of GDP per capita (%)	4
Reserves/imports	Ratio of foreign reserves to monthly imports (months)	4
Government budget	Ratio of government budget surplus to GDP (%)	4
Domestic credit	Growth rate of domestic credit (%)	4
Current account	Ratio of current account surplus to GDP (%)	4
FDI flow/debt	Ratio of net FDI inflow to total debt (%)	4
FDI stock/debt	Ratio of FDI stock to total debt (%)	5

Sources: (1) Santaella (1995). (2) International Monetary Fund, *Annual Report* (Washington, D.C., various years). (3) International Monetary Fund, *International Financial Statistics Yearbook* (Washington, D.C., various years). (4) World Bank, *World Data* (Washington, D.C., 1995), CD-ROM. (5) United Nations, *World Investment Report* (New York, 1995).

Table 9A.4 Summary Statistics for Variables in Table 9.6

Variable	Mean	Standard Deviation
b9497	0.35	0.48
e9497	0.41	0.49
Short-term debt	15.07	14.25
Debt	0.80	0.92
Growth rate	1.10	4.14
Reserves/imports	3.57	2.75
Domestic credit	51.15	292.08
Current account	−9.40	10.49
FDI flow/debt	4.05	5.63
FDI stock/debt	17.08	18.82

Table 9A.5 Correlation Matrix for Variables in Table 9.6

Variable	(1)	(2)	(3)	(4)	(5)	(6)	(7)	(8)	(9)	(10)
1. b9497	1.00									
2. e9497	0.26	1.00								
3. Short-term debt	0.06	−0.00	1.00							
4. Debt	−0.17	0.00	−0.02	1.00						
5. Growth rate	−0.09	−0.23	0.15	−0.19	1.00					
6. Reserves/imports	0.05	0.00	−0.01	−0.28	0.04	1.00				
7. Domestic credit	−0.07	−0.08	0.05	−0.08	0.08	0.19	1.00			
8. Current account	0.08	−0.10	0.09	−0.50	0.23	0.32	0.12	1.00		
9. FDI flow/debt	−0.21	−0.02	0.22	0.23	0.43	0.02	−0.06	0.03	1.00	
10. FDI stock/debt	−0.21	−0.06	0.30	−0.05	0.15	−0.11	−0.06	−0.10	0.64	1.00

Table 9A.6   Summary Statistics for Variables in Table 9.7: Current Values

Variable	Mean	Standard Deviation
ER	0.12	0.32
IMF	0.13	0.34
Short-term debt	14.60	11.94
Debt	0.54	0.42
Growth rate	1.61	5.75
Reserves/imports	3.41	3.11
Government budget	-4.32	5.83
Domestic credit	47.93	228.25
Current account	-6.79	8.53
FDI flow/debt	4.03	9.44

Table 9A.7   Correlation Matrix for Variables in Table 9.7: Current Values

Variable	(1)	(2)	(3)	(4)	(5)	(6)	(7)	(8)	(9)	(10)
1. ER	1.00									
2. IMF	0.20	1.00								
3. Short-term debt	0.04	-0.01	1.00							
4. Debt	0.14	0.18	-0.06	1.00						
5. Growth rate	-0.21	-0.12	0.02	-0.21	1.00					
6. Reserves/imports	-0.03	-0.10	0.18	-0.29	0.17	1.00				
7. Government budget	-0.03	-0.05	0.04	-0.26	0.14	0.37	1.00			
8. Domestic credit	0.22	-0.01	0.04	-0.02	-0.08	0.02	-0.02	1.00		
9. Current account	0.06	-0.00	0.19	-0.29	0.09	0.38	0.30	0.03	1.00	
10. FDI flow/debt	-0.11	-0.13	-0.06	-0.26	0.19	0.27	0.21	-0.00	0.08	1.00

Table 9A.8   Values of Macroeconomic Variables for Calculating Probabilities in Table 9.8

Variable	Korea	Indonesia	Thailand	Malaysia	Philippines	Mexico[a]
Short-term debt (%)	58.9	24.8	40.8	41	26.6	23.1
Debt/GNP	0.26	0.534	0.504	0.392	0.649	0.332
Growth rate (%)	5.9	6.1	5.2	5.3	5	-2.1
Reserves/imports (months)	2.65	6.73	6.27	4.09	3.52	4.1
Government budget (%)	-1.1	0	1.5	-0.5	-0.1	-1.7
FDI flow/debt[b] (%)	-1.36	3.24	1.26	11.13	1.99	4.15
Domestic credit (%)	19.3	22.7	14.03	12	40.2	11.48
Current account (%)	-4.7	-4	-8.5	-7.4	-4.4	-6.42

Source: Compiled by Park and Lee (1998) from various primary sources.
Note: Values are for 1996 except as noted.
[a] For Mexico, values are for 1993.
[b] For FDI flow/debt, values are for 1995.

References

Aitken, Brian, and Ann Harrison. 1994. Do domestic firms benefit from foreign direct investment? Evidence from panel data. Policy Research Working Paper no. 1248. Washington, D.C.: World Bank.

Basu, Susanto. 1995. Procyclical productivity: Increasing returns or cyclical utilization? NBER Working Paper no. 5336. Cambridge, Mass.: National Bureau of Economic Research.

Blomström, Magnus, and Ari Kokko. 1996. The impact of foreign investment on host countries: A review of the empirical evidence. Policy Research Working Paper no. 1745. Washington, D.C.: World Bank.

Blomström, Magnus, and Hakan Persson. 1983. Foreign investment and spillover efficiency in an underdeveloped economy: Evidence from the Mexican manufacturing industry. *World Development* 11:493–501.

Borensztein, E., J. de Gregorio, and J.-W. Lee. 1998. How does foreign direct investment affect economic growth? *Journal of International Economics* 45:115–35.

Caves, Richard E. 1974. Multinational firms, competition and productivity in host-country markets. *Economica* 41:176–93.

Choi, I. B., and J. T. Hyun. 1991. Effects of foreign direct investment on productivity: The case of manufacturing industries in Korea and Taiwan (in Korean). Policy Report no. 91-05. Seoul: Korea Institute for International Economic Policy.

Chung, W., W. Mitchell, and Bernard Yeung. 1994. Foreign direct investment and host country productivity: The case of the American automotive components industry. Discussion Paper no. 367. Ann Arbor: University of Michigan, Institute of Public Policy Studies.

Collins, Susan M., and Barry P. Bosworth. 1996. Economic growth in East Asia: Accumulation versus assimilation. *Brookings Papers on Economic Activity,* no. 2:135–203.

Djankov, Simeon, and Bernard Hoekman. 1998. Avenues of technology transfer: Foreign investment and productivity change in the Czech Republic. Discussion Paper no. 1883. London: Centre for Economic Policy Research.

Feldstein, Martin. 1998. Refocusing the IMF. *Foreign Affairs* 77 (March/April): 20–33.

Fischer, Stanley. 1998. The Asian crisis: A view from the IMF. Address at the midwinter conference of the Bankers' Association for Foreign Trade.

Frankel, Jeffrey A. 1998. The Asian model, the miracle, the crisis and the FUND. Address at the U.S. International Trade Commission, 16 April.

Frankel, Jeffrey A., and Andrew K. Rose. 1996. Currency crashes in emerging markets: An empirical treatment. *Journal of International Economics* 41:351–66.

Globerman, Steve. 1979. Foreign direct investment and "spillover" efficiency benefits in Canadian manufacturing industries. *Canadian Journal of Economics* 12: 42–56.

Haddad, Mona, and Ann Harrison. 1993. Are there positive spillovers from direct foreign investment? Evidence from panel data for Morocco. *Journal of Development Economics* 42:51–74.

Harrison, Ann. 1996. Determinants and effects of direct foreign investment in Côte d'Ivoire, Morocco, and Venezuela. In *Industrial evolution in developing countries,* ed. Mark J. Roberts and James R. Tybout. New York: Oxford University Press.

Hong, Kyttack. 1997. Foreign capital and economic growth in Korea, 1970–1990. *Journal of Economic Development* 22 (June): 79–89.

Hong, Sung-Duck, and Jung-Ho Kim. 1996. *Long-run trend on total factor productivity in manufacturing* (in Korean). Seoul: Korea Development Institute.

Kim, June-Dong. 1997. Impact of foreign direct investment liberalization: The case of Korea. Working Paper no. 97-01. Seoul: Korea Institute for International Economic Policy.

Krugman, Paul. 1998. What happened to Asia? Cambridge: Massachusetts of Technology. Mimeograph.

———. 2000. Fire-sale FDI. In *Capital flows and the emerging economies,* ed. Sebastian Edwards. Chicago: University of Chicago Press, forthcoming.

Lee, Jong-Wha. 1995. Government interventions and productivity growth in Korean manufacturing industries. NBER Working Paper no. 5060. Cambridge, Mass.: National Bureau of Economic Research.

Lee, Yung Joon, and Hyoungsoo Zang. 1998. Urbanization and regional productivity in Korean manufacturing. *Urban Studies* 35:2085–99.

NBER (National Bureau of Economic Research). 1998. Lessons from the Asian currency crises: Risk related to short-term capital movement and the "21st century-type" currency crisis. Report of the NBER Subcommittee on Asian Financial and Capital Markets of the Committee on Foreign Exchange and Other Transactions. Cambridge, Mass.: National Bureau of Economic Research.

Park, D., and C. Lee. 1998. The crisis in Korea: Was it avoidable? Seoul: Seoul National University. Mimeograph.

Pyo, Hak K. 1997. Estimates of fixed reproducible tangible assets in the Republic of Korea, 1953–1996. Seoul: Seoul National University. Mimeograph.

Sachs, Jeffrey D. 1997a. IMF is a power unto itself. *Financial Times,* 11 December.

———. 1997b. The wrong medicine for Asia. *New York Times,* 3 November.

Santaella, J. A. 1995. Four decades of fund arrangements: Macroeconomic stylized facts before the adjustment programs. IMF Working Paper no. 95/74. Washington, D.C.: International Monetary Fund.

Comment   Hong-Tack Chun

Kim and Hwang examine whether FDI in Korea has positive effects on productivity in manufacturing industries. In addition, they investigate whether FDI plays a role in preventing currency crisis.

In their investigation of the productivity effects of FDI in Korea, they use TFP as a measure of productivity in manufacturing industries. TFP is calculated as a residual in the conventional growth accounting framework. Growth in TFP is assumed to be a function of the growth rates of the FDI stock and the royalty stock, which is used as a proxy for imported technology from foreign countries. They use a random-effects model with instruments to avoid possible endogeneity between productivity effects and the independent variables. They found that for both the OLS and the random-effects model, growth in the FDI stock has a positive but insignificant effect on TFP growth in manufacturing industries.

I have two comments on the productivity effects of FDI in Korea. My first comment is on the explanation for their finding that industry aggre-

Hong-Tack Chun is a senior fellow at Korea Development Institute.

gate data do not show a significant effect of FDI on productivity, contrary to case study evidence. As the authors suggest, this might be due to aggregation of data at the industry level in that the experiences of individual firms are not sufficient to have an impact at the aggregate level. Currently, firm-level analysis is almost impossible because data are lacking. However, a subsector-level analysis may show a significant productivity effect because FDI is concentrated in a few subsectors, such as the chemical, electrical and electronics, and transport equipment industries.

My second comment is on the specification of the TFP equation. R&D expenditures by large Korean firms have increased rapidly since the mid-1980s. Human capital has also increased in Korea. Rapid growth in R&D expenditures and human capital might have affected both TFP and FDI. This suggests that a variable for R&D expenditure or human capital, or variables for both, should be included in the TFP equation to avoid the omitted-variables problem.

Let me turn to the role of FDI in a currency crisis. Kim and Hwang apply the probit estimation method of Frankel and Rose (1996) to pooled data from 1973 to 1994 for eighty-four developing countries to see whether FDI has an effect in preventing currency crashes and IMF rescue loans. The estimation results for currency crashes and IMF rescue loans are similar to those of Frankel and Rose.

The authors also calculate the predicted probabilities of currency crashes and IMF arrangements in six crisis-ridden countries, five Asian countries and Mexico, using the estimated coefficients and values of independent variables for 1996. They find that the probabilities of currency crisis and IMF arrangements in Korea are the highest among these countries. They conclude that the high predicted probabilities of currency crash and IMF arrangements for Korea can be attributed to Korea's relatively high proportion of short-term debt and low ratio of FDI flow to total debt. In addition, they argue that a higher proportion of capital inflow in the form of FDI could help to reduce the likelihood of future crises.

A Frankel and Rose–type model examines the statistical correlation between independent variables and a dependent variable without a structural mechanism that causes currency crisis. Therefore, the estimation results might have been affected by the omission of an important independent variable, and an estimated correlation between a independent and dependent variable may not imply a causal relation. Furthermore, one should not apply estimation results from a Frankel and Rose–type model directly to a particular country without examining the structural mechanism that caused a currency crisis in that country. In the Korean case, it is now well known that a combination of terms-of-trade shock, policy missteps, and low foreign exchange reserves relative to short-term external debt led to the currency crisis. It is doubtful that a higher net inflow of FDI alone would have prevented the crisis, although the crisis might have been less severe with a higher net inflow of FDI.

Reference

Frankel, Jeffrey A., and Andrew K. Rose. 1996. Currency crashes in emerging markets: An empirical treatment. *Journal of International Economics* 41:351–66.

Comment   Yuri Nagataki Sasaki

In the wake of the Asian currency crisis, many papers have sought a way to prevent such crises. This paper gives us a clue to finding the way.

The paper is composed of two parts. The first part, a historical overview of FDI policy and the trend of FDI in Korea, offers a very convenient survey of the history and background of FDI policy in Korea. The second part examines the productivity effects of FDI in Korea and the role of FDI in a currency crisis.

I have some comments on the second part of the paper, sections 9.4 and 9.5. In section 9.4, the effect of FDI on productivity is examined and contrasted with the effect of royalties on productivity. Section 9.5 examines the role of FDI as a safety net during a currency crisis and explains that FDI plays this role in contrast with other forms of debt.

First, as the authors point out, it is said that foreign firms tend to locate in more productive sectors, and estimates of the impact of FDI on the productivity of domestic industries may often be biased upward. This paper uses industry-level data, not firm-level data, so the coefficients of FDI change are possibly biased upward.

Second, the paper shows that FDI has had a positive effect on the TFP growth of Korea. But if the TFP growth rate of Korea is very low, FDI may play a very limited role in its total growth. For example, Young (1995) reported that average TFP growth of manufacturing in Korea during the period 1966–90 was estimated at 3 percent. Young also showed that TFP growth in East Asia is not as high as in the G-7 countries and concluded that East Asian countries may not enjoy learning-by-doing externalities.

Third, the paper mentions that the predicted sign of royalty change, gamma in equation (3), or β_2 in table 9.5, is negative because royalties reduce R&D. But there is no evidence that royalties reduce R&D and that FDI does not have a similar effect on R&D. It would be better to explain the difference between the effect of FDI and that of royalties. Or if one can get data on R&D in Korea, it might be interesting to test the effects of royalties and FDI on R&D directly.

Fourth, table 9.1 shows that FDI inflows into Korea have increased time

Yuri Nagataki Sasaki is associate professor in the Department of Commerce at Takachiho University.

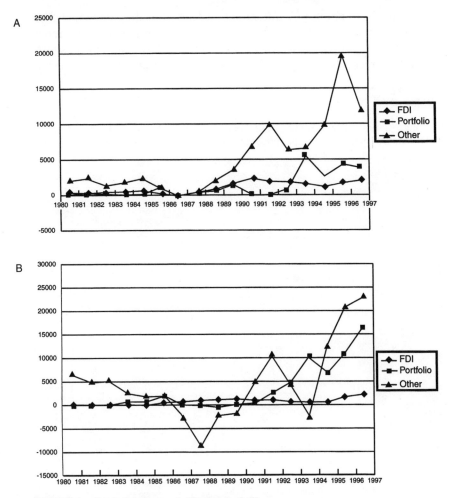

Fig. 9C.1   Capital inflows: *A*, Thailand; *B*, Korea

after time, as the Korean government has liberalized FDI policy. Although the data are annual and the sample size is small, it would be better to add some dummies to the equation to measure the effects of policy change.

My last comment is on section 9.5: This paper proposes that the Korean government promote FDI in order to raise the ratio of FDI to total debt. But another way to raise the FDI ratio is to decrease other debts, especially short-term debt. Large amounts of short-term debt—which can be promoted by countries in various ways, for example, by creating international banking facilities or by pegging exchange rates—have a strong impact on currency crisis. Figure 9C.1 shows FDI inflow, portfolio investment liabilities, and other liabilities in Thailand and Korea during

1980–96. These graphs are not strong evidence, but they show that FDI was stable but other debts grew rapidly just before the Asian currency crisis. Thus rapid growth in other debts, including large amounts of short-term debt, seems to have been one important factor in inducing the crisis.

Reference

Young, A. 1995. The tyranny of numbers: Confronting the statistical realities of the East Asian growth experience. *Quarterly Journal of Economics* 110:641–80.

Effects of Outward Foreign Direct Investment on Home Country Performance
Evidence from Korea

Seungjin Kim

10.1 Introduction

Most studies of outward foreign direct investment (OFDI) have been conducted for advanced countries such as the United States, Sweden, and Japan. The reason is simple. These countries have invested much abroad and thus issues related to their OFDI have merited a wide range of studies. By contrast, research on the OFDI of developing countries is almost nonexistent because such nations have been mostly recipients rather than exporters of direct investment. Since the mid-1980s, however, some East Asian developing countries have been experiencing a surge in OFDI, which makes it worthwhile to launch a study of the OFDI of developing countries. Excluding Singapore, the Asian newly industrialized countries (NICs) have already transformed themselves into net exporters of direct investment despite starting as net importers. Korea was a net importer of direct investment through the 1980s, but since 1990, it has recorded more OFDI than inward foreign direct investment (IFDI) on a flow basis. Over that time span, its OFDI has increased at a rapid pace, making OFDI a topic of discussion in Korea.

The two main questions to be tackled in this paper are the following: What role did Korean OFDI play in its economic performance? What are the characteristics of Korean OFDI? In contrast to developed countries, sufficient data are lacking for Korea, making a rigorous study difficult. Given this shortcoming, to be expatiated on later, this paper tries to approach the questions stated above in a persuasive manner.

The remainder of the paper is organized as follows. Section 10.2 outlines

Seungjin Kim is a research fellow of Korea Development Institute.

the trends, structures, and motives of Korean OFDI. Section 10.3 examines evidence of the effects that Korean OFDI has on home investment and exports. Section 10.4 points out key characteristics supporting the evidence and compares the situation with those in developed countries such as Sweden and the United States. Section 10.5 provides a summary and conclusion.

10.2   Korean Outward Foreign Direct Investment: Trends, Structures, and Motives

Korea started directly investing abroad in 1968, but its annual outflow was very insignificant (less than $200 million) until the mid-1980s because of governmental controls on foreign exchange outflows and incapability on the part of firms. Korean OFDI began to expand in 1986 when the relevant restrictions were lifted. Over the next decade, OFDI increased exponentially, amounting to $4.2 billion of investment outflow in 1996 (fig. 10.1).

This surge was due to the rising cost of production, the need for better market access, and the enhanced capabilities of firms, as well as the relaxation of regulatory measures. The share of Korean OFDI stock in the total OFDI stock of developing countries increased from 2.0 percent in 1985, to 3.1 percent in 1990, and then to 4.9 percent in 1996.

Despite the increase, however, Korea's ratio of OFDI stock to GDP in 1995 was around 2.2 percent, far below those of other NICs, as well as those of developed countries, including Sweden, the United States, and Japan (table 10.1).

Why did Korea invest less abroad than developed countries and other NICs in terms of the size of its economy? First, Korean firms have weak capabilities, so-called small bases of ownership advantage. In general, de-

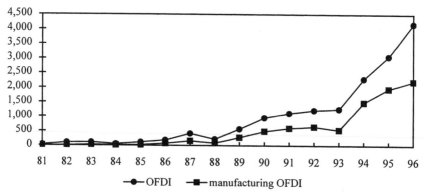

Fig. 10.1   Trend of Korean OFDI, 1981–96 (million U.S. dollars)
Source: Bank of Korea (1997).

Table 10.1   **Outward FDI Stock as a Percentage of GDP, 1990–95**

Country	1990	1995
World	8.10	9.90
Developed countries	9.80	11.50
Germany	10.10	10.80
Sweden	21.50	31.20
United Kingdom	23.60	27.40
United States	7.90	9.80
Japan	7.00	6.00
Developing countries	1.80	4.50
Hong Kong	18.50	88.80
Korea	0.90	2.20
Singapore	25.80	38.40
Taiwan	8.20	11.20

Source: United Nations (1997).

veloped country firms with superior knowledge or technology to invest more abroad to exploit such advantages. The ownership advantages of Korean multinationals have long been in technologies forgotten by developed countries but not yet adopted by latecomers. However, some large conglomerates in the electronics and automobile sectors have recently developed knowledge-intensive technologies, thus strengthening their technological bases. Second, Korean OFDI, most of which is undertaken by large conglomerates with much use of capital-intensive technologies, has been less sensitive to rising wages than that of other NICs whose multinational firms have employed labor-intensive technologies. Although a number of small and medium-size enterprises in Korea are in labor-intensive industries that face pressures from rising wages and have responded like their counterparts in the other NICs, they account for only a small proportion of the country's total OFDI. OFDI by Korean conglomerates is intended more to establish market share in host countries (i.e., in Southeast Asia and developed countries), or to gain access to new technologies and skills, and less to acquire cheaper labor. Third, the small amount of IFDI has placed little pressure on Korean firms to go multinational. The government has protected domestic markets by restricting IFDI and imports, providing an uncompetitive market environment in which domestic firms can make sufficient profits without going multinational.

The motives of foreign production have changed over time. Korean multinationals have typically established foreign affiliates to avoid trade barriers and reduce transportation costs at an early stage of foreign production. After the mid-1980s, they started setting up foreign affiliates to exploit wage differences. Simultaneously, they also moved production to foreign sites to get closer to their customers, which became necessary in order to adapt to local tastes or production standards. Moreover, some multinationals have acquired developed country firms to obtain advanced technologies that otherwise would take too much time and money to develop. These motives are sometimes pursued simultaneously and are thus hard to separate in explaining the foreign production behavior of some multinationals. In particular, a few conglomerates have started to adopt regional strategies seeking lower costs and better market access, blurring the distinction between the two motives.

Korean OFDI has been most concentrated in the manufacturing sector, followed by wholesale trade. The sectoral distribution of the outward investment of Korean manufacturing firms in 1990 and 1996 is presented in table 10.2.

Mechanical equipment was the most important sector in both years, and its percentage increased significantly during the period. Metals was the second largest sector in 1990, but its share dropped by a lot during the period. The share of textiles and clothing fell slightly but occupied the second position in 1996.

Table 10.3 presents data on the geographical distribution of Korean OFDI in 1990 and 1996. OFDI to Asia jumped rapidly during that period, and as a result, Asia has become the most important OFDI region. In particular, China has become the prime destination for Korean manufacturing OFDI and the second most popular OFDI region in all industries. The percentage of OFDI to Europe also increased during the period examined. In particular, Eastern Europe has become a strategic investment region, reflecting a recent trend of investing in emerging markets. North America's attractiveness to Korean OFDI has declined, leaving it the second most important region. Among countries, the U.S. share of Korean manufacturing OFDI has dropped to the second, but the United States remains the prime target for total OFDI.

Table 10.2   **Sectoral Distribution of OFDI by Korean Manufacturing Firms, 1990–96 (percent)**

Sector	1990	1996
Food and beverages	6.6	4.5
Textiles and clothing	13.7	12.3
Shoes and leather	4.8	4.2
Wood and furniture	2.5	2.1
Paper and printing	1.6	1.6
Petrochemicals	13.3	8.5
Nonmetals	3.8	5.2
Metals	23.3	9.1
Mechanical equipment	27.2	44.9
Others	3.2	7.6
Manufacturing	100	100

Source: Bank of Korea (1991, 1997).

Table 10.3   **Geographical Distribution of Korean OFDI, 1990–96 (percent)**

	All Industries		Manufacturing	
Region	1990	1996	1990	1996
North America	47.3	31.5	49.8	20.7
United States	34.6	29.5	28.7	18.8
Canada	12.8	2.0	21.0	1.9
Europe	6.5	15.3	6.3	14.6
European Community	4.3	9.5	5.5	6.1
Eastern Europe	0.1	2.8	0.1	4.8
Asia	30.6	44.0	35.3	58.5
Japan	2.2	2.2	0.3	1.1
China	1.0	19.4	2.0	29.0
ASEAN	23.4	13.1	28.0	17.5
Indonesia	18.2	7.8	16.9	8.8
Malaysia	2.1	2.2	4.5	3.7
Philippines	1.6	1.9	3.5	2.9
Thailand	1.4	1.3	3.1	2.1
Latin America	5.2	4.0	5.0	4.3
Mexico	0.0	0.7	0.0	1.1
Africa	1.9	2.0	1.1	1.1
Oceania	6.1	2.3	1.0	0.5
Middle East	2.4	0.9	1.6	0.3
Total	100.0	100.0	100.0	100.0

Source: Bank of Korea (1991, 1997).

10.3   Effects of Korean Outward Foreign Direct Investment on Home Country Performance

In this section, we examine the evidence of the effects of Korean OFDI on home investment and exports, reflecting its financial-side effects and real-side effects.

10.3.1   Domestic Investment

OFDI may detract from a home country's capital stock. Whether OFDI takes place at the expense of domestic investment depends on how that investment is financed. However, indirect effects, including investment financed through repatriation of profits or brought about by increased foreign demand for exports, also have to be taken into account. The evidence regarding the effects of OFDI on domestic investment is mixed. Stevens and Lipsey (1992) demonstrated a strong positive correlation between fixed investment at home and abroad by U.S. multinationals. However, the positive relation between domestic and foreign investment likely results from the positive relation between both types of investment and a parent firm's internally generated funds. This evidence, at least, suggests that OFDI does not necessarily have negative effects on domestic investment.

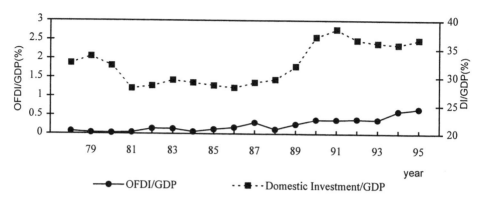

Fig. 10.2   Foreign investment and domestic investment, 1978–95
Sources: Bank of Korea, *National Accounts* (Seoul, various years); Bank of Korea (1997).
Note: Domestic investment refers to total fixed investment.

In contrast, Feldstein (1995) showed that outward investment and domestic investment are at least partial substitutes. Svensson (1993) also showed that in the 1980s, OFDI by Swedish multinationals had a negative effect on the size of Sweden's capital stock.

Unfortunately, in Korea, no firm-level data are available for a rigorous analysis of the relation between outward and domestic investment by Korean firms. Looking at the trends of outward and domestic investment over 1978–95 in figure 10.2, we can see that outward and domestic investment did not go in opposite directions. Domestic investment increased by a large margin over the 1986–90 period, during which outward investment increased steadily due to the relaxation of capital outflow restrictions. Both types of investment also show similar growth patterns after 1990. This, of course, does not tell much about the relation between outward and domestic investment. Nevertheless, outward investment does not seem to have had a large negative impact on domestic investment for the following reasons. First, an increasing part of outward investment by Korean firms tends to be financed from external resources. In 1995, the share of home sources in total financing of OFDI amounted to less than 40 percent, and in particular, the share was less than 20 percent for the large conglomerates that account for most Korean OFDI.[1] In the case of U.S. multinationals, about 20 percent of the value of foreign-affiliate assets is financed through cross-border capital outflows from the United States (Feldstein 1995). Although Korea had a larger share of cross-border financing than the United States and Japan, it increasingly financed its OFDI from

1. In 1995, the five largest conglomerates accounted for approximately 60 percent of Korea's total OFDI stock.

foreign sources.[2] Second, the size of outward investment has been very small relative to that of domestic investment, and export creation effects of outward investment also exist.

10.3.2   Exports

Foreign production can replace exports of a single product. But it usually generates demand for other products, such as capital goods or intermediate goods and services. These products may be provided by other parts of the parent company, its suppliers, or independent firms at home. So foreign production can be either export replacing or export supporting. Most analytical evidence relates to developed countries, including the United States and Sweden. The majority of studies showed that OFDI had an overall positive effect on home exports, suggesting that the export-creating effect of OFDI outweighed the export-replacing effect (Lipsey and Weiss 1981; Swedenborg 1979; Blomström, Lipsey, and Kulchycky 1988). In contrast to the numerous studies for developed countries, very few studies have addressed the case of developing countries. Questions about the effects of OFDI on home exports and employment in Korea have received much attention since OFDI by Korean firms surged in the early 1990s. Nevertheless, there is a dearth of detailed studies due to lack of data.[3] While data on the amount of foreign investment exist, no information is available on foreign affiliate activities, such as production, exports, and sales. No firm-level data are available either. Such deficiencies have made it difficult to undertake rigorous studies of the home country effects of OFDI by Korean firms. However, given the available data, we will try to estimate the empirical relation between OFDI and exports. Investigating the graphical relation between OFDI and exports will precede the regressional analysis of their relation.

Figure 10.3 tells us how OFDI and exports in particular industries as ratios to the production size of the industry, have evolved between 1990 and 1994. There appears to be no substitution between OFDI and exports, represented as ratios to production size, of the total manufacturing industry. However, this graph shows only a simple trend of two variables, not

---

2. As the portion of large-scale outward investments of some conglomerates financed abroad increased, the Korean government implemented controls on foreign financing in late 1995. It introduced self-financing obligations and controls on foreign financing through payment guarantees by parent firms out of concern that firms might undertake excessive OFDI and so weaken the home base of production or that the failure of a foreign business might lead to the failure of the parent providing a payment guarantee. Ironically, the government had no superior knowledge with which to judge whether a firm had made an overinvestment, and moreover, restrictions on foreign financing could have substituted for domestic investment resources. Self-financing obligations were lifted in 1997, but some controls on foreign financing through payment guarantees by parents remain.

3. Kim and Kang (1997) found no significant relationship between OFDI and exports.

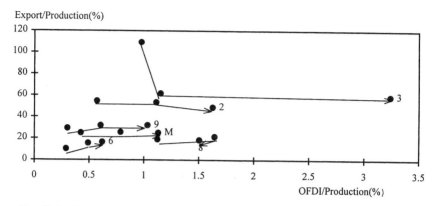

Fig. 10.3   Exports and OFDI of major industries, 1990, 1992, and 1994

Sources: Bank of Korea (1997) and information from Korean Bureau of Tariffs and Bureau of Statistics.

Note: 2, Textiles and clothing; 3, shoes and leather; 6, petrochemicals; 8, metals; 9, mechanical equipment; and M, manufactures.

suggesting that OFDI has not decreased home exports. Major industries show varying trends. During 1990–92, in textiles and clothing and shoes and leather, OFDI increased while exports decreased. In contrast, both OFDI and exports increased in petrochemicals, metals, and mechanical equipment during the same period. We can observe a similar sectoral pattern during 1992–94, except that OFDI and exports for metals both decreased. We need to be cautious in interpreting sectoral trends. In the case of textiles and clothing and shoes and leather, we cannot say that OFDI decreased exports. Rather, it seems more probable that OFDI increased but exports decreased as these sectors lost their comparative advantages. OFDI may have increased exports, instead. In the case of mechanical equipment, we cannot say that OFDI increased exports. Both OFDI and exports may have increased as the sector gained competitive advantages. Consequently, movements of OFDI and exports tend to be influenced by common factors. The cross-sectional correlation between OFDI and exports, represented as ratios to production size, turned out to be positive (.78) in 1994.

Figure 10.4 shows how OFDI and exports to particular countries, represented as ratios to the GDP of the destination were correlated in 1994. The correlation between OFDI and exports turned out to be positive (.38), meaning that Korea exported more to countries in which it invested more. This does not imply that OFDI had a positive effect on exports. Variables affecting OFDI and exports in the same direction may have produced the positive correlation.

An econometric study will help us to understand the systematic relation

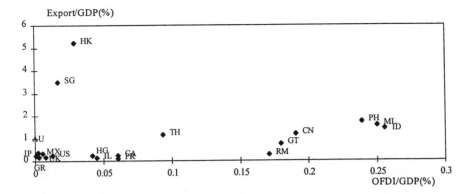

Fig. 10.4   Exports and OFDI to major countries, 1994

Sources: Bank of Korea (1997); World Bank, *World Development Report* (Washington, D.C., 1997); information from Korean Bureau of Tariffs.

Note: JP, Japan; AU, Australia; GR, Germany; MX, Mexico; UK, United Kingdom; US, United States; SG, Singapore; HK, Hong Kong; HG, Hungary; IL, Ireland; CA, Canada; PR, Portugal; TH, Thailand; RM, Romania; GT, Guatemala; CN, China; PH, Philippines; ML, Malaysia; and ID, Indonesia.

between OFDI and exports. As mentioned earlier, lack of data prevents us from doing more in-depth analysis. A systematic relation will be sought using the amount of outward investment and exports.

The export equation to be estimated takes GDP of a destination, GDP per capita of a destination, and a dummy representing EC membership as independent variables.[4] GDP and GDP per capita are the country characteristic variables that seem to significantly affect OFDI as well as exports. The EC dummy reflects Korean firms' tariff-jumping OFDI in EC countries. Besides these variables, distance, relative wages, tariffs and nontariff barriers could affect exports, but they will not be included in the estimation because relevant data are lacking. So the export equation takes the following form:[5]

$$(1) \qquad EX_{ij} = f(GDP_j, GDPC_j, OFDI_{ij}, EC_j),$$

4. ASEAN could be a dummy variable but it is inferior to an EC dummy for the purpose of my study. I included the EC dummy to reflect tariff-jumping OFDI by Korean firms and to keep the effects of a trading bloc from being transferred to the effects of OFDI. ASEAN, in 1992, agreed to form a free trade area and has been taking steps to complete the AFTA (ASEAN Free Trade Area). So it seems inappropriate to regard ASEAN as a complete trading bloc in 1994, the year for which values were taken for all variables in the estimation. Furthermore, Korean OFDI to the ASEAN region was not in general motivated by tariff jumping but by wage differences, while its OFDI to the EC region was largely motivated by tariff jumping.

5. This specification helps us to examine how exports to country *j* are affected by OFDI to country *j*. So the results of the regressions have nothing to do with the story of *chaebols* (large conglomerates) expanding exports and OFDI through favorable loans or cash flows.

where EX_{ij} is exports of industry i to country j; GDP_j and $GDPC_j$ are, respectively, GDP and GDP per capita of country j; $OFDI_{ij}$ is outward foreign direct investment of industry i to country j; and EC_j is the dummy variable representing EC membership.[6] The variables EX_{ij}, $OFDI_{ij}$, GDP_j, and $GDPC_j$ take 1994 values for fifty-seven destinations and nine industries. The coefficient of GDP is expected to be positive because GDP reflects market size. Exports will increase as market size increases. The coefficient of GDPC may be positive or negative, depending on the income elasticity of demand. The coefficient of EC is expected to be negative because the European Community, as a trading bloc, discourages exports to the region. Finally, the coefficient of OFDI may be positive or negative, which is to be confirmed in this econometric study.

The results of the regressions are as follows (see the appendix). OFDI turns out to have a positive relation with exports in the regression using all destinations or all destinations and industries. The coefficients of GDP and EC are, respectively, positive and negative as expected. The positive effect of OFDI on exports appears to be far greater for developing countries than for developed countries. The coefficient of OFDI is strongly positive in the regression using a group of developing countries as destinations, while it is insignificantly positive in the case of developed countries. The impact of OFDI is prominent in such industries as shoes and leather, textiles and clothing, petrochemicals, and mechanical equipment. The effects are, however, insignificantly negative in metals and food. If we take the textiles and clothing and shoes and leather industries and call them labor intensive, we can see that the impact of OFDI on exports is greater for labor-intensive industries than for industries overall. The effect of OFDI in labor-intensive industries toward developing countries is strongly positive, but the effect of OFDI in labor-intensive industries toward developed countries is insignificantly positive. In contrast to the conventional wisdom that OFDI in labor-intensive industries toward developing countries reflects an exodus of such industries and the subsequent weakening of their export bases, the effect of OFDI on exports turned out to be positive. This implies that OFDI created new exports of intermediate goods in the same industries, an effect that seems to exceed its replacement effect.

In spite of the results, all regressions described above have limitations because of omitted variables that could affect both OFDI and exports. Although we included GDP and GDP per capita to stop their effects from being transferred to the effect of OFDI, we cannot exclude the possibility that omitted variables may have affected exports in the name of OFDI. In order to reduce such a possibility, we regress export variation between

6. The European Community includes France, Italy, Germany, Belgium, the United Kingdom, Portugal, the Netherlands, Ireland, and Spain.

1992 and 1994 on OFDI variation, GDP variation, and exports in 1992. That is, the new export equation we estimate is

$$(2) \qquad \Delta EX_{ij} = f(\Delta GDP_j, EX92, \Delta OFDI_{ij}),$$

where ΔEX_{ij}, $\Delta OFDI_{ij}$, and ΔGDP_j represent the variations of exports, OFDI, and GDP between 1992 and 1994. EX92 is the 1992 (initial) value of exports and plays the role of absorbing the effects of omitted variables.

The results of the new regression, in table 10.4, show similarities to those of the former regressions. Consequently, we found no evidence that Korean OFDI substituted for exports. If the coefficients for the variables other than OFDI were eccentric or even if they had negligible influence where we expected them to be important, some doubt would be cast on the coefficients for OFDI, because it would be likely that some effects of country characteristics entering the trade equation were being absorbed by the OFDI variable. Coefficients that looked reasonable would add to our confidence in the measures of the effect of OFDI. However, the effect of OFDI on exports may have to be compared to what would have happened to exports without OFDI. The econometric study may infer what would have happened to exports without OFDI from exports to countries where no OFDI took place. But the econometric study gives limited information on the counterfactual situation without OFDI due to omitted variables. The positive coefficients of OFDI may result from the omission of variables that could have increased both OFDI and exports. Differencing equations between two points in time can reduce the influence of omitted variables, but it is not likely to exclude their effect completely.

However, the econometric study combined with figure 10.4 hints that the effect of OFDI is likely to be positive. The regression for all destinations tells us that OFDI to country j had a positive effect on exports to country j. If omitted variables that could have increased both OFDI and exports produced the positive coefficient, the omitted variables are probably policy variables of host countries representing their openness to trade and investment. In figure 10.4, the ratio of OFDI and exports to GDP

Table 10.4   **Coefficients of OFDI and OFDI Variation**

	OFDI	ΔOFDI
All countries	0.32 (5.58)	0.13 (2.21)
All countries and industries[a]	0.24 (4.60)	0.25 (3.73)
Developed countries[a]	0.04 (0.58)	−0.02 (0.21)
Developing countries[a]	0.38 (5.51)	0.26 (3.08)
Labor-intensive industries[b]	0.53 (4.69)	0.35 (2.56)

Note: Numbers in parentheses are *t*-values.
[a]Industry dummies were used.
[b]Textiles and clothing; shoes and leather.

tends to be higher in developing countries, such as Indonesia, Malaysia, the Philippines, and China, than in developed countries, such as the United States, the United Kingdom, and Germany. Since it is hard to say that these developing countries are ahead of the developed countries in their openness to trade and investment, the open policy of a host country is unlikely to have had a large impact.

10.4   Characteristics of Korean Outward Foreign Direct Investment That Support Home Country Effects

In this section, we examine what characteristics of Korean OFDI contributed to its home country effects. We propose four characteristics: the low ratio of OFDI to GDP, the high share of developing countries, the increasing importance of overseas financing, and simple integration strategies.

10.4.1   Low Ratio of Outward Foreign Direct Investment to GDP

There has been much concern about the "hollowing out" of manufacturing industries as OFDI flows have surpassed IFDI flows since 1990. Korean OFDI has grown faster than world OFDI overall and than OFDI from developed countries. The annual average growth rate of Korean OFDI for 1991–96 was 27.4 percent; the corresponding figures were 12.5 percent for the world overall and 10.2 percent for the developed countries. However, Korean OFDI has not grown faster than OFDI from other developing countries. The annual growth for such countries during the same period was 52.4 percent. Moreover, OFDI from Korean firms has been small in terms of the size of the country's economy. The ratio of OFDI stock to GDP in Korea is lower than in the other NICs, not to mention developed countries. Therefore, the economic effects of OFDI do not seem to be greater in Korea than in other nations.

10.4.2   High Share of Developing Countries

The developing country share of Korean manufacturing OFDI was 71.5 percent in 1996, much higher than the developing country share of manufacturing OFDI from developed countries. In textiles and clothing and shoes and leather, the developing country shares were over 90 percent. In mechanical equipment and petrochemicals, the developing country shares were 66.6 percent and 83.0 percent, respectively. Why is a big part of Korean OFDI directed toward developing countries? Most Korean multinational firms have smaller bases of ownership advantage, and their advantages derive from adaptation and experience rather than proprietary technology and brand names. Korean multinationals lacking proprietary assets exploit the weak ownership advantages in developing countries. Most OFDI toward developed countries is made by a few conglomerates with proprietary assets or brand names. What do high developing country shares imply about the role of OFDI in home country performance? First, OFDI has contributed to an increase in exports from Korea. More specifically, OFDI to developing countries tends to induce more exports of intermediate goods from the home country because local firms are unable to supply these goods. Moreover, the degree to which OFDI substitutes for exports may be lower because the low-cost advantages of developing countries would give a narrower chance to home exports even without OFDI to the region. Second, OFDI has been upgrading the composition the workforce between "blue collar" and "white collar" jobs—between the unskilled and the skilled. Exports of blue-collar or unskilled jobs are inevitable as Korea loses its comparative advantages in activities that make intensive use of blue-collar or unskilled labor, while demand for skilled labor or white-collar workers to manage foreign subsidiaries tends to increase.

10.4.3 Increasing Importance of Overseas Financing

We see, in table 10.5, that overseas financing as a share of total investment financing was approximately 55 percent in 1994, which is low compared to the U.S. and Japanese figures. This seems to be related to the

Table 10.5   **OFDI Financing by U.S. and Japanese Transnational Corporations, 1994 and 1992 (million U.S. dollars)**

	United States, 1994	Japan, 1992	Korea, 1994
Transnational corporations	51,007	16,925	376
	(24.9)	(25.2)	(16.1)
Equity outflows	12,666	17,166	–
	(6.2)	(25.5)	
Reinvested earnings	31,730	–	–
	(15.5)		
Intrafirm loans	6,611	−238	–
	(3.2)	(−0.4)	
Other home sources	−22,808	4,088	689
	(−11.1)	(6.1)	(29.5)
Overseas sources	177,041	46,263	1,270
	(86.2)	(68.7)	(54.4)
Host country sources	59,394	3,041	–
	(28.9)	(4.5)	
Sources in other countries	117,647	43,222	–
	(57.3)	(64.2)	
Total	205,240	67,276	2,335
	(100.0)	(100.0)	(100.0)

Sources: United Nations (1997) and information from Korean Ministry of Finance and Economy.
Note: Numbers in parentheses are percentages of total OFDI financing.

high share going to developing countries as well as restrictions on foreign financing. The underdevelopment of capital markets in developing countries makes it difficult to finance operations locally. Recently, Korean multinationals, especially large conglomerates, have increased their use of foreign funds, which contributed to an increase in overseas investment at less expense to domestic investment.

10.4.4   Simple Integration Strategies

Most Korean multinational firms are currently at the stage of simply connecting parent firms and foreign subsidiaries and having parent firms export a considerable amount of intermediate goods to their foreign subsidiaries. Some Korean conglomerates, however, have started to adopt advanced, complex strategies through which they efficiently allocate a variety of value-added activities within and across regions to increase their market shares. Foreign subsidiaries are becoming more localized to increase local sourcing and, in addition, exporting more to third countries. Export-creating effects through exports from parents to foreign subsidiaries are expected to decrease. Moreover, parents' exports to third countries are also expected to be replaced by exports from foreign subsidiaries.

10.5   Summary and Conclusion

We could not find any evidence that OFDI by Korean multinational firms had a detrimental effect on home country performance. Even though Korean multinational firms depend less on foreign funds than do developed country firms, overseas investment does not seem to have significantly crowded out domestic investment because the amount of OFDI was small relative to domestic investment and the demand for domestic investment increased as a result of increased exports. Moreover, these firms are financing an increasingly large part of overseas investment from abroad. The OFDI of Korean multinational firms was also discovered to have a positive effect on exports. The high share in OFDI of developing countries and close associations between parents and foreign subsidiaries seem to have contributed to the positive effect on exports through increased exports from parents to foreign subsidiaries.

As pointed out above, the lack of evidence that OFDI has harmful effects on home country performance can be attributed to the fact that Korean OFDI has been in its infant stage: OFDI is not big enough to significantly affect the domestic economy, and the strategies associated with OFDI are not complex enough to substitute for exports on the net balance. The question arising from this context is naturally, Can this situation continue to hold as Korean OFDI increases and its strategies become more complex? The answer depends on how large a portion of OFDI will be involved in complex strategies in which foreign subsidiaries become more independent and play stronger roles as export bases within their multinational firms. A few business conglomerates have already initiated complex strategies on a regional scale in which both local sourcing and foreign subsidiaries' exports have increased. It is not clear at this stage how far and how fast the strategies will go and how many firms will be able to pursue these strategies.

Appendix

Table 10A.1   OLS Estimation of Export Equation I

		Coefficients					
	Intercept	GDP	GDPC	EC	FDI	$\bar{R}^2$	N
All countries	−1.65	0.71	0.09	−0.56	0.32	0.82	57
	(−2.35)	(7.67)	(0.82)	(−3.41)	(5.58)		
All countries and industries	−1.62	0.77	−0.01	−0.58	0.24	0.71	167
	(−2.30)	(9.83)	(−0.14)	(−3.74)	(4.60)		

Note: Numbers in parentheses are *t*-values.

Table 10A.2   OLS Estimation of Export Equation II

		Coefficients					
	Intercept	GDP	GDPC	EC	FDI	$\bar{R}^2$	N
Developed countries	−4.57	0.88	0.66	−0.34	0.04	0.89	50
	(−2.14)	(6.51)	(1.02)	(−2.93)	(0.58)		
Developing countries	−3.57	0.81	0.21		0.38	0.71	117
	(−3.30)	(7.53)	(1.82)		(5.51)		

Note: Numbers in parentheses are *t*-values.

Table 10A.3 **OLS Estimation of Export Equation III**

			Coefficients				
	Intercept	GDP	GDPC	EC	FDI	$\bar{R}^2$	N
Food and beverages	−6.73 (−3.32)	1.41 (5.49)	−0.50 (−1.74)	−0.53 (−1.36)	−0.11 (−0.61)	0.74	16
Textiles and clothing	−1.66 (−1.53)	0.58 (5.66)	0.27 (1.77)	−0.45 (−1.36)	0.39 (4.57)	0.75	28
Shoes and leather	−6.10 (−2.27)	0.73 (2.54)	0.44 (1.30)	0.001 (0.002)	0.60 (2.72)	0.57	19
Furniture and wood	−5.09 (−2.70)	1.60 (6.42)	−0.82 (−3.95)		−0.57 (−2.61)	.087	8
Paper and printing	−0.10 (−0.04)	0.92 (4.20)	−0.82 (−3.57)	−0.48 (−1.35)	−0.02 (−0.12)	0.67	9
Petrochemicals	−1.86 (−0.79)	0.71 (3.11)	−0.15 (−0.67)	−0.49 (−1.22)	0.38 (2.43)	0.48	21
Nonmetals	−3.44 (−1.12)	−0.11 (−0.26)	0.51 (1.26)	−0.59 (−0.56)	1.42 (2.85)	0.59	13
Metals	−6.21 (−1.89)	1.52 (3.60)	−0.71 (−1.61)	−1.27 (−1.97)	−0.13 (−0.52)	0.56	15
Mechanical equipment	−0.58 (−0.64)	0.67 (5.77)	0.15 (1.27)	−0.48 (−3.20)	0.16 (2.71)	0.80	38
Labor-intensive[a] industries	−2.91 (−2.00)	0.57 (4.10)	0.29 (1.49)	−0.13 (−0.34)	0.53 (4.69)	0.54	47
Capital-intensive[b] industries	−0.78 (−0.63)	0.65 (4.48)	−0.01 (−0.08)	−0.52 (−2.34)	0.27 (3.22)	0.48	74

Note: Numbers in parentheses are *t*-values.
[a]Textiles and clothing; shoes and leather.
[b]Petrochemicals; metals; mechanical equipment.

Table 10A.4 **OLS Estimation of Export Equation IV**

			Coefficients				
	Intercept	GDP	GDPC	EC	FDI	$\bar{R}^2$	N
Labor-intensive/ developed countries	−11.53 (−1.62)	1.02 (2.62)	1.52 (0.66)	−0.11 (−0.29)	0.15 (−0.88)	0.81	11
Labor-intensive/ developing countries	−4.05 (−2.24)	0.51 (3.23)	0.52 (2.32)		0.70 (5.44)	0.58	36
Capital-intensive/ developed countries	−7.72 (−1.65)	0.22 (0.66)	2.67 (1.99)	−0.12 (0.41)	0.29 (1.69)	0.43	24
Capital-intensive/ developing countries	−3.37 (−1.98)	0.84 (4.68)	0.11 (0.68)		0.31 (3.31)	0.54	50

Note: Numbers in parentheses are *t*-values.

Table 10A.5   **OLS Estimation of Export Variation Equation I**

		Coefficients				
	Intercept	ΔGDP	EX92	ΔFDI	$\bar{R}^2$	N
All countries	0.52	1.08	−0.06	0.13	0.25	50
	(2.37)	(3.64)	(−2.26)	(2.21)		
All countries and industries	0.22	1.65	−0.03	0.25	0.20	130
	(0.80)	(3.70)	(−0.08)	(3.73)		

Note: Numbers in parentheses are *t*-values.

Table 10A.6   **OLS Estimation of Export Variation Equation II**

		Coefficients				
	Intercept	ΔGDP	EX92	ΔFDI	$\bar{R}^2$	N
Developed countries	−0.43	1.66	0.05	−0.02	0.59	39
	(−1.53)	(3.06)	(1.60)	(−0.21)		
Developing countries	0.12	1.09	−0.003	0.26	0.11	91
	(0.31)	(1.65)	(−0.07)	(3.08)		

Note: Numbers in parentheses are *t*-values.

Table 10A.7   **OLS Estimation of Export Variation Equation III**

		Coefficients				
	Intercept	ΔGDP	EX92	ΔFDI	$\bar{R}^2$	N
Textiles and clothing	0.94	0.07	−0.10	0.23	0.26	22
	(2.57)	(0.10)	(−2.25)	(2.54)		
Shoes and leather	0.19	−0.28	−0.04	0.94	0.33	14
	(0.30)	(−0.21)	(−0.50)	(2.57)		
Mechanical equipment	0.82	1.31	−0.09	0.17	0.27	30
	(1.70)	(1.97)	(−1.63)	(2.60)		
Labor-intensive industries	0.66	0.46	−0.08	0.35	0.21	36
	(1.79)	(0.62)	(−1.82)	(2.96)		
Capital-intensive industries	−0.19	1.16	0.02	0.21	0.19	57
	(−0.57)	(2.20)	(0.46)	(3.33)		

Note: Numbers in parentheses are *t*-values.

Table 10A.8   **OLS Estimation of Export Variation Equation IV**

		Coefficients				
	Intercept	ΔGDP	EX92	ΔFDI	$\bar{R}^2$	N
Labor-intensive/	−1.76	1.15	0.17	0.86	0.66	7
developed countries	(−3.40)	(0.54)	(2.89)	(3.12)		
Labor-intensive/	0.68	−0.78	−0.06	0.27	0.24	29
developing countries	(2.06)	(−1.14)	(−1.41)	(2.74)		
Capital-intensive/	−0.75	−1.80	0.09	−0.03	0.23	22
developed countries	(−1.61)	(2.05)	(1.50)	(−0.34)		
Capital-intensive/	−0.25	0.10	0.04	0.27	0.28	35
developing countries	(−0.55)	(0.12)	(0.73)	(3.37)		

Note: Numbers in parentheses are *t*-values.

References

Bank of Korea. Various years. *Overseas direct investment statistics yearbook.* Seoul: Bank of Korea.

Blomström, M., R. Lipsey, and K. Kulchycky. 1988. U.S. and Swedish direct investment and exports. In *Trade policy issues and empirical analysis,* ed. R. Baldwin. Chicago: University of Chicago Press.

Feldstein, M. 1995. The effects of outbound foreign direct investment on the domestic capital stock. In *The effects of taxation on multinational corporations,* ed. M. Feldstein, J. R. Hines, Jr., and R. G. Hubbard. Chicago: University of Chicago Press.

Kim, J., and I. Kang. 1997. Outward FDI and exports: The case of South Korea and Japan. *Journal of Asian Economics* 8.

Lipsey, R., and M. Weiss. 1981. Foreign production and exports in manufacturing industries. *Review of Economics and Statistics* 63:488–94.

Stevens, G., and R. Lipsey. 1992. Interactions between domestic and foreign investment. *Journal of International Money and Finance* 11.

Svensson, R. 1993. Domestic and foreign investment by Swedish multinationals. Working Paper no. 391. Stockholm: Industrial Institute for Economic and Social Research.

Swedenborg, B. 1979. *The multinational operations of Swedish firms.* Stockholm: Almqvist and Wicksell International.

United Nations. 1997. *World investment report.* New York: United Nations.

Comment   Mariko Sakakibara

Kim poses two major research questions: What role did Korean OFDI play in the country's economic performance? What are the characteristics of Korean OFDI? Performance is measured in this paper by exports and domestic investment. The author is especially concerned about the possibility that OFDI might decrease exports. These are important research issues.

Kim concludes that "we could not find any evidence that OFDI by Korean multinational firms had a detrimental effect on home country performance." He finds no evidence that Korean OFDI substituted for exports. Nor does he find any evidence that OFDI decreased domestic investment. I am sympathetic to this author, who made great efforts given limited data availability.

I would like, however, to raise some issues. The first issue concerns the data. Kim uses FDI data collected by the Bank of Korea (Korea's central bank). OFDI reporting to the Bank of Korea is mandatory for investments that exceed approximately $10 million, though this cutoff changes over time. Once OFDI is reported, companies have an obligation to report the profitability of their investments. There is a strong incentive, therefore, for Korean firms to avoid reporting OFDI. In fact, many investments are made in groups of amounts below the cutoff at one time. The most pessimistic estimation suggests that half of all Korean OFDI might not be covered by these data.[1] This sample is likely to have a bias toward large companies, namely, *chaebols,* or Korean conglomerates. The paper even states that five *chaebols* account for 60 percent of Korea's OFDI stock, indicating the possibility of sample selection bias.

The basic setup is

$$EX_{ij} = f(GDP_j, GDPC_j, OFDI_{ij}, EC_j),$$

where i represents an industry and j represents a host country. The sign on EC is expected to be negative because it is assumed here that Korean firms are motivated to conduct tariff-jumping OFDI. This is a crude assumption because the effects of tariff jumping should be industry specific. Kim worries about the possibility of omitted variables, so he runs

$$\Delta EX_{ij} = f(\Delta GDP_j, EX92, \Delta OFDI_{ij}).$$

Mariko Sakakibara is assistant professor at the Anderson Graduate School of Management of the University of California, Los Angeles.

The author is grateful to Dong-Sung Cho at Seoul National University for helpful comments on this article.

1. E.g., though the official record shows that there were approximately 750 cases of OFDI by Korean firms in the Quingtau area of China as of the end of 1995, keen observers in the Chinese market estimate that there were at least 2,000 investment cases by Korean firms in that area (Cho 1997).

He finds the coefficients on OFDI and ΔOFDI to be positive and statistically significant.

The problem here is that taking the first difference does not solve an omitted-variables problem, nor does the inclusion of exports in 1992. It is possible that an omitted variable drives both OFDI and exports by Korean firms simultaneously.[2] Given the limited coverage of the data, the prime candidate for an omitted variable is an indicator of a *chaebol's* growth maximization orientation. Some evidence supports this possibility. For example, favorable bank loans are given to large firms for domestic and foreign investment, and for export financing. This is because of the very limited disclosure requirements imposed on Korea firms, which results in profitability data not being available for lenders. The primary criterion for banks in their loan approval is the size of the borrower's revenue. In addition, *chaebol* leaders seek social recognition from overseeing the largest conglomerates. The rivalry between the chairmen of Samsung and Hyundai is well documented. Both of these examples suggest growth maximization not profit maximization by *chaebols*.

A possible scenario here is that when *chaebols'* profits, cash flow, or borrowing capacity increases, we would observe increases in both exports and OFDI. This scenario also fits with Knickerbocker's (1973) oligopolistic reaction in FDI. A *chaebol* is likely to seek all investment opportunities, domestic or overseas, to maximize its size. In addition, we should note the high domestic exit costs. Up until the 1997 Korean economic crisis, firing by Korean firms was illegal. Korean firms could not fire workers unless they declared bankruptcy. The only way a Korean firm could fire a worker was to sign an "honorable retirement" contract and make severance payments equal to the sum of the employee's three-year salary plus one month's salary times the number of years served. This prohibitively high exit cost suggests the possibility that firms could not decrease domestic production even if they increased OFDI. As a result, an increase in both exports and OFDI can be observed. If any of the variables suggested above are not available, domestic sales as a proxy for those variables should be used as a control, as suggested by Lipsey and Weiss (1984).

The major contribution of this paper is to identify the characteristics of Korean OFDI. Given the data, OFDI is driven by *chaebols,* concentrated in China, the ASEAN countries, and to some extent the United States, and focused on mechanical equipment (perhaps consumer electronics and semiconductors) and textiles and clothing. This kind of OFDI tends to be

2. Though Kim claims that this specification is to be used to examine how exports to country *j* are affected by OFDI to country *j*, the omitted-variables bias remains if country *j* is a favorable (or unfavorable) destination for both exports and OFDI for industry *i*, which appears to be the case here. In addition to the possibility explained in the text, the omitted variables might be the ones that reflect the increasing comparative advantages of an industry, and policy variables of host countries are only one kind of many possible omitted variables.

associated with the export of intermediate goods. For example, when Korean wage levels increased, the Korean garment industry shifted its domestic garment production to China or the ASEAN countries and shipped Korean textiles to these countries for final sewing.

This paper does not explain the causes of OFDI and exports by Korean firms, however. It is not clear whether the current structure of Korean OFDI and its positive association with exports will continue in the future. In the long run, Korean firms might relocate their production of intermediate goods to China or the ASEAN countries. If the final products produced by Korean subsidiaries are exported to third countries or to Korea, that will directly reduce Korean exports. As Korean firms begin to invest in developed countries, the current structure of FDI undertaken to seek cheap labor may not be sustainable. In addition, I would be concerned about growth maximization and overinvestment by the *chaebols.* What is happening now is that as of the end of May 1998, $40 billion of outstanding debt is held by Korean firms, and as of the end of 1997, the average debt-to-equity ratio of the thirty major *chaebols* was 518.90 percent, far beyond a sustainable level. A pessimistic view might be that Korean OFDI has a detrimental effect on home country performance for reasons different from those explained in this paper.

References

Cho, D. S. 1997. Empirical studies on the formation of firm-specific competitive advantages in Korean corporations (in Korean). *International Business Journal* 8:127–49.

Knickerbocker, F. T. 1973. *Oligopolistic reaction and multinational enterprise.* Boston: Harvard University, Graduate School of Management, Division of Research.

Lipsey, R. E., and M. Y. Weiss. 1984. Foreign production and exports of individual firms. *Review of Economics and Statistics* 66:304–8.

Comment   Chong-Hyun Nam

I think Kim's paper is interesting in two major respects. One is that it deals with outward foreign direct investment from a supposedly capital-scarce developing country, Korea; the other is that it attempts to investigate the effects of outward foreign direct investment on home country rather than host country performance.

I have only a few comments about the paper. First of all, I think that the paper's theme and analysis need to be more focused. As I understand

Chong-Hyun Nam is professor of economics at Korea University.

it, foreign direct investment in Korea, both inward and outward, has been quantitatively too minor to have any significant impact on macroeconomic variables. So it may not be too rewarding to explore its macroeonomic effects on such variables as domestic investment and employment at an aggregate level. If one wants to analyze its impact, however, I think the issue can best be addressed in the context of a general equilibrium framework, accounting for direct as well as indirect effects. But I do think it is quite worthwhile and interesting to investigate the impact of foreign direct investment on trade at a disaggregated industrial level.

My second comment is that the paper would gain much if it could explain why the accumulated stock value of foreign direct investment in Korea, both inward and outward, has been kept at such an exceptionally low level compared to not only developed countries but also developing countries. As can be seen in table 10.1, for instance, despite its recent surge, the stock value of outward foreign direct investment from Korea for 1990–95 stands at only 2.2 percent of GDP, about one-half of that for developing countries on average.

Obviously, a number of factors, both formal and informal, must have worked against Korea's inward and outward foreign direct investment. I suspect, however, that Korea's rather restrictive regulatory policies toward foreign direct investment have much to do with its poor performance in such investment. I think it is very important to unveil these policies and to discuss some of the potential economic costs borne by Korea due to such policy failures. I should also point out that the relatively small amounts of Korean inward and outward foreign direct investment by no means imply that capital flows, both inward and outward, were also small in Korea. In fact, Korea has relied heavily on foreign capital throughout its development over the past several decades; this dependence was a major cause of the recent financial crisis in Korea. Capital outflows have also grown substantially in recent years in Korea. Both capital inflows and outflows, however, often took the form of loans or portfolio investment than of foreign direct investment. Again, it would be interesting to explain why.

Another point I want to make is that Kim's paper presents interesting empirical evidence that Korea's outward direct investment did not hamper but rather promoted its exports, particularly in such labor-intensive industries as textiles and clothing and shoes and leather, contrary to the common expectation. Kim argues that outward foreign direct investment in Korea might have created new exports of intermediate goods that belong to the same industry classifications. I wonder whether this finding holds true for data periods other than 1994. I also think it would be interesting to examine the effects of outward foreign direct investment on Korea's imports as well, at a disaggregated industrial level and on a bilateral basis. I suspect that the motivation behind some of Korea's outward foreign direct investments is to produce parts and components or other resource-based intermediate goods more cheaply abroad and to ship them back to parent firms in Korea.

Finally, I think it would be interesting to examine how investment motives and environments faced by Korean firms have been changing over time and how Korean firms have been responding to such changes. For instance, in recent years, *chaebols* in Korea have made bold and aggressive outward foreign direct investments in high-tech industries in the United States and elsewhere, mainly for the purpose of acquiring advanced technologies and increasing access to larger overseas markets. According to Kim's paper, the five largest *chaebols* made up more than 60 percent of Korea's total outward foreign direct investment in 1995 alone, and more than 80 percent of this outward foreign direct investment was financed by foreign resources. I wonder whether these outward foreign direct investments have served their intended objectives and whether they have been cost-effective.

Foreign Direct Investment and Industrial Restructuring
The Case of Taiwan's Textile Industry

Tain-Jy Chen and Ying-Hua Ku

11.1 Introduction

Whether or not foreign direct investment (FDI) causes domestic industry to "hollow out" (deindustrialize) is a question that has long been debated in the literature but that remains unanswered. The debate has focused on the relation between FDI on the one hand and employment and exports on the other. Some argue that FDI creates jobs at the headquarters, which provides technical and managerial services to overseas subsidiaries (Lipsey 1995). FDI may even protect unskilled jobs at home if skill-intensive work like R&D is conducted abroad (Blomström, Fors, and Lipsey 1997). FDI also enables investing companies to preserve export market shares that would otherwise be lost to local competition or competition from low-wage countries (Lipsey and Weiss 1984). Others argue that FDI is tantamount to industry dislocation and the export of jobs from home (Bluestone and Harrison 1982).

In this paper, we take a direct look at the relation between FDI and the domestic industrial structure. Following Mucchielli and Saucier (1997), we view FDI as a Schumpeterian innovation whereby industrial production is reorganized across borders in order to gain a competitive edge. Indeed, Schumpeter called "the conquest of a new source of supply of raw materials or half-manufactured goods" (1934, 66) an innovation. Since any innovation is a "constructive destruction" process, it inevitably has some impact on the domestic industry, benefiting some firms and factories while hurting others. Therefore, it should not be surprising if FDI brings about

Tain-Jy Chen is professor of economics at National Taiwan University and a consultant at Chung-Hua Institution for Economic Research. Ying-Hua Ku is a research fellow at Chung-Hua Institution for Economic Research.

some redistribution in the economy. And like any successful innovation, successful FDI creates transitory profits for the innovators, tempting their competitors to follow suit until profits are completely dissipated.

If FDI is something innovative that brings competitive advantages to the investors, firms that choose not to follow suit must come up with some counterinnovations at home or risk losing their market shares and consequently their workforce. Therefore, FDI by an individual firm is likely to have an extensive impact on the whole industry through innovations and counterinnovations. The key to understanding how FDI may affect the domestic industry, therefore, lies in an exploration of the nature of the restructuring associated with FDI-induced innovations.

Industrial restructuring associated with FDI may occur on three different levels. First, some firms may introduce new product lines to replace old ones transplanted overseas. This is done in an effort to exploit the power of their firm-specific assets, which are often embodied in their employees, especially in the skilled ones. Laying off workers runs the risk of leaking special know-how to competitors. Therefore, arrangements will be made to deploy workers to new production units. Usually, such a placement plan is well thought out before a foreign investment project is undertaken. This is the case of intrafirm restructuring.

Second, relocated overseas production may be linked forward or backward to domestic industries (Rodríguez-Clare 1996). Through this linkage, overseas production may nourish downstream or upstream industries at home. This is intraindustry restructuring. The key to this type of restructuring is vertical integration between home and overseas production. Involved in intraindustry restructuring may be intrafirm transactions or interfirm linkages. Most multinational firms prefer to source from their home markets, particularly the headquarters, to reduce adjustment costs in overseas production. This provides the impetus for intraindustry restructuring.

Third, the resources released from the relocated industries may be channeled to new industries. This follows from the classical assertion that resources find their own way toward full employment. When one industry declines, other industries take its place automatically in accord with the country's comparative advantages. This is intersectoral, or economy-wide, restructuring.

In this paper, we study only intrafirm restructuring, using the case of Taiwan's textile industry as an example. The study shows that firms that undertook FDI gained market share and employment share at home relative to firms that did not. Loss of employment in Taiwan's textile industry was mainly attributable to the exit of failing firms rather than to FDI. All firms responded to rising labor costs in Taiwan by increasing specialization, but those engaged in FDI proceeded further. FDI firms also switched their major product lines more frequently and changed overall product composition more extensively than their non-FDI firm counterparts. The evidence suggests that FDI accelerates the restructuring process, which is probably inevitable under prevailing macroeconomic conditions. Firms that choose to make overseas investments also choose a fast track for restructuring and take high jumps over technological hurdles, while those choosing not to engage in overseas production choose a "gradual" approach to restructuring and make only marginal changes in production technology.

11.2   Foreign Direct Investment and the Restructuring of Taiwan's Textile Industry

Before 1980, the textile industry was Taiwan's largest manufacturing industry and largest export sector. Starting in the mid-1980s, rising wages made labor-intensive operations in the textile industry uncompetitive, and many textile firms responded by undertaking FDI in lower wage countries. FDI set off a restructuring process that has completely reshaped the textile industry. Production shifted from garments to fabrics and textile fibers with the method of production becoming more capital intensive and the value added generally increasing. There has been extensive turnover among individual firms since FDI began, and the surviving firms have recomposed their product lines to cope with the new climate of competition. This experience makes the textile industry a perfect case for the study of the relation between FDI and industrial restructuring.

FDI in the textile industry started with garment firms that relocated to nearby Southeast Asian countries and China with the simple aim of salvaging their export markets. After a massive relocation of garment operations, fabric manufacturers found it difficult to service overseas markets from Taiwan. Some decided to make FDI in the clusters of garment operations in Southeast Asia and China in order to better serve their old customers or to explore new patrons in the same locations. FDI by fabric manufacturers brought with it the dyeing and finishing operators that create the textures and colors distinctive of the Taiwanese industry.

When the local fabric industry reached a certain level of output, spinning operators from Taiwan also started to appear. Spinning operations are more capital intensive than weaving and garment operations. Unlike FDI in weaving and garments, where a large number of small investors congregated in the same locations, FDI in spinning was undertaken by a small number of relatively large firms, scattered throughout different countries. Each was to serve a cluster of local weaving and garment firms.

Finally, fiber producers from Taiwan also joined these clusters to cap the agglomeration process. Because fiber production is even more capital intensive and technologically demanding than spinning, FDI takes place only when the local market is large enough to guarantee economies of scale and competition is such that local production is more advantageous than export. By 1997, Taiwanese fiber producers had made three major investments: in Thailand, Malaysia, and the Philippines.

FDI has brought about a dramatic change in the textile industry in Taiwan. Table 11.1 lists the employment and output values of three subsectors of the textile industry, namely, synthetic fibers, spinning and weaving (knitting), and garments for 1986–96. It can be seen that total employment in the textile industry fell from 473,662 in 1986 to 287,065 in 1996, a drop of 186,597 jobs, equivalent to 40 percent of the 1986 employment level. Most jobs were lost in the garment sector. The output value of all textile products increased slightly over 1986–96, but its share in manufactured output decreased from 21.6 to 12.2 percent (data not shown). If "deindustrialization" is defined as "the dismantling of a country's manufacturing base" (Caslin 1987, 240) and if dismantling is taken to mean a rapid decline in output share, then Taiwan's textile industry is a classic case of deindustrialization. But a closer examination reveals that structural change seems to characterize the trend in the industry more vividly than absolute or relative decline. The composition of textile output shifted dramatically between 1986 and 1996, with the garment sector declining as synthetic fibers and spinning and weaving gained.

Overseas production was an apparent catalyst for domestic restructuring, as manifested in the pattern of exports. In 1986, garments accounted for 55.8 percent of Taiwan's textile exports, shrinking to only 19.8 percent in 1996. Taking the place of garments was exports of fabrics and yarn, whose share of total textile exports increased from 40.6 percent in 1986 to 73.9 percent in 1996. The destination of textile exports also shifted dramatically. In 1986, the U.S. market absorbed 36.8 percent of Taiwan's exports of textile products, of which garments took the lion's share. The U.S. market share had shrunk to only 15.9 percent by 1996, as Taiwan's exports were supplanted by those from Southeast Asia and China. In turn, the market share of Taiwan's exports of fabrics and yarn to this region rose from 23.4 percent in 1986 to 53.8 percent in 1996 (Chen et al. 1997, 201–8).[1]

In the following subsections, we will outline the restructuring process in each subsector of Taiwan's textile industry, focusing on how domestic restructuring was brought on by FDI. The outline is based mainly on interviews given by Taiwanese firms operating in Southeast Asia.

---

1. Southeast Asia includes Malaysia, Thailand, the Philippines, Vietnam, and Singapore. China includes Hong Kong. Direct trade between Taiwan and China during the sample period was prohibited, and indirect trade between them was usually transshipped through Hong Kong. Exports to Hong Kong were taken to be exports to China in our calculations.

Table 11.1   **Employment and Output Value of Taiwan's Textile Industry, 1986–96**

Year	Fibers		Spinning and Weaving		Garments		Total	
	Employment	Output	Employment	Output	Employment	Output	Employment	Output
1986	16,945	1,897	185,328	7,560	271,389	5,457	473,662	14,913
1987	27,217	2,545	186,277	9,802	247,175	7,138	460,669	19,485
1988	26,575	2,711	186,365	9,517	226,427	6,136	439,367	18,364
1989	24,839	3,222	174,234	6,842	196,000	6,693	395,073	16,757
1990	24,330	2,918	159,763	10,444	171,771	5,672	355,864	19,034
1991	23,916	3,700	155,292	12,633	160,067	6,299	339,275	22,633
1992	23,547	3,672	157,273	11,974	146,684	5,443	327,504	21,090
1993	22,560	3,092	153,241	10,253	139,142	4,777	314,943	18,088
1994	22,974	3,996	155,768	11,866	137,897	4,449	316,639	20,311
1995	23,654	5,206	149,832	12,002	126,901	3,946	300,387	21,154
1996	23,412	4,389	143,756	11,884	119,897	3,863	287,065	20,136

Sources: Employment from Directorate General of Budget, Accounting and Statistics, *Monthly Report on Wages and Salaries*; output value from Ministry of Economic Affairs, *Monthly Industry Report.*

Note: Employment reported in number of persons; output value reported in million U.S. dollars.

11.2.1 Garments

Garment firms were the frontrunners of Taiwanese FDI. After relocating production lines overseas, most garment firms reduced or removed their domestic production capacity. In general, larger firms and those possessing brand names in the domestic market were more capable than others of retaining domestic production after FDI. Taiwan continued to export some garments, partly because export quotas in the United States, Canada, and Europe served to protect Taiwan's market shares, partly because of Taiwan's unique production environment. A flexible production network cultivated over long years of experience in serving export markets gave Taiwan the unique capability to switch product lines swiftly and deliver products promptly. Even small garment firms maintained small-scale production capacity in Taiwan to produce for short orders after they had invested abroad. Production lead time was shorter in Taiwan because of a well-knit network comprising suppliers and subcontractors who could divide jobs in a very efficient and flexible manner.

If a garment firm was too small to maintain even small-scale production at home, it at least kept an office in Taiwan to provide logistical support to overseas production. Logistical support mainly consists of such marketing and procurement functions as accepting orders, making samples, participating in trade fairs, and procuring and collecting materials in preparation for overseas production. Making samples, for instance, is a very important part of soliciting orders. Normally, when a potential client indicates an intention to purchase a certain type of product, multiple samples need to be prepared quickly for the client to inspect and to choose from. Taiwan is known for its superior ability to supply small-volume, large-variety orders. For the small-volume market, the capacity to make samples fast and creatively is essential in the competition for orders. Making samples entails design capability in transforming the vague ideas of clients into a visualization of real products, and this capability needs to be maintained at the headquarters to ensure a nimble response to market demand.

Logistical support in the procurement of parts and materials in preparation for production is also essential to the flexibility of overseas production. When an order is accepted and planned to be carried out in an overseas subsidiary, parts and materials not available at the overseas location need to be procured and shipped there "just in time." Note that even in overseas production, quick delivery constitutes a competitive edge for Taiwanese subsidiaries over local firms, as both groups face the same wages. Any disruption in the supply of parts and materials will delay the delivery schedule and undermine the core competitiveness of Taiwanese subsidiaries. For example, most Southeast Asian subsidiaries of Taiwanese garment firms purchase fabrics from Taiwan, and procurement is conducted by parent firms. It is advantageous to import fabrics from Taiwan because

Taiwanese suppliers provide more variety, accept smaller orders, and promise shorter delivery time. Only such general purpose parts as buttons and zippers are procured locally. Logistical support from Taiwan's local networks provides linkages that allow Taiwanese suppliers to restructure themselves and survive despite a massive relocation of production.

The initial production of overseas subsidiaries of Taiwanese garment firms is furnished by orders transferred from parent companies. Gradually, overseas subsidiaries accumulate new assets and explore new sources of clients. To beat off local competitors, logistical support from the parent firm and the unique resources available from Taiwan's production networks become their weapons. New clients typically come from export markets, and original equipment manufacturer (OEM) contracts are the typical form of engagement. Diversification and enlargement of the customer base enable home and overseas operations to be horizontally integrated, whereby firm-specific know-how is shared.

Although most Taiwanese garment firms are export oriented, domestic-market-oriented firms do exist, and their FDI pattern is distinctive. When undertaking FDI, this type of firm exploits local markets or obtains low-cost products through direct production for resale to Taiwan. Such firms usually hold brand names. Together with overseas production, they strengthen their marketing capability and enlarge their marketing channels to enhance the value of their brands. Unlike export-oriented firms, which emphasize cost reduction, this type of firm emphasizes product value enhancement. Through FDI, they gain better access to local markets, lower their production costs, and expand their global production capacity, all of which serve to enhance the value of their brands.

Moreover, these firms often have an internationalization strategy in market development and labor sourcing. They are reminiscent of U.S. and European firms for which international subcontracting was a major strategy for reorganizing production in the 1970s and 1980s (Mytelka 1991). For this type of firm, the responsibilities of the headquarters are more demanding and more diverse than those associated with export-oriented investors. In addition to procurement, production allocation, design, R&D, and marketing coordination are all conducted at the headquarters.

In any event, relocated garment firms maintain close links with domestic industries. They purchase a large proportion of their fabrics from Taiwan, contributing to the expansion of fabric production in Taiwan. This linkage allows Taiwanese subsidiaries to hone a keener competitive edge than their local peers.

11.2.2   Fabrics

Weaving (knitting) firms relocated either by following in the footsteps of their main customers or by making independent moves in response to rising labor costs at home. The overseas products of Taiwanese weaving firms were usually export oriented. A few firms that aimed at local markets often found their main competition came from imported Taiwanese fabrics. Local production gave them the advantage of market proximity, but imported fabrics from Taiwan had the edge in quality and product variety.

In Taiwan, the production of fabrics was normally accomplished by weaving and dyeing firms independently, with the latter acting as a subcontractor to the former. Only very large fabric firms had integrated weaving and dyeing operations. When weaving firms relocated abroad, they often had difficulty finding subcontractors to perform dyeing and finishing functions for them. Even if there was one, its technology was likely to be geared toward domestically consumed fabrics and unsuitable for exports. Local dyeing and finishing concerns were also unaccustomed to the speed and punctuality of delivery required by export orders. For example, in Southeast Asia, local fabric firms were usually established with in-house dyeing and finishing operations. Specialized and independent dyeing and finishing subcontractors were not as common as in Taiwan. Subcontracting dyeing and finishing jobs to an integrated fabric firm ran the risk of products being emulated. The response of Taiwanese weaving firms to this problem was to establish their own dyeing and finishing divisions, making overseas operations more integrated than home operations.

Unlike overseas subsidiaries of garment firms, which procured a majority of their fabrics from Taiwan, weaving firms bought most of their yarn from local suppliers, many of which were Taiwanese subsidiaries. Overseas production of fabrics was normally differentiated from Taiwanese production by quality, tilting toward low-end products. In general, locally produced yarn was good enough to meet low-end demand. Production of yarn was capital intensive, and the investment scale tended to be large. A few Taiwanese subsidiaries of yarn producers in Southeast Asia were able to take care of most of the demand from local Taiwanese weaving firms, with the rest supplemented from Taiwan. The close working relations between Taiwanese subsidiaries of spinning and weaving firms stood in sharp contrast to the largely segregated operations of weaving and garment investors.

Fabrics made by Taiwanese weaving firms were either directly exported or made into garments for export. Only a small fraction was locally consumed. Because the customer base was partly formed by local garment firms, Taiwanese weaving subsidiaries were much more adapted to local conditions than were garment firms, which more or less operated in export enclaves.

Unlike garment firms, most weaving firms retained their home operations after investing abroad. Relocation of some low-end product lines prompted Taiwanese operations to move upward to higher end products. Horizontal differentiation of domestic and overseas production was the norm. Overseas production complemented domestic production in terms of product variety and production capacity. In general, parent firms and overseas subsidiaries accepted orders independently and swapped production capacity when needed. To increase the degree of product differentiation, many weaving firms in Taiwan also integrated fabric design, dyeing, and printing operations at home. More commonly, they invested in new weaving and knitting machines to improve productivity. This resulted in increased capital intensity and overall plant modernization in the fabric industry after the mid-1980s.

Improvements in design capability were also evident in Taiwan's fabric industry. In the old days, the possession of production capacity seemed to be enough to attract orders from international buyers. Nowadays, Taiwanese fabric producers have to keep abreast of world fashion, to design their own products, and to participate actively in international fairs in order to attract orders. In the past, trading firms collected fashion information and provided samples to fabric producers to ask for an allotment of production capacity. Nowadays, fabric producers present their own samples, albeit mimics of international fashion products, to trading firms in order to solicit business and sometimes bypass trading firms and appeal directly to international merchandisers.

11.2.3   Yarn

Yarn production was more capital intensive and the scale of investment larger than that of apparel and fabrics. Initial investment by Taiwanese yarn producers was often made by transplanting old-vintage machinery and equipment from Taiwan. New machinery and equipment made in Taiwan and other advanced countries would be purchased, however, when local production capacity was expanded after the initial investment. Relocation of existing production capacity from Taiwan was prompted by rising labor costs and land value in Taiwan, which rendered some yarn production inefficient. A shift from cotton-based spinning to manmade-fiber-based fabrics also made some cotton yarn production capacity obsolete in Taiwan.

The overseas subsidiaries of Taiwanese yarn producers were mostly local market oriented; only a small fraction of their products were exported. Customers in local markets included local firms and Taiwanese subsidiaries, but local firms usually outweighed Taiwanese subsidiaries in sales.

Product lines in overseas yarn production were diverse. Mixed yarns based on manmade fibers, such as T/C (polyester-cotton mix) and T/R (polyester-rayon mix), were most common. In initial operations overseas, manmade fibers were mostly imported from Taiwan, and cotton was imported from cotton-producing countries. Recently, some Southeast Asian countries have established or expanded their local production capacity of textile fibers by enticing direct investment or obtaining technology transfers from multinational firms. As a result, local Taiwanese yarn subsidiaries have also started procuring textile fibers from local or regional manufacturers. Countries with the capacity to produce textile fibers were inclined to erect trade barriers to hinder imports and to induce the localization of procurement.

FDI certainly reduced yarn production in Taiwan. Total spindles fell from a peak of 4.8 million to 3.3 million in 1996. Capacity utilization also diminished for the remaining spindles. Some capacity was dismantled instead of being relocated overseas. For spinning firms that maintained bicountry or multicountry plants, domestic production was still comparable or even larger than overseas, however, because of active investment in new-vintage and superior equipment.

The restructuring of the domestic spinning industry led to a change in product composition. The share of cotton yarn decreased while the share of polyester-based yarn increased. The sharpest increase was observed in the production of draw textured yarn (DTY) of polyester, output of which increased from 335,923 metric tons in 1986 to 883,005 metric tons in 1996. In recent years, Taiwanese spinners have all but bought out the whole production capacity of the world's two major manufacturers of DTY machines, Barmag of Germany and Murata of Japan (Taiwan Textile Federation 1998, 116–17). The rapid increase in DTY production was made possible by the capacity expansion of its upstream material, preoriented yarn (POY). Capacity expansion of POY by fiber manufacturers was mainly geared toward rapidly expanding demand in China. This expansion led to a cost reduction in POY, which boosted the competitiveness of DTY and trickled down to the downstream products of polyester-based fabrics. The buoyant fabric industry maintained close links to the clusters of garment manufacturers in China and Southeast Asia, explaining the looming share of fabric exports in Taiwan's textile trade.

11.2.4 Fibers

Taiwan's FDI in manmade textile fibers took place in Thailand, Malaysia, and the Philippines, each by a single company. These three Taiwanese subsidiaries all specialized in polyester fibers. Indonesia had the largest textile market in Southeast Asia, but there was no Taiwanese direct investment in manmade fibers there. Some indigenous textile fiber firms had technology cooperation programs with Taiwanese manufacturers, and some employed Taiwanese technicians to improve productivity and quality. There were also joint-venture textile fiber producers using technology furnished by the joint venture partners, notably those from Japan. The significant presence of local firms and the Indonesian government's divestiture policy, which requires foreign investors to relinquish their ownership over time, discouraged direct investment from Taiwan.

The manmade fiber industry was considered strategic in most developing countries. Tariff protection and nontariff barriers, such as licensing controls on imports and domestic entry, were often employed to protect local industries, including those in which multinational firms had invested. Trade barriers made local presence necessary to compete in the local market. Major competition for Taiwanese subsidiaries came from Japanese subsidiaries. Although the Japanese subsidiaries might have had a technological edge, in terms of product quality, Taiwanese subsidiaries resorted to a larger scale of production to gain cost advantage. For example, Taiwan's Tuntex in Thailand endured Japanese competition and obtained a market share of roughly 40 percent in polyester fibers in 1997, mainly through price competition. Taiwan's Hualon in Malaysia has monopolized the local market so far, although a majority of its products are exported to regional markets, China and Europe.

In spite of FDI, domestic investment in manmade fibers was vibrant. In 1986, Taiwan produced NT$44.2 billion worth of manmade fibers. In 1996, the product value increased to $85.8 billion. The quantity of manmade fibers produced was 1.24 million metric tons in 1986 and 2.60 million metric tons in 1996. Most expansion was accounted for by polyester fibers, of which Taiwan's production capacity was ranked first in the world in 1996. Expanding capacity to keep unit cost down was the main strategy of Taiwan's synthetic fiber producers, unlike their Japanese counterparts, who pursued product differentiation more earnestly than investment in capacity (Japan, Ministry of International Trade and Industry 1994).

11.3 Microdata Analysis

In this section, we analyze firm-level data to uncover the pattern of restructuring within Taiwan's textile industry. We draw data from the government's annual censuses of manufacturing plants. We take 1992 as the initial point of observation and 1995 as the end point. The choice of 1992 is dictated by the fact that this is the earliest survey year that provides data on FDI. The 1995 survey provides the most recent data available. The time span from 1992 to 1995, although short, is long enough to trace out the major restructuring path of the industry, as we will see later.

Table 11.2 lists the number of firms and plants in the sample. Only firms that own a textile plant are included in the sample, but textiles need not be the company's main business. By textiles, we mean the manufacturing of synthetic fibers, spinning and weaving (knitting), and garments. The census was conducted at the plant level. We consolidate plant-level data into firm-level statistics, on which our analysis is based. The quality of the 1992 census is relatively poor as it contains a large number of missing observations on employment and sales.[2] We delete observations where both employment and sales values are absent. In comparison, the quality of the 1995 census is relatively good, with only a few missing observations.

As can be seen from table 11.2, 6,054 textile firms were observed in

2. The census is meant to cover the population of all manufacturing plants, but inevitably, some plants refuse to answer census questions, provide incomplete information, or simply cannot be located. These missing observations are mainly for smaller plants.

Table 11.2   **Textile Firms and Plants in the Sample**

| | 1992 | | | 1995 | | |
Category	Firm	Plants[a]	Textile Plants	Firm	Plants[a]	Textile Plants
FDI firms	213	279	267	173 (167)	239 (227)	228 (222)
Non-FDI firms	5,841	6,197	6,086	4,866 (4,735)	5,339 (5,072)	5,201 (5,041)
New entrants[b]				2,272 (2,409)	2,343 (2,622)	2,295 (2,461)
Total	6,054	6,476	6,353	7,311	7,921	7,724

[a]Plants include textile plants and other plants owned by textile firms.

[b]New entrants are firms entering the textile industry in 1992–95 by establishing new plants. If entry by acquiring or merging with existing textile plants in 1992 is included, the numbers are shown in parentheses. In this case, the acquired or merged plants are also deducted from the calculation of survivors, where the corresponding numbers of firms and plants are also shown in parentheses.

the 1992 census. Among them 213 firms indicated that they sometimes undertook FDI before 1992.[3] The proportion appears to be small, but those undertaking FDI are relatively large firms and are more likely to operate multiple plants compared to the rest of the industry. Among the 213 firms in the FDI group, 173 survived until 1995. Meanwhile, among the 5,841 firms in the non-FDI group, 4,866 survived.

Note that census data are plant-level data. Plants that changed affiliating companies are considered to have been acquired by or merged into new companies. In calculating the number of survivors in 1995, these plants are treated as being "survived" by the new companies, which in turn, are part of the survivor group. If the "new" companies were nontextile firms in 1992 that acquired or merged with textile plants to become part of the textile industry in 1995, we may wish to treat them as new entrants rather than surviving firms from 1992 (see Dunne, Roberts, and Samuelson 1988, for a similar treatment). In this case, the number of survivors decreases to 167 firms for the FDI group and 4,735 for the non-FDI group. This implies that out of 213 FDI firms in 1992, 46 exited the market, whereas 1,106 out of 5,841 non-FDI firms did the same, including those acquired by or merged into other firms. The exit rate is 21.6 percent for the FDI group and 18.9 percent for the non-FDI group.

Between 1992 and 1995, 2,272 new firms entered the textile industry

3. The census asked whether the company had engaged in any FDI before the time of survey. The exact time of investment was not identified. The 1993 census also provided similar data. We used the 1992 census as the basis by which to cut the sample into the FDI group and non-FDI group, according to which differences in performance in subsequent years were examined. The comparison is subject to the disturbance that some firms may have undertaken FDI between 1992 and 1995 but been classified in the non-FDI group. Statistics indicate that Taiwanese overseas investment peaked around 1991 and 1992 (Chen et al. 1997); hence the number of FDI cases occurring in 1992–95 tends to be small compared with the cumulative number in 1992.

Table 11.3   **Employment by Different Groups of Firms in the Textile Industry**

Category	Number of Firms	Employment (persons)	Share (%)	Employment per Firm
		1992		
FDI firms	213	41,228	12.6	193.6
Non-FDI firms	5,841	228,459	69.8	39.1
Unobserved or error	–	57,817	17.7	–
Total	–	327,504	100.0	–
		1995		
FDI firms	173	38,917	13.0	225.0
Non-FDI firms	4,886	193,953	64.6	39.7
New entrants	2,272	59,060	19.7	26.0
Unobserved or error	–	8,457	2.8	–
Total	–	300,387	100.0	–

Source: Employment from Directorate General of Budget, Accounting and Statistics, *Monthly Report on Wages and Salaries.*

by establishing new plants, while 137 firms entered through merger and acquisition. New entrants, including the latter group, accounted for 33.0 percent of the stock of firms in 1995. Rapid exit and entry is a characteristic of Taiwan's industry and is an important contributor to the industry's improvement in efficiency (Aw, Chen, and Roberts 1997).

Now let us look at employment in the textile industry, shown in table 11.3. In 1992, total employment was 327,504, of which 12.6 percent was provided by firms that engaged in FDI and 69.8 percent by firms that did not, and 17.7 percent was unaccounted for due to missing observations. In 1995, total employment decreased slightly to 300,389, of which 13.0 percent was contributed by FDI firms that had survived (including plants that survived through merger and acquisition), 64.6 percent by non-FDI firms that had survived, and 19.7 percent by new entrants through establishment of new plants, while unaccounted employment was a negligible 2.8 percent.[4] These statistics show that despite attrition through exit, the share of employment in the textile industry contributed by FDI firms did not diminish. The assertion that foreign investors export jobs can be easily refuted in our case. In fact, if we look at employment provided by each firm, average employment by FDI firms actually increased from 193.6 per-

4. A textile plant may be acquired by (or merged into) a textile or a nontextile firm. A textile firm that expands by acquiring existing textile plants is naturally included in the survivor group, and its corresponding employment in the newly acquired plants is counted as part of the contribution by the survivor group to overall employment. It is logical to also treat employment by existing plants that are merged into nontextile firms in the contribution by the same group. Sales of the survivor group, reported below, are treated in the same manner.

Table 11.4   Sales by Different Groups of Firms in the Textile Industry

Category	Number of Firms	Sales (million NT$)	Share (%)	Sales per Firm (million NT$)
		1992		
FDI firms	197	54,242	10.1	275.3
Non-FDI firms	5,124	340,255	63.5	66.4
Unobserved or error	–	141,188	26.3	–
Total	–	535,685	100.0	–
		1995		
FDI firms	173	86,728	15.7	501.3
Non-FDI firms	4,886	405,989	73.3	83.1
New entrants	2,272	76,353	13.8	33.6
Unobserved or error	–	−15,535	−2.8	–
Total	–	553,535	100.0	–

Source: Sales from Ministry of Economic Affairs, *Monthly Industry Report.*

sons in 1992 to 225.0 persons in 1995.[5] We do not know whether major employment shedding had taken place before 1992, but these results at least indicate that FDI firms are not more susceptible to downsizing than non-FDI firms. On the other hand, average employment of new entrants (through new plants) is smaller than for any existing group of firms.

Next, let us look at market share in terms of sales as listed in table 11.4. The 197 FDI firms that provided sales data had a combined market share in 1992 of 10.1 percent. In comparison, the non-FDI firms took 63.5 percent of the market. The market share of surviving FDI firms rose to 15.7 percent in 1995, while that of their non-FDI counterparts rose to 73.3 percent. Both gained at the expense of failing firms. The average sales of surviving firms increased during the period, particularly among FDI firms.[6] Yamawaki (1992) reported that similarly Japanese textile and clothing firms significantly increased in size in 1965–83 by way of restructuring in response to rising wages in Japan. Torre (1986, 117) also reported that size is an important factor contributing to successful adjustment to rising production costs by clothing firms in developed countries because it permits firms to centralize a number of production services, which then could be provided to various plants at significant savings. New entrants through new plant establishments, despite their large number, took only 13.8 per-

5. These numbers do not include employment in nontextile industries.
6. According to *Commodity Price Statistics Monthly in Taiwan Area of the Republic of China* (June 1998), the wholesale price index of textile products rose 14.9 percent in 1992–95 while that of apparel and accessories rose 10.7 percent. If we use the wholesale price index of textile products to deflate nominal sales value, average sales of FDI firms rose 58.7 percent in real terms during the period while that of non-FDI firms rose 8.9 percent.

Table 11.5   **Distribution of Product Lines**

	1992		1995	
Number of Lines	All Products	Textile Products	All Products	Textile Products
1	4,277	4,311	4,539	4,441
2	671	642	389	356
3	191	173	125	106
4	102	95	52	50
5	45	42	14	11
6	30	25	13	11
7	12	10	6	4
8	6	6	0	0
9	6	6	0	0
10	4	2	0	0
Greater than 10	9	7	6	4
Total lines	7,504	7,173	6,200	5,876
Number of firms	5,353	5,319	5,144	4,986
Lines per firm	1.4	1.35	1.21	1.18

cent of the market in 1995. The pattern that new entrants tend to contribute only marginally to employment and sales is also found in U.S. industry data. Diversification and expansion (including that through merger and acquisition) by existing firms are found to be the major driving force of industrial growth in the U.S. industry (Dunne et al. 1988).[7]

To understand the nature of restructuring, let us first look at the distribution of product lines in the industry. Product line is defined by the seven-digit commodity code in Taiwan's official commodity classification. It distinguishes, for example, woven fabrics from knit fabrics, ladies' wear from men's wear, and further distinguishes woven fabrics made of different materials. Table 11.5 lists the distribution of product lines in the sample. It can be seen that most firms operate a single product line; only about one-fifth of the firms operate multiple product lines. As a whole, the average firm operated 1.35 textile product lines in 1992. Even if nontextile products were included, the average number of product lines was merely 1.40. From 1992 to 1995, the average number of product lines decreased, indicating that the average firm became more specialized in this period.

Table 11.6 confirms this trend. In this table, we trace the product lines of firms that survived from 1992 to 1995. New entrants, either through new plant establishment or through merger and acquisition, are excluded. It can be seen that the number of product lines of the average FDI firm

7. Dunne et al. (1988) reported that by averaging across industries, new entering firms between two census years (five years) account for approximately 16 percent of industry output, but 40 percent of the number of firms of each census year. In their paper, new entering firms include new entrant firms and existing firms that diversify into the said industry. New entrants alone account for only about 8 percent of industry output.

Table 11.6   **Product Lines per Firm, 1992-95**

	All Products		Textile Products	
Category	1992	1995	1992	1995
FDI firms	2.01 (163)	1.89 (139)	1.82 (163)	1.69 (136)
Non-FDI firms	1.39 (4,334)	1.20 (3,721)	1.33 (4,314)	1.18 (3,636)
Total	1.41 (4,497)	1.23 (3,860)	1.35 (4,477)	1.20 (3,772)

Note: Only firms that operate in both 1992 and 1995 are included in the statistics. Numbers in parentheses are sample sizes.

decreased from 2.01 in 1992 to 1.89 in 1995. The average non-FDI firm had significantly fewer product lines, but the trend was the same: decreasing from 1.39 lines in 1992 to only 1.20 lines in 1995. Fewer lines among the non-FDI group were largely attributable to their smaller firm size. If we count the number of four-digit industries operated by each firm, the average number of industries operated by each firm also decreased from 1992 to 1995. Similar findings were reported by a study of the U.S. manufacturing industry over 1963–82 (Dunne et al. 1988).

In essence, Taiwanese textile firms chose to specialize in a few product lines and resorted to equipment modernization, process innovation, and product differentiation to create a new competitive edge under immense pressure from rising wages. Mytelka (1991) reported a similar pattern of restructuring by the Italian textile industry in an effort to weather competition coming from East Asian producers. Ghadar, Davidson, and Feigenoff (1987, 76) also reported that U.S. textile and clothing firms attempted to increase specialization in segments where they enjoyed leadership positions in order to combat import competition. When wages were low in Taiwan, textile firms took any OEM orders that could fill their idled capacity; when wages rose and labor-intensive operations were no longer profitable, concentration on a few niche products was desirable because in order to protect their threatened competitive margin, firms had to acquire new resources, and resources are always limited and costly. Specialization allowed firms to strengthen their core competitiveness with limited resources. Gollop (1997) also reported that increased plant specialization in narrow product lines was a major determinant of recent U.S. manufacturing productivity growth. Over the 1963–87 period, decreased product heterogeneity accounted for about 17 percent of productivity growth, second in importance only to technical change and equaling the contribution of scale economies. Studying large U.S. companies in the second half of the 1980s, Lichtenberg (1992) also found that de-diversification contributed to productivity growth of the companies studied.

We may use a more formal index of product line concentration (or diversification), the Herfindahl index, to further verify the trend of specialization. The Herfindahl index takes into account not only the number of product lines but also the distribution of sales among all production lines. The greater the Herfindahl index, the higher the degree of product concentration or the lower the degree of diversification. We calculate the Herfindahl index for each group of firms and list the results in table 11.7. Again, only surviving firms are included in the calculation. This principle applies to all indexes to be elucidated in the rest of the paper.

It can be seen that the Herfindahl index increases across the board between 1992 and 1995, suggesting that all firms had to become more specialized during this period. FDI firms are shown to be more diversified than non-FDI firms in general, and this pattern persisted over 1992–95. This may be largely attributable to the larger size of FDI firms because firm size has been shown to be positively correlated with degree of diversification (Amey 1964). In 1992, the Herfindahl index (for textile products alone) was 0.8367 for FDI firms and 0.9284 for non-FDI firms. The indexes increased to 0.8622 and 0.9552, respectively, in 1995.

Another "paper trail" of industrial restructuring is shifts in major product lines between 1992 and 1995. By major product line we mean the product line that accounts for the largest proportion of a company's total sales revenue. A shift in major product line indicates a major change in the company's business orientation.

Table 11.8 indicates the extent of major product line shift between 1992 and 1995. It can be seen from the table that among all textile firms, 41.1 percent shifted major product lines in 1992–95. This defuses our concern that we may be looking at a period in which industrial restructuring was rather dormant. Indeed, the restructuring taking place in the sample period was remarkable. Comparing firms engaged in FDI with those holding out, the FDI group underwent more extensive restructuring. Among the FDI group, 53.4 percent of firms switched major product lines in 1992–95, while among the non-FDI group, only 40.7 percent of firms did so. The evidence suggests that FDI is often accompanied by more thorough re-

Table 11.7   **Herfindahl Index of Product Line Concentration**

Category	1992	1995
FDI firms		
All products	0.8225 (163)	0.8495 (139)
Textile products	0.8367 (163)	0.8622 (136)
Non-FDI firms		
All products	0.9225 (4,334)	0.9512 (3,721)
Textile products	0.9284 (4,314)	0.9552 (3,636)
All firms		
All products	0.9184 (5,353)	0.9517 (5,144)
Textile products	0.9241 (5,319)	0.9558 (4,983)

Note: Numbers in parentheses are sample sizes.

Table 11.8 Shifts of Main Product Line, Subsector, and Sector, 1992–95 (number of firms)

Shift	All Firms	FDI Firms	Non-FDI Firms
Product line shift			
Shift	1,601 (41.1)	70 (53.4)	1,531 (40.7)
Do not shift	2,291 (58.9)	61 (46.6)	2,230 (59.3)
Total	3,892 (100)	131 (100)	3,761 (100)
Subsector shift			
Shift	752 (19.3)	31 (23.3)	721 (19.1)
Do not shift	3,152 (80.7)	102 (76.7)	3,050 (80.9)
Total	3,904 (100)	133 (100)	3,771 (100)
Sector shift			
Shift	297 (7.6)	15 (11.3)	282 (7.5)
Do not shift	3,607 (92.4)	118 (88.7)	3,489 (92.5)
Total	3,904 (100)	133 (100)	3,771 (100)

Note: Subsector shift indicates a shift between four-digit industry codes. Sector shift indicates a shift between fiber, weaving and spinning, and garment industries. Numbers in parentheses are percentages of firms in category.

structuring and that firms making overseas investment are less likely to avoid reorienting their businesses.

A similar pattern is observed if we define business orientation in a broader sense. For this, we look at the major subsector from which the sample firms derived their sales. By subsector, we refer to the four-digit industry classification in accord with Taiwan's official industrial code. Subsector refers to industries such as cotton textiles (spinning and weaving), polyester textiles, knit garments, and the like.

Table 11.8 also indicates that the textile industry underwent extensive restructuring, even at the subsector level. As a whole, 19.3 percent of textile firms switched subsector in the sample period. Again, FDI firms were more likely than their non-FDI counterparts to switch subsectors, such as from cotton textiles to polyester textiles. Nearly a quarter (23.3 percent) of FDI firms switched subsectors while only about one-fifth (19.1 percent) of non-FDI firms did so.

If we divide the textile industry into three main sectors, namely, fibers, spinning and weaving (yarn and fabrics), and garments, in accord with two-digit industry demarcation lines, to examine whether the shift in four-digit industry has crossed sectoral lines, the result remains robust. Switching between sectors is naturally less common but is, nevertheless, significant. Table 11.8 shows that 7.6 percent (297 cases) of textile firms in the sample switched sectors in 1992–95. Once again, firms that had invested abroad were more likely to switch sectors than those that had stayed home. Production sector switches occurred mostly from garments to spinning and weaving, and from textile to nontextile industries. In other words, shifts within the textile industry were mostly vertical movements toward upstream production. Shifts of major business from textile to nontextile industries occur more often in the non-FDI group (65 out of 282 cases) than in the FDI group (2 out of 15 cases).

In studying the largest U.S. firms, Berry (1975, 74) concluded that four-digit interindustry activity was most conducive to corporate growth but that this activity is normally confined within the border of two-digit industry groups. Gorecki's study of British industry between 1958 and 1963 also found that "enterprises diversified to a large extent within a group of industries that could be considered homogeneous in a technical sense" (1975, 143). Our finding is in general conformity with these conclusions, but cases of firms jumping industry borders seem to be more pervasive in Taiwanese industry.

It is worth nothing that restructuring within the garment sector may be relatively difficult for Taiwanese firms. Torre (1986, 90), for example, reported that successful adjustments of the garment industries in developed countries in the 1970s and 1980s entailed either "moving up the market" by incorporating better product design, higher quality, more elaborate materials and accessories, and better distribution networks and consumer services or reducing costs through offshore subcontracting. Both cost reduction and product value enhancement options are formidable tasks for Taiwan's no-brand manufacturers, who themselves serve as international subcontractors. In contrast, restructuring is relatively easy in the weaving and spinning sector because there is some room for Taiwanese firms to make process innovations and expand capacity. Garment firms that have difficulties restructuring within the garment sector may wish to jump to weaving and spinning, taking advantage of knowledge relevant to the textile industry.

Switching main product lines is only a crude measure of product line shift. It provides a discrete number (zero or one) to indicate whether there is a switch. Firms shifting weights between product lines without changing major product always get a measure of zero. We therefore need a more sophisticated measure to capture shifts in product line composition. To this end, we calculate the share of each product line in total sales and measure changes in these shares between 1992 and 1995. Naturally, some product lines have their shares increased while others have them decreased. Since the shares of all product lines sum to one, the shares gained by the rising product lines always equal the shares lost by the declining product lines. We therefore take the combined shares gained by the rising product lines as a measure of product composition change and call it the "composition change index."

The index can be understood from figure 11.1. In figure 11.1, we spread product lines along the horizontal axis, assuming, for simplicity, that these

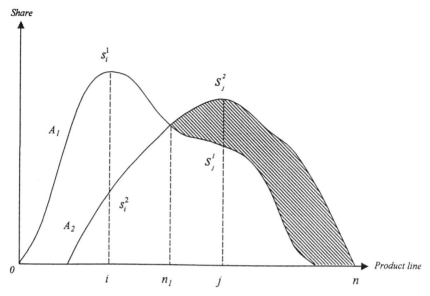

Fig. 11.1   Measuring changes in product composition

product lines are continuous. The product lines manufactured in period 1, together with their respective shares, are depicted by contour A_1. Since the shares of all products sum to one, the area under A_1 is unity. Similarly, product lines manufactured in period 2 are depicted by contour A_2. For the ith product line, its share decreases from period 1 (S_i^1) to period 2 (S_i^2). For the jth product line, its share increases from period 1 (S_j^1) to period 2 (S_j^2). Our index measures total shares gained by product lines such as the jth, or the area below the period 2 contour and above the period 1 contour, shaded in the figure.[8]

Note that the composition change index always lies between zero and one. If the composition of product lines does not change, the index is zero; if all product lines have been replaced, the index is one. The measure applies to single- as well as multiple-product firms. For single-product firms, the measure is identical to the "major product shift" index described in table 11.8.

As a side measure, we also calculate the number of product lines that increased their shares of sales between 1992 and 1995 as a proportion of the combined number of product lines in these two years. This measure is named the "product line change index." In figure 11.1, for instance, the total number of product lines in the two periods is n, and the number of

8. We are indebted to Chien-Fu Chou of National Taiwan University for suggesting such a measure.

Table 11.9   **Changes in Product Line Composition**

Category	Composition Change Index (%)	Product Line Change Index (%)	Sample Size
FDI firms			
Single plant	0.4857 (0.4654)	0.3020 (0.2512)	98
Multiple plants	0.5858 (0.3692)	0.4208 (0.2052)	31
Total	0.5082 (0.4503)	0.3306 (0.2455)	129
Non-FDI firms			
Single plants	0.3946 (0.4678)	0.2272 (0.2486)	3,093
Multiple plants	0.5423 (0.4280)	0.3658 (0.2217)	256
Total	0.4058 (0.4665)	0.2380 (0.2495)	3,349

Note: Numbers in parentheses are standard errors of the sample.

product lines that increased their shares is $n - n_1$; hence the product line change index is $(n - n_1)/n$. Both indexes are presented in table 11.9.

It can be seen from table 11.9 that both indexes suggest that product shifting is more pervasive among firms that undertook FDI. The composition change index is 0.5082 for FDI firms against 0.4058 for non-FDI firms. This indicates that over half of the sales revenue of FDI firms in 1995 came from new production or uneven expansion of old product lines. The statistics also indicate that firms with multiple plants underwent more sweeping changes in product composition than those with a single plant. This is not surprising because multiple plants provide more room for adjustment and restructuring.[9]

The product line change index shows a similar pattern, that is, more sweeping changes taking place among FDI firms. The index shows that among the FDI group, 33.06 percent of product lines were either newly introduced or gained production share between 1992 and 1995. In comparison, only 23.80 percent of the product lines of non-FDI firms fall into this category. From this index, we can also infer that 66.94 percent of the product lines of FDI firms were abandoned or lost production share in 1992–95, while 76.20 percent of the product lines of non-FDI firms received the same treatment. This suggests that more attrition and dismantling of product lines took place among non-FDI firms. As FDI is usually accompanied by product line relocation, investing firms are likely to introduce new product lines to replace outgoing ones or to expand remaining product lines to fill the vacuum left by relocation. In contrast, firms that

9. Changes in relative prices, in addition to changes in production costs, lead to restructuring in product composition. Part of change in product mix may be a natural response to change in relative prices without "reorganization" of the production structure or "retooling" of the production technology. Hence, our index needs to be interpreted as a broad measure of restructuring in response to both price signals and cost factors.

stayed away from FDI restructured themselves by selecting a few niche product lines for expansion and upgrading. Our data show that 95 new product lines were introduced by 129 FDI firms between 1992 and 1995, with each firm introducing an average of 0.736 lines, while only 1,468 new product lines were introduced by 3,349 non-FDI firms in the same period, with an average of 0.438 new lines per firm. In fact, non-FDI firms tend to resort to capacity expansion in a few emerging product lines, whether they be old or new. These product lines are conducive to process innovation or the realization of scale economies. This can be seen from table 11.10.

Table 11.10 lists the ten most rapidly growing product lines in 1992–95 and the contributions by various groups of firms to their growth. By "most rapidly growing" we refer to the largest increases in terms of the absolute value of sales. Six of these product lines are polyester-based products, whether fibers, yarn, or fabrics. Capacity expansion of non-FDI firms in these areas is apparent, as non-FDI firms contribute the lion's share to the growth in output. In comparison, FDI firms only contributed marginally to growth in these segments of the industry. Even new entrants (including those entering through merger and acquisition) contributed more than the FDI group. Meanwhile, exit from these emerging industry segments is negligible, except for cotton-polyester mix yarn.

Among the ten top emerging product lines, three lines were in the garment sector, where production was nonexistent in 1992. These were newly introduced products. FDI firms contributed significantly to growth in two of them. Antonelli (1995) argued that in response to rising factor costs, firms restructure themselves by considering the trade-off between switching costs and innovation costs. The former refer to costs of changing techniques within a given technology set, and the latter refer to costs of changing production technology. A firm's accumulated knowledge specific to existing production techniques is critical to this choice. Although our study focuses on restructuring of product lines and ignores technology changes, our results seem to suggest that FDI firms have endowment advantages in innovation costs over switching costs. The endowment advantages that reduce innovation costs for them may be firm-specific assets such as organizational strength and technological capability. With these advantages, FDI firms are more inclined to switch product lines by adopting new technologies than to switch production techniques within existing product lines. To the extent that firms with more endowment advantages are more inclined to make overseas investments (Caves 1971), the fact that FDI firms are more apt to restructure themselves may simply be a result of these advantages, rather than of FDI actions per se. Even if this is the case, FDI is still an important indication of the restructuring process, although it is not the root of restructuring. The evidence presented above at least illustrates the differences between domestic restructuring that is associated with FDI and restructuring that is not.

Table 11.10   **Top Ten Growth Product Lines, 1992–95 (million NT dollars)**

Commodity Code	Product Line	1995 Sales	1992 Sales	Increase 1992–95	Contribution by FDI Firms (%)	Contribution by Non-FDI Firms (%)	Contribution by New Entrants (%)	Contribution by Exits (%)
1360014	Textured filament yarn of polyesters	50,556	30,942	19,614	0.7	92.2	9.6	−2.6
1360201	Polyester woven fabrics	33,315	18,765	14,550	10.6	65.0	26.0	−1.5
2121020	Polyester staple fiber	31,050	16,890	14,160	−0.1	85.2	14.9	0
2121012	Polyester filament	21,262	9,321	11,941	−0.3	100.3	0	0
1360140	Cotton-polyester mix yarn	20,366	13,595	6,771	15.1	75.4	23.2	−13.8
2121013	Partially oriented filament yarn of polyesters	17,628	9,071	8,557	0	72.9	27.1	0
2121002	Nylon filament	16,733	4,765	11,968	74.5	14.8	18.0	−7.3
1419090	Outerwear made of other fabrics	9,078	0	9,078	25.2	39.6	35.2	0
1342320	Knit women's underwear	8,313	0	8,313	42.2	32.2	25.7	0
1342110	Knit sportswear	6,396	0	6,396	7.1	78.1	14.8	0

Note: The contribution of each group of firms is measured by the change in their sales as a percentage of the increase in total sales in respective product lines.

Since some indicators seem to suggest that more extensive and sweeping restructuring occurred in FDI firms, it would be desirable to put all the indicators together and formally test whether there was indeed a difference associated with FDI. To do this, we perform a principal component analysis on several indicators that we have presented above to obtain an aggregate measure of restructuring. We then conduct analysis of variance (ANOVA) to test whether there is a significant difference between FDI and non-FDI firms. The restructuring indicators included in the principal component analysis are (1) change in the number of product lines, (2) change in the Herfindahl index, (3) change in the main product line, (4) change of subsector, (5) change of sector, (6) composition change index, and (7) product line change index.

The standardized scoring coefficients resulting from the principal component analysis are listed in table 11.11. It can be seen that all coefficients are positive except for change in the number of product lines. This is be-

Table 11.11   Tests of Difference between FDI and Non-FDI Firms

Principal Components Analysis of Restructuring Indicators

Indicator	Scoring Coefficient (standardized)
Change in number of product lines	−0.02171
Change in Herfindahl index	0.02324
Change in main product line	0.27659
Change of subsector	0.22165
Change of sector	0.16227
Composition change index	0.27964
Product line shift index	0.25641

Analysis of Variance by FDI

Category	Mean Loading Score	Sample Size
FDI firms	0.3118	124
Non-FDI firms	−0.0119	3,261
F-statistic	12.56	

Analysis of Variance by Size and FDI (mean loading score)

Category	Large Firms[a]	Small Firms	Significant Difference?
FDI firms	0.2864 (90)	0.3791 (34)	No
Non-FDI firms	0.0691 (1,100)	−0.0531 (2,161)	Yes
Significant difference?	Yes	Yes	

Note: Numbers in parentheses are sample sizes.

[a]Large firms are firms employing thirty persons or more. The rest are small firms.

cause the number of product lines decreased over 1992–95 and a larger negative value actually indicates a higher degree of change. The rest of the indicators are consistently positive, where larger values suggest higher degrees of restructuring.

From the appropriation of scoring coefficients, each firm is given a loading score based on the principal components of these seven indicators. The loading score is standardized with zero mean and unit variance, and ANOVA can be performed to see whether there is a significant difference between FDI and non-FDI firms. We list the mean score for each group in table 11.11. It can be seen that the mean score is 0.3118 for FDI firms and −0.0119 for non-FDI firms. The F-statistic for the null hypothesis that the two groups come from the same population is 12.56, indicating that there is a significant difference at the 1 percent level between the two groups of firms. Since a greater loading score indicates a higher degree of restructuring, the result suggests that firms that invested abroad before 1992 underwent deeper and more extensive restructuring in 1992–95 compared to those that had not taken a similar course.

Since FDI firms are generally larger than non-FDI firms, this difference in restructuring may be attributable to size rather than FDI activity. We therefore introduce another dimension into the ANOVA by separating the sample by size, in addition to FDI. Firms that employ fewer than thirty employees are called small firms, and the rest are called large firms. A four-way classification of ANOVA is also presented in table 11.11. It can be seen that there is a significant difference in terms of mean loading score between the FDI and non-FDI classes whether they be large or small firms. Meanwhile, size makes no difference to mean leading score among the FDI firms. Size only matters for the non-FDI group, where large firms are shown to have a significantly higher loading score. This suggests that it is FDI, rather than firm size, that accounts for the difference in the degree and extent of restructuring.

11.4 Concluding Remarks

We view FDI as a Schumpeterian innovation whereby an old production structure is dismantled in favor of a new one. Therefore, FDI is always accompanied by restructuring. Restructuring may take place at the firm, industry, or economy-wide level. In this paper, we examine the firm-level restructuring of Taiwan's textile industry between 1992 and 1995 and find that restructuring was indeed extensive and sweeping. We find that the average textile firm reduced its number of product lines and increased its concentration of product line distribution as measured by the Herfindahl index. About half of the textile firms under our observation switched their main product lines in the short time span of three years. More than one-fifth of the textile firms switched between four-digit industry categories.

Some even moved from downstream operations to upstream operations, such as from garments to weaving, to take advantage of new schemes in the international division of labor. In fact, the product mix of the whole textile industry has been reshuffled to an amazing degree. For an average textile firm, nearly half of sales revenue comes from newly introduced product lines or from disproportional expansion of existing product lines. When compared with textile firms that did not undertake FDI, those investing abroad show a significantly higher degree of restructuring by all indexes.

There is no evidence that overseas investment led investing firms to shed jobs from domestic operations. In fact, there is even some indication that FDI enables firms to increase employment at their headquarters. Most job losses in Taiwan's textile industry during the sample period were attributable to the exit of firms, and there is no evidence that FDI contributed to exit either. Firms that undertook FDI were also likely to expand sales in domestic markets, casting doubt on the assertion that "FDI hollows out domestic industry."

However, this paper falls short of uncovering intrinsic differences in terms of the nature of restructuring, except for product line shift. Scanty evidence suggests that non-FDI firms resort more often to capacity expansion and process innovation whereas FDI firms are more keen on new product introduction and technology change. More research in this area is desirable.

References

Amey, L. R. 1964. Diversified manufacturing businesses. *Journal of the Royal Statistical Society,* ser. A, 127:251–90.

Antonelli, Christiano. 1995. *The economics of localized technological change and industrial dynamics.* Economics of Science, Technology and Innovation, vol. 3. Dordrecht and Boston: Kluwer.

Aw, Bee-Yan, Xiaomen Chen, and Mark Roberts. 1997. Firm-level evidence on productivity differentials, turnover and exports in Taiwan's manufacturing. University Park: Pennsylvania State University, Department of Economics. Working paper.

Berry, C. H. 1975. *Corporate growth and diversification.* Princeton, N.J.: Princeton University Press.

Blomström, Magnus, Gunnar Fors, and Robert Lipsey. 1997. Foreign direct investment and employment: Home country experience in the United States and Sweden. *Economic Journal* 107:1787–97.

Bluestone, Barry, and Bennett Harrison. 1982. *The de-industrialization of America.* New York: Basic Books.

Caslin, Terry. 1987. De-industrialization in the U.K. In *Current controversies in economics,* ed. Howard Vane and Terry Caslin, 265–92. Oxford: Blackwell.

Caves, Richard. 1971. International corporations: The industrial economics of foreign investment. *Economica* 38:279–93.

Chen, Tain-Jy, et al. 1997. *Taiwan's outward investment in Southeast Asia and its effect on industrial development.* Taipei: Chung-Hua Institution for Economic Research. Unpublished project report.

Dunne, Timothy, Mark Roberts, and Larry Samuelson. 1988. Patterns of firm entry and exit in U.S. manufacturing industries. *Rand Journal of Economics* 19 (winter): 495–515.

Ghadar, Fariborz, William H. Davidson, and Charles S. Feigenoff. 1987. *U.S. industrial competitiveness: The case of textiles and apparel.* Lexington, Mass.: Lexington Books.

Gollop, Frank. 1997. The pin factory revisited: Product diversification and productivity growth. *Review of Industrial Organization* 12:317–34.

Gorecki, P. K. 1975. An inter-industry analysis of diversification in the U.K. manufacturing sector. *Journal of Industrial Economics* 24 (2): 131–46.

Japan. Ministry of International Trade and Industry. 1994. *Sekai Seni Sangyo Jijo* (World textile industry affairs). Tokyo: Ministry of International Trade and Industry.

Lichtenberg, Frank. 1992. Industrial de-diversification and its consequences for productivity. *Journal of Economic Behavior and Organization* 18:427–38.

Lipsey, Robert. 1995. Outward direct investment and the U.S. economy. In *The effects of taxation on multinational corporations,* ed. Martin Feldstein, James R. Hines, Jr., and R. Glenn Hubbard. Chicago: University of Chicago Press.

Lipsey, Robert, and Merle Weiss. 1984. Foreign production and exports of individual firms. *Review of Economics and Statistics* 66:304–8.

Mucchielli, Jean-Louis, and Philippe Saucer. 1997. European industrial relocations in low-wage countries: Policy and theory debate. In *Multinational firms and international relocation,* ed. Peter Buckley and Jean Louis Mucchielli. Cheltenham, England: Elgar.

Mytelka, Lynn K. 1991. Technological change and the global relocation of production in textiles and clothing. *Studies in Political Economy* 36:109–43.

Rodríguez-Clare, Andrés. 1996. Multinationals, linkages, and economic development. *American Economic Review* 86:852–73.

Schumpeter, Joseph. 1934. *The theory of economic development.* Oxford: Oxford University Press.

Taiwan Textile Federation. 1998. *Development plans and assistance programs for the textile industry.* Unpublished report for a project commissioned by the Bureau of Industrial Development, Taiwan.

Torre, Jose de la. 1986. *Clothing-industry adjustment in developed countries.* London: Macmillan.

Yamawaki, Hideki. 1992. International competition and Japan's domestic adjustments. In *New silk road: East Asia and world markets,* ed. Kym Anderson, 89–118. Cambridge: Cambridge University Press.

Comment   Yum K. Kwan

This paper has to do with outward FDI of Taiwan's textile industry. Adopting the view that FDI is a Schumpeterian innovation, Chen and Ku emphasize the impact of outward FDI on the domestic industrial structure, using the textile industry as a case study. The data consist of two

Yum K. Kwan is associate professor of economics at the City University of Hong Kong.

surveys of firms, one conducted in 1992 and the other in 1995. Firms are classified into two groups, FDI firms and non-FDI firms, according to whether they have invested abroad or not. The two groups are then compared by a number of characteristics, including employment and sales; distribution, number, and concentration of product lines; and indicators of restructuring such as shifts of main product line, subsector, and sector, among others. The comparison shows that FDI firms undertake more rapid restructuring than non-FDI firms. The authors interpret this as evidence that FDI leads to restructuring and even accelerates the restructuring process.

At first glance, what could be more natural than doing a pairwise comparison of the kind so skillfully exploited by the authors in tables 11.2 through 11.11, since the objective is to ascertain the effects of FDI on industrial structure? In the jargon of experimental design, the exercise is to measure the "treatment effect" of FDI on industrial structure, where the FDI firms constitute the "treatment group" and the non-FDI firms the "control group." If the firms were randomly assigned into the two groups (i.e., making outward FDI or not) by some superior authority—as in a textbook experimental design setting—the authors' approach would be the right way to go. But presumably, firms do make FDI decisions purposefully so that they are in fact *self-selecting* themselves into the two groups. In other words, being an FDI firm or not is an endogenous variable—and it should be taken into account as such in the analysis—rather than exogenous as is implicitly assumed by the authors. Ignoring data self-selectivity, as the authors do in this paper, unfortunately, leads to biased samples and usually exaggerated treatment effects. Econometric issues related to the problem of self-selectivity have been extensively studied in the literature (especially in labor economics); see Maddala (1983, chap. 9) for a survey.

Similarly, the issue of survival bias (another kind of sample selectivity) also applies here. For an existing firm, it is unlikely that the decision to quit or stay is independent of the decision to invest abroad. Ignoring the simultaneity by comparing only surviving firms, as in the paper, will again lead to sample selection bias.

Reference

Maddala, G. S. 1983. *Limited dependent and qualitative variables in econometrics.* Cambridge: Cambridge University Press.

Comment   Munehisa Kasuya

An Overview

This paper tries to analyze the effect of FDI on employment, sales, and restructuring of the home country industry by using firm-level data. It obtains a lot of findings that are very interesting, stimulating, and useful. I would like to summarize these before making a few comments.

First, Chen and Ku criticize the hypothesis that "FDI is tantamount to industry dislocation and the export of jobs from home" by examining the relation between FDI firms and shares of employment and sales. That is, the data on employment in table 11.3 show that "there is no evidence that overseas investment led investing firms to shed jobs from domestic operations." Those data refute the assertion that foreign investments export jobs. The data on sales in table 11.4 show that FDI firms "were also likely to expand sales in domestic markets." Those data cast doubt on the proposition that "FDI hollows out domestic industry."

After the analysis of employment and sales, the paper moves to the topic of restructuring. The data on restructuring in tables 11.5 through 11.11 indicate that "FDI firms show a significantly higher degree of restructuring." Based on these statistical correlation analyses, the authors conclude that FDI induces restructuring.

Comments

Chen and Ku are trying to support the hypothesis that "FDI induces a higher degree of restructuring." I think the hypothesis is theoretically plausible because firms with more choices of production factors are supposed to be able to reach more efficient production levels by rearranging production factors. What I want to comment on first is not the hypothesis but the methodology of the empirical analysis.

If we want to support the hypothesis, we should use firms that have the same attributes with the exception of FDI. If firms have different attributes, we should control for those different attributes. Without such control, we might mistake the effects of those different attributes on restructuring for the effect of FDI on restructuring. This kind of control has already been done in the paper. The authors control firm size effects in the ANOVA because "FDI firms are generally larger than non-FDI firms" and "the difference may be attributable to size rather than FDI activity."

Meanwhile, the authors suggest that FDI firms may have "endowment advantages." I am confused by this statement. That is, I am afraid that the endowment advantages could be a variable to be controlled like firm size. Differences in restructuring may be attributable to endowment advantages

Munehisa Kasuya is a senior economist in the Research and Statistics Department, Bank of Japan.

rather than FDI activity, like firm size. Of course, there are several possibilities. We could assume that FDI causes endowment advantages. Under this assumption, we could conclude that FDI induces restructuring without controlling endowment advantages. However, we could also assume that there is no causality or even assume that endowment advantages cause FDI. Under these assumptions, we should control endowment advantages. Even if we cannot tell which possibility is correct, I do not think this kind of reservation would require us to reject the conclusions of the paper. However, it might be better for us to be more careful in deriving implications.

My second comment is on the data indicated in table 11.2. Based on these data, the paper analyzes several characteristics of FDI firms. I am afraid that we could not get information of FDI except the data for 1992. However, I am also afraid that we could not reject the possibility that new FDI firms entered between 1992 and 1995 from among the non-FDI firms of 1992. If there were new FDI firms after 1992, the comparison between 1992 and 1995 could include a kind of bias.

My third comment is on the "unaccounted data" in table 11.3. The author suggests "the share of employment contributed by FDI firms did not diminish" after comparing 13.0 percent for 1995 with 12.6 percent for 1992. However, the unaccounted data amount to 17.7 percent. I am afraid that the difference in shares of employment could be smaller than those unaccounted data.

My next comment is on the composition change index in table 11.9. By using the composition change index, the authors suggest FDI firms show a higher degree of restructuring. I think the share data used in making the index include the information of price changes. However, I do not think price changes mean restructuring in general, although price changes can lead to restructuring. It would be more comfortable for us to interpret the index as a broad measure of restructuring.

Last but not least, I would like to confirm again the contributions of this paper. Even if there are some limits in data availability, by using firm-level data very efficiently and intensively, this paper makes important contributions to the field of empirical analysis of restructuring induced by FDI.

Foreign Direct Investment and Economic Growth in Taiwan's Manufacturing Industries

Vei-Lin Chan

12.1 Introduction

In endogenous growth theory, which explains growth by endogenizing technological change, foreign direct investment (FDI) and international trade are considered to be major channels for transmitting ideas and new technologies. This paper analyzes the Taiwanese experience regarding these potential factors of growth. Its primary purpose is to evaluate the role of FDI in explaining economic growth in Taiwan and to ascertain whether movements in FDI help to predict movements in economic growth. The effects of other pertinent factors, such as fixed investment and volume of exports are also analyzed.

The features of this study are the following. The first concerns the data set. Most empirical studies in endogenous growth use cross-country macro-aggregate data; as such, they seldom consider differences across industries within a country. This paper uses more disaggregated manufacturing industry panel data, which are formed by pooling all time-series and cross-sectional data at the two-digit industry level. As far as I know, this data set has not been used before in the growth literature about Taiwan.

The second feature has to do with methodology. This paper conducts a number of Granger causality tests regarding manufacturing sector data. The main hypothesis concerns whether FDI "Granger causes" economic growth. This is more informative than merely ascertaining a positive asso-

Vei-Lin Chan is an associate research fellow of the Institute of Economics, Academia Sinica.

The author is deeply indebted to Anne Krueger for her stimulating comments on the paper. Thanks are also due to Sheng-Cheng Hu, Takatoshi Ito, and Robert Lipsey for their valuable help with the paper, and to other conference participants for their helpful comments.

ciation between, say, FDI and economic growth. We can find similar discussions of the role of fixed capital formation or trade in economic growth using cross-country data in King and Levine (1994), Carroll and Weil (1994), Blomström, Lipsey, and Zejan (1996) and Frankel and Romer (1999).[1]

Our test results support a causal relation from FDI to economic growth. Furthermore, we would like to ascertain the channel through which FDI affects growth. Two kinds of channels are possible from pure theoretical reasoning. First, FDI could induce technology transfer, thus causing an advance in technology, which in turn promotes economic growth in the host country. Or, second, FDI may induce fixed investment or exports and thus affect economic growth through increased aggregate demand. Now, which of these two possible channels reflects the Taiwanese situation?

A brief review of the relevant literature is in order. Based on growth accounting, earlier empirical studies overwhelmingly supported the view that factor accumulation plays a dominant role in the extraordinary performance of East Asian countries (see, e.g., Kim and Lau 1994; Young 1995; Collins and Bosworth 1996). This view is now under debate due to the findings of Klenow and Rodríguez-Clare (1997), Rodrik (1997), and Hsieh (1999), which have stated that technological progress accounts for a significant portion of workers' productivity growth in East Asia.

A number of studies have investigated the role of FDI in growth. Findlay (1978) and Wang (1990) suggested that FDI would promote economic growth through its effect on technology adoption (see Kozumi and Kopecky 1980; Wang and Blomström 1992; Malley and Moutos 1994). Markusen and Venables (1997) showed that FDI is complementary to local industry and would stimulate development in host economies through several channels. Their analytical work was consistent with the case study by Hobday (1995), which included industries in Taiwan. Recently, a cross-country regression by Borensztein, De Gregorio, and Lee (1998) has supported the view that FDI affects economic growth through technology diffusion.

Among studies on Taiwan, Ranis and Schive (1985) examined the role of FDI in Taiwan's development from 1952 to 1980 by industrial case study. They found that FDI played an important role in Taiwan's early economic development and thus confirmed that FDI is an efficient channel of technology transfer from overseas to Taiwan. Using 1986 and 1991 survey data for Taiwan, Chen, Hsu, and Chen (1999) found that FDI has no or even has negative effects on labor productivity when examining the competing channels of technology adoption. Thus it seems that the role

---

1. In fact, some of them find that the positive association between fixed capital formation and economic growth is mainly due to the effect of economic growth on fixed capital formation instead of a causal relation from fixed capital formation to economic growth.

of FDI in Taiwan's economic development needs further clarification through time-series data.

As regards the role of domestic investment, an interesting question concerns whether FDI crowds out or crowds in domestic investment. Due to competition for physical and financial resources or competition in the product market, one may view subsidiaries and multinational corporations (MNCs) and domestic investment as substitutes. On the other hand, on account of the linkage effects due to a cheaper intermediary good produced by subsidiaries and MNCs, or the spillover effects of foreign capital that would stimulate domestic investment, foreign investment and domestic investment could also be complements. The overall effect may go either way. Tu (1989) found a crowding-in effect in the overall economy, but a crowding-out effect in Taiwanese manufacturing industries. Similarly, FDI and exports can be complements or substitutes. International trade signifies the movement of commodities, and FDI signifies the movement of capital. From this point of view, international trade and FDI are substitutes. But if the object of FDI is to cut costs of exports by utilizing cheaper labor in export-oriented industries, exports and FDI are complementary. Hence, which relation is true is an empirical question.

Now we can state the second part of our results. We find causal relations from fixed investment and exports to economic growth. But the hypotheses that FDI affects economic growth by inducing more investment and exports are not supported by our test results. This seems to indicate that FDI affects growth through technological progress.

The remainder of the paper is organized as follows. Section 12.2 provides an overall picture of Taiwan's growth experience and specific data on the manufacturing sector and FDI. Section 12.3 states the model and discusses the data. Section 12.4 summarizes the empirical results. Section 12.5 concludes the paper.

12.2 Some Background Material about Taiwan

12.2.1 General Background

Taiwan has experienced rather high growth rates in the past four decades (see, e.g., Tsiang 1984). In the 1950s, the agricultural sector accounted for 30 percent of total GDP, and the main exports were agricultural or processed agricultural products, which accounted for 80 percent of total exports. The share of agricultural sector GDP in total GDP declined rapidly. It was for example, 7.7 percent in 1980 and a mere 3 percent in 1997. The Taiwanese economy took off in the mid-1960s. With a two-digit average GDP growth rate in the manufacturing sector, Taiwan gradually transformed itself into a newly industrialized economy. The manufacturing sector has become the largest single sector in Taiwan's economy.

But recently its share in GDP declined a little due to the rapid growth of the service sector.[2]

Because of the active export-promoting policy, the values of exports and imports are quite high relative to GDP in Taiwan. This reflects the "processing nature" of Taiwan's industries. Moreover, since the mid-1960s there has been an active policy of encouraging FDI by giving tax credits and setting up export-processing zones. FDI was concentrated in labor-intensive industries in the 1960s, and in more diversified and sophisticated industries afterward.

12.2.2   Manufacturing Sector

This paper will focus on the manufacturing sector, which has been the leading sector in Taiwan's economy. Table 12.1 shows the contribution of the manufacturing sector and two-digit industries to growth. On average, the manufacturing sector grew faster than the overall economy before the 1980s, but slower than the overall economy in the 1990s, due to the rapid expansion of the service sector. Manufacturing's percentage contribution to the total GDP growth rate rose from 30 percent (3.02 out of 9.79 percent) in the 1960s to around 40 percent in the 1970s and the 1980s (4.20 out of 10.23 percent and 3.11 out of 8.15 percent, respectively). In the 1990s, manufacturing contributed 20 percent (1.28 out of 6.32 percent) of the GDP growth rate. The manufacturing sector accounted for 3 to 4 percentage points of the total GDP growth rate before the 1980s and barely 1.3 percentage points after the 1980s. The change reflects the trend of industrial restructuring in Taiwan since the late 1980s.

It is also interesting to note the shift in the role of capital-intensive versus labor-intensive two-digit industries in the manufacturing sector. While a capital-intensive industry such as electronics (ELE) contributed 47 percent (1.89 out of 4.03 percent) of the manufacturing GDP growth rate in the 1990s, the contributions of traditional industries (such as TEX, APPAREL, LEATHER, WOOD, and PAPER) to manufacturing became negative. Note that before 1990, the percentage contribution of electronics to manufacturing was no more than 15 percent. This shift partly reflects the fact that these labor-intensive industries moved their production to Southeast Asia and China. These moves may have to do with the rapid appreciation of the New Taiwan dollar and rising production costs since the 1980s. (See table 12.1 for details.)

---

2. Taiwan has experienced industrial restructuring since the late 1980s. GDP of the service sector (which includes commerce, transport, storage and communications, government services, finance, insurance, business services, and personal services) as a percentage of total GDP has risen dramatically from a steady 46 percent over 1952–86 to 63.1 percent in 1998. In the meantime, GDP of the manufacturing sector as a percentage of total GDP has fallen from a peak of 39.4 percent in 1986 to 27.0 percent in 1998.

Table 12.1   **Contribution to Economic Growth Rate of Manufacturing Sector, 1962–96 (percent)**

Industry	1962–96	1962–69	1970–79	1980–89	1990–96
GDP growth rate	8.75	9.79	10.23	8.15	6.32
Manufacturing GDP growth rate	11.03	16.15	14.34	8.51	4.03
Contribution of manufacturing GDP to total GDP growth rate	3.04	3.02	4.20	3.11	1.28
Contribution of two-digit industry GDP to manufacturing GDP growth rate[a]					
FOOD	1.36	3.52	1.18	0.61	0.24
TEX	0.96	1.69	1.48	0.57	−0.08
APPAREL	0.46	0.49	0.97	0.37	−0.20
LEATHER	0.11	0.03	0.28	0.13	−0.09
WOOD	0.30	0.62	0.51	0.17	−0.16
PAPER	0.39	0.47	0.65	0.39	−0.08
CHEM	1.64	2.23	1.92	1.51	0.74
Petroleum[b]	1.08	2.05	0.79	0.90	0.65
NMP	0.44	0.68	0.53	0.32	0.19
FMP	1.02	0.52	1.59	1.00	0.81
MEQ	0.42	0.52	0.48	0.38	0.26
ELE	1.66	1.79	1.83	1.24	1.89
TRAN	0.69	1.06	0.79	0.67	0.14
INS	0.51	0.47	1.34	0.26	−0.28

Source: National Income, Taiwan Area, the Republic of China.
[a]For two-digit industry abbreviations, see appendix.
[b]Petroleum and coal products.

12.2.3   Foreign Direct Investment

FDI had at least a two-digit average growth rate in every decade. Growth in FDI slowed a bit in the 1970s and 1990s. The average share of FDI going to the manufacturing sector peaked in the 1970s; and even though this average share then lost 30 percentage points within the next two decades, the manufacturing sector still receives most FDI in the 1990s. This decline in average share is due to a shift in FDI from the manufacturing sector to the banking, insurance, and service sectors in the past decade. (See table 12.2 for details.)

Japan and the United States are two major sources of foreign capital; investment from these two countries together accounts for at least half of FDI in Taiwan. They are also the world's most important source countries of capital outflow. In general, the United States provides more capital in the PAPER, CHEM, and ELE industries, and Japan provides more capital in the remaining manufacturing industries and in the service sector. (See table 12.3 for more details.)

The overall ratio of FDI to fixed investment was not so high and has

Table 12.2   **Industry Distribution of FDI by Decade, 1953–97**

Industry	1953–97	1953–59	1960–69	1970–79	1980–89	1990–97
Growth rate of total FDI (%)	293.28	346.58	1,022.78	15.61	33.12	13.69
Growth rate of FDI into manufacturing (%)	456.98	667.95	1,538.00	21.11	32.39	23.05
Share of manufacturing FDI in total FDI (%)	79.16	77.11	86.68	90.23	76.92	60.51
Share of two-digit industries FDI in manufacturing FDI[a] (%)						
FOOD (1954)	8.79	33.06	4.78	0.61	5.57	6.80
TEX (1953)	3.79	14.29	2.02	2.55	0.92	1.94
APPAREL (1961)	0.82	0.00	1.74	0.77	0.46	0.89
LEATHER (1961)	0.25	0.00	0.24	0.17	0.12	0.73
WOOD (1963)	0.30	0.00	0.17	0.40	0.29	0.63
PAPER (1966)	0.38	0.00	0.37	0.33	0.74	0.34
CHEM (1954)	28.77	38.03	41.87	17.88	26.85	20.30
NMP (1961)	1.71	0.00	0.89	2.46	2.65	2.12
FMP (1961)	7.74	0.00	5.58	10.11	10.85	10.36
MEQ (1954)	8.10	0.35	2.53	12.74	15.07	7.34
ELE (1958)	38.26	14.29	39.81	51.99	36.49	42.37
TRAN (1993)	0.88	0.00	0.00	0.00	0.00	4.97
INS (1993)	0.22	0.00	0.00	0.00	0.00	1.21

Source: Statistics on Overseas Chinese and Foreign Investment, Technical Cooperation, Outward Investment, Outward Technical Cooperation, and Indirect Mainland Investment, the Republic of China.
[a]Values in parentheses are years that data start to be nonzero.

Table 12.3   **Sources of FDI, 1952–97 (percent)**

	Asia			North America			
Industry	Hong Kong	Japan	Other	United States	Other	Europe	Other
Total	7.66	28.40	5.53	26.48	12.82	12.93	6.18
Banking, insurance, trade, and services	11.65	29.26	7.26	18.95	12.77	15.69	4.44
Manufacturing	6.32	28.64	3.50	31.30	8.40	14.89	6.95
FOOD	8.99	22.95	5.51	19.66	14.26	10.50	18.12
TEX	6.40	34.75	12.87	7.46	24.50	11.28	2.74
APPAREL	10.75	49.01	4.81	3.63	28.32	3.37	0.10
LEATHER	3.20	5.04	0.00	3.18	80.62	4.95	3.01
WOOD	31.34	37.89	5.06	2.29	13.22	10.20	0.00
PAPER	11.68	14.00	0.00	55.17	12.56	2.02	4.57
CHEM	6.20	22.43	0.97	32.88	5.34	25.57	6.61
NMP	19.82	36.95	4.06	12.66	4.31	21.45	0.74
FMP	5.24	30.91	1.32	14.43	7.96	6.18	33.95
MEQ	5.62	47.85	1.54	17.92	15.18	8.22	3.67
ELE	4.53	28.81	6.51	43.67	7.55	8.68	0.24
TRAN	20.06	56.14	2.28	7.11	8.71	5.66	0.04
INS	6.67	39.07	17.47	5.47	23.87	7.46	0.00

Source: See table 12.1 source.

Table 12.4   **FDI as a Percentage of Gross Investment by Two-Digit Manufacturing Industry, 1961–96**

Industry	1961–96	1961–69	1970–79	1980–89	1990–96
Manufacturing	13.22	17.15	13.57	12.21	9.08
FOOD	5.49	2.58	0.60	10.06	9.66
TEX	1.76	0.94	2.13	1.22	3.07
APPAREL	8.81	15.37	4.34	4.88	12.37
LEATHER	59.48	201.71	23.20	1.90	10.71
WOOD	2.55	1.35	2.21	2.08	5.25
PAPER	1.36	2.32	0.69	1.72	0.56
CHEM	18.65	35.11	11.55	16.32	10.98
NMP	6.59	2.94	9.54	8.14	4.85
FMP	15.98	16.24	31.61	8.20	4.43
MEQ	45.77	23.85	64.36	63.68	21.82
ELE	76.20	160.42	78.07	36.71	21.68
TRAN	1.21	0.00	0.00	0.00	6.20
INS	0.85	0.00	0.00	0.00	4.35

Source: See table 12.2 source.

declined. It was no more than 20 percent in the 1960s and only about 9 percent for the manufacturing sector in the 1990s.[3] FDI is not a major source of capital for most manufacturing industries. Domestic investment is much more important for manufacturing industries. Among them, CHEM, MEO, and ELE have higher ratios of FDI to fixed investment than other industries across different decades. (See table 12.4.)

12.3   Model and Data

12.3.1   Model

We perform the Granger causality test on the pooled time-series and cross-sectional data of two-digit manufacturing industries. The bivariate variable model is given by

$$(1) \quad Z_{it} = \alpha_0 + \sum_{j=1}^{p} \alpha_j \cdot Z_{i,t-j} + \sum_{j=1}^{p} \beta_j \cdot X_{i,t-j} + f_i + \lambda_t + \varepsilon_{it},$$

where i and t denote industries and years, respectively. The dependent variable is Z. The explanatory variables include the lagged dependent variable and the variable X. We consider the specification of industry and time fixed effects: f_i is the industry fixed effect and λ_t is the time fixed effect.

3. Since FDI is computed on an approval basis, not on an actual arrival basis, it is possible that the ratio of FDI to fixed investment exceeds 100 percent for particular industries in particular periods (e.g., as shown in table 12.4, the ratio was 160 percent for ELE in the 1960s).

The term ε_{it} is a disturbance. The Granger causality test is used to determine whether the addition of the lagged variable X (i.e., p restrictions on the coefficients of the lagged variable X) is statistically significant using both F-tests and Wald (χ^2) tests. The theoretical model does not provide guidance on the appropriate lag length p. For the panel data, we arbitrarily choose lag length p to be two and four.

Note that the results may be sensitive to the model specifications. To test for Granger causality from variable X to variable Z, the multivariate model for panel data is estimated and given by

$$(2) \quad Z_{it} = \alpha_0 + \sum_{j=1}^{p} \alpha_j \cdot Z_{i,t-j} + \sum_{j=1}^{p} \beta_j \cdot X_{i,t-j} + \sum_{m=i}^{n} \sum_{j=1}^{p} \gamma_j \cdot Y_{j,m,t-j}$$
$$+ f_i + \lambda_t + \varepsilon_{it}.$$

Explanatory variables include the lagged dependent variable Z, the variable X, and the variables Y_m, $m = 1, \ldots, n$, which are the relevant variables. Among the variables Y_m, H_t is the human capital stock proxy, assumed to be common to all two-digit industries.

Equations (1) and (2) are estimated using OLS. The OLS estimates of equations (1) and (2) are biased in the presence of industry fixed effects and the lagged dependent variable. But Nickell (1981) has shown that the bias is inversely related to the number of sample periods. Our sample period spans twenty-three years, so the bias in the estimate is likely to be small. We thus can ignore this problem.

We first perform the Granger causality test from FDI to growth in real GDP. We also perform the Granger causality test from fixed capital formation and exports, respectively, to economic growth. To avoid bias due to excessive zero values, we consider eleven two-digit industries only when the model includes FDI.

In a multivariate model, various combinations of human capital, fixed investment, exports, and FDI would alternatively be used as explanatory variables in equation (2). The human capital proxy and fixed investment have been shown to positively affect economic growth in numerous empirical endogenous growth studies. Moreover, traditional trade theory argues that export expansion affects economic growth positively by increasing resource allocation efficiency and capacity utilization. Recent studies have emphasized the role of exports as a channel for promoting technical change. Most empirical results support a positive and significant effect of export expansion on economic growth.[4] The causality result should be carefully explored due to some econometric problems. One is the possibility that trade is endogenous, which would cause a simultaneity problem. Frankel and Romer (1999) have dealt with this problem by using a geographical factor and have still supported the hypothesis that trade raises

---

4. See Harrison (1996) for a survey of relevant empirical studies.

income using cross-country regression. Their method is not applicable to the present situation in which we deal with only one country. And the issue of simultaneity is not treated in this paper. The analysis focuses on testing whether FDI "Granger causes" economic growth while controlling for human capital, fixed capital formation, and exports at the two-digit industry level in Taiwan's manufacturing sector.

We further investigate whether FDI affects economic growth by increasing fixed investment and exports. We perform Granger causality tests from FDI to fixed investment and exports, respectively. The presence of a growth effect of FDI and the absence of positive causal relation from FDI to fixed investment and exports suggest that FDI promotes economic growth through technological improvement instead of accumulation of capital and increase in exports.

12.3.2 Data

The econometric analysis will use the following variables: for each industry, GGDP is growth in real GDP, FDIY is the ratio of approved investment by foreign nationals to GDP, INVY is the ratio of fixed capital formation to its own GDP, EXPY is the ratio of exports to GDP, and JH and SH are proxies for the human capital stock. Table 12.5 reports summary statistics on GGDP, FDIY, INVY, EXPY, and TEXPY for the manufacturing sector and two-digit manufacturing industries. TEXPY is the ratio of exports for the individual two-digit manufacturing industry to total exports in the manufacturing sector. It provides information on trade share for an individual industry relative to other manufacturing industries.

Over our sample period, 1973–94, traditional industries such as FOOD, TEX, APPAREL, and WOOD had lower average GDP growth rates while newly developed industries such as FMP and ELE had higher two-digit average GDP growth rates. FDIY is much lower than INVY for every industry, as shown in table 12.5. MEQ, ELE, and CHEM had much higher average FDIY than other industries. MEQ was the only industry with FDIY that was more than half of its INVY.

The industries ELE, CHEM, APPAREL, and INS, which had the highest average TEXPY, were the major export manufacturing industries. They accounted for about 59 percent of exports in manufacturing. However, in terms of the ratio to industry's own GDP, INS, LEATHER, ELE, and APPAREL had high average export shares EXPY. The fact that EXPY is higher than 100 percent percentage points for many industries may appear odd at the first glance, but it just reflects the general "processing nature" of Taiwan's industries.

12.4   Empirical Results

Table 12.6 reports the results of causality tests for the panel data. *P*-values for *F*-tests (*upper numbers*) and Wald tests (*lower numbers*) of the

Table 12.5 **Summary Statistics of Variables in Manufacturing Industries, 1978–94 (percent)**

Industry	GGDP Mean	GGDP S.D.	FDIY Mean	FDIY S.D.	INVY Mean	INVY S.D.	TEXPY Mean	TEXPY S.D.	EXPY Mean	EXPY S.D.
Manufacturing	8.3	7.0	1.8	0.8	18.2	4.4	100.0	–	122.5	11.3
FOOD	5.6	8.0	1.0	1.0	11.1	1.7	6.1	2.6	57.8	13.2
TEX	5.6	13.5	0.4	0.4	24.0	17.2	8.9	2.0	125.9	24.0
APPAREL	4.0	14.1	0.3	0.3	4.3	2.1	12.2	4.0	90.16	64.5
LEATHER	11.1	18.3	1.0	1.0	7.8	2.3	2.4	0.7	217.7	70.6
WOOD	5.0	18.9	0.3	0.3	12.3	3.5	4.9	2.3	191.1	71.6
PAPER	7.2	11.2	0.3	0.3	20.8	6.9	0.8	0.2	22.9	6.5
CHEM	10.0	9.5	1.8	1.8	25.7	7.7	12.6	1.4	104.1	17.1
NMP	9.6	9.1	4.0	4.0	20.3	6.8	1.8	0.4	53.9	19.4
FMP	13.2	18.3	0.9	0.9	31.5	20.6	7.5	1.8	91.0	16.3
MEQ	9.9	8.9	9.1	9.1	14.9	3.9	5.0	1.7	166.3	22.4
ELE	11.7	15.9	3.1	3.1	16.0	2.5	22.1	5.0	207.7	33.7
TRAN	10.0	12.7	–	–	16.2	11.2	4.1	1.1	78.6	16.5
INS	8.1	20.1	–	–	7.6	1.9	11.8	2.0	240.0	36.6

Source: See table 12.2 source.

Table 12.6   **Granger Causality Tests for Annual Panel Data**

Relation and Lag	Model				
	I	II	III	IV	V
FDIY→GGDP[a]					
$p = 2$	0.23	0.14	0.15	0.08	0.08
	0.17	0.03	0.03	0.04	0.05
$p = 4$	0.52	0.80	0.46	0.63	0.25
	0.41	0.01	0.01	0.01	0.14
INVY→GGDP[b]					
$p = 2$	0.23	0.23	0.23	0.20	0.20
	0.28	0.18	0.32	0.15	0.08
$p = 4$	0.03	0.72	0.03	0.61	0.01
	0.01	0.01	0.01	0.00	0.01
EXPY→GGDP[c]					
$p = 2$	0.02	0.02	0.02	0.02	
	0.01	0.01	0.01	0.00	
$p = 4$	0.05	0.03	0.66	0.03	
	0.01	0.01	0.00	0.01	
FDIY→INVY[d]					
$p = 2$	0.05	0.07	0.06		
	0.03	0.04	0.59		
$p = 4$	0.32	0.33	0.38		
	0.22	0.21	0.51		
FDIY→EXPY[e]					
$p = 2$	0.16	0.17	0.13		
	0.11	0.12	0.85		
$p = 4$	0.97	0.96	0.91		
	0.95	0.94	0.47		

[a]Model I is a two-variable model that includes GGDP and FDIY. Models II and III are four-variable models that include GGDP, FDIY, INVY, and JH and GGDP, FDIY, INVY, and SH, respectively. Models IV and V are five-variable models that add EXPY to Models II and III, respectively.

[b]Model I is a two-variable model that includes GGDP and INVY. Models II and III are three-variable models that include GGDP, INVY, and JH and GGDP, INVY, and SH, respectively. Models IV and V are four-variable models that add EXPY to Models II and III, respectively.

[c]Model I is a two-variable model that includes GGDP and EXPY. Model II is a three-variable model that includes GGDP, EXPY, and INVY. Models III and IV are four-variable models that add JH and SH to Model II, respectively.

[d]Model I is a two-variable model that includes FDIY and INVY. Model II is a three-variable model that includes FDIY, INVY, and GGDP. Model III is a four-variable model that includes FDIY, INVY, GGDP, and EXPY.

[e]Model I is a two-variable model that includes FDIY and EXPY. Model II is a three-variable model that includes FDIY, EXPY, and GGDP. Model III is a four-variable model that includes FDIY, EXPY, GGDP, and INVY.

Granger causality tests are based on a least squares with dummy variables estimation. Model I is a bivariate model. The others are multivariate models as described in notes to the table.

Regarding the Granger causality test from FDIY to GGDP, the test results are somewhat sensitive to the choices of model specification, lag length, and test statistic. In all cases, the p-values of the F-statistics are larger than those of the χ_2 statistics in the respective GGDP equations. The addition of explanatory variables somewhat lowers both sets of p-values. Most χ_2 test statistics reject the null hypothesis that all of the coefficients on lagged FDIY are zero. The significant estimated coefficients are all positive. The results support a causal relation from FDIY to GGDP in a multivariate model.

In the Granger causality test from INVY to GGDP, most test statistics for the case $p = 4$ reject the null hypothesis that all of the coefficients on lagged INVY are zero. The evidence indicates that the coefficients on later lags are likely to be nonzero. Thus it takes a long time for fixed capital formation to affect economic growth.

For the Granger causality test from EXPY to GGDP, all but one test statistic suggest that EXPY Granger-causes GGDP. The results are quite robust with respect to the choices of model specification, lag length, and test statistic. The evidence hence strongly supports a predictive role for export share. These results are consistent with findings of earlier empirical studies that indicate that exports promote economic growth in developing countries.

In summary, at the two-digit industry level in Taiwan's manufacturing sector, Granger causality tests suggest causal relations from FDI, fixed investment, and exports to economic growth. The result that fixed investment plays a major role in promoting economic growth in the manufacturing sector supports capital fundamentalism. The significant causal relations from FDI and exports to economic growth also support the belief that total factor productivity matters in the process of economic growth.

We further investigate whether the presence of a positive causal relation from FDIY to GGDP is through capital accumulation or through exports. Most test statistics support the causal relation from FDIY to INVY when $p = 2$. This causal relation disappears for a longer period (i.e., $p = 4$). We therefore conclude that FDI does not Granger-cause fixed investment. Also, note that most estimated coefficients of FDIY are negative. They imply that the substitution effect dominates the complementary effect. Our finding of a crowding-out effect in Taiwanese manufacturing is consistent with those of Tu (1989). Finally, none of the statistics support a causal relation from FDIY to EXPY. Both sets of results indicate that FDI does not promote economic growth by increasing total capital accumulation or exports. The channel of technology improvement is the key to the growth effect of FDI.

12.5 Conclusion

The source of economic growth has long been a central issue in economics. Recently, endogenous growth theory has provided a new direction from which to study the determinants of economic growth. And FDI is one of the channels emphasized by R&D-based endogenous growth theory. This paper investigates the causal relation from FDI to GDP growth in the Taiwanese manufacturing sector while controlling human capital, fixed capital formation, and exports at the two-digit industry level. The results based on comprehensive panel data of two-digit industries support in general a causal relation from FDI. Furthermore, our results do not find a positive causal relation from FDI to fixed investment and exports. This indicates that FDI promotes economic growth, not by increasing total capital accumulation or exports, but, more likely, through the channel of technology improvement. This would be quite consistent with R&D-based endogenous growth theory.

Therefore, this paper represents a step forward in clarifying the role of FDI as a source of economic growth in Taiwan. The evidence, as it stands, for technological advancement as the channel through which FDI affects growth is still rather indirect. Future research is needed to provide more direct evidence on this matter. For example, one could assess, using Taiwanese macrodata, the effects of FDI on technology advancement and of technology on growth.

Currently, the Taiwanese government aims to promote Taiwan as an Asian-Pacific Regional Operations Center (APROC). One objective of the APROC project is to overcome bureaucratic inertia on reform, which has been a major impediment to the efficacy of Taiwan's government. Another objective is to promote economic relations between Taiwan and Southeast Asia. It will be interesting to see how the APROC project can attract FDI to Taiwan and can stimulate the advancement of operational technology in Taiwan.

Appendix

Data Sources

For each individual two-digit manufacturing industry, GGDP is growth in real GDP, and INVY is the ratio of fixed capital formation to its own GDP. Data are from *National Income, Taiwan Area, the Republic of China*. EXPY is the ratio of exports to GDP. Export data come from *Monthly Statistics of Exports and Imports, Taiwan Area, the Republic of China*. To explain economic growth, recent empirical studies on endogenous growth have emphasized educational attainment measures as human capital proxies to augment the labor input measure in the production function. We use primary and secondary school enrollment rates, JH and SH, respectively, as proxies for the human capital stock. Data are from *Monthly Bulletin of Manpower Statistics, Taiwan Area, the Republic of China.*

FDI in the manufacturing sector has been overwhelmingly dominated by foreign nationals. Also, in channeling funds into Taiwan's economy, overseas Chinese investment has been intended to provide scarce capital rather than to transfer technology. The early restrictions on investment in service industries by foreign nationals are another reason. Therefore, FDI used in the analysis refers to investment made by foreign nationals only. FDIY is the ratio of approved investment by foreign nationals to GDP. Statistics on approved FDI are from *Statistics on Overseas Chinese and Foreign Investment, Outward Investment, Technical Cooperation, Outward Technical Cooperation, Indirect Mainland Investment, Guide of Mainland Industry Technology, Investment Commission, Ministry of Economic Affairs, the Republic of China.*

The manufacturing sector is disaggregated into thirteen industries: foods, beverages, and tobacco (FOOD); textiles (TEX); wearing apparel and accessories (APPAREL); leather and fur products (LEATHER); wood and bamboo (WOOD); paper, paper products, and printing processing products (PAPER); rubber, plastic, and chemical products (CHEM); nonmetallic mineral products (NMP); basic metal products and fabricated metal products (FMP); machinery and equipment (MEQ); electric and electronic machinery (ELE); transportation equipment (TRAN); and precision instruments and miscellaneous manufacturing (INS).

According to Taiwan's 1991 official industrial classification for manufacturing, there are twenty two-digit industries. One issue concerns the Chinese Petroleum Corporation, a public corporation in the petroleum and coal product industry, which has enjoyed a monopolistic position. We hence exclude petroleum and coal products from our data set. To match the classifications of two-digit manufacturing industries for international trade, FDI, and real GDP data as closely as possible, several two-digit industries are pooled due to the availability of data.[5] The sample period of this compatible data set is 1972–94. Approved FDI for TRAN and INS have nonzero values only in 1995 and 1996. Thus these two industries will be also excluded from our econometric analysis.

5. The classification of two-digit manufacturing sectors for export and import data is based on the *Standard Classification of Commodities of the Republic of China (C.C.C.).* This commodity classification has changed several times. To match the classification for import and export data to that of real GDP data, we choose the classification that has only eighteen two-digit industries in manufacturing and covers the period from January 1972 to June 1995. The number of manufacturing subsectors for FDI is thirteen because data for basic metals and metal products are pooled. So the sample period is 1972–94 and the number of subsectors in manufacturing is thirteen. Four subgroups are subject to the availability of export and import data: (1) rubber and plastic products; (2) wood, bamboo, and rattan products; (3) paper allied products and printed matter; and (4) beverage and tobacco products.

References

Blomström, Magnus, Robert E. Lipsey, and Mario Zejan. 1996. Is fixed investment the key to economic growth? *Quarterly Journal of Economics* 111:269–76.

Borensztein, Eduardo, Jose De Gregorio, and Jong-Wha Lee. 1998. How does foreign direct investment affect economic growth? *Journal of International Economics* 45:115–35.

Carroll, Christopher D., and David N. Weil. 1994. Saving and growth: A reinterpretation. *Carnegie-Rochester Conference Series on Public Policy* 40:133–92.

Chen, Been-Lon, Mei Hsu, and Jing-Yi Chen. 1999. Technology adoption and technical efficiency in a developing economy: Foreign investment led versus export performance promoted. In *Economic efficiency and productivity growth in the Asia-Pacific region,* ed. Tsu-Tan Fu, Cliff J. Huang, and C. A. Knox Lovell. Cheltenham, England: Elgar.

Collins, Susan M., and Barry P. Bosworth. 1996. Economic growth in East Asia: Accumulation versus assimilation. *Brookings Papers on Economic Activity,* no. 2: 135–203.

Findlay, Ronald. 1978. Relative backwardness, direct foreign investment, and the transfer of technology: A simple dynamic model. *Quarterly Journal of Economics* 92:1–16.

Frankel, Jeffrey A., and David Romer. 1999. Does trade cause growth? *American Economic Review* 89:379–99.

Harrison, Ann. 1996. Openness and growth: A time-series, cross-country analysis for developing countries. *Journal of Development Economics* 48:419–47.

Hobday, Michael. 1995. *Innovation in East Asia: The challenge to Japan.* London: Aldershot.

Hsieh, Chang-Tai. 1999. Productivity growth and factor prices in East Asia. *AEA Papers and Proceedings* 89:133–38.

Kim, Jong-Il, and Lawrence J. Lau. 1994. The sources of economic growth of the East Asian newly industrialized countries. *Journal of the Japanese and International Economies* 8:235–71.

King, Robert G., and Ross Levine. 1994. Capital fundamentalism, economic development, and economic growth. *Carnegie-Rochester Conference Series on Public Policy* 40:259–92.

Klenow, Peter J., and Andrés Rodríguez-Clare. 1997. The neoclassical revival in growth economics: Has it gone too far? In *NBER macroeconomics annual 1997,* ed. Ben S. Bernanke and Julio J. Rotemberg. Cambridge, Mass.: MIT Press.

Koizumi, Tetsunori, and Kenneth Kopecky. 1980. Direct foreign investment, technology transfer and domestic employment effects. *Journal of International Economics* 10:1–20.

Malley, Jim, and Thomas Moutos. 1994. Prototype of macroeconomic model of foreign direct investment. *Journal of Development Economics* 43:295–315.

Markusen, James R., and Anthony J. Venables. 1997. Foreign direct investment as a catalyst for industrial development. NBER Working Paper no. 6241. Cambridge, Mass.: National Bureau of Economic Research.

Nickell, S. 1981. Biases in dynamic models with fixed effects. *Econometrica* 49: 1417–26.

Ranis, Gustav, and Schive Chi. 1985. Direct foreign investment in Taiwan's development. In *Foreign trade and investment,* ed. Walter Galenson. Madison: University of Wisconsin.

Rodrik, Dani. 1997. TFPG controversies, institutions, and economic performance in East Asia. NBER Working Paper no. 5914. Cambridge, Mass.: National Bureau of Economic Research.

Tsiang, S. C. 1984. Taiwan's economic miracle: Lessons in economic development. In *World economic growth,* ed. A. C. Harberger, 301–24. San Francisco: ICS Press.

Tu, Jenn-hwa. 1989. Foreign direct investment and private fixed capital formation in Taiwan. In *Proceedings of the conference on Taiwan's trade and exchange rate.* Taipei: Academia Sinica.

Wang, Jian-Ye. 1990. Growth, technology transfer, and the long-run theory of international capital movements. *Journal of International Economics* 29:250–71.

Wang, Jian-Ye, and Magnus Blomström. 1992. Foreign investment and technology transfer: A simple model. *European Economic Review* 36:173–55.

Young, Alwyn. 1995. The tyranny of numbers: Confronting the statistical realities of the East Asian growth experience. *Quarterly Journal of Economics* 110: 641–80.

Comment   Mari Pangestu

This paper examines the basic relations between trade, fixed investment, FDI, and economic growth for the case of Taiwan and confined to the manufacturing sector. Chan uses a rich data set and utilizes the standard Granger causality test to prove causality among these variables. The author concludes that there is a causal relation from FDI to economic growth through technology improvement rather than through increasing total capital accumulation or exports.

The lack of role for FDI with regard to exports is surprising given that in the early years of Taiwan's export promotion strategy, FDI was actively encouraged through various export promotion policies and incentives. Further explanation is needed as to why FDI's role with regard to exports was not found to be significant. It could be that FDI was important to export growth in the earlier period, when the main motivation was employing low-cost labor and using Taiwan as an export base, and much less so afterward, due to the changing nature of FDI going to Taiwan. It could also be due to the nature of the relation between FDI and domestic companies in subcontracting and owner equipment manufacturing relationships. Furthermore, it is entirely possible that technological advancement through FDI had an important impact on competitiveness and productivity, and therefore on exports and growth.

Similarly, FDI was also not important for capital accumulation, and here an explanation of what *has* been important for capital accumulation would be useful, such as the roles of domestic savings and investment.

It is also not clear why the tests undertaken for exports and fixed investment were not also applied to human capital, as the link between FDI and human capital is potentially important.

Mari Pangestu is an economist at the Centre for Strategic and International Studies, Jakarta.

The interesting result with regard to the role of FDI in technological advancement and thus indirectly growth needs to be further explored because of its important policy implications. Chan does point out that the evidence as it stands provides only indirect evidence with regard to the effect of technological advancement through FDI on growth. In addition to analyzing further the relation between the effects of FDI on technological advancement and of technology on growth using macrodata, it would be worthwhile to look at the nature of the interaction of technological advancement through FDI with exports, productivity, and competitiveness. Such quantitative results could also be supplemented by a discussion of case studies of particular sectors, industries, and companies or subsets of companies.

Another area of future research would be to analyze possible sectoral differences in whether FDI affects economic growth through increasing exports or fixed investment. For instance, FDI is expected to play a role in increasing exports for export-oriented sectors such as garments and electronics.

The policy implications are also important and need to be drawn out more. The promotion of Taiwan as a regional headquarters may attract the types of FDI that can contribute to technological advancement. However, other policies need to be identified and discussed further. For instance, are there particular sectors or even companies that should be targeted to contribute to technological advancement in Taiwan? If so, then active sector- or incentive-specific approaches may be needed, much like those undertaken by the Economic Development Board in Singapore. More general policies can maximize the impact of technological advancement on growth, such as policies that maximize the potential for domestic linkages and spillovers, education policy, and incentives for R&D.

Comment   Masatsugu Tsuji

The purpose of this paper is to estimate the effects of domestic investment, trade, and FDI on economic growth in Taiwan's manufacturing sector. Chan selects thirteen major industries in the manufacturing sector and analyzes them with panel data. The paper thus provides a comprehensive study. Using time-series data, the author fully applies the Granger causality test. The analysis follows such fundamental procedures in time-series analysis as the unit root test, the cointegration test, and the error correction model. The conclusion is that FDI in the electric and electronic ma-

Masatsugu Tsuji is professor of economics at the Osaka School of International Public Policy, Osaka University.

chinery industry (ELE), currently one of the country's major industries, is the most influential factor in Taiwan's economic growth. It is of interest to see how each individual industry affects the economy differently.

I have been engaging in research on the growth and industrial transformation of the machine tool industry in East Asian economies such as Japan, Korea, Taiwan, and China. Although my method of research is entirely different, I have learned much from this paper. My approach is based on microdata obtained by field research. I visited factories, job shops, and company headquarters and interviewed workers on assembly lines, R&D researchers, managers, and top management. According to Chan's classification, the machine tool industry is part of the machinery and equipment industry (MEQ). According to table 12.2, the amount of FDI in MEQ as a percentage of total manufacturing investment ranks third following ELE and CHEM during the sample period. There is, however, an interesting contrast between ELE and MEQ. ELE affects the growth of real GDP (GGDP), but MEQ does not. On the other hand, domestic investment in MEQ affects GGDP, but that in ELE does not. The author does not interpret the results in detail. From my field research, I can interpret this difference between the two industries as follows: Japanese machine tool builders are highly reluctant to transfer technology to other countries. They are afraid of a "boomerang effect," so they supply core devices, or "black boxes." Thus the Japanese machine tool industry is one of the least globalized. When we refer to FDI, we must recognize many differences in characteristics such as nationality, industry, and the management of individual firms. Since macrodata erase those differences, care should be taken when interpreting the conclusions of the paper.

The following are comments on the technical aspects of the estimation: First, the Granger causality test does not indicate a quantitative relation among variables but rather a qualitative one. The estimated results may not reveal a quantitative relationship; they show only that there is some relation of investment, trade, and FDI with GGDP. In order to estimate quantitative influence, the author must conduct a supplementary analysis, such as estimating the impulse reaction function. If such an analysis were integrated into the paper, it would have more extensive results. It may also be advisable to directly estimate the usual structural equations and compare the coefficients of the variables. This method seems to be rather simple but meets the purpose of the author's research.

Another interesting point is found in the methodology—for example, the application of the Granger causality test to panel data. The following question naturally arises: Why does Chan adhere to the fixed-effects model a priori? Usually in panel data analysis, the fixed-effects model and the random-effects model, for instance, are tested using the Hausman test. The suitable model is then selected according to the results of that test.

Contributors

Kenzo Abe
School of Economics
Osaka University
1-7 Machikaneyama
Toyonaka, Osaka 560-0043 Japan

René A. Belderbos
Department of Management Science
Faculty of Economics and Business
    Administration
Maastricht University
PO Box 616
6200 MD Maastricht, The
    Netherlands

Lee Branstetter
Department of Economics
University of California
Davis, CA 95616

Giovanni Capannelli
Fellow in Residence, University of
    Malaya European Studies
    Programme
Asia-Europe Centre
University of Malaya
50603 Kuala Lumpur, Malaysia

Vei-Lin Chan
Institute of Economics
Academia Sinica
Taipei 11529 Taiwan

Tain-Jy Chen
National Taiwan University
Department of Economics
21 Hsu-Chow Road
Taipei, Taiwan

Leonard K. Cheng
Hong Kong University of Science and
    Technology
Department of Economics
Clear Water Bay
Kowloon, Hong Kong

Hong-Tack Chun
Korea Development Institute
207-41 Chongnyangni-Dong,
    Dongdaemun-Gu
PO Box 113 Chongnyang
Seoul, Korea

Kyoji Fukao
Institute of Economic Research
Hitotsubashi University
Naka 2-1, Kunitachi-shi
Tokyo 186-0004 Japan

Shin-ichi Fukuda
Faculty of Economics
University of Tokyo
Hongo, Bunkyoku
Tokyo 113 Japan

Toshihiko Hayashi
Osaka School of International Public
    Policy
Osaka University
1-16 Machikaneyama
Toyonaka, Osaka 560-0043 Japan

Yuzo Honda
School of Economics
Osaka University
1-7 Machikaneyama
Toyonaka, Osaka 560-0043 Japan

Sang-In Hwang
Korea Institute for International
    Economic Policy
300-4 Yomgok-Dong, Socho-Ku
Seoul 137-800 Korea

Takatoshi Ito
Institute of Economic Research
Hitotsubashi University
Naka 2-1, Kunitachi
Tokyo 186-8603 Japan

Munehisa Kasuya
Bank of Japan
2-1-1, Hongoku-cho
Nihonbashi, Chuo-ku
Tokyo 103-8660 Japan

Hiroki Kawai
Keio University
Faculty of Economics
2-15-45 Mita
Minato-ku, Tokyo 108-8345 Japan

June-Dong Kim
Korea Institute for International
    Economic Policy
300-4 Yomgok-Dong, Socho-Ku
Seoul 137-800 Korea

Seungjin Kim
Korea Development Institute
PO Box 113, Cheong Ryang Ri-Dong
Dongdaemoon-Gu, Seoul 130-012
    Korea

Fukunari Kimura
Keio University
Faculty of Economics
2-15-45 Mita
Minato-ku, Tokyo 108-0073 Japan

Akira Kohsaka
Osaka School of International Public
    Policy
Osaka University
1-21 Machikaneyama-cho
Toyonaka, Osaka 560-0043 Japan

Anne O. Krueger
Department of Economics
Stanford University
579 Serra Mall
Landau Economics Bldg., Room 153
Stanford, CA 94305

Ying-Hua Ku
Chung-Hua Institution
No. 75 Chang-Hsing Street
Taipei 106 Taiwan

Yum K. Kwan
Department of Economics and
    Finance
City University of Hong Kong
Tat Chee Avenue
Kowloon, Hong Kong

Robert E. Lipsey
NBER
365 Fifth Avenue, 5th Floor
New York, NY 10016

Chong-Hyun Nam
Department of Economics
Korea University
5-1 Anam-dong, Sungbuk-ku
Seoul 136-701 Korea

Hock Guan Ng
Department of Accounting and
    Finance
University of Western Australia
Nedlands WA 6907 Australia

Eiji Ogawa
Department of Commerce
Hitotsubashi University
Kunitachi, Tokyo 186-8601 Japan

Yumiko Okamoto
Kobe University
Graduate School of International
    Cooperation Studies
Kobe 657-8501 Japan

Mari Pangestu
Centre for Strategic and International
    Studies
Jalan Tanah Abang 111/23-27
Jakarta 10160 Indonesia

Mariko Sakakibara
Anderson Graduate School of
    Management
University of California, Los Angeles
110 Westwood Plaza, B508
Los Angeles, CA 90095

Yuri Nagataki Sasaki
Department of Commerce
Takachiho University
2-19-1 Omiya, Suginami-ku
Tokyo 168 Japan

Akiko Tamura
Department of Economics
Hosei University
4342 Aihara-machi
Machida, Tokyo 194-0298 Japan

Masatsugu Tsuji
Osaka School of International Public
    Policy
Osaka University
1-21 Machikaneyama
Toyonaka, Osaka 560-0043 Japan

Shujiro Urata
School of Social Sciences
Waseda University
1-6-1 Nishiwaseda
Shinjuku
Tokyo, Japan

Shang-Jin Wei
World Bank
Room MC 2-615
1818 H Street NW
Washington, DC 20433

Mahani Zainal-Abidin
Faculty of Economics and
    Administration
University of Malaya
50603 Kuala Lumpur, Malaysia

Laixun Zhao
Faculty of Economics
Hokkaido University
Sapporo 060-0809 Japan

Author Index

Subject Index